Culture and Communication

James M. Wilce's new textbook introduces students to the study of language as a tool in anthropology. Solidly positioned in linguistic anthropology, it is the first textbook to combine clear explanations of language and linguistic structure with current anthropological theory. It features a range of study aids, including chapter summaries, learning objectives, figures, exercises, key terms, and suggestions for further reading, to guide student understanding. The complete glossary includes both anthropological and linguist terminology. An appendix features material on phonetics and phonetic representation. Accompanying online resources include a test bank with answers, useful links, an instructor's manual, and sign language case study. Covering an extensive range of topics not found in existing textbooks, including semiotics and the evolution of animal and human communication, this book is an essential resource for introductory courses on language and culture, communication and culture, and linguistic anthropology.

JIM M. WILCE is Professor of Anthropology at Northern Arizona University. He is the author of three books, *Eloquence in Trouble* (1998), *Crying Shame* (2008), and *Language and Emotion* (Cambridge University Press, 2009). He is also the editor of *Social and Cultural Lives of Immune Systems* (2003) and the book series *Studies in Discourse and Culture* (2005 to 2016).

Culture and Communication

An Introduction

JAMES M. WILCE

Northern Arizona University

CAMBRIDGE
UNIVERSITY PRESS

CAMBRIDGE
UNIVERSITY PRESS

University Printing House, Cambridge CB2 8BS, United Kingdom

One Liberty Plaza, 20th Floor, New York, NY 10006, USA

477 Williamstown Road, Port Melbourne, VIC 3207, Australia

4843/24, 2nd Floor, Ansari Road, Daryaganj, Delhi – 110002, India

79 Anson Road, #06-04/06, Singapore 079906

Cambridge University Press is part of the University of Cambridge.

It furthers the University's mission by disseminating knowledge in the pursuit of education, learning, and research at the highest international levels of excellence.

www.cambridge.org
Information on this title: www.cambridge.org/9781107031302
DOI: 10.1017/9781139381581

First published 2017

Printed in United Kingdom by TJ International. Padstow Cornwall

A catalogue record for this publication is available from the British Library

Library of Congress Cataloging-in-Publication Data
Names: Wilce, James MacLynn, 1953- author.
Title: Culture and communication : an introduction / James M. Wilce.
Description: University of Cambridge : Cambridge, [2017] | Includes bibliographical references and indexes.
Identifiers: LCCN 2016043384 | ISBN 9781107031302 (hardback : alk. paper) | ISBN 9781107628816 (pbk. : alk. paper)
Subjects: LCSH: Intercultural communication. | Language and culture. | Communication, International. | Anthropolgical lingusitics.
Classification: LCC P94.6 .W525 2017 | DDC 302.2–dc23 LC record available at https://lccn.loc.gov/2016043384

ISBN 978-1-107-03130-2 Hardback
ISBN 978-1-107-62881-6 Paperback

Additional resources for this publication at www.cambridge.org/wilce

CONTENTS

DETAILED CONTENTS

FIGURES

TABLES

PREFACE

A young woman in South Asia performs a traditional dance, full of hand motions that "speak" to her audience. A student posts an update to her Facebook page and receives responses within moments. Emerging drowsily from sleep, a couple ask each other how they slept, while halfway around the world, in a village made up of longhouses, other people emerge from sleep and a ritual dream-telling occurs.

Participants in a university course discuss language and communication. Someone approaches a few friends who, as it happens, had been talking about the very man approaching them now. He asks what they had been discussing. They say, "Oh, nothing. We were just talking."

Opening Up Culture and Communication

In these two paragraphs, I have introduced the topic of culture and communication in a way that illustrates a theme I develop throughout this book: We not only communicate with each other in many ways, in many **media**, all the time, but we also *communicate about our communication* – we engage in **metacommunication**. (Note that bolded words like this are defined in the Glossary at the end of this book.) As exotic as metacommunication might sound, it is really quite ordinary and pervasive in our lives.

This book is intended for students on **anthropology**, linguistics, or communication courses receiving their first exposure to **linguistic anthropology** – to "culture and communication" as seen through the lens of linguistic anthropology. If anthropology is *the study of humankind from many angles*, linguistic anthropology is *the anthropological field that mines the practices of communication – language in particular – for their sociocultural significance. It studies human life, human culture, and human societies through the social production, exchange, circulation, and reception of signs in society.*

Linguistic Anthropology: Features of My Tribe

My tribe – linguistic anthropologists or "linganths" – is as exotic as any other. Note that I associate "tribe" here with "the exotic" – in a purely tongue-in-cheek manner! I use "tribe" elsewhere in this book in the technical anthropological sense (Ranjan 2012).

My tribe works well with others, in the sense of having related interests and sometimes approaches to what we do. At the same time, my linganth tribe is also unique in what we do, in how we explore and reflect on the interconnections between culture and communication. I want to introduce you here to some of the important elements of both our commonalities with others and our uniqueness.

Our Commonalities

My tribe joins other tribes in the hard work of analyzing such things as human interaction (also studied by conversation analysts) and music and culture (also studied by ethnomusicologists). My tribe shares with folklorists an interest in traditional **performance**. Along with sociologists and psychoanalysts, linganths study *identity* and, more and more frequently, the *process* of **identification** (Smith 2010) – of identifying *with* someone or *as* this or that (Kulick 2009). Linganths, finally, share with communicologists specializing in media studies an interest in trendy new media and the communities that create and are created by those media.

Additionally, linguistic anthropology is one of the four subfields of anthropology, so my linganth tribe's work overlaps, unsurprisingly, with the work of archaeologists, biological anthropologists, and, especially, social and cultural anthropologists (*anthropologists focused on society on the one hand and culture on the other*).

And, since anthropology is a social science, linguistic anthropologists share common concerns with political scientists, social psychologists, and sociologists, to name but a few examples. Thus, linguistic anthropology links the fine details of face-to-face interaction and communication on old and new media with the great questions of the social sciences – What is power? Who "has" it? How do people become good representatives of their **society** rather than of humankind more generally? How does social inequality come about, and how and why does it last? What are the mysteries of everyday life and how does the mundane relate to community-creating ritual and to world-shattering events? Language and other forms of communication play key roles in all of these.

Finally, linguistic anthropology is not only a social science but also, in some ways, a humanistic discipline. So you will find much in this introduction to linguistic anthropology that may remind you of humanistic studies of **culture**, history, **poetics**, rhetoric, and music.

If at times our self-positioning between a variety of academic disciplines, in both the sciences and the humanities, leaves us with our feet in two boats (or many boats), linguistic anthropologists can also be said to enjoy the richness of all of these perspectives together.

Our Uniqueness

What sets linguistic anthropology apart from other disciplines is the way we **contextualize** *communication, especially language, in relation to culture.*

In describing the distinctive and defining work of our tribe, linguistic anthropologist Alessandro Duranti hits the nail on the head:

> [These] contributions on the nature of language as a social tool and speaking as a cultural practice have established a domain of inquiry that makes new sense of past and current traditions in the humanities and the social sciences and invites everyone to rethink the relationship between language and culture. (1997:1)

As we explore *Culture and Communication* together, you will find many examples of what Duranti is describing. Hopefully, you will find them as interesting, even exciting, as I do.

As you read this book, you will also find a different style of writing than you might be expecting – I use words like "you" and "I" (or "me" or "my") and sometimes "we" (or "us" or "our"). Although the presence of "you"s and "I"s, "me"s, and "my"s – and "we"s, "us"s, and "our"s – may surprise you, it is no accident. Indeed, it signals that linguistic anthropology is a different kind of science than some – neither a set of opinions nor a so-called hard science, but one of the "human sciences."

Now that you know something about how this book is situated in a particular discipline, which is situated among many disciplines, let me introduce you to the book's major themes.

Overarching Themes: Reflections on Reflection

Although this is a textbook, and thus fulfills its obligation to introduce our field in a way my fellow linguistic anthropologists can recognize and validate, *Culture and Communication* also reflects my "take" on the topic. For example, I describe communication in relation to *the scientific study of signs* known as **semiotics**. Taking a semiotic approach to communication means saying much about language in the context of other human (and even nonhuman) sign systems.

This book also demonstrates the many ways in which *communication is action* – and *all human action communicates*. It reveals the multilayered nature of **discourse** (i.e., language in use, or speech and writing deployed in events of social interaction), always as a particular form of communication.

I use the word "multilayered" here to mean **reflective** or self-reflexive – capable of reflecting on itself. Indeed, the kinds of things we do with language *reflect* various realities and are quite *likely to be reflected on*. Thus, the book peels back the layers of language, uncovering how language is uniquely suited to reflect on the world – the supposedly prelinguistic or nonlinguistic world "out there" – *but also on itself*. Unlike other forms of communication, language is very capable of focusing on speaking, signing, and other forms of "languaging" (Becker 1991). So, just as people like to reflect on what people do, in this book, we reflect on what people do with that unique toolkit we call language.

As we begin this introduction to *Culture and Communication*, you may find yourself wondering:

- What *is* culture?
- What *is* communication?
- How are communicating and communing related?
- If communication is more than conveying information – if indeed communicating is a form of **social action** – what does it accomplish?

We do explore those questions here, along with others that are still more vexing:

- When we speak about our feelings, are we "expressing ourselves" (our subjectivity, our inner life), or are the words, kisses, and grimaces by which we "express ourselves" somehow the feelings in and of themselves?
- If subjectivity is an important area of anthropological concern – and it is – how much more important is intersubjectivity (shared experience, feelings, and thoughts, which all add up to sharing a sense of "what's going on here")? How can anthropologists interested in communication and language get at both subjectivity and intersubjectivity?
- How do members of a community or participants in shared or **social activities** – activities defined by speaking, signing, or writing as well as others like eating (Cavanaugh et al. 2014) or playing chess (Desjarlais 2011) – manage to understand each other?
- How do members of communities come to share common feelings and values? How do they commune with each other?
- How is "the social" (the complexity of interaction that brings about enduring relations, all the phenomena pertaining to society or societies) born? For that matter, how are we to understand the relationship between society and persons? And is "the social" transformed by social media?

Many people I know, including beginning students, assume that human beings are first and foremost private creatures (i.e., that it makes sense to speak of "the individual," with an emphasis on "the"). In fact, many people conceive of **the social** as the sum total of the actions of distinct individuals. By contrast, this book shares the broad social science assumption that *we become who we are in a dialectic or two-way process*.

Taking this idea further, we not only *adapt* to our physical and social environments but, in both micro and macro processes, *shape* our environments. And both are manifestations of **agency** or action. Linguistic anthropologists explore how we are shaped by, for instance, the **micro-interactions** we have as babies with our caregivers (Gratier and Trevarthen 2008; Ochs 1988; Schieffelin 1990; Trevarthen 1979) and by interacting in/with the wider circles of participation into which we grow and from which we learn, by listening, speaking, and other forms of "doing"/"acting."

So we focus here on action, especially *interaction*. And we explore **subjectivity** (our inner life), but particularly **intersubjectivity**. Finally, we consider how we create understanding. Here in the world of human beings, we connect with one another – even when such connecting means sharing misunderstanding or conflict.

To borrow a metaphor from Clifford Geertz (2000), introducing you to culture and communication from a linguistic anthropologist's perspective is like trying to sail a boat upwind: We must tack back and forth – from signs to metasigns (see Chapter 3), from first communicative **moves** to second moves (as in a game), from linguistic and interactional details to questions of "what is at stake" locally and globally in acts of communication. This is the path we travel in this book – from examining what makes everyday speech, song, **ritual**, great political **oratory**, or globally circulating media (Chapter 11) what it is (normal, prestigious, stigmatized, beautiful), to reminding ourselves of the local *and* global stakes in communication – it is this rich and interwoven journey that reveals all that is linguistic anthropology.

Λ Preview of What's to Come

Overall, this book introduces you to the **anthropological perspective** on communication known as linguistic anthropology. Although "linguistic" implies a focus on language alone, this subfield of anthropology actually studies other forms of communication as well. So it is *that* broad anthropological perspective on which I will be focusing throughout this book.

You will also be introduced to one of the defining concepts of anthropology – **culture**. In this book, I often assert the value of looking at cultural *processes* and not just *products*. The book offers ways to avoid treating such concepts as language and culture as things (i.e., "objectifying" or **reifying** them). Thus, I try to use "processualizing" terms – words that emphasize process rather than product, such as "communication," "identification," and "languaging." The central achievement of human linguistic communication – and, perhaps more than any other kind, face-to-face communication – is **intersubjectivity**, which for now we can define as shared experience. This shared experience is often bound up in mutual **identification**, in which we feel and act upon a sense of commonality. Identification is typically complex and even conflicting. It is certainly a process rather than a thing, whereas statements such as "language shapes our identity" can easily sound like one thing determines another thing. Thus, keep in mind as you read this book that, when I use words like "culture," or "language," that sound like things – and I do so frequently – *these terms are shorthand for complex processes more accurately labeled with such odd terms as **languaging***.

With that as a brief overview, let me describe the basic concepts that each chapter covers.

Chapter 1 explores terrain that is, on the one hand, typically dealt with in anthropology textbooks, particularly defining "culture." Such words are deceptively familiar. Popular discourse too often confuses culture and society, too often using "cultures" to mean populations or groups. In this book, I explain that a population is a society, and culture is a catch-all term for *all* of the things that define a particular society – its ideas, values, modes, and patterns of action (including communication as action), and the material manifestations of all of these. In talking about these manifestations, keep in mind that we may only experience language via its material forms (for instance, sound waves conveying spoken language, light waves coming off of this page, and the areas of the brain associated with language).

Chapter 2 introduces "communication." It starts with a critique of a popular model of communication that locates meaning in individual minds and, in some way, envisions sentences and other building blocks of language as pipelines through which the mental things called "meanings" travel. In this **conduit model** – critiqued by me in Chapter 3 and by Reddy (1979) – the pipeline (i.e., specific languages and even more specific grammatical forms) in no way influences the ideas or meanings being conveyed through the conduit. Chapter 2 explores two alternative models that linguistic anthropologists prefer over the conduit model. The **pragmatic** or **practice** approach looks at speech, writing, and communication more generally as forms of action. Viewing communication as **semiosis** draws on Charles Peirce's (1931–1958) understanding of the process of forming **signs** and of their circulation and effects.

Chapter 3 continues to explore Peirce's model of semiotics, centering on the triad of signs or **sign-vehicles** (signs themselves), objects (which sign-vehicles represent in some way), and **interpretants** (signs' effects). Peirce liked triads, the best known of which is the trio of sign types or modalities – **icons**, **indexes**, and **symbols**. Each of them "means" in a different way: by virtue of the sign's similarity to its object (**iconicity**), by virtue of proximity or of some tangible relationship (**indexicality**), and by virtue of cultural convention (**symbolicity**). Chapter 3 also asserts the fundamental importance of the process of semiotic reflection, the capacity of signs in some systems (language, in particular) to reflect overtly on themselves or on the sign system of which the reflecting sign is a part. This chapter then turns to the historical and cross-cultural diversity of sign theories.

Chapter 4 opens up the subject of language. Textbooks that address language tend either to treat it as a system (i.e., a set of structures with no apparent relevance to social relations or culture) or to include very little about the various levels of **linguistic structure**. By contrast, Chapter 4 offers a serious introduction to the details of linguistic structure – **phonetics** and **phonology**, **morphology**, **syntax**, **semantics** and **pragmatics**, and **textuality** (structure at the highest level, that of discourse) – while demonstrating the subtle and not-so-subtle ways in which this uniquely structured human invention called language becomes a tool for accomplishing social and cultural work. I focus particularly on the ways in which ritual oratory around the world tends to take advantage of linguistic structure in creating poetic effects through what is called **parallelism**.

Chapter 5 covers the evolution of communication and, specifically, language. The chapter's uniqueness is in doing so from the perspective of linguistic anthropology rather than linguistics, biological anthropology, or cognitive science. Textbooks typically approach the evolution of language both as a manifestation of the large brain size that characterizes *Homo sapiens sapiens* and as a crucial tool for the highly complex social interactions that became necessary in our evolution. Clearly, these two phenomena overlap or are mutually constitutive, and each is relevant to topics central to linguistic anthropology. The chapter also introduces "**Theory of Mind**."

The first phenomenon, which is the topic of Chapter 6, contributes significantly to the ways in which language becomes a crucial cultural resource. And that is central to the way that linguistic anthropologists approach language. This phenomenon is also related to **linguistic relativity**, or the sometimes vexing question associated with Edward Sapir and Benjamin Lee Whorf of how linguistic diversity might be linked to perceptual or cognitive diversity. The treatment of these issues in Chapter 6 differs from that in other textbooks insofar as it draws on work being done today.

This contemporary work in linguistic anthropology entails and requires a contemporary toolkit – the topic of Chapter 7. Linguistic anthropologists share many methods and theories with other anthropologists, including methods used by sociocultural anthropologists, such as **participant observation** and **interviewing**. However, Chapter 7 also emphasizes a particular form of interviewing especially suited to linguistic anthropology – the **playback interview**, a method pioneered by Bambi Schieffelin (1979). Just as we use participant observation and interviewing in our own unique way, we linguistic anthropologists make digital video and audio recordings and transcribe them – but transcribe them in ways best adapted to our particular research goals.

After this methodological shot in the arm, we go back to developing our models of human communication. Chapter 8 expands on earlier chapters' treatments of language as a tool for social action (Duranti 1997:1–2; 2003) – an expansion that well reflects linguistic anthropologists' increased emphasis on that theme. To revisit what was said about the two-sided relationship between language as a reflection of modern human brains – a capacity residing in the brain – and as a means by which we enact our humanity and reinforce and even expand on our brain-based cognition, Chapter 8 emphasizes the social over the individual, external communication over (sometimes) internal thought. It revisits the theme of semiotics, and particularly the three sign modes – **iconicity**, **indexicality**, and **symbolicity**. This time, however, the relevance of those modalities to human social life takes center stage. This chapter explores how signs and their use or workings help create the sociocultural realities we inhabit. It shows how the sign-types "iconicity" and "indexicality" both break down into two subtypes, and it introduces the idea that human social interaction typically involves many channels of communication in use simultaneously (semiotic "multimodality").

Chapter 9 builds on that survey of human social semiotics. If Chapters 5 through 8 are in part about language-based communication as a reflection of our humanity – evolved as it is to incorporate a complex interaction between the brain and the rest of the body – then Chapter 9 addresses communication as the enactment of culture, the embodiment of society. It introduces dynamic ways to view the phenomena discussed in previous chapters, especially iconicity as "iconization" and "society" as "socialization." It introduces the process of **socialization** by which cultural insiders pass on to children, newcomers, and adults in changing roles the knowledge they need to navigate particular cultural worlds successfully. More specifically, it introduces **language socialization**, which refers to the many times when socialization works *through the use of language* (e.g., when parents tell children to wash their hands before eating) and, of at least equal importance, those times when insiders such as parents and other caregivers overtly train children how *to use language* in socially appropriate ways (Schieffelin and Ochs 1986).

Chapter 10 puts **performance** under the lights and examines its power as a cultural force. It defines performance in ways that go far beyond what actors, stand-up comics, or musicians, for example, do. In fact, every time you say something to make a friend laugh, you are engaging in performance. (Whereas those of us from the so-called West often believe that performance and sincerity are incompatible, many communities around the world regard performance – especially in the sense of speaking in a manner that is appropriate to a **context** – as admirable, and they find the Western obsession with sincerity hard to understand.) Chapter 10 reintroduces readers to the concept of **performativity** – the ability of language-in-use to accomplish things and even, in the eyes of cultural insiders, to move the world, the cosmos. This chapter also presents a brief history of performativity and theorists in and beyond anthropology who have developed the concept.

Chapter 11 covers cutting-edge work on globalization in relation to language and media. It turns out that, to grasp the sorts of sea changes that "cultural globalization" entails requires taking into account both media, its spread (sometimes called "mediation"), and the increasing degree to which what spreads around the globe and through our media partakes of emotion. Our world is more and more interconnected, and languages and new *forms* of language are spreading at breakneck speed. Chapter 11 emphasizes the significance of the intensifying co-occurrence of these communicative forms in complex single events. Globally mobile and interconnected actors are, more and more, using multiple languages and multiple communicative media in single situations (Jacquemet 2005:64–65). Chapter 11 explores recent work by linguistic anthropologists at the complex intersections of globalization, media (i.e., mediated communication), "mediatization," and emotion. This work recognizes that our focus on "face-to-face" conversation involving two people in the same place and time – and our implicit or explicit claim that such talk is the most typical and important example of communication from an anthropological perspective – ignores large swaths of culturally and emotionally significant communicative activity (Agha 2007). Thus, contemporary linguistic anthropologists study **new media** and particularly "social media" – both of which refer to Web 2.0 (Wesch 2007) in which users create their own new content (posting it on blogs, YouTube, Facebook, and so on) – as well as "old" media (e.g., print and broadcast media). Chapter 11 explores the burgeoning interplay between linguistic anthropology and studies of media and mediatization.

Chapter 12 offers ways in which the book's concepts of culture and communication can be fruitfully applied, as in **applied anthropology**. These include linguistic anthropologists collaborating with indigenous groups who are breathing new life into their traditional languages, helping children diagnosed with autistic spectrum disorders (and their families) better manage everyday life, and helping medical practitioners, their patients, and patients' families and partners consider new ways of communicating.

Dealing as they do with such rich areas of inquiry, these chapters combined should take you on a journey of discovery – one I hope you enjoy!

Pedagogical Features

To assist and maximize your learning, this book also contains a number of features that you will notice as you read. Each chapter starts with Learning Objectives and an Introduction and ends with a Conclusion, Summary, Questions, and Exercises. Each chapter also includes a section titled Additional Resources, with annotations explaining the importance of each publication included there.

The Conclusions section of each chapter summarizes and synthesizes its content. These sections also point forward and backward to the content of following and previous chapters, to situate each chapter in relation to the whole. While the Conclusions tie together and describe the significance of each chapter, the Summaries list each chapter's key concepts. These Summaries can be important tools of self-assessment, allowing you to gauge what you have learned as you read.

In addition to these chapter-linked features, at the end of the book you will find a Glossary of key terms. And when you see a word bolded in the text, you will know you can find it defined in the Glossary.

Finally, I have included an Appendix that explains the somewhat mysterious International Phonetic Alphabet (IPA), since its symbols appear in various parts of this book. The IPA is a scientific tool. Whereas the roman alphabet as used in English spelling is inconsistent at best, each IPA symbol always represents one sound, and only, and precisely, that sound. This Appendix provides a glimpse into the specifics of how it is used, by linguistic anthropologists among others.

I also want to mention the website associated with this book, where you can find online auxiliary material related to the text (see www.cambridge.org/wilce).

ACKNOWLEDGMENTS

Preparing a textbook like this can take many years – and many before the many. During that time, countless individuals and groups have contributed, each in their own ways, to shaping me and my thinking.

Because I want to stress that this book comes only partly from me, I begin with words of gratitude to my students, my teachers, and friends both on and off "the field."

In looking back on my many years of professional preparation before writing this book, I am thankful for my doctoral studies at the University of California–Los Angeles (UCLA). It is hard to convey how excited I was to embark on the study of anthropology – particularly linguistic anthropology. At UCLA, I learned the content of the discipline and how to teach it – indeed how to teach. From Paul Kroskrity, my first linguistic anthropology teacher, my friend, and mentor-in-chief, I learned to link language with art – verbal art. To Paul, my warm and heartfelt thanks for countless face-to-face meetings and for our always helpful threads of correspondence over the years (even before email became our standard means). Thanks also to Sandro Duranti, who also modeled and taught the methods and theory of linguistic anthropology. And to the members of my "linganth" cohort, who shared in the scintillating seminars that helped develop my thinking.

As I launched my career in teaching and research, I was fortunate to encounter a whole new set of teachers-at-large – elders who contributed to my growing vision of culture and communication through their roles as editors of, and commentators on, my publications. Fond thanks to those who have been so generous in helping me develop my own vision – Don Brenneis, Charles Briggs, Michael Herzfeld, Jane Hill, Judith Irvine, Bruce Mannheim, Susan Philips, and Michael Silverstein. Also, Bambi Schieffelin helped me to launch a richly fulfilling book series, sustained by a wonderful editorial board, which has allowed me to learn about the publication process from a different vantage point.

Of course, my fieldwork experiences, particularly in Bangladesh and Finland, have taught me myriad other kinds of lessons. I am grateful to the residents of Habibur Rahman Bari, who taught me Bangla. Likewise, I thank Tiina-Maija Jäskeläinen, Anu Salmu, Jussi and Anne Mänkki, and Aku Talikka for teaching me Finnish. Among those who gave me guidance in the field and challenged my intellectual models were Pirkko Fihlman, Tuomas Rounakari, Sirpa Heikkinen, Aira Vasikaniemi, and Aino Pusa. As can happen in anthropological fieldwork, my relationships with Gazi Nazrul Islam Faisal in Bangladesh and Heidi Haapoja in

Finland began formally and evolved into friendships that always included new lessons for this linguistic anthropologist in the wonders of their respective languages and cultures.

I have also learned from years of professional collegiality and exchanges of ideas. For long, rich sessions of dialogue about the concepts that eventually found their way into this book, thanks also to Betty Sue Brewster, Aaron Denham, Bob Desjarlais, Heikki and Lea Laitinen, Leila Monaghan, Daniel Negers, and Olga Solomon. I shall always remember the help I received in understanding Finnish folklore from Aili Nenola, Aleksandra and Eila Stepanova, and Frog, as well as from Pertti Anttonen and his doctoral and post-doctoral students at Helsinki University.

Of course I have learned from students throughout my years of teaching and, most recently, from students' specific responses to this book. I thank my colleague Janina Fenigsen and her students for their feedback and my own students for theirs. Among those graduate students, current and former, first mention goes to the co-author of Chapter 12, Martina Volfová. Many other students have given invaluable feedback, including Sable Schwab, Erica Rockhold, Christine Kirby, and Kevin Shaw. You have filled this book with your personal touch. In doing so, you have helped me convey linguistic anthropology's often challenging lessons, reminding me that both passion and humility are required, as well as knowledge, to effectively teach subject matter that fascinates me.

Numerous other gifts of learning have come my way over the years. Special lessons in the values of passion and humility – and the nature of the soul, of poetry, and myth – have come to me via Brad Olson. And sadly, many givers of these gifts have since passed away. I will forever appreciate Tom Brewster and Hans Ruyter, who encouraged my interest in languages, and John G. Kennedy, who encouraged my interest in emotion during my graduate student years. I am also indebted to Wasu and F. Majumdar in Bangladesh; Karen Armstrong and Anna-Leena Siikala in Finland, and my dear friend and teacher in Finland, Ensio Fihlman. I will always be grateful for each of your unique contributions to my life and my ideas!

I thank Andrew Winnard at Cambridge University Press for suggesting the original idea for this textbook and Cambridge editors Claire Eudall, Valerie Appleby, Rosemary Crawley, Rachel Cox, and Jacqueline French for their gracious encouragement and gentle guidance all along the way. Thanks also to the anonymous reviewers for their astute comments and suggestions. The book is far better for their wisdom.

Finally, as I hope to convey here, being a linguistic anthropologist involves gaining deep human relationships, sometimes even families, wherever one studies culture and communication. Families by ties of blood and love remain cherished as well. I am grateful to my family, especially my wife Sarah Wilce, for support and help throughout this process. I can never fully express my appreciation.

I ask the forgiveness of those who are on this page unnamed but in my heart still thanked.

1 Society, Culture, and Communication

LEARNING OBJECTIVES

After reading this chapter, you should be able to do the following:

- Define culture and society in such a way as to distinguish them clearly from each other.
- Describe the problems that can result from using the term "culture" inaccurately.
- Understand the difference between terms like language and languaging.
- Contrast the American idea of ritual with that of social scientists, especially anthropologists.
- Define signs in relation to metasigns and language in relation to metalanguage.
- Understand communication-centered approaches to culture.

Introduction

In this first chapter, we explore the argument for studying **communication** from the perspective of culture and society – which is another way of saying that we explore languages as "forms of life" (Wittgenstein 1958).

We begin by defining culture and society in such a way as to carefully distinguish between the two as different but interacting types or orders of reality. Along these lines, this chapter explores speaking as a **social activity** and language as a cultural resource (Duranti 1997:1–2).

In this chapter, I also advocate studying what we often call "identity" or even "identities" – social, cultural, and personal – from the perspective of **identification** (meaning *actions, often laden with emotion, linking oneself to another individual, group, or practice*).

I further call for the **processualization** of not just identity, but culture, society, and language. That does not mean I completely eliminate these more familiar terms, but I do emphasize them as denoting the *products* of processes because it is crucial to give process its due.

With all of that in mind, let's get back to directly considering the terms culture and society. Both are notoriously difficult concepts to pin down – even before processualizing these concepts (for instance, by replacing "culture" with "enculturate/enculturation"). Thus, the distinction between culture and society can easily

Figure 1.1 Societies are made up of individuals in interactional patterns together. (Yenpitsu Nemoto/Getty Images)

be blurred. By taking care to avoid such blurring, I aim to help you understand the intersection of culture, society, and communication as a foundation for understanding the rest of this book.

Society

English speakers use the term "society" routinely in the course of our everyday lives. Indeed, we may give it a variety of meanings, depending on how we individually choose to use it. For the purposes of this book, however, we need a shared understanding of the word.

Obviously, "society" is similar to the word "social," and we use both words to refer to something beyond the individual. (See Figure 1.1.) In fact, "social" comes from the Latin word *socialis* meaning allied, whereas "society" comes from the Latin *societas*, meaning a union for a common purpose (Lewis and Short 1891). With these Latin derivations in mind, let's look at some definitions for "society":

- "The aggregate of persons living together in a community, [especially] one having shared customs, laws, and institutions" (OED Online 2016b).
- "… an enduring and cooperating social group whose members have developed organized patterns of relationships through interaction with one another" (Merriam Webster Dictionary 2016).
- "… an encompassing level of social organization that can include, for example, multiple ethnic groups" (Barth 1969:16–17).

From my perspective, society is the word for a very high level of social organization – a population with which people identify and through which they accomplish necessary tasks to an extent that would be impossible for individuals or small groups.

All of these definitions hint at something crucial to our understanding: *The underpinning of society is interaction, and interaction requires communication.*

We have many terms to describe human societies, such as "villages," "towns," "cities," "communities," and "countries" (or "nation-states"). These human societies rely on living, breathing, cultural phenomena of various sorts. Crucial among these phenomena are multiple systems of communication. Indeed, one of the six models of culture that linguistic anthropologist Alessandro Duranti (1997) proposes is *culture as communicative system*.

I do need to clarify one thing: "The social" is not confined to our species. Because the social is that realm of organismic reality in which complex interactions make collective achievements possible   beyond that which any individual organism could achieve alone – we recognize that ants, for instance, are social creatures who live in societies. So do termites (in "colonies") and baboons (in "troops"), among others.

Culture

If "society" is an organized population that transcends an aggregate of individuals, what is "culture"? Again, this is a word we use often – and in a variety of ways. In fact, it is not uncommon for some people to use the words society and culture interchangeably. But for the purposes of our shared conversation in this book, we need a definition that we can all use, all of the time – a definition that clearly distinguishes between society and culture.

As you might imagine, the word "culture" is closely related to "cultivate," derived from the Latin *cultivus*, meaning 'tilled soil'. Of course, in English, "cultivate" has changed from a strictly agricultural focus to something broader over time – for instance, cultivating language and literature, ideas, customs, and artistic expressions of a group or, as we might say, a society.

So how is the word "culture" itself defined? Here are two perspectives.

- "The distinctive ideas, customs, social behaviour, products, or way of life of a particular nation, society, people, or period" (OED Online 2016a).
- "… that complex whole which includes knowledge, belief, art, morals, law, custom, and any other capabilities and habits acquired by man [*sic*] as a member of society" (Tylor 1871:1–2).

However, such definitions are today considered **esssentializing** or *objectifying* of a process ("culturing") or a dimension ("the cultural") that cannot be defined simply.

Thus, I insert a relatively recent definition, by Ulf Hannerz, which perhaps represents the far end of the spectrum from the previous definitions. Hannerz's vision of culture is one that

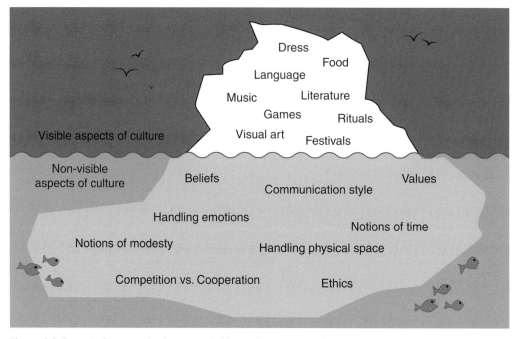

Figure 1.2 Some indicators of culture are visible, and some are under the surface. (Slide 6, Introduction to clinical cultural competence. Clinical Cultural Competency Series. Courtesy of the Centre for Innovation and Excellence in Child and Family Centered Care at SickKids Hospital)

> suggests that the flow of culture between countries and continents may result in another diversity of culture, based more on interconnections than on autonomy. It also allows the sense of a complex culture as a network of perspectives, or as an ongoing debate. People can come into it from the diaspora, as consultants and advisors, or they can come into it from the multiform local cultures, from the bush. The outcome is not predicted. Creolization thought is open-ended. (1992:266)

Each of these definitions provides a useful window on this oft-used (oft-*mis*used) term. My definition, which we use throughout this textbook, is this: *Culture denotes the set of principles guiding human thought and action together with the products of thought and action in a society and in the now-continuous intersocietal encounters.*

As you can see, the word "culture" includes many things. You may have heard archaeologists talk about "material culture," the physical "stuff" of a group or society. And then there is everything else – the stories, customs and traditions, values and beliefs, social practices, and of course language. (See Figure 1.2.) We discuss all of this and more, in detail, from many different angles, throughout this book.

To help us clarify our understanding, it is also useful to talk about what culture is not. It is *not* a space, a sphere, a territory, or a population. Various cultures, instead, are "organizations of diversity," as Anthony F. C. Wallace argues. Wallace's recognition of the complex processes by which individuals grow up and relate to the organization of life (i.e., culture) in their society was a touchstone of his life's work: "The organizing of diversity emerges as a developmental process that provides ... an arena for conflict and culture change" (2009:254). Recent descriptions of culture echo Wallace's, stressing that culture is a world of practices and ideologies that are to some extent fought over (Wallace and Grumet 2004).

Directly or indirectly, the following perspectives on culture reflect these underlying features – namely, culture as:

- a "glue" that holds a particular society together;
- a circulatory phenomenon (something that circulates across time and space);
- a process or, more accurately, a complex nexus of processes;
- sets of rules that operate in various activities from, say, hopscotch to drinking scotch;
- a set of practices, signs, values, and ideologies.

Concepts of Culture and Society – and the Problems They Raise

If we are concerned with human societies and with culture-making, culture-sharing, and cultural values –*as all anthropologists are* – then we must view **the cultural** (the levels of human reality defined by culture) and **the social** (the human and infrahuman levels of reality defined by complex interactions structured over time and manifest as **social structure**) as intertwined parts of a whole. Alfred Kroeber says it thus: "Just as culture presupposes society, so society presupposes persons. It is an assemblage of individuals – plus something additional – that something which we and termite societies share" (1949:183).

Yet, even in the early twentieth century, Kroeber was concerned that scholars too often confused or conflated **culture** (*ideas, practices, and products*) with society (*a group of people held together by culture*). His is a concern that I share strongly as well. That's why, in this section, we explore some of the ways this confusion of terms is problematic and then more generally how misunderstandings of the word "culture" itself can cause harm.

We start with the problem of conflating the common (i.e., too generalized) meaning of culture with what more careful anthropologists call "society." At least for most of the twentieth century, **cultural anthropologists**, among others, have marginalized the concept of society or treated it as a concern only for sociologists. Instead, as we are beginning to see, *"culture" and "society" are in a complex dialectical relationship* – cultural notions govern societies and how they populate their institutions and subgroups. Focusing on these interrelationships results in a more useful understanding that *societies are collectives bound together through cultural phenomena.*

It is worth noting that it is really the word "culture" that is most misunderstood and misused. The term "society" is less often misused – although society is sometimes left out of the conversation entirely.

An anthropology of culture without a clear vision of society can miss the social distribution of power and wealth – to which ways of speaking, and speaking about speaking, contribute. In fact, it is enormously important for anthropologists to focus not only on isolated cultural practices and beliefs (which the uninitiated might even consider quaint or exotic) but also on social hierarchy, global power structures, and the **ideologies** (i.e., the cultural ideas related to, and typically supportive of, the structures of power characterizing a society) that maintain them.

Let us consider a very troubling example of how some national and international authorities think about culture. Sadly, this thinking echoes some of the most unfortunate passages in the work of an otherwise outstanding anthropologist and human being – Franz Boas. In some of his writings (1917), Boas treats culture as a kind of "jail" or "jailor" (Bauman and Briggs 2003:282–283) – something that entraps us, preventing us from seeing "the truth."

Briggs and Mantini-Briggs' (2003) account of a cholera epidemic in Venezuela shows the damage that can result from thinking in terms of culture-as-jailor. In trying to stop the cholera epidemic, public health officials tried to communicate to the public about ways to reduce the spread of cholera. Unfortunately, the unexamined cultural biases in these communication efforts resulted in another kind of damage: Briggs and Mantini-Briggs document how communication pieces, including flyers and leaflets, from these public health officials *indirectly spread the notion* that indigenous cultural beliefs and practices rendered indigenous people "ignorant" as well as polluted and polluting.

In other words, in contrast to public health and other government officials' imagination of themselves as "sanitary citizens," the discourse of public health – in Venezuela and far beyond – constitutes indigenous people as "unsanitary subjects." And, in that discourse, they "seemed to be intrinsically linked to a particular package of premodern or 'marginal' characteristics – poverty, criminality, ignorance, illiteracy, promiscuity, filth, and a lack of the relations and feelings that define the nuclear family" (Briggs and Mantini-Briggs 2003:33). (See Figure 1.3.)

Briggs and Hallin assert that news media transmit to the general public "instructions from medical professionals and the state on how to behave as a 'responsible consumer' in an environment of scarce medical resources" – maintaining that "the form of the information flow is hierarchical, and patients are imagined paternalistically, as ignorant and irresponsible" (2007:57). As a result, in Venezuelan public health pamphlets, the indigenous peoples of Venezuela, especially those of the Orinoco River delta, were essentially identified as the *cause* rather than the *victims* of the deadly epidemic. This framing of "culture as a form of ignorance" shifts the blame for the victims' illnesses away from the Venezuelan government officials (e.g., public health officials) who ensured a grossly

Figure 1.3 Living conditions – not choices, habits, or culture – contribute to the spread of diseases like cholera and malaria. This Indian child is standing beside an open sewer. (Howard Davies/ Getty Images)

unequal distribution of hygiene-related infrastructure, medical resources, and so on (Briggs and Mantini-Briggs 2003:5). Instead, the blame is shifted to the indigenous people who are seen as "blinded" by their "jailor" – meaning their "traditions" or "culture."

Let's look for a moment at this flawed logic from an even more general perspective. This representation of culture-as-jailor is an example of what Briggs and Mantini-Briggs refer to as "cultural logic" or **cultural reasoning** – a set of attitudes held by elites, such as national and international public health officers, who substitute "culture" for **race** (*a social category projected falsely onto biology* [American Anthropological Association 2016]) in an era when it has become untenable to attribute stupidity, for instance, to a "race." (For evidence against the notion of race as a scientific or biological category and its usefulness in racism as a "cultural project," see Hill 2009.) Briggs' concerns about widespread and damaging uses of the term "culture" are shared by other anthropologists. Abu-Lughod's essay "Writing against Culture" (1991) and Ortner's discussion of attempts to replace "culture" with "ideology" (1984) come to mind.

As unfortunate as this widespread echoing of Boas on the notion of culture is, there is little to be gained by abandoning it altogether, which some anthropologists have advocated. More accurately, what we *can* and *must* do is to reject an

essentialist view of culture. Popular views treat culture as an "essence" equally distributed among all "members of a culture." Of course, talking about a culture having "members" is absurd if we recognize culture as a set of activity systems, processes, products, and ideologies, but not as a group of people, as we have been discussing.

But what does essence mean in this context? It is a way of referring to the nature of "X" – something very important to defining X, something that is inside every copy of X. This view of culture imagines essence as a kind of "substance" inside everyone affiliated with a given "culture." People thus affiliated are then thought to manifest this internal cultural essence in their thoughts and actions. The expectation is that we will find an overwhelming homogeneity "inside" a culture. This can result, for instance, in Venezuelan public health workers declaring the indigenous people of the Amacuro River delta as problematic in a cholera epidemic simply because the "essence of their culture" keeps them from seeing and understanding the means of cholera's transmission.

Taking problems with the word "culture" further, we see that some of the ways it is commonly misused are reifying. **Reification**, from the Latin *res*, meaning 'thing', treats a dynamic process such as culture as a static object – not as the glue that holds a population together or as *a complex interlocking set of processes*, but as the kind of thing one might check off on a census form, thus making "culture" auditable. Medical, psychiatric, and public health studies, among others that are based on such a concept, can thus never be sensitive to the internal complexities of culture. (See Chapter 12.)

Not only is the word culture, as popularly conceived, problematic, but this is even more true of the word "cultures," which may conjure up images of small, exotic indigenous groups living in far-off jungles, unchanged since the beginning of time. This image reduces complex and dynamic systems to populations with supposedly distinct boundaries. In fact, though, the cultural is rarely isolated and does not respect boundaries. In this age of **globalization** (discussed at length in Chapter 11), the boundaries of nation-states are at best porous.

In fact, we know that globalization today involves mass migrations, the diversification of the world's large cities, and a rapid flow of goods and ideas around the world. As people (i.e., members of societies) are in constant motion around the world, so are their cultural concepts, products, and practices. And, although we tend to think this current period of globalization is unique, there is evidence for earlier explosions of globalization dating back thousands of years. To think realistically about society, culture, and their interconnections, we must today be aware of ongoing "waves" of globalization, starting from classical Greece (Friedman 1994) or with the "Sanskrit Cosmopolis" (Pollock 1996), resulting in the sharing and mixing of cultural concepts, products, and practices over time. That is what it takes for us to truly grasp the notion of culture as dynamic and ever-evolving, rather than static.

A Sign-Centered Approach to Society, Culture, and Communication

We turn now to a discussion of signs. Why is it important to do so? Because *Culture and Communication* is about more than language, and its lessons in language are enriched by a sign-centered approach. It reflects a semiotic linguistic anthropology.

I bring to this book an interest in all human signs (and some animal signs as well) – an interest in all forms of communication. I am convinced that we can understand culture *and* communication only by grasping culture *as* communication. That means studying languaging and culturing as forms of signing.

This book advocates treating society and culture as systems of signs – or more accurately, as communicative systems, systems of signing. One important theory of signs and signing, upon which I draw more than any other, is that of Charles Sanders Peirce, who referred to processes surrounding signs as **semiosis**. He wrote, "A sign is something which stands to someone for something in some respect or capacity" (Peirce 1931–1958:2.228 [CP 2.228]). (Note that it is conventional in citing Peirce's *Collected Papers* to use the abbreviation CP, along with the volume – in this case "2" – and paragraph number – in this case "228." I follow this convention throughout the book.)

So Peirce is saying that sign is always a combination of a thing that carries meaning, the thing represented, and an understanding of how the sign means. Key to such theories is the recognition that our signs and our signifying activities are layered. Thus, for any given sign$_1$ – say, a Japanese communicative **style** oriented to politeness (Clancy 1986) – there are metasigns (signs$_2$) about signs$_1$. I am speaking, for example, of metasigns positively evaluating children and adults who successfully and gracefully perform the ideal (polite) Japanese communicative style. Those metasigns (signs$_2$) are not the end of the process at all. My writing about them becomes a new sign (sign$_3$) in a new context, a process called **recontextualization** (Bauman and Briggs 1990).

Semiotic Reflexivity

Social relations rely not just on "simple" signs, but reflexive signs (i.e., metasigns). Among all human communicative systems I know of, we can manage in only one to explicitly reflect on the sign system we are using. I know of no explicit musical reflections/evaluations/critiques of music. But there is language about language, especially talk (linguistic metasigns$_2$) about talk (linguistic signs$_1$). This potential of one utterance, for example, to reflect on another (like "Damn!" followed by "Oops, I'm sorry I swore") is called the **reflexive**, reflective, or **metalinguistic capacity** of language. The function of "Damn!" as an utterance of its own is "expressive." (For a commonly used model of six **functions** of language, see Jakobson 1990.)

Reflexivity applies to more than just language. Anthropologist Greg Urban (2001) places reflexivity at the heart of his model of culture. A culture, according to Urban, is a set of ideas embodied in material objects – including spoken or written utterances – which we always and only encounter in their material (audible or visible) form. These sets of ideas that constitute culture face the challenge of moving across time (as culture is transmitted from generation to generation) and space. Drawing on the physics of motion and specifically a metaphoric invocation of momentum and inertia, Urban envisions **metaculture** as a kind of gas pedal and brake rolled into one. Metaculture – "culture about culture" – may accelerate or slow the motion of cultural ideas, products, and so on. Examples of metaculture include advertisements (which are metacultural in relation to what they advertise, such as a popular brand of jeans) and book and film reviews (which are metacultural in relation to the "merely cultural" books or films being reviewed).

The "simply cultural$_1$" objects (blue jeans, books, and films) are all material objects. All of them happen to be commodities as well. And they are all complex signs. They "say" many things in many ways. Metaculture is what causes these **signs** to accelerate or decelerate. Again, "culture$_2$ about culture$_1$" is at the level of **metasign** or **metacommunication** – the level of signs about signs or communication about communication.

Among cultural elites and non-elites in this postmodern era, the one metacommunicative label that is probably most important to the way we human actors talk about cultural items/performances is "authentic." "Authenticity" (Fenigsen and Wilce 2015; Lindholm 2008, 2009; Wilce 2017) is a sign$_2$ (a metasign) that denotes a particular relationship between two signs$_1$, such as an older "traditional" performance and another performance intended to either echo the first performance in particular or reflect the tradition that produced the first. To label the second performance "authentic" is to acknowledge that the second succeeded in its intent, as it was received and perceived by some legitimate or duly authorized audience. Such an audience would itself be an example of a group authorized to make judgments about the authenticity of some bit of culture (whether or not it represents "their culture"). Note that the judging of authentic cultural production can be a "local" or a "global" process.

Viewing Culture through the Lens of Communication

This section treats culture as dynamic processes mediated by communications as sign systems. In it, I outline and describe many complex intertwinings of culture and communication that linguistic anthropologists study.

I begin by providing a foundational definition of culture as *systems of shared meanings and interactions that both produce and "re-produce" social structures*. From there, we explore culture and language as toolkits whose constituent tools both shape and are shaped by their uses. These analogies serve as preparation to understand the concept of ritual – in an anthropological sense – as a means to create and transform social realities through language use. In this way, ritual drives the processes that form culture, language, and identity. Following this section, I conclude the chapter by examining how these dynamic processes fit within and relate to a society's economic systems.

Culture in, and Consisting of, Activity Systems

Earlier in this chapter, we successfully distinguished society from culture. Now we must still locate culture. Many scholars locate the phenomenon of culture within a society. However, there are advantages to the very different approach taken by Marjorie H. Goodwin (1990), who might have found inspiration in the twentieth-century philosopher Ludwig Wittgenstein. Goodwin looks for culture in *activities*, rather than groups. An activity system could, for instance, include what workers at a construction site do and say – an example described by Wittgenstein (1958). One worker, the philosopher wrote, might call out "brick!" as an abbreviated request for another worker to pass the speaker a brick.

Goodwin has studied children's playground activities, like hopscotch games in which squares are drawn on a flat surface and players can be called "Out!" – sometimes with intense feeling. These two activities, which draw on different sorts of communicative resources and follow different rules, are what Wittgenstein calls different "**language games**." So, rather than thinking of a group that is stuck with a single "culture" or set of rules that manifests similarly in all of its various activities, Wittgenstein and Goodwin suggest that we find culture (an "organization of diversity," as I mentioned above) in various activities, each of which is constrained by unique communicative resources and governed by fairly unique sets of rules (metacommunicative or **metasemiotic** principles).

Linguistic anthropologist Michael Moerman (1988) claims to find culture in "a grain of sand," by which he means *at the most micro level of sociality* (i.e., **conversation**). Sociocultural life involves "being on the same wavelength," sharing perspectives, aligning **subjectivities**, and thus achieving **intersubjectivity**. Those who have studied conversation for decades have discovered that the process of sharing perspective or being/staying "on the same page" is not mysterious or mystical. They argue, instead, that not only do we supply each other with utterances that communicate information for a conversational partner to react to, but that, in each turn at talk, we draw on previous turns. (See Figure 1.4.) Each turn draws its meaningfulness from the previous turn (and other previous turns). At the same time, each turn also forms the context for the next turn (Maynard and Heritage 2005). This give-and-take continues. Each turn faces backward and forward. Thus, for example, the way I respond to your just-ended turn gives you information about how I have interpreted it and may tell you that you need to "repair" what you said – if, for example, my response

Figure 1.4 Conversation involves not only taking turns but framing responses based on information we get from our conversational partner.

indicates I have misunderstood. This give-and-take of conversational talk is the fundamental form of social life. However, while conversation (re)produces the social, *its structures also fundamentally reflect culture* – cultural ideas about talk, its purpose, and its participants.

Together with Charles Goodwin (Goodwin and Goodwin 1987), Marjorie H. Goodwin (2006) studied for four decades hopscotch, jump rope, and other children's activities along with the speech activities that surround and make those activities possible. Goodwin and Goodwin have no rosy picture of childhood – not even of girls, said by many to grow up "nicer" than boys. Having studied girls' arguments and how they are like and unlike those of boys, Goodwin and Goodwin reject the notion that children, and girls in particular, are always happy – and kind – on the playground. That being noted, however, they still find that these girls' and boys' arguments manifest something about the nature of conversation in general – in particular, a striking form of collaboration or co-production that they call "format tying" (1987). Despite its specificity and its micro nature, format tying is nonetheless a tool as well as an achievement of sociality, as shown in the following four separate, but similar examples.

CHOPPER: Get your four guys.
MICHAEL: You get *three* guys.

DENIECEY: An that happened *last* year.
TERRI: That happened *this* year.

MICHAEL: How'd you lost those two games.
CHOPPER: *One* game.

ROBBY: You got on a blouse too. I can see the sleeves.
TERRI: I got a *sweater* on dear heart.

(Goodwin and Goodwin 1987:211)

Format tying involves what others call **parallelism**, with which we deal later in this book. Note for now that format tying involves a second speaker making use of a first speaker's words. This sort of thing happens in many conversations. What is of special interest in the preceding example, however, is that the first speaker's turn-**structure** is borrowed or copied by the second speaker for the purpose of disagreeing with what the first speaker said. Here, structural collaboration (the sharing of structure) is the means to building a conflict.

What **conversation analysts** have done since the 1960s is to accumulate more and more evidence about how society and culture work. We collaborate, as societies must, via cultural tools (i.e., by sharing a common culture, often perceived as a common set of cognitions). But those tools and cognitions that make up culture are manifested in "grains of sand" (i.e., in the microstructures of face-to-face interaction). The children in the transcript above are not *agreeing*, but they *are* on the same wavelength. They share an understanding of the topic of conversation; in fact, they collaborate in producing that topic. We know they are cognitively aligned to each other because they demonstrate it verbally.

Culture (or Language) as Toolkit

We have seen in the preceding section how the complex reality that we call culture can be seen as a set of activity systems. Building on that possibility, we can also treat "a culture" – and "a language" (given its relationship to culture) – as a *toolkit*, a set of tools that people might use in activity systems, tools that shape and are shaped by those activities.

The toolkit model is relevant to discussions of **linguistic relativity**, which we survey in Chapter 6. "Linguistic relativity" refers to the claim that particular sets of linguistic resources influence cultural patterns of perception. The toolkit metaphor comes to life when we imagine being stranded on a desert island with, for instance, just a hammer or just a saw. Clearly, two of us on two such islands with one unique tool each would prove that what is easily constructable depends in large part on the tool in hand. Hence the saying, "If all you have is a hammer, the whole world looks like a nail." Soviet-era literary critic Vladimir N. Volosinov didn't think in terms of a toolkit, but his words certainly fit here: "It is not experience that organizes expression, but the other way around – expression organizes experience" ([1929] 1973:85). Thus, having a variety of linguistic tools allows for a greater variety of cultural perceptions and responses.

The long history of linking linguistic habits to cultural habits of perception belongs to the tradition of cultural anthropology. Additionally, the "culture/language as toolkit" model can also be helpful to the analysis of power. (Although distinct in many ways, anthropologies of perception and power come together in **practice theory**, which we discuss in Chapter 2. We return to the theme of power in relation to language and mind in Chapter 6.)

The toolkit model leads us to wonder what acts one can perform with the linguistic (e.g., grammatical) resources of a certain language. Are these acts equally performable by, for example, elites and non-elites? All societies are internally differentiated to some extent; they all divide labor, if only, for instance, by gender. Some societies, ours certainly included, are highly stratified; individuals and social groups are ranked. What do urban American varieties of English – that spoken in Pittsburgh (Johnstone 2016), in Boston's "Southie" neighborhood (Nagy and Irwin 2010), or in places where "Black Language" is accepted (Alim 2006) – offer their users as they jostle for position, as they rank and are ranked, as they accept or resist acts of domination? As another example, what tools does the Samoan language have? Linguistic tools that enable speakers to assign responsibility bluntly and openly for a particular act may – as in Western Samoa (Duranti 1994) – be largely limited to traditional elites.

Culture in Ritual

I want to explore the idea that culture may be most visibly at work in **ritual** – and then to consider what ritual can tell us about communication. First, though, we must examine what we mean by ritual.

Many people I encounter in the United States use the term ritual to denote an act with limited meaning, one that involves "hollow" or "insincere" repetition/recitation of "mere" words, as, for instance, the Pledge of Allegiance may be recited at the beginning of a school day. As another example, the words of the Lord's Prayer are the epitome of sacred language for many Christians, but those words represent "empty ritual" for Pentecostals, described by Shoaps (2002:45), and perhaps for others as well. However, social scientists, myself included, could hardly disagree more with this view of ritual, which may reflect early Puritanical ideas in Europe but would by no means be agreed to by a global range of people.

Instead, social scientists see in ritual both *society at its most social* and *cultural activity at its most intense*. To those who participate in and believe in its power, ritual can transform the world (Silverstein 2003a). Crucially, rituals derive their power from their deployment of very particular, sometimes unique or esoteric, sets of signs. After all, not just anyone in any context can say "I hereby declare the defendant guilty," or "I now pronounce you partners for life," or a similar phrase. Such utterances – strings of linguistic signs that are quite unique to their respective ritual contexts (trials and weddings) – are familiar to us, yet at the same time, they are recognizable as sacred, or at least very special.

Such signs may be visible-and-visceral for **ritual specialists** – those with special ritual knowledge, such as, for instance, judges and priests in European countries or shamans (Paul 1950) and north African marabouts (Rasmussen 1992). They may be similarly visible-and-visceral to other ritual participants, as in a Christian wedding in the United States or Kaluli dance in Papua New Guinea in which the audience is moved to burn the dancers (Schieffelin 1976). Another kind of example involves ritual songs that are understood among the Kaluli to be like bird songs and are used to express and help to overcome a community's grief (Feld 1990). (The understanding of the similarity between songs of grief [i.e., laments] and bird song comes from a shared repeating melody of a particular bird [the Beautiful Fruit Dove] and of Kaluli lament.)

To understand ritual means recognizing that – from the perspective of participants – ritual often *brings about* what it appears simply to *talk* about. We can see this in ritual moments in American history. For instance, Lincoln's Gettysburg Address and Dr. Martin Luther King Jr.'s "I Have a Dream" speech both transformed their context and moved a divided nation toward the possibility of reunification. The Gettysburg Address uses a historical here-and-now contrast with a "there-and-then" to describe a future that transcends history – an eternal life (Silverstein 2003a). It is worth noting that Silverstein uses the descriptor "eternal," which is not found in Lincoln's Address but nicely captures the meaning of its final words: *that this nation under God shall have a new birth of freedom, and that government of the people, by the people, for the people shall not perish from the earth.*

So how do rituals bring about what they appear to simply talk about? They *transform* as they *perform*; they carry out acts that are central to the social order. Linguistic anthropologists use the term **performative** to capture the magical force of ritual speech in particular and ritual communication more broadly. By performative, we mean *not* that rituals are staged or that they are particularly dramatic, but simply that they are experienced as *accomplishing things*, specifically the things that they refer to (as in Lincoln's indirect reference to the eternal).

This power is called **performativity**. Let us explore an example of performativity to help make this clear. Very often in ritual, such as in a naming ceremony, the particular act of speech we hear follows quite precisely the formula laid down by the philosopher J. L. Austin (1962) for a performative utterance. In the christening of a ship (see Figure 1.5) of the National Oceanic and Atmospheric Administration, Catherine Silver likely not only christened the ship but did so with the precise words, "I christen thee the Henry B. Bigelow!" By the proper ritual utterance of such words, new social realities come about – in this case, the ship's name as a new social fact. The christening utterance itself does the performing and/or transforming, as all performative utterances do.

From this perspective, it is as true to say that beliefs emerge from rituals as to say the opposite. And it is here that we see how *society* (social action) and *culture* (rules for that action, grounds for belief, and the reproduction of both action and belief) come together, each making the other possible.

Figure 1.5 The christening of this ship *Henry B. Bigelow* is an example of ritual performativity. (Courtesy NOAA)

Culture, Language, Communication, and Identification as Dynamic Processes

When you see a book titled *Culture and Communication*, as this book is, you may think of "culture" as a thing, and perhaps "communication" too. Many people do. However, in this book I shift our focus from words that sound like *things* (e.g., words like culture) to related words that bring to mind *processes*.

To explain, we are used to using words like culture and cultures, society and societies, language and languages, identity and identities, and communication (whose meaning changes if you add an /s/). For some of these words, we have verbs or processual nouns that we can use to express more dynamic forms: communicative and communicating, socialize and socialization, and identify and identification – all of which make us think of *processes*. But for some "thingy words" (as I often describe them) like culture, we don't have a ready-to-use word that describes the dynamic processes we talk about in this book. ("Culturing" probably brings to mind making yogurt instead.) And you have probably never heard a word like "languaging."

But to be able to really understand key concepts in this book, we need to use some new and some unfamiliar terms, always with the aim of expressing less of a "thingy" view and instead a more dynamic view.

Focusing on a dynamic view involves shifting away from **essentialization** (treating a group as though all of its members share some distributed essence or substance equally), **reification** (taking a complex process and treating it as a thing), and **nominalization** (converting verbs or whole phrases into thing-like nouns). Instead, I offer a new way of talking and thinking about the building blocks of what we call culture – not abandoning, but *revivifying* "culture," "language," and "identity." Bringing them to life.

How does taking a dynamic view of **communication** help us as we seek to understand **culture**? Despite the apparent usefulness of the terms "culture," "identity," and "language," we stand to gain even more by considering the potential value of terms like, for instance, "languaging" (Becker 1991). "Humankind is a languaging species. This means that as human beings we use language to achieve our goals. Every time we use language, we change the world a little bit" (Jørgensen et al. 2011).

So changing the world includes changing ourselves as well as what we think of as "our language." Focusing not on languages as things, but rather on *using* language and using it in ever-changing ways, may help us to go beyond more static ways of viewing our communicative world (i.e., beyond perspectives that reify communicative activities or processes, reducing them to "things").

What appear to be rather stable entities (things) are more accurately the *results* of activities and processes. Focusing on "language" and "identity" as things is like reducing photosynthesis to oxygen and light, human reproduction to babies, or all of the human activities involved in political argument, campaigning, and voting to one end result – the final vote count. What plants, pregnant mothers, and voters go through – particularly what they *do* to produce things and transform their worlds – is far too important for us to neglect.

As a final note here, I do need to say that at times I turn to old (not so processualized) terms like "languages" and "societies" – not because I think that, at their core, these are static "things," but because they are both hard *and* soft, theorizable as structural or structured *as well as* loose, soft, ever-evolving, emergent, processual phenomena. (I'll talk more about this in the discussion of post-structuralism in Chapter 2.)

Beyond Identity: Dynamic Process(es) of Identification

So far in this chapter, we have explored some of the basic concepts we build on throughout this book: culture, society, signs, language, ritual, and dynamic processes. Now we look at **identification** and what is typically referred to as "identity" (e.g., "personal identity" or "cultural identity"). There is much to explore here, and we tackle this concept from several different angles.

Introducing the Dynamics of Identification

You are probably familiar with a link between culture and identity, although most of us do not step back to analyze what we mean by "cultural identity." It does perhaps sound "natural" – at least more than "cultural identities." But both terms have meanings that we explore here.

First, though, let's talk about identity. Most commonly, we use the verb "to identify" in the sense of recognizing or categorizing something or someone – for example, pregnant women (or pregnant couples) (Kirby 2012). Likewise, we tend to use "identification" for the act of recognizing or categorizing. Yet we can also talk about "someone identifying *with*" some person or persons or "someone identifying *as*" some kind of person.

For some, the word identification calls to mind a specialized meaning – namely, what the founder of psychoanalysis, Sigmund Freud, saw as unconscious processes like "repression" and "projection." Thanks to Freud and his followers, these terms became embedded in American English, as did the idea that they were psychological phenomena living in the deep unconscious. In linguistic anthropology, however, we focus on the process of identification that we can locate in communicative interaction.

So what kind of process is this process of identifying (with or as)? Oddly, it is a process involving *paradox*. It, first of all, inherently involves the paradox of being yourself and yet, to another person, being "someone else." Additionally, though, part of being you involves – in a profound and mysterious way – being you precisely by being identified complexly, negatively and positively, with someone else. (The paradox of identification is exemplified by the statement, "Today, we are all Haitians," following the 2010 earthquake there. Although this wasn't literally true, it expressed identification by people all over the world with those in the midst of tragedy.)

Additionally, identification is never a simple matter in terms of *polarity* (i.e., do I or don't I identify with someone or with some cultural notion or practice?). Instead, identifications are complex and contradictory.

When a daughter feels a deep identification with her mother, she might experience an attraction to her mother or a desire to be like her. The same feeling might indeed characterize the strong identification that ritual participants feel toward a ritual, its language, the community that practices it, and that community's culture. Participants in any activity system experience a pull toward that system and/or a push away from it, a pull toward the larger sociocultural system of which it is a part and/or a push away from it. Identifications are push-and-pull relationships, combining attraction and repulsion – just as two magnets attract or repel each other, depending on their mutual orientation. To use some examples of mutual attraction, we could say that identifying *with* a community of refugees, *as* a Navajo, or *as* a construction worker, for instance, is a bit like saying that communities, ethnic labels, or social roles exert an attraction like that of a magnetic or gravitational force.

Languages and the actions we perform with them are resources in "enacting" identity (i.e., *identifying with* or *as* some category). Languages or linguistic varieties can also be objects of identification. They can have a magnetic attraction for their speakers, and we often perceive identification in acts of speaking.

Learning to identify by means of linguistic acts, and with varieties of language, is central to the sociocultural process of becoming (i.e., **socialization**). As I see it, and as the social sciences generally do, socialization is what adults, insiders, or experts do *to* novices. As a result, the process of socialization is the process by which we become competent members of our communities, competent social actors and cultural navigators.

Identity Passed On, Thus Still with Us

One of the defining features of culture is that it is learned – or, from another perspective, culturally transmitted. (This sets human culture apart from the cooperative activities of, say, bees or termites, which are genetically transmitted.) In other words, we become culturally competent actors in a particular community through the process of socialization – and that implies coming to identify not only with our community and its culture but also with certain linguistic varieties. For instance, Eira and Stebbins have investigated lines by which "authentic" tradition is passed down among speakers of Sm'algyax, a language spoken in British Columbia and Alaska.

> The traditional model of knowledge transfer continues to be applied to some cases of Sm'algyax acquisition in the Tsimshian community today. Given the fact that many members of the community come to learning the language as adults, and as part of seeking to find out more about their heritage, it is a natural model to identify with. (Eira and Stebbins 2008)

Indeed, language is often said to signal our identities. But identity development is also what settles out over time. In this book, I focus on *processes* as well as what "precipitates out" of the solution or the "chemical" processes of human social life. Although this settling-out process may appear to yield a thing-like result, as illustrated in Figure 1.6, in fact, settling out is an *ongoing* process. As Diana Fuss writes: "Identification is a process that keeps identity at a distance, that prevents identity from ever approximating the status of an ontological given, even as it makes possible the formation of an *illusion* of identity as immediate, secure, and totalizable" (1995:2).

Dynamizing Our Word-Tools: Processualization

In this book, I point beyond thing-like identities and toward processes by which we identify *with* or *as* – in other words, the psycho-social-communicative processes whereby we feel connected with others. We can identify with someone or something (including some form of language) or as someone or something (like a particular social role). For example, I personally identify *with* academia and with bird-watching. I identify *as* a father, a husband, a son, a photographer, and a speaker of American English. And not all forms of identification involve "real-world" connections, as shown in Figure 1.7.

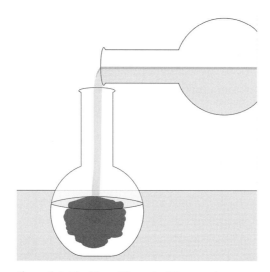

Figure 1.6 Identity settles out of the ongoing processes of our lives, much like the chemical precipitation process shown here. (Charissa Pray)

Figure 1.7 Boy identifies with a superhero that he has likely seen some media representation of. (Peter Muller/Getty Images)

Communicating, languaging, socializing, speaking, performing, doing rituals, making magic happen with words – these are the processes we explore here. Whether we are looking at the details of a face-to-face interaction between two people or at the global flows of people, ideas, products, and languages in relation to global power, we are always concerned with activity, emotion, feeling, dominating, gossiping, loving, connecting, communing.

To use a metaphor, we could say that social actors – or communities of such actors or their cultures – are a bit like planets, stars, solar systems, or galaxies, which all have gravity. Even the tiniest thing has gravity – or, more precisely, undergoes gravitational attraction from and to other objects and also subjects other objects to the pull of its gravity, however small that force may be. We, as social actors (human beings), are not just pulled this way or that, but we also do some pulling of our own. In the remainder of this book, we return repeatedly to communicating and its role in acts of identifying-as-something or identifying-with-something or -someone.

In speaking of how we identify *with*, say, a way of speaking, or how we identify *as* daughters, believers, or athletes, we approach the issue of what it feels like to be a person – a person in a particular cultural setting using a particular language. What approach to "language" and "personhood" can help us understand the subjectivity of social beings – say, of two interlocutors – as well as their attempts at intersubjectivity in their ongoing relationship? (Note that I always use the term "subjectivity" to denote our inner life, never in a derogatory way as it is sometimes used in common parlance.) The approach we need must be one that recognizes the role of language in who and what we are constantly becoming – not just persons, but a dynamic center of "personing" through our ever-shifting ways of speaking. The approach we need must focus, too, on how identification – for instance, with elders and peers as speakers of a particular variety of language – is part of the same "personing," the same becoming, individuating, and "I–Thou" relating (Buber [1923] 2004).

When we speak of *using language*, we emphasize a human activity that spawns other, related activities and processes. People do not simply "have" thing-like "identities." Instead, we take on identities, for instance, by using language in a variety of ways – *identifying with* "one's own" group, "one's own" language, or even some "other" group and its language. That identification can be positive or negative. For example, you may have heard about some group thinking of its own "linguistic variety" as inferior, dropping its own variety in favor of some other, or even experiencing shame in relation to its group's speech (Bonner 2001). Some people from Brooklyn, for instance, pay dialect coaches to lose their Brooklyn accents. (It's important to me to make clear that linguistic anthropologists use the term "linguistic variety" in a neutral way, to refer to distinct languages, separate dialects of one language, and different speech registers that are used in different situations in particular communities. We do *not* use "linguistic variety" – let alone "dialect" – to judge any such variety to be inferior.)

Taking this activity focus further prompts us to explore how our self-identifications shift as we use language – and how ways of speaking *enact* identifications of various sorts. The activities identifying *with* (Kulick 2006) and identifying *as* (Fuss 1995) something or someone are *enacted* in and through language. Here we can think of a simple example, like uttering the pronouns "we," "us," or "our." Or we can explore a complex example, like **code-switching** – for example, switching among Tewa, Hopi, and English within a single conversation among the trilingual people of Tewa village on the Hopi reservation in northern Arizona (Kroskrity 1993). Such *acts of identification* may engender a push and/or a pull, shame and/or pride, in relation to "our" way of communication or "our language."

Examples of Identification in Cultural Contexts

Let's look now at some real-world examples of identification, first related to consumer capitalism and then in the ritual context of christening.

In economies today that rely heavily on consumer spending, what we identify with not only reflects our culture but also, to some degree, *makes* our culture what it is – one focused on purchasing products or, increasingly, purchasing experiences. That is, in consumer-capitalist societies today, acts of purchase and consumption are central to producing "identities."

In Chapter 9, we discuss **registers** – packages of signs (often different sorts of signs) that together send signals about what sort of "social persona" is culturally associated with those registers. Here, I only point out that commodity registers, or registers whose central elements or signs are commodities, are often what enable us simultaneously to conform and assert our uniqueness.

> All commodity formulations and their fragments (products, services, discourses about them) are recontextualized [repeated in or placed in a new context] and transformed through the activities of those acquainted with them. Many commodity formulations come to be treated as common culture. (Agha 2011:22)

In consumer-capitalist societies, culture has become a blend of wholesale copying and small divergences. We possess – or at least appear to possess, though we may rather be *possessed by* – what Blommaert and Varis (2015) call "culture as accent." Speaking in certain ways can be part of the process of forming this "accent," but its features are probably never just linguistic.

For example, we often think of culture as a way of life – quite rightly so. If we substitute for "way of life" the single word "lifestyle," we are now using a word that helps to describe culture in this period of late capitalism. To say that cultures are crucially manifest in what we increasingly call lifestyles indicates an understanding of culture as a product or set of products that we own and/or display as *social* signs or sign-sets, therefore identifying us as part of a particular status group. Think not only of advertisements for fine wines, cheeses, or blends of coffee, but also the forms of language that have grown up around elitist consumption of such products. (For instance, see NPR 2012 for an example of "coffee talk.")

It's interesting to note that sometimes lifestyle advertisements can invoke other, unexpected, cultural perspectives – and identifications. Such is the story of a shoe name's competing meanings. In a story appearing in March 2012, a *Los Angeles Times* reporter wrote that Nike had announced a new line of shoes called "Black-and-Tan" to be sold (among other places) in Ireland. The company thought the color terms were innocent, recalling only a drink involving creamy Guinness.

> To Americans, a "black and tan" usually refers to a creamy stout beer, such as Guinness, stacked atop a pale ale. And no doubt many an American will down one this weekend in honor of St. Patrick's Day, under the mistaken belief that it's a nod to the Irish. But you might not want to order a black and tan in Ireland. To the Irish the colors are those of a murderous unit of the British Army. The Black and Tans, so nicknamed because of their uniforms, were part of a British escalation of violence and brutality against the Irish in the 1920s. The forces are "remembered for brutality" and "a systematic reprisal policy," according to *History Ireland.* (Lynch 2012)

In the end, Nike apologized for the offensive name. However, the idea of a shoe sharing the name of the British Army unit did not seem so bad to some in Ireland.

> Over at Irish Central [apparently a website catering to Irish-Americans] where news of the Nike gaffe was well read, one sly commenter named "hotdubliner" suggested that Nike critics have it all backward: "I say wear them proudly! The only place a 'Black and Tan' belongs is underfoot! Every time you kick a ball or pound them down by dancing them into the ground, hold that vision of divine retribution finally having its day!" (Lynch 2012)

Indeed, we are what we drink, what we wear, what we put on our feet. Semioticians (see Chapter 3) use the word "signs" to cover many things, but in consumer-capitalism we are also surrounded by literal signs that glow, blink, or pop up on our computers or handheld devices. Yet, as contemporary as these signs are, and as modern as the culture of ads and "shop-'til-you-drop" is, products and brand names often become entangled with older forms of society and culture. What we drink or wear, and the ad campaigns that influence our drinking and shoe-buying, can bring out old feelings about identifying as, for example, "Irish" or "British" – by processes that linguistic anthropologists call **decontextualization** and recontextualization (Bauman and Briggs 1990).

Let me give one last example of identification, this time in the **context** of ritual. Christening is of interest to students of culture and communication because it is an

Figure 1.8 A baptismal performance conveys a change in status that all in attendance recognize. (Vano Shlamov/AFP/Getty Images)

instance of performativity, a "magical" use of words that brings about a new reality – in this case, a new name, one that officially "sticks."

As such, it also entails an act of identification. There is, of course, the obvious sense, that we can now identify a ship by its name because it is painted on the side, for example. But there is more. A christening involves an officiant who identifies with someone else, who might also identify with someone else again – with each successive person or entity being more powerful. In the case of a federally sponsored American ship christening, for instance, we might hear, "in the name of the United States." Whereas, in a baptismal or baby christening – a situation that is not altogether different – the words might be something like "We christen you in the name of the Father, the Son, and the Holy Spirit. Amen." (See Figure 1.8.) In both cases, an argument could be made for a necessary and profound identification between the officiant and the ultimate authority that officiant represents, be it civil or religious.

Turning our Attention: Phenomenology

For human beings, *identifying with* something or someone involves, at the very least, some focus on the object of identification. This focus is of the same sort that phenomenologists have described in relation to perception; it is a turning, a directing of attention, that is not only embodied or physical but also mental or subjective.

For anthropologists Desjarlais and Throop, phenomenology is "the study of phenomena as they appear to the consciousnesses of an individual or a group of people; the study of things as they appear in our lived experiences" (2011:88). Among understudied "things as they appear" are experiences of language in use and associated processes of identification (Webster 2010). Kockelmans notes that, "It has been said that phenomenology is an attempt to give a direct description of our experience as it is in itself" (1999:665). He goes on to say he finds the generality of this statement objectionable, preferring to note that there are *many* phenomenologies (1999:666).

In **phenomenology**, this orientation-toward-something is called an **intention**. This is quite a different use from that which is common in so-called Western societies, where intention is typically used in a strictly individualistic, inward, psychological sense. For phenomenologists, by contrast, the most basic form of intention is an orienting of oneself *toward* something. And drawing explicitly or implicitly on their understanding of intention as focusing on or orienting to something, phenomenologists argue that "perception [is] a constituting process" (Csordas [1988] 1990:9). We see what we focus on, as demonstrated in Figures 1.9a and 1.9b. Hence, communication often involves finding a mutual orientation. That orientation is what phenomenologists call an "intentional act."

Duranti describes the significance of this two-part illustration by starting with the affirmation that multiple attitudes toward an object are possible at the same moment. Duranti (2009:209) then explains that

> [Figure 1.9a] schematically represents the possibility of multiple (in this case, for simplicity, only two) ways of relating or "intending" the same Object. When the type of intentional act we entertain toward something or someone changes, for example, from admiration to fear [Figure 1.9b], from disapproval to approval, from seeing it as something alien to seeing it as a member of a familiar group, we are experiencing an intentional modification, that is, the "phenomenon" – in the sense of what it appears to be for us – changes as a result of our way of relating to it. We can schematically represent this event by adding a time variable t to the two intentional acts in [Figure 1.9b].

Let's try an example to help make this clearer. In Figure 1.9a, Duranti's unnamed object might be a form of language, one on which I might have only a tenuous grip (Graber 2012; McEwan-Fujita 2010). Let's say I might not be able to perform this form of language in such a way as to allow me entrance into some prestigious social

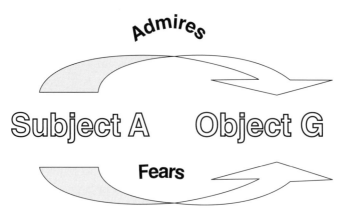

Figure 1.9a This is one way of relating to or "intending" an object, thus helping to make it what it is or seems to be. (Adapted from Duranti 2009:209)

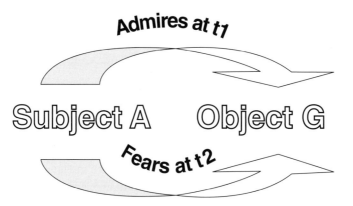

Figure 1.9b Our way of relating to the same object may change over time (i.e., t1 versus t2). (Adapted from Duranti 2009:209)

club or a neighborhood bar in Cambridge, Massachusetts, near Harvard University. Approaching this club or the bar, I might perform contrastive intentional acts toward, say, "Harvard English" or "working-class (Southie) Bostonian" – one indexing a fear of, and the other admiration toward, one linguistic form or the other.

If we imagine this example involving a potentially simultaneous pair of "intentions," the following involves a different kind of time or temporality. As in Figure 1.9b, I might – after honing my skills in either form of language (say, for acting in a film or to achieve the status of an insider or "native speaker" – shift my intentional stance or orientation toward it from fear to admiration.

I must explain this concept of intentionality because it is a very different one from the one we encounter in popular and even academic discourse. Speakers, hearers, and all those who have ideas about any particular way of speaking or form of language, identify with that particular way of speaking or languaging. That identification, like other acts of identification, can be contradictory or tension-filled. Put differently, speakers and hearers think about forms of language, orient toward them, or "intend" them. Again, I am using "intend" as phenomenologists do – namely, as a synonym for orienting toward an object in a particular way. Duranti (2009) refers to stances or orientations toward objects as "intentional acts" – not acts performed "on purpose," as we say, but acts involving orientation, or a change of orientation, toward some object. Duranti (2009:209–210) stresses the profound "constituting" significance of these acts, quoting Wittgenstein: "To 'see as' is the same as to have an 'attitude' toward something" (1958:205, 214).

CONCLUSION

In this chapter, we explore concepts central to anthropology in general (such as "culture" and "society") and to linguistic anthropology in particular ("communication" viewed through the lenses of culture and society). Not only does clarifying what exactly we mean by "culture" and "society" enable us to better understand "communication," but the inverse is also true. Viewing culture through the lens of communication is one way to underscore the dynamic nature of culture. (We look at this most closely in the section titled "Culture in, and Consisting of, Activity Systems" earlier in this chapter.) That dynamism is crucial for us to understand, as it is central to the remainder of this book.

As the first chapter in this book, Chapter 1 sets the tone for what is to come. It challenges our perceptual habits – mental habits like experiencing the words "cultures," "languages," and "identities" as if they referred to *things*. It stakes out a contrasting agenda – exploring culture and communication as complex and tightly interwoven *processes*. I emphasize in this chapter that, despite the value of concepts like culture, society, and communication, they can at times be controversial and essentializing, if not downright dangerous. It is that danger which Briggs and Mantini-Briggs (2003) ascribe to cultural reasoning – not the way people who share a particular culture think, but the way elites get away with essentializing representations of people by invoking the concept of culture (instead of race, for example).

In introducing linguistic anthropology, this book – particularly this chapter – provides the sort of map needed to avoid the dangers that introductory textbooks sometimes overlook. I hope that this "map" also guides you to areas rich with excitement and to paths that may move us forward toward playing a constructive role in enhancing understandings between people – the sort of understandings that can only result from grasping others' "forms of life," which, as we saw at the outset of this chapter, is to say others' "languages."

SUMMARY

After reading this chapter you should have a good grasp of the following themes:

• Languages as forms of life.

- Human communication as inextricably bound up with society and culture.
- A "sign-centered" perspective on society and culture.
- The junction of culture and communication – culture as communicative activity and as toolkit and the intersection of communication and culture in identification.

QUESTIONS

1. What do Briggs and Mantini-Briggs mean when they say a certain institution is using "cultural reasoning"? How does the concept of cultural reasoning pertain to the dangers that lie in the use of the term "culture"?
2. What is the useful term coined by Greg Urban to describe an advertisement in relation to the subject of the advertisement – for example, blue jeans or a newly released movie? What is the relationship of that term and metalanguage?
3. What does it mean to "locate culture in *activity systems*"? What does locating culture in activity systems contrast with? What is one advantage to the activity systems approach to culture?
4. What are the implications of looking at culture or language as toolkits?
5. The concept of ethnicity often implies a blood relationship. Does culture also?
6. Using only the words of this chapter, define intersubjectivity. How does the text define it? What synonyms seem to occur with it?
7. What is the advantage of replacing the word language with "languaging," talk with talking, communication with communicating, communion with communing?
8. How can each of the approaches to culture mentioned in this chapter be only about culture (defined as we do in this chapter)? In your answer, demonstrate your ability to keep "culture" distinct from "society."

EXERCISES

1. Throughout this book, you will find words beginning with "meta" (e.g., meta-communication). The prefix "meta-" signals that a word of which it is the first part pertains to reflecting. When "meta-" is part A and a noun like "communication" is part B, then A signals that the compound word involves B reflecting on B.
   By yourself or in groups, invent a realistic scenario in which members of some social group talk in a certain way (we'll call that "level 1"), while members of a second social group reflect on (e.g., evaluate or criticize, which we'll call "level 2") the "facts" of level 1. Then someone comments ("level 3") on the "level 2" comment/evaluation/criticism. Is level 1 likely to be an objective fact, not a fact, or something like a "social fact"? Is there any end to the potential levels or layers of reflection?
2. Search for and read about the psychological syndrome that involves identifying with someone we might assume would be hated and feared. What is this called?

How does it illustrate the distinct phenomenon of identification as opposed to identity?

3. Have you been in a chemistry class where adding one liquid to another results in "precipitation" out of a solution? (See Figure 1.6.) Write a paragraph describing how this example works as a metaphor for "identity" and "identification." Which parts of the chemistry example correspond to what in the world of human life, in which we encounter identities and identification?

4. This exercise pertains to Figure 1.5. First read the following excerpt from a story about the christening of this ship. Then complete the instructions that follow.

> VT Halter Marine, Inc. and NOAA today launched the second of four planned NOAA fisheries survey vessels. The ship was christened *Henry B. Bigelow* by Catherine Silver of Winnacunnet High School in Hampton, N.H., on behalf of the ship's sponsor, Mrs. Judd Gregg, wife of the senior senator from New Hampshire. The ship will be one of the most technologically advanced fisheries survey vessels in the world when placed in operation in late 2006 ... "The christening of Henry B. Bigelow is a significant milestone in the modernization of our NOAA fleet," said retired Navy Vice Admiral Conrad C. Lautenbacher Jr., Ph.D., undersecretary of commerce for oceans and atmosphere and NOAA administrator. "We appreciate the contribution Mrs. Gregg has made as the ship's sponsor and we are delighted that Ms. Silver was able to represent her, maintaining the close connection between the school and the vessel." (From NOAA Magazine 2005)

Instructions: On a sheet of paper, arrange the names of the persons mentioned in the excerpt from the lowest position to the highest, in order of power or authority. Speculate as to Ms. Catherine Silver's experience, knowing in a sense she was taking the place of the wife of then-Senator Judd Gregg. In what way might a form of "identification" be at work between ceremonial officiants and the authorities they invoked in naming this ship?

ADDITIONAL RESOURCES

Alexander, Jeffrey C., and Steven Seidman, eds. 1990. *Culture and Society: Contemporary Debates*. Cambridge University Press.

Alexander and Seidman have collected a superb set of essays that illustrate a range of approaches to culture and society.

Kroeber, Alfred Louis. 1949. The Concept of Culture in Science. *The Journal of General Education* 3(3):182–196.

Kroeber's essay offers a classic treatment of emergent structure, from the biological to the social, and to the cultural.

2 What Is Communication?

LEARNING OBJECTIVES

After reading this chapter, you should be able to do the following:

- Understand communication as action and as semiosis; be able to explain their differences and similarities.
- Understand communication as communion and as **mutual attunement**.
- Understand two different ideas of the **sign** – those of Ferdinand de Saussure and of Charles S. Peirce.
- Understand the three types of sign in Peirce's thought.
- Distinguish **semantic** and **pragmatic meaning**, using the concepts of performativity and **deictic** words.
- Define **structuralism** and **phenomenology**, and explain their relevance to culture and communication.
- Understand dynamism as it applies to language, speech, and context.

Introduction: Models of Communication beyond the Conduit

In Chapter 1, we made reference to communication as a key to the production and reproduction of human societies. In Chapter 2, we focus more intently on communication, offering two models that transcend an older "conduit" model that still tends to dominate an unreflective view of communication.

First, though, let's talk briefly about the term "model." A model is a verbal or graphic representation that helps explain or make understandable some concept or theory – in our case, a way of imagining culture and communication and how they interact. A "theory," by contrast, answers a scientific problem in a conceptual way and can be applied with some consistency. As you undoubtedly know, in the sciences, theories are not guesses, but plausible visions that have been, and continue to be, applied and tested in relation to the phenomena of interest – in our case, to culture, society, and language.

As an example, let's look at the **conduit metaphor**. This model envisions communication as a transfer of content (ideas, information, feelings) between

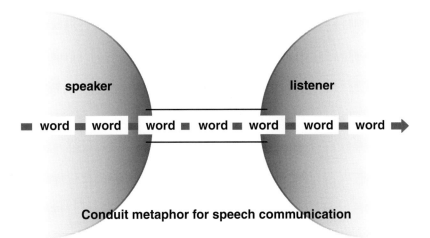

speaker · listener

word · word · word · word · word · word · word ➡

Conduit metaphor for speech communication

Figure 2.1 This conduit metaphor is an outdated model for how speech communication works. (William Benzon © 2015)

two people through a "conduit," such as language, that is presumed to be completely value-neutral (see Figure 2.1). However, the conduit model (Reddy [1979] 1993) – an idea that was in circulation during Saussure's lifetime, long before his famous "Course" was published ([1916] 1959:11) – is no longer accepted in linguistic anthropology or communication studies, even though it still lingers on in popular thought.

The conduit model represents a theory of information transfer. But the theory does not hold up: Neither "information" nor the "conduit" exist as things. Additionally, neither is passive; instead, both are active. So what shall we invoke in place of the conduit model? How *do* we conceptualize communication?

A number of alternative models do exist, including a communication-as-action model and a semiotic model. In this chapter (Chapter 2), we first explore animal communication, because communication among nonhuman animals is so clearly action-oriented. We then explore communication as activity or action. Finally, we foreshadow the semiotics discussion. I then devote Chapter 3 to exploring semiotics systematically.

Communication as Action or Practice: Before Human Communicative Systems

In this section, we contemplate communication involving nonhuman animal partners. Specifically, we explore animal-to-animal communication systems, especially systems of calls, including those known as alarm calls. (We return to this topic when discussing the evolution of communicative systems in Chapter 5.)

Figure 2.2 Prairie dog producing an alarm call. (Shafer and Hill/Getty Images)

Animals do not waste time and energy. However, they do expend energy when necessary, for example, by making alarm calls in situations of grave danger. That just makes evolutionary sense. In Flagstaff, Arizona, where I live, many species – including prairie dogs (Figure 2.2) and chickadees (Figure 2.3) – frequently expend energy to produce alarm calls.

Animals use their energy in ways that matter to their survival. In eating, fighting, mating, and playing, animals are doing something important. (The play of younger animals, especially, seems to serve almost universally as a means of practicing skills needed to survive and thrive as adults.)

Also in their efforts to survive, animals *communicate*. In fact, there are no believable accounts of animals using their communicative systems to share information for no particular purpose. So, perhaps by looking at animal sign systems, especially in the wild, we can reinforce our understanding of the pragmatic approach to communication that we will be discussing in the next section.

Many species of birds in the wild have evolved distinctive systems for signaling danger to their conspecifics (other members of their species). We consider here the chickadee (see Figure 2.3) as an example. The name "chickadee" is, interestingly, an apparent attempt to imitate its call (Templeton, Greene, and Davis 2005). In other words, it exemplifies what we call onomatopoeia, an imitative word – a special case

Figure 2.3 Variations in the black-capped chickadee's alarm call tells other chickadees how serious the current threat is. (Brian Lasenby/Shutterstock).

of the sign-type that Peirce called **icons**, imitative signs, signs that represent their **objects** by some sort of resemblance.

Not only is the chickadee's English name iconic; its alarm calls are too. Of course, their **function** is indexical: They point to something, always in their here-and-now context, that their conspecifics must notice and flee. Although any alarm call is by function an index, the **structure** of chickadee alarm calls is iconic of the *degree* of threat to which the calls bring urgent attention: The greater the threat, the more intense the call. To explain, owls are chickadees' most dangerous predators, but different species present different degrees of danger to the sparrow-sized chickadees. The small pygmy owl is an agile flyer, so it is a greater threat than the much larger great-horned owl. Warning conspecifics of the presence of highly mobile pygmy owls involves multiplying the number of *dee* "syllables" in the chick-a-dee call (dee, dee, etc.). It is in that way that signal-intensity resembles threat-intensity or that the intensity of the sign maps directly onto its object. Sign and object share a common quality – degree of intensity – although that quality is measured quantitatively in the size of the owl and the length of the string of *dee* syllables (Templeton et al. 2005).

Birds are only distantly related to humans, in that both descend from reptiles. Yet our more closely related cousins, the **primates** (and we ourselves), also have alarm systems. For instance, capuchin monkey alarm calls (www.youtube.com/watch?v= ArKLQiMSpT4) operate on the same principle as those of the chickadees. Both systems involve an imitative or one-to-one relationship between some quantitative dimension of the signal and a measure or ranking of the threat posed by an intruder species. The "noise," "duration," and "frequency range" of the more urgent calls are all greater, exemplifying call-threat iconicity (Fichtel et al. 2005:173; Templeton et al. 2005).

I do want to note before we move on that it is not possible, desirable, or necessary to know what sorts of "meanings" might be in animals' heads apart from their communicative behavior. Instead, good science leads us to focus on the behavior, the action itself, and to discard the conduit model. As to what might take its place, let's dive now into the first of our two alternatives and explore it in some detail.

First Alternative Model: Communication and/as Action

All human action communicates. And all communication is action. In the following sections, we explore two approaches that roughly correspond to this pair of assertions. First, we consider "practice theory," a theory of the significance of action-as-practice. By practice, theorists mean embodied, collectively meaningful forms of action – all of which are forms of communication. We then consider communicative pragmatics, an important domain of theory aimed at uncovering communication as action.

As we will see, practice theory is implicitly about language, while a theory of pragmatics is explicitly about language, down to the very forms of speech-in-interaction.

Communication and Action: Practice Theory

Recent accounts of language and communication in linguistic anthropology have drawn on **practice theory**, deriving from Anthony Giddens and a chain of predecessors. Practice theory insists that social reality is both hard and soft, both product and process, and reflects both structure and what Giddens (1979) calls "structuration" or "the duality of structure."

Giddens (1938–present) drew on the work of the slightly older Pierre Bourdieu (1930–2002) and ultimately Marx, as Ahearn (2012:23) makes clear:

> Consider Marx's famous words in "The Eighteenth Brumaire of Louis Bonaparte": "Men make their own history, but they do not make it just as they please; they do not make it under circumstances chosen by themselves, but under circumstances directly found, given and transmitted from the past" (Marx [1852] 1978:595). In place of the word "history" in this remark, one could easily substitute "language," "society," or "culture," and the statement would remain equally insightful. At the core of what is known as "practice theory" is this seeming paradox: that language, culture, and society all apparently have a pre-existing reality but at the same time are very much the products of individual humans' words and actions.

Ahearn is essentially saying that individuals – agents in their own right – seem to constantly bump up against "structure." "Agency refers to the socioculturally mediated capacity to act" (2001:112). **Structure** *appears* to make **agency** impossible. The reality is more complex. (Remember, we're talking about a paradox here.)

It is only within structure that human action can take place, and, at the same time, human **social activity** reproduces or transforms the structure within which it operates. We cannot communicate more than simple ideas without sharing a structure like the English language or American Sign Language, and yet such structures are always changing because we (especially children) keep messing with them (e.g., messing with English by insisting on saying 'sensible' things like "childs" instead of "children," or "goed" instead of "went"). This never-finished quality is what leads some (e.g., Becker 1991) to write of "languaging" rather than language. Whereas the term's origin goes back much further, and Becker himself appears to attribute it to Maturana and Varela (1980), Becker develops the concept in particularly intriguing ways. To think not of "language" but of "languaging" is to consider this phenomenon "not as an abstract accomplished fact but '*in statu nascendi*' – not as an already-always existing thing ('THE English language,' for example) – but as something that is always in *a state of being born*" (Becker 1991:232).

A giant of late twentieth-century sociology and anthropology, Pierre Bourdieu ([1972] 1977, 1991), drew much of his inspiration from structuralism and **phenomenology** (introduced in Chapter 1 as "the study of things as they appear in our lived experiences" (Desjarlais and Throop 2011:88). Structuralism leaked into the study of language from Ferdinand de Saussure. But what is structuralism?

"Structuralism" refers to a theory of signs or communication in which relationships between signs receive particular attention. The great structuralist insight is that we never encounter a single isolated sign, nor indeed do signs have meaning in and of themselves. Rather, the structuralist argument is that signs take on meaning in relation to the system of which they are a part (see Figure 2.4). Moreover, structuralists like Saussure argue that what is important about an individual sign is less what it *is* than what it is *not* or what it *contrasts* with. In the study of the sounds of languages (i.e., phonology) – at least in the version of **phonology** envisioned by Roman Jakobson and by American structuralists like Edward Sapir – polar contrasts between sounds are what give them their significance. The English sound /t/ is made without the vibration of the vocal folds (i.e., it is "voiceless" or whispered). From a structuralist perspective, its significance is, in large part, this: It is not a /d/ (a sound produced in the same manner and at, or by, the same part(s) of the mouth as /t/, the difference being only in regard to /d/ being voiced).

The "structures" on which structuralism focuses are sets "of phenomena . . . treated as a structural whole[s]" and governed by "inner . . . laws," by virtue of their emergent nature as a system (Jakobson 1929:11, as cited by Percival 2011:244). (By "emergent" we mean such phenomena as "the social" or what societies achieve collectively that would be impossible even for all of them as individuals. For example, in Chapter 1, I mentioned termite societies; their emergent achievements

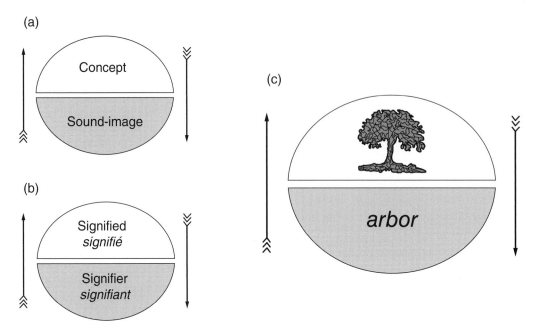

Figure 2.4 The Saussurean sign, in which each dyad explains the binary relationship in a slightly different way: The signifier *is* a sound-image and "arbor" *is* the sound-image for tree in French. (Adapted from Saussure [1916] 1959:66–67)

include huge mounds.) Structures are sets of linguistic features (phonetic, **lexical**, and poetic,) or cultural features (such as systems of kin terms) (Trawick 1990). So structures are relationships defined by contrastive features; unfortunately, Lévi-Strauss treated these structures as if there were no real problem in abstracting them from their contexts. As he himself put it, "These structures – or, more accurately, these structural laws – are truly atemporal" (Lévi-Strauss 1963:202).

Saussure is known for his *two-dimensional*, highly mentalist, model of the sign, or sign relations (i.e., the relationship between the "vertical" axis or the axis of choice) and the "horizontal" axis (that of co-occurrence). He called the first the paradigmatic and the second the syntagmatic axis. This distinction is useful, but limited and limiting. What do people's choices of what sign to put in a "slot" reveal? There is indeed social-situational significance in *choices*. Echoing Agar (1996), we might imagine ordering from a menu as an example of the two axes. One might order an expensive wine or the cheapest beer or something else fizzy. Note, however, that in ordering wine with dinner, connoisseurs will say that one's choice of white versus red wine should be determined by whether one is eating white or red meat as an entrée. Another example: There is great social significance in the choice between shouting out "Chow time!" versus writing on fine stationery, "You are invited to dine ..." Or choosing a greeting "slot" – shall I say "Yo!" or "Hello!"? **Context** matters, but not just in the way we usually think it does. It matters not just as some "thing" that shapes communicative choices, but as something actively created through communicative choices, such as the choice between saying "Yo!" and "Hello!"

The syntagmatic axis involves stringing things together. In the sociocultural worlds in which we actually use language, we do so not in isolated words or sentences, but in the context of practices. **Genres** can be viewed as communicative practices – things people do with sign systems like spoken or written language, film, or music. Genres often have locally assigned names – journal articles, lectures, personal essays, sermons, spells, fairy tales, and laments are examples of discourse genres. In the living breathing context of speech-in-interaction – take, for example, interactions between parents and children involving reading or telling a story – conventionalized "strings" create anticipation. Even very young children no doubt know what sort of story is coming when they hear "Once upon a time." The opening words **index** the genre – in this case, a fairy tale.

The concept of "indexing," which is crucial in this book to understanding culture and communication, is Peirce's (Hoopes 1991), not Saussure's (Preucel and Bauer 2001). Peirce provides us with more powerful tools to understand signs and semiosis (communication) than Saussure did. Peirce brought signs and semiosis out of our heads and into the world. Peirce would have rejected Saussure's emphasis on "the **arbitrary** nature of the sign" (Saussure 1959:67) and on Saussure's lack of interest in the very phenomena that would call that arbitrariness into question. At least in the work of his interpreters, Peirce's concept of indexing is bound up with sociocultural phenomena. To say that certain words index the genre that gives shape to a text (an oral or written story, for example) is to say that such words as "once upon a time" remind listeners in a particular community with a particular culture of many stories called "fairy tales."

In explaining structuralism, I have bent it quite a bit: Although I have explained this theory in relation to activities (ordering from a menu, telling and hearing stories), Saussure himself was fonder of structures in the abstract (or in the mind) than he was of the *social* dynamics of sign use. Saussure's anthropological devotee, Claude Lévi-Strauss, also tended to analyze cultural elements outside of real time and space, outside of the flow of real human actions (including communicative actions) in history.

Now we can return to Bourdieu, whose theory of human social life we call *post*structuralist. Why poststructuralist? Bourdieu, like Saussure, was drawn to visions of structure. However, whereas the structuralism of Saussure and Lévi-Strauss tends to be ahistorical, poststructuralist or **practice theory** embraces a dynamic and historical model. And whereas Saussurean structuralism lends itself to individualist and cognitivist models of sign use, poststructural approaches regard "practice" as a social phenomenon best understood within a **materialist** framework. Bourdieu located the roots of practice – always *the practice of some social fraction* (e.g., a group defined as a social class in a particular society) – in that group's "objective conditions." Central among these are the historical, material, and economic circumstances that help define the group. However, as Bourdieu argues, a group's history is transformed and in large degree forgotten as its history becomes embodied in the form of a cluster of "sensibilities," which Bourdieu called the **habitus**. "The structures constitutive of a particular type of environment (e.g., the material conditions of existence characteristic of a class condition) produce habitus, a system of durable, transposable dispositions" (Bourdieu [1972] 1977:72). Not rules, but embodied leanings or dispositions guide the activities – and judgments of those activities – that mark the activities as part of a sociocultural system. Note that, where rules determine actions, dispositions guide without determining. This bears some affinity to paired "moves" in conversation – for example, an answer is expected to follow a question – as long as we don't turn "expectations" (or preferences) into psychological concepts.

Practice in poststructuralist theory is a *shared* form of **social action** – e.g., forms of human communication, and, specifically, the particular forms of human communication that dominate a given community. Borrowing from Bourdieu, linguistic anthropologist William Hanks (1996) calls for the study of communication as communicative practice. This means, on the one hand, attending to the fairly automatic uses of the body in communicating – such as uses of the mouth in forming the sounds that define one's speech not only as *French*, for example, but as "working-class French" (Bourdieu 1977, 1991). (See Chapter 8 for a detailed discussion of Bourdieu's example.)

On the other hand, the communicative practice model seeks to understand the universal practice of *reflecting on* and *evaluating* others' ways of communicating. These reflexive practices – so common in our social lives – are what linguistic anthropologists call "linguistic" (or "communicative" or "semiotic") ideologies, rooted in shared values, cultural ways of orienting us to the world.

A practice-theoretic approach to communication is not the only approach that regards speech and other ways of communicating as forms of *action*. In fact, linguistic anthropologists argue that the best way to study speech as a form of social action is to examine it in the context of *interaction*. Face-to-face conversation, while by no means the only context for our linguistic communication (see Chapter 11), is a good place to start if our quest is to understand action-in-interactive-context. And this, in turn, leads us to engage more intensively and explicitly than Bourdieu did with *social* phenomenology and sociocultural models of **intersubjectivity** (Desjarlais 1996; Desjarlais and Throop 2011; Schutz 1967; Throop 2010).

Linguistic anthropologists and others influenced by **conversation analysis** study the exquisitely timed "dance" of interaction. That dance involves exchanging something – not dance moves or money, but conversational turns. Somehow, in thousands of interactions, conversational partners manage to exchange turns at talk without overlapping each other and without leaving an appreciable gap or pause. We may attribute that exquisite timing to a kind of social contagion or to observable cues – changes in vocal pitch or intonation, pausing, and so on – that tell a listener that the speaker's turn-at-talk could happily end now. This cues the listener of an opening in the conversation that she or he might wish to jump into.

In any case, conversation analysis and forms of linguistic anthropology inspired by it are making exciting discoveries about interactively situated action. I discuss this in more detail in the next section.

A Pragmatic Approach to Communication/Signs

When we define *language* as a set of cultural tools for doing things and *speaking* as a form of doing social things (i.e., as a form of social action), we are making a distinction compatible with that between **pragmatic** and **semantic meaning**, which goes back at least to Charles Morris (1938).

Linguistic anthropologists often use *pragmatic* as a near-synonym for linguistically **indexical** or **performative**. Indexical signs reflect their surrounding context and draw their meaning from it, or they help create the very context in which they take on meaning. In language, indexical phenomena include spatial and temporal **deictics** (i.e., words like "here" and "there" or "now" and "then"). These deictic words sometimes rely for their interpretation on context (particularly in this case of sharing an "extralinguistic" context, the context *beyond language* including the visible presence of people together and what is visible to them together). By contrast, other deictics, such as first-**person** plural pronouns (like the English "we") shape their extralinguistic contexts. Almost any use of "we" *creates* even as it *reflects* context. It reinforces or even creates an idea of a particular group bound together in solidarity and, in the process, suggests the existence of another group that may not be mentioned but is implicit, namely some "they" (i.e., outsiders). The effect-producing significance of words and larger units of language – their impact on, or ability to influence, the extralinguistic context – is their pragmatic meaning. (In Chapter 8, I expand on these two sorts of indexicality or pragmatic meaning.)

Two culturally particular examples may shine a light on the pragmatic meaning of communicative acts. For the Puebloan peoples of the American Southwest, there is a right time and a wrong time for telling what are known as Coyote stories. When performed at the right time (in the winter when things lie dormant), their pragmatic meaning includes an effect on a truly extralinguistic context – the growth of the crops in the next season (Kroskrity 2009b; see Chapter 10, this volume).

A second example of pragmatic meaning concerns a shift in how much deference or honor (called "honorification," the use of "speech levels" or respect forms; Wilce and Fenigsen 2015) one uses in speaking to another. When I first lived in Bangladesh and was learning the Bangla (also known as "Bengali") language, I had a tutor. When we began working together, we each used the highest of three levels of honor one can perform in Bangla, signaled by *apni*, the respectful or distant form of the second-person pronoun "you." We agreed later to address each other as *tumi*, also second-person "you," but indicative of less formality and more equality as well as intimacy. I never felt comfortable using *tui*, the lowest of the three "honorific forms," in five years of life in Bangladesh – even to children – nor did any

Bangladeshis ever seem comfortable with the idea. (Note that "person" is a common way to refer to speaker [first-person], addressee [second-person], or referent [third-person].) (See Chapter 8 for more discussion of **honorifics**.)

A shift such as I have just described – either from high to low honor or vice versa – will have at least the potential *to shift the social relationship* in which the (non)honorific speech occurs. This is its performative significance, its "effectiveness in context" – its pragmatic meaning.

The same lesson is aptly illustrated in the story told by linguistic anthropologist Laura Ahearn (2012:4–7, 80–82) about a turning point that occurred during a Nepali wedding. It involved the groom, who was receiving linguistic-cultural "coaching from his elders" (2012:5), downshifting from the highest honorific version of the Nepali second-person singular pronoun to the lowest, as he requested his bride to release for the guests' consumption all of the pounded rice that she had prepared, which she at first refused, in traditional fashion. The final step in the groom's request, from the relatively neutral-to-distant to the relatively demeaning-or-intimate *tā* form of the "you" pronoun (the Nepali equivalent of Bangla *tui*), produced the desired result – shifting the nonlinguistic context, including the bride's behavior, the groom's feelings regarding pronoun use, and the overall progress of the ritual.

What can we see in Ahearn's example? The rice that was in the bride's possession and indeed her tenacious grip on it, the speech forms the groom used to address her (forms that were passed to him from his elders), and the bride's final release of her pounded rice to the groom for distribution to the guests – all of these are signs. More accurately, they are all, simultaneously, communicative actions and indeed "moves" in a specific **language game** (Wittgenstein 1958) or an interactive sequence (Goodwin and Goodwin 1992:94). They thus exemplify communication as we have discussed in this book – *actions embedded in interactions*.

The use of "high" honorifics to pay deference or of "low" forms to demean (potentially) is related to using "**diminutive**" and "**augmentative**" forms. Spanish diminutives are, in form, suffixes and include, for example, *-ito* and *-eño*. In terms of function, they usually express endearment. Suffixes that are augmentative are often pejorative in function. Spanish examples of these suffixes include *-ón* (*-ona*), *-azo*. Importantly, both honorifics and diminutives can express attitude toward a referent (something about which or whom one is talking) and not only an addressee (someone to whom one is speaking). We explore the diminutive–augmentative functions and their structural means in Chapter 4.

Second Alternative Model: Semiosis

Philosopher Charles Peirce offers a sign-centered or semiotic model. Central to Peirce's model of signs (see Figure 2.5) is the question of their *effect*.

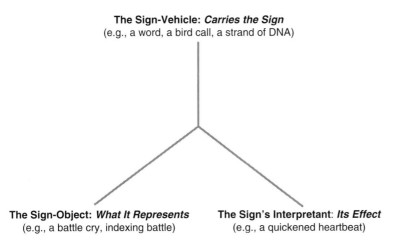

The Sign-Vehicle: *Carries the Sign*
(e.g., a word, a bird call, a strand of DNA)

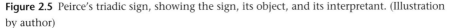

The Sign-Object: *What It Represents*   **The Sign's Interpretant**: *Its Effect*
(e.g., a battle cry, indexing battle)   (e.g., a quickened heartbeat)

Figure 2.5 Peirce's triadic sign, showing the sign, its object, and its interpretant. (Illustration by author)

As we shall see, his model is not unrelated to the "pragmatic" approach to communication that we examined in the previous section. However, Peirce preferred the term "semiosis" to communication. For the moment, let us treat communication and semiosis as sister terms, if not synonyms. Peirce defined semiosis as "an action, or influence, which is, or involves, a cooperation of three subjects, such as a sign, its object, and its **interpretant** [*not* interpretation or interpreter]" (Peirce CP 5.332). These three entities work together to constitute the sign and communicate meaning. To better understand Peirce's triadic definition of the sign, let us consider an example of linguistic communication. Imagine that, in a **conversation**, one person says to the other, "It looks like a storm is coming." Each word is a sign, but so is the sentence as a whole. Its object is what it refers to – a certain "it" (the sky, presumably) that looks a certain way. The interpretant may be a mental effect, or possibly even a physical effect, or a combination of the two. A listener or **interlocutor** who has a deep-seated fear of tornados may experience his or her heart beating faster upon hearing this sentence. This example easily fits our commonsense notion of communication, and we can readily see that there is no end to the number of possible interpretants.

Now let's consider an example of semiosis in Peirce's sense that does not exemplify our everyday idea of communication. When two moving things collide, they enter into a two-way relationship with each of them moving in a new direction. This movement in a new direction reflects each being a sign of the other – or more accurately, an interpretant of the other thing. The interpretant is both an important part of the sign as well as its external effect – and a sign in and of itself. Hence we see that collisions are just as "sign-ificant" (just as much signs) as are ideas communicated via sentences.

Having looked at a straightforward conversation example (a storm is coming) and a rather extreme example (collisions), we next explore situations involving easily

Figure 2.6 Behavioral synchrony is a part of communication in everyday life. (Laurence Mouton/ Getty Images)

recognizable "communication," but a kind of communication that Peirce had in mind in defining semiosis – communication or semiosis as a model for understanding the mutual effects of two people interacting with each other. In the section that follows, we see that Peirce's model of semiosis not only can fit something we easily recognize as communication but can also help us better understand communication.

Behavioral Synchrony and Mutual Attunement as Communication

Scholars have known since the 1960s that face-to-face communication between two individuals *is* a kind of coordination, *reflects* coordination, and at the same time *helps produce* coordination. Coordination can even mean doing the same thing at the same time – "**behavioral synchrony**" (Gerard 1943; Rosenblatt 1969) – as shown in Figure 2.6.

Relations of "**mutual attunement**" – a phrase apparently first used over a century ago (Herrick 1911) – are complex signs, complex forms of communication. For example, when a mother and infant enter, as they often do in societies around the world, into behavioral synchrony, not only does that synchrony result from signals passed from one to another and vice versa, but their mutual orientation *is* a sign.

Conversational interlocutors, let's say a pair or a trio of people involved in conversation with each other, can even enter into respiratory synchrony (Lyon 1994). Who knew that breathing could be a social activity?

Recently, a group of Japanese neuropsychologists found a new manifestation of "interpersonal synchrony" – called eye-blink entrainment. "Entrainment" is used here as a near-synonym of "attunement" or "synchrony." It is defined by Phillips-Silver, Aktipis, and Bryant as "spatiotemporal coordination resulting from rhythmic responsiveness to a perceived rhythmic signal" (2010:5). "When viewing close-up video clips with sound, listeners synchronized their blinks to the speaker's blinks, especially at breakpoints of his speech" (Nakano and Kitazawa 2010; Nakano et al. 2011:2784). They found that the eye-blinks of adults diagnosed with Autism Spectrum Disorder (ASD) who were included in the experiment "did not synchronize with the speaker's blinks while viewing speech. This was in contrast to the eye-blink synchrony observed in the control participants" (Nakano et al. 2011:2788).

The experiment that Nakano, Kato, and Kitazawa carried out involved only listening while watching a videotape of a person speaking – far different than the **naturally occurring** talk that linguistic anthropologists prefer to study. And the lack of naturalness might be quite significant in this case; since the eye-blinks of experimental subjects were never observed while they were *speaking*, the experiment was perhaps not able to capture the two-way nature of speaker–listener coordination. The authors thus explain eye-blink entrainment "during breakpoints" as careful attunement among the control group to the speech – and movement of eyes and lips – of one speaker. The control group processed information coming from the movement (and pauses in movement) of eyes and lips together, while those diagnosed with ASD did not (Nakano et al. 2011:2789).

Coordination is communication, semiosis. For instance, the synchrony of a caregiver's behavior with that of the infant's passes no information of the sort we think of in relation to language (no complete thought, argument, claim, or assertion). Nonetheless, the routine achievement of such coordination between infant and caregiver (e.g., a father or mother) not only leads to a healthy relationship but has such personal developmental benefits as promoting a sense of security in the infant (Reyna et al. 2012:671).

In all of these examples, it would oversimplify the phenomenon to say that one interlocutor is merely following the other. Instead, in the magic of human interaction, two people often fall into a shared pattern of action – indeed, that is what "interaction" means. And the sharing or mutuality reflects precisely what Peirce had in mind in his definition of semiosis, particularly in his use of the term "interpretant."

It is when shared action (i.e., true *interaction*) involves very clear rhythmic synchrony – a reflection of mutual influence – that communication and "communion" meet. We return to the theme of "communion" later in this chapter.

Semiotic Modalities

Whether or not scholars of communication today take Charles Peirce as their inspiration, many are now examining the phenomenon of communicative multimodality or multimodal semiosis – the simultaneous use of several modes or channels in carrying out communication within human interactions.

Throughout this book, we recognize language as the human communicative modality, or sign system, par excellence. At the same time, this newer research in multimodal semiosis reminds us that the use of spoken or signed language is *never isolated*. Therefore, we locate language within a broader framework of communication.

As we have noted, communication via other modalities almost always continues *simultaneously* with speaking. And these other modalities can range from the subtle to the highly noticeable. Subtle, and common, modalities include gesture and other visual and embodied sign systems (posture, eye gaze/facial orientation). Less subtle modalities can include laughter and crying, silence, music, dress and body decorations, and contemporary modalities from film and online streaming video to texting – and graffiti, as Phillips discusses in her book *Wallbangin'* (1999).

Things get even more interesting when we realize that people can use one sign mode to comment on, mock, or **recontextualize** a sign produced in another mode. And, in the flow of face-to-face interaction, it is quite possible not only to experience many communicative modalities in near-simultaneity, but also to experience a sign in one "channel" as complementing or playing with ("troping on") a sign in another.

The following section provides a fascinating example of this interchannel communication or interchannel sign play. The example is captured in a YouTube video excerpted from Gérard Miller's film *Rendez-vous chez Lacan*. This segment (www.youtube.com/watch?v=VA-SXCGwLvY) represents footage from an interview with Suzanne Hommel, a woman who underwent psychoanalysis in 1974 with the famous French psychoanalyst Jacques Lacan. Hommel's encounter with Lacan takes place some decades after her experience of living in fear of the German Gestapo.

It is helpful to know that Lacan loved word play, "academic trickster" that he was (Trawick 1990:143). Yet, in this example, an event of communication involving Lacan and his patient Hommel also became the occasion of multimodal communicative play.

In the video, Hommel is shown recounting a moment in analysis where she tells Lacan that she wakes up every morning at 5 a.m., which was the time when the Gestapo came "to get the Jews in their houses." At that moment, Lacan jumps up and strokes her cheek. Why? His act involved a **trope** or play on words – here, a play on the word "Gestapo," which Hommel had used. But it also involved a gesture that reinterpreted the word. When Lacan gently stroked her cheek – an act that in French can be rendered *geste à peau* – which sounds nearly identical to Gestapo – he was engaging in interchannel sign play. And play can be powerfully therapeutic.

Communicating and Communing: The Broader Social Context of Language

As we have just seen, language is rooted in the broader, more inclusive category of communication, and thus it behooves linguistic anthropologists to treat it as such. At the risk of being labeled "mystical," this recognition must also include "communing" – and indeed, new phenomenological approaches in linguistic anthropology stress intersubjectivity (basically, shared subjectivity, awareness, or experience). Scholars invoke the term "intersubjectivity" to talk about everything from the raw *potential* for mutuality and understanding to the *achievement* of close communicative coordination and a high degree of actualized (and interactively produced) mutual understanding (Duranti 2010). If this be *communion*, it certainly involves *communicating*.

In 1985, the psychiatrist R. D. Laing – often identified with the "anti-psychiatry" movement (Boyers 1971) – demonstrated this quasi-sacred, quasi-ritual, therapeutic quality of coordination-as-communion. In the excerpt that follows, Laing is referring to an event in a 1985 "Evolution of Psychotherapy" conference – an annual event held in Phoenix, Arizona, that Amantea (1989) calls "The Lourdes of Arizona." Laing had successfully requested that conference organizers allow him to demonstrate his therapeutic approach to persons diagnosed with schizophrenia. In a separate chapter written by Laing in Amantea's (1989) collection, Laing reflects on this event:

> I specified that I required a person to interview who was not on medication ... [T]he organizers could find no such person until Christy turned up ...
>
> The main point [of the interaction] is in the rhythm, the tempo – the timbre and pitch of the words ... There is between Christy and me, a music of words. There are, as well, kinesics – concerted movements involving arm, hand, finger, leg, the positions of our bodies in the chairs, set at 90 degrees to each other.
>
> The point is that the rapport which seemed to so many [among the thousands of psychotherapists gathered in the auditorium] so "mysterious," "mystifying," or "mystical" (the "love" to which Salvador Minuchin referred in his remarks) is there on video for all to see and to analyze in detail. There is a lot of technique there. Many people like Christy do not connect with "content" alone, if ... the therapist ... is effectively selectively inattentive to 99 percent of the sight and sound of the patient/client. (Amantea 1989:141–142)

According to Farber (2006), when Christy accepted Laing's invitation to appear with him onstage in front of all the psychotherapists attending the 1985 conference, Laing had the sense that he and Christy shared a sense of communion that went beyond words and was difficult to explain or talk about. But Farber (2006) reports that Laing added:

> It makes all the difference if there is a sense of communion which is unspoken . . . If that is absent . . . it will come to nothing . . . whether it's behavioral therapy, psychoanalytic therapy or whatnot etc. etc. . . . It doesn't get anywhere with those people who find it difficult to live in the world . . . and can see how stupid it all is, how ugly it all is, how inexpressibly confused it all is, and yet are just regarded as crazy and mad for realizing that, and are either locked up or run away.

Laing's own commentary (in the essay on Christy that he authored for Amantea's book) indicates that he believed in the therapeutic potential – indeed, the loving, healing potential – of coordination that was based, in this case, apparently on the conscious intent of Laing as therapist.

Both Lacan and Laing have reputations as nonconformists in their respective fields (psychoanalysis and psychiatry). Yet a number of others, in fact whole schools of thought and practice, have emphasized the therapeutic potential of communion, synchrony, and attunement. "Transpersonal Psychotherapy" is the title not only of an academic article (Hammer 1974) but of *The Journal of Transpersonal Psychology* as well.

Synchrony and attunement was also the research topic of a dynamic group of investigators led by anthropologist Gregory Bateson. The project, which went on for many years, was called "Natural History of an Interview" (McQuown [1956] 1971). Among the publications that refer to it are two that are respected in the field of conversation analysis (Kendon 1990; Streeck and Scott Jordan 2009).

I believe linguistic anthropology, with its interpretive and human sciences nature, is a field of study that can tolerate a degree of mystery – something that certainly characterizes the therapeutic potential of interactive synchrony.

CONCLUSION

It may be widely imagined that communication involves people using some sort of pipeline or conduit (e.g., language) through which they send meaningful information, as if the conduit had no effect on the process. However, this model is no longer accepted in academic circles today.

So this chapter discusses two other models, starting with a pragmatic approach to communication – treating communication as activity or practice. When we talk, we don't just say things about a world separate from or existing independently of our talk – we act *in* and *on* our world(s). To refer to communication as practice is to evoke something habitual, something patterned and, in fact, reflecting *shared* patterns. Communicating is just one of many *social* practices that define a community and its culture (norms, ideas, practices, products). The practice approach also represents an attempt to get beyond the limitations of "either/or" and "determinism" versus "free will" dichotomies. We have seen how we inherit and inhabit worlds – worlds not only of things but of practices, including ways of speaking – that are not of our making. And yet, we act upon these worlds every time we commit an act of communicating.

A second way to understand communication derives from the semiotics of Charles Peirce. Peirce used the term "semiosis," which we first explored as a rough synonym of communication, then as the production and circulation of signs and their effects. Not only can signs *have* effects, but also sometimes *the effect is the sign*. All signs have "interpretants," and these are frequently sign-effects. However, an interpretant may play a double role as the effect of one sign *and* as a new sign in and of itself.

In this chapter, we have also seen how human behavioral synchrony or mutual attunement is itself a sign. The achievement of mutual attunement may well be an effect of proximity between a caregiver and an infant, for example, but it can also have its own effects. An infant who participates in exchanges of identical behavior or behavioral synchrony with a caregiver may, as a result, experience calming. Children may thus know about synchrony, attunement, and intersubjectivity decades before having any possible exposure to these terms. The sort of coordination achieved in face-to-face interaction, not only between parents and their infant children, but between two or more adults, begins to take on the quality of "communion."

We also looked in this chapter at the themes of semiotic modalities or channels (e.g., speaking, writing, gesturing) and their interplay. When communication becomes communion (intersubjectivity, mutual attunement), multiple communicative or semiotic channels are typically involved.

Building on our discussions here, we see in later chapters (especially Chapter 7) some scientifically observable **(ethno)methods** for achieving close coordination in conversation. This coordination involves face-to-face conversationalists beginning a turn at talk at the very moment when a prior speaker ends his or her turn, with no gap or overlap between the second and first utterances. This is just one example of the ideas we explore, based on what we have learned in this chapter, throughout the rest of the book.

SUMMARY

After reading this chapter, you should have a good understanding of the following themes:

- **Peircean** semiotics versus Saussurean **semiology**.
- Structuralism versus phenomenology.
- Communication as practice.
- Semiosis as sign production, circulation, and effects.
- Human behavioral synchrony or mutual attunement.
- Multimodality or multimodal semiosis.
- Communication as communion.

QUESTIONS

1. What kinds of communicative, developmental, and/or mental disorders disrupt the ability to engage in behavioral synchrony or experience mutual attunement?
2. Which of Peirce's three kinds of sign relationships involves the ability to map in a one-to-one correlation a sign form (such as the number of "dee" syllables in a chickadee alarm call) onto that form's meaning (in this case, seriousness or intensity of the threat stimulating the alarm)?
3. How could "communion" be the subject of scientific study (that is, the object of a linguistic anthropology analysis)?
4. Think of a situation, event, or phenomenon that is best analyzed via Saussure's semiology or via Peirce's semiotic. What would the relevant advantage be in relation to that situation?
5. How do the "pragmatic" approach and the approach centering on "semiosis" shed new light on, and complicate commonsense ideas of, communication?

EXERCISES

1. Listen to the following National Public Radio story (www.npr.org/2013/08/25/214831942/heart-of-iranian-identity-reimagined-for-a-new-generation). What is Ferdowsi's Shahnameh? When was it composed? What do we learn about the sacred from the NPR discussion of the release of the English translation? What are the two means of communication in this example that partake of the sacred?
2. This exercise gives you practice in identifying the semantic versus the pragmatic meanings of words and utterances. For this exercise, let's agree that "eat" and "dine" *refer to* or *denote* the same act; that is, they share the same *semantic* meaning. Imagine two invitations, one using "eat" and the other using "dine." In two sentences, describe the pragmatic difference and justify the assumption that there is no semantic difference between the two verbs.
3. Watch the brief video of Suzanne Hommel talking about Jacques Lacan's use of gesture as communication (www.youtube.com/watch?v=VA-SXCGwLvY). How was it that Hommel came to perceive Lacan's gesture as a trope or play on the word "Gestapo"? How common is the French phrase *geste à peau*? What can you discover in your answer to these empirical questions? Have you ever used or witnessed such an intersemiotic play of signs?

ADDITIONAL RESOURCES

Caton, Steven C. 1990. *"Peaks of Yemen I Summon": Poetry as Cultural Practice in a North Yemeni Tribe*. Berkeley and LA: University of California Press.

Caton has written a beautiful ethnography of poetry. If you can read only a small part of the book, read the first chapter in which Caton sketches the story of his ethnographic work in a Yemeni tribe.

Duranti, Alessandro. 1997. *Linguistic Anthropology*. Cambridge University Press.

Duranti's textbook is a superb introduction to the field, particularly for graduate students.

Goodwin, Marjorie H. 2006. *The Hidden Life of Girls: Games of Stance, Status, and Exclusion*. Malden, MA: Blackwell Publishers.

Goodwin's second ethnography challenges dominant representations of girls as it offers a close-up of their play. The ethnography is as rich as Caton's, but much closer to home for most readers.

Gumperz, John, and Dell Hymes, eds. 1972. *Directions in Sociolinguistics: The Ethnography of Communication*. New York: Holt.

In their 1972 classic, the editors bring together a range of scholars collaborating in the definition of the **ethnography of communication** *as a new field.*

3 Semiotics and Sign-Types

LEARNING OBJECTIVES

After reading this chapter, you should be able to do the following:

- Distinguish between icons, indexes, and symbols, and discuss examples of their co-occurrence.
- Provide reasons to use the word "symbol" narrowly rather than as an umbrella term for all signs and sign-types.
- Discuss the significance of context in relation to language and indexicality.
- Discuss the relative frequency of icons and indexes among animals.
- Understand why symbols might be evident only in the human world.
- Describe the history of sign theories and their importance to cultures, particularly religious ideas and practices.
- Discuss the intellectual traditions associated with Saussure, Jakobson, Peirce, and Bateson.

Introduction

We live in a world of signs. It is a world that can be explained in reference to the "semiotic" (now, more typically "semiotics") of Charles Sanders Peirce (pronounced "purse"). Diverse phenomena – from the turning of sunflowers toward the sun to the process whereby DNA is transcribed as RNA (ribonucleic acid), which in turn is translated into proteins – can all be understood in terms of sign relations (Ji 2002).

This chapter covers the following themes: signs, metasigns, and their dynamic relations one to another; semiotics or sign theories in history and culture; the sharply different sign theories of Ferdinand de Saussure and Charles Peirce; and Peirce's most famous triad (icons, indexes, and symbols), which he conceived of as three sign modalities.

Signs

Signs seem to breed and multiply in Peirce's theory. As we discussed in Chapter 2, signs include **interpretants**; but they also *produce* interpretants, which are themselves new signs. Peirce distinguished several kinds of interpretants, including the "dynamical interpretants" (i.e., dynamic effects like that of the sun on the sunflower). Such is Peirce's vision of **semiosis** or sign production-reception-circulation – a "live-action" process-oriented model provided by the great philosopher himself. Keep in mind throughout this chapter, however, that although we talk about icons, indexes, and symbols as though they are things (sign-things), by the end of the book it should be clear that what is most interesting are the *processes* by which people produce (and use, circulate, and consume) signs, processes by which complex relationships are made to appear as icons. (We discuss "iconization" more in Chapter 9.)

Often words and larger units of language denote and refer – that is, they pick out something in the world and say something about it. When thinking about what language is and what it does, we tend to think that its "denotative-referential" function is the whole story. Until the philosopher J. L. Austin described language as a tool for doing things, philosophers of language fell into the same trap, treating sentences like "The sky is blue," whose obvious function is denotative-referential, as typical.

For pre-Austinian philosophers of language, such falsifiable assertions represented the primary, if not the only, function of language. But in fact, communication, or semiosis, is as likely to involve a sign *affecting* something as to merely serve a denotative-**referential** function (to say something about something) or to convey information between interlocutors (those engaged in conversing with each other).

As I noted previously, the sign's interpretant is a new sign in and of itself. The sun is a sign that determines certain effects – for example, in a sunflower (CP 2.275) – and thus the sunflower becomes a **representamen** of the sun:

> If a sunflower, in turning toward the sun, becomes by that very act fully capable, without further condition, of reproducing a sunflower which turns in precisely corresponding ways toward the sun, and of doing so with the same reproductive power, the sunflower would become a Representamen of the sun.

This is not to say that the sunflower is an **icon** of the sun (resembling it), let alone a **symbol** thereof. For Peirce, the flower is an **index** of the sun in that flower and sun share a physical context in which the sun determines at least something about the flower.

The relationship between "representamens" and "signs" is complex. Peirce (CP 2.242) wrote, "[A sign] is a representamen of which some interpretant is a cognition of a mind." Whereas here Peirce makes signs a subclass of representamens, at other times he seems to use representamen and sign interchangeably. All signs, after all, *represent*.

If DNA and sunflowers can be signs, it is all the more true that animals, including human animals, exchange signs regularly. Note, however, that people – and, to some extent, most mammals – stay busy circulating metasigns along with lower-level signs, and that's what we turn to next.

Metasigns

The relationship between x and *meta-x* – something (even a thought or reflection) and a reflection on that something – may seem impossibly abstract. But in fact we cannot think or speak without it, and nor can mammals play without the power of metasignaling (Bateson 1972:185–187) – and all mammals apparently play. Polish and German versions of the term **metalanguage** first appeared in philosophical writings in the 1930s, before Anglophone philosophers began using the term. Use of the prefix "meta-", however, has a much longer history and is quite widespread today. Invoking "metacognition" is now very common in schools of education, but it appears to have been a somewhat newer trend, starting in the 1970s.

Gregory Bateson was the first scholar in the field of culture and communication to demonstrate the power of analyzing the *sign–metasign* relationship. To be specific, Bateson wrote about the relationship between communication and **meta-communication** (i.e., communication that reflects on, or is about, communication). It is worth noting that during his long career, Bateson studied many phenomena pertaining to culture and communication – carrying out ethnographic fieldwork in Papua New Guinea ([1936] 1958), analyzing the nature of schizophrenia, and studying how dolphins learn in captivity.

The world, or at least the human world, requires frames in order to be interpretable. Bateson, invoking the notion of the **figure-ground** relationship developed by Gestalt psychologists, put it like this: "[M]ental processes resemble logic in *needing* an outer **frame** to delimit the ground against which the figures are to be perceived" (1972:188; emphasis in original). (For an example of how the sociologist Erving Goffman developed the idea of "frame analysis" and applied it to conversation, see Goffman 1974 and 1981.)

To understand Bateson's claim, think of literal framing and how differently one might react to the following two images, one which might be framed in an art museum (Figure 3.1a) and the other which, though similar to the first, might be found on the museum bathroom's wall (Figure 3.1b). When we see a literal frame around a pattern formed by paint, charcoal, or other media, our attention is pulled toward the thing that is framed.

Let's examine another example, one that moves quite a bit further from literal framing. In Figure 3.2, the word "Godot" serves as a kind of frame in itself, as a metasign that helps us interpret the basic sign, "Be right back." That metasign reference, of course, is the title of Samuel Beckett's play *Waiting for Godot* (Beckett 1956).

Human communication – particularly when it is face-to-face – is typically multimodal. Participants simultaneously use modalities like spoken language, nonlinguistic sounds like "Hmmm," along with body orientation and gesture. In fact, speech itself encompasses multiple modalities. What marks an American English sentence or utterance as sarcastic or ironic is typically a stand-out (i.e., "marked," Jakobson and Pomorska 1990) **prosodic** pattern including **intonation** (perhaps a

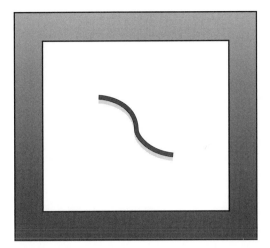

Figure 3.1a Framed squiggle in an art museum. (Illustration by author)

Figure 3.1b Unframed squiggle on museum's bathroom wall. (Illustration by author)

singsong speech melody) and/or voice quality (e.g., **nasalization**). Linguistic anthropologist Jane Hill (citing Sperber and Wilson 1981) writes, "Irony is best understood as a dialogic phenomenon, as the representation of 'What someone else might say'" (1995b:117).

These vocal features are not part of what we think of as language. Instead the marked intonation or voice quality "wraps up" or "frames" words like "Oh great!" in order to cue listeners as to how to interpret the words. The total message thus consists of the frame and what is framed. Without metacommunication or framing, we are at a loss, unable to interpret even the most commonplace utterances.

The problem with the metaphor of an image in a literal frame or an utterance in a figurative frame is that both focus on stable, fixed signs. The metaphor falls short when it comes to modeling natural communication in all of its dynamism. If we think of a frame or metacommunicative signal as something that helps us interpret what is "in" the context, we must keep in mind Lindstrom's insightful comment that in any particular instance of human social interaction, the communicative "context rolls as people talk" (1992:103). Paying attention to the history of sign theories can help us see a kind of scrolling at a macro level.

Figure 3.2 Here the word "Godot" effectively provides a frame for the words above it. (Thor Swift Photography)

Flying in the face of our tendency to see language as text and physical setting (or some such) as context, and adding one more to the list of phenomena that can be considered context, it is worth considering the perspective of neuroscientists like Gendron et al. This research team asserts that "there is accumulating evidence that words shape perception in a variety of domains." They add that "emotion words act as a context during emotion perception" and that "the conceptual knowledge associated with emotion words influences the initial encoding of emotion percepts" (Gendron et al. 2012:314).

Signs and Sign Theories across History

Throughout human history, particularly written history, we have evidence of a concern with signs – what things signify, stand for, represent, or communicate and how they do so. Indeed, we find the *concept of sign(s)* across cultures of the past. Sign theories are metasigns, **metasemiotic** concepts that are signs of their own sort – signs about signs. Wherever human beings have lived, they not only have used signs, but also have had clear metasemiotic concepts. Typically, those metasemiotic ideas are best called **ideologies**, ideas related to the unequal distribution of power in the societies that produce the ideologies.

Figure 3.3 Pictograph from Chauvet-Pont-d'Arc Cave in southern France may represent a theory of signs. (Patrick Aventurier/Getty Images)

Before we move on, I call your attention to an important feature of the prefix "meta-": Any word resulting from the addition of "meta-" in the reflexive sense that concerns us here must be an instance of the thing (noun) modified by the prefix. For example, only some bits of language can qualify as metalanguage. An instance of metalanguage must be language about language.

Sometimes we must infer the concept – the metasemiotic concept – that underlies fantastic artistic productions which predate writing. At times, we might even see evidence of multiple conflicting sign theories. The history of human thought is a history of such multiplicity, if not outright conflict.

For example, scholars have multiple theories to explain rock art left by small groups of people hundreds or thousands of years ago. The term **rock art** includes not only scratchings and etchings, called petroglyphs, but also paintings on open-air rock faces or inside large caves, called pictographs.

What is the purpose or nature of beasts so vividly painted that they look as though they might leap off of the European cave wall on which we may be lucky enough to see them? (See Figure 3.3.) Some rock art scholars assert that such paintings are likely to have been more than mere depictions. The act of painting on cave walls might well have been a ritual act aimed at magically attracting game to the cave's vicinity. (Note that experts consider such rock art to be the product of *Homo sapiens*. Together with other "artistic" products in the archaeological record, these are considered indicators of fully modern human brains with the capacity to produce fully modern language, as we will see in Chapter 5.)

We can't be sure that such a theory of signs (or, in this case, of "art") motivated these prehistoric users. Yet I mention it here to underscore the importance of communication (making or deploying signs) not only as a means of designating or referring to things in the world but as a means of *doing* things in the world. Signs, be they of the linguistic sort or some other, serve both functions in every human society.

Let us now turn our gaze from prehistoric sign users to some examples from the present. When two or more societies clash – as they certainly have in the American Southwest, for instance, where Native American groups such as the White Mountain Apache live – the use of signs is quite often at the heart of the clash. Sadly, clashes between groups like the White Mountain Apache and powerful outsiders (Euro-Americans) sometimes reappear within tribes, in the form of those whose perspective and actions toward their indigenous language appear, at least superficially, to be "White" and ("traditional") Native.

Marybeth Nevins is a linguistic anthropologist who has long worked with the White Mountain Apache people. She has written (see Nevins 2004, 2013) of the vexing questions facing that community, questions that arise from dominant American ideologies of language and learning: Is it appropriate to teach the Apache language in schools – for example, to spell out the Apache word for *bear* and write it on a white board, or to use computers to motivate Apache youth to learn their grandparents' language? Or will doing these things rob the bear of its vital reality – and likewise destroy the language – by ripping it out of the traditional contexts in which it was learned?

In another example of present-day societal conflicts, anthropologist Jane Hill has studied what she calls **Mock Spanish** for over two decades. Increasingly in the last fifteen years, she sees Mock Spanish as an example of "the everyday language of White racism" (Hill 2009). By contrast with *overt* racist language, such as racial slurs, Mock Spanish is a "covert racist discourse" (Hill 2009). As such, it is invisible. Hill asserts that White English speakers in the southwestern United States do not recognize certain common uses (or *misuses*) of Spanish as racist. But, as Hill writes, Mock Spanish – like other forms of covert racist discourse – subtly "works to reproduce negative stereotypes of members of people of color, in this case, members of historically Spanish-speaking populations in the United States" (2009:119). Non-Hispanic English speakers in the United States have been for centuries *somewhat* aware of Mock Spanish and the pejorative "work" it does. Hill (1995a) provides examples dating back to the late eighteenth and early nineteenth centuries, but her clearest example is from Jerome Hart's book, *Vigilante Girl*, in which a character refers to "'buckayro' Spanish. It ain't got but thirteen words in it, and twelve of them are cuss words" (Hart 1910:60). The use of words like *mañana*, *cerveza*, and *cojones* in contemporary English work subtly to associate Spanish speakers with negative stereotypes.

Hill finds unresolved questions in ordinary Americans' ideas about ways of talking, which we can appropriately call **language ideologies**: Are "racist slurs" (i.e., words perceived by their targets as demeaning and degrading) simply tools for referring quite innocently to a social group? Such a claim is embedded in arguments that "it was just a slip of the tongue, and nothing bad was intended," or "words will never hurt me." On the other hand, White Americans sometimes recognize that offensive words (e.g., racial slurs and all sorts of labels for ethnic and gendered Others) can indeed be intentionally used as "sticks and stones." This ideology, which Hill calls **performative**, recognizes that words *are* actions, capable of wounding others. It is yet another case involving not only metasemiotic concepts, but clashing visions of semiosis within one society.

The issue of competing ideologies about racist slurs is not so different from that which has recently divided the White Mountain Apache tribe internally – only the actors are different. As Nevins argues, disagreements over language policy, specifically over different approaches to language revitalization, are often cast in terms of Apache versus White ways of speaking, acting, and behaving. "Reflections on differences" between White and Apache norms "are germane to language maintenance because they comprise a local exegetical tradition on Apache and English languages that inform concerns about Apache language loss as well as local reactions to language programs" (Nevins 2013:23).

The preceding paragraphs, about histories of sign theories, remind us that the past reaches into the present. Among those who study sign theories of the past, archaeologists or specialists in ancient civilizations that had written records have a significant advantage over those whose concern is prehistory: Ideas about signs are often preserved in the written records of literate societies, though we should beware of making overly sharp distinctions between literate and non-literate societies (Street and Besnier 2008).

It appears as though, when sign theories did emerge in literate societies, there were two particular stimuli for their development – a desire to know about things that by nature are *invisible* and a desire to know about the *future*. In the following paragraphs, we look at several examples of how those two desires have been given voice across time and space.

For example, written texts on medicine and **divination** (e.g., "divinatory tracts" from Mesopotamia) tried to answer a question like "If this, then what?" with "this" or "X" as the omen and "what" as the "oracle" or prediction. Studying signs in ancient medicine, at least in Greece, might seem similar to what is done in biomedicine today – Greek physicians scrutinized signs for what they revealed about patients' conditions. But whereas biomedicine today interprets sets of signs as indicators or indexes of a *diagnosis*, the Greeks of the classical period believed their sign system gave them a *prognosis* or prediction of the course of illness. Deriving "knowledge" (Greek, *gnosis*) is the goal in both cases, but these different kinds of knowledge lead to different modes of action.

The ancients naturally had their theories of – and debates over – language too. Is language able to convey, or link people to, reality? Plato didn't think so: "Language is not a sufficiently valid tool for attainment of knowledge of reality" (Manetti 2010, summarizing Plato's view). The Mahayana school of Buddhist thought and Hinduism see this differently though. Keep in mind that Buddhism arose in the midst of, and in reaction to, Hinduism, in India. Perhaps it was, at least in part, a particular Hindu understanding of sacred words, consisting of sacred sounds (like *Om* ॐ), that provoked Buddhist skepticism. A very ancient strand of Hindu thought affirms that it is sound which most powerfully conveys the sacred. Beck (1993:6) describes the following soundscape or sonic "scene" – one as current as the latest Twitter feed, but also one whose theological underpinnings date back a thousand years and more. So, we suspect, do the enactments of the scene below:

> Drums, bells, gongs, cymbals, conch shells, flutes, lutes, and a wide assortment of vocalizations are often heard simultaneously, blending together to create a vibrant sonic atmosphere within the Hindu temple, home, or sacred space. The initial impression to an outsider, or non-Hindu, is one of cacophony and profane chaos, an irrational ensemble of noise without order, rhyme, or reason. On closer inspection, however, one finds that what are being heard are specific sets of "prescribed sound," backed by an arsenal of oral and written sacred tradition. Consequently, whole categories of "proscribed sound" are restricted from holy encounters. (Beck 1993:1–6)

Interestingly, Beck's description happens to be very much like what I heard during Hindu *pujas* (rituals, sacred ceremonies) when I lived in Bangladesh in the 1990s, conducting ethnographic fieldwork there.

In South Asia, we find continuity between centuries-old religious rituals and philosophical discourse and their contemporary echoes. For instance, we could consider medieval Hindu writings on what gives poetic words their transformative or even healing power. An example of an ancient Sanskritic theory of **poetics**, aesthetics, or – as we might say – *signs* is the *dhvani* theory, the theory that poetry's seductive power lies in its suggestiveness (Bruce M. Sullivan, personal communication, June 2013). Or we could look at contemporary Yolmo (Nepali-Buddhist) shamanic rituals designed to restore a wandering *bla* ('soul') back to its body in contemporary placetime (Desjarlais 1996).

In either case, what we would find is a cultural concept of many signs working together to **sacralize** (make sacred) a place or event. It is worth noting that Desjarlais experienced first-hand the chanting of lamas designed to bring back a wandering *bla*. In fact, he apprenticed himself to a Tibetan-Buddhist lama/**shaman/ritual specialist** during his fascinating fieldwork in Nepal. He describes the chanting as consisting of "a point by point appeal to the imagination. Each image, standing alone, acts as a lure" (1996:154). In other words, *Yolmo wa* (the Yolmo people) understand these signs as enticing the soul to return to its body. We return to Desjarlais' description of Yolmo theories of signs in Chapter 6.

To sum up the historical-cultural account I have provided in this chapter thus far, many societies have paid intense attention to signs and have developed elaborate sign theories. Some of us have encountered these *semiotic* theories growing up in a community defined by a holy book or body of scripture; others of us might have had grandparents who were poet-philosophers. In any case, we find explicit theories of signs in the classical philosophy of Greeks and Romans as well as in the Hebrew Bible, the New Testament, the Qur'an, and in ancient commentaries and reflections on the holy books.

But why do we use the noun **semiotics** or the adjective **semiotic**? The terms and their various forms are borrowed rather directly from Greek. According to the *Oxford English Dictionary*, "Greek σημειωτικός [semeiotikos] significant; also, concerned with the interpretation of symptoms … σημειοῦν [semeioun] to interpret as a sign, σημε ον [semeion] sign" (OED Online 2016). Profound religious or theological questions, such as how people could encounter the divine and understand divine communications – theories of divine revelation (e.g., in Papua New Guinea, Slotta 2014) – are semiotic issues. But theories of meaning, significance, and signs grew up in rather more secular philosophical traditions as well – in ancient Sanskrit theories of language and how it works, for example.

It was therefore no arbitrary intellectual event when American philosopher Charles Peirce worked across several decades before and after 1900 to develop what he called his theory of "semeiotic." Today we refer to such theories and, for example, to Peirce's sign theory as semiotics. Linguistic anthropology owes a great debt to Peirce, though not only to him. The contributions of Roman Jakobson and Gregory Bateson are also important to the development of semiotic anthropology (i.e., an anthropological approach to culture and communication).

Human Communication and Peirce's Trichotomy of Sign Modes

In the following section, then, we compare Peirce's "semiotic" and Saussure's "**semiology**." Peirce's model of the sign is triadic – more accurately, triads structure Peirce's thinking at all levels. The subsections below include introductions to each of Peirce's three semiotic modes – iconicity, indexicality, and symbolicity – a triad that contrasts with Saussure's thinking , which, for the most part, excludes iconicity and indexicality, as what Saussure calls "motivated," meaning not arbitrary ([1916] 1959:69).

Note, too, that I strongly disagree with the tendency, in both popular and anthropological contexts, to use the word "symbol" as a cover term for signs, *including* indexes and icons. This tendency might derive from Saussure. At any rate, despite the profound difference between Saussurean and **Peircean** thought – a difference that helps explain why linguistic anthropologists prefer Peirce's "semiotic" over Saussure's "semiology" – I agree (as did Saussure and Peirce) on the importance of what Peirce calls symbolicity.

Saussure and Peirce

By this point in the book, you have read a great deal about Peirce and a bit about Saussure. Let me briefly underscore their differences before continuing along a decidedly Peircean path. Unlike Peirce's *triadic* relationship between sign, object, and interpretant – a relationship that leads to an open-ended, nonfinite world of signs (since every sign gives rise to a unique interpretant) – Saussure's model is *dyadic*. He speaks of signifiers – linguistic signs like "tree" that stand not for any particular tree, but for a signifier – e.g., the general idea of "tree." (See Chapter 2.)

It is true in this case that the signifier, which is a sonic sign (tree), has no inherent or necessary relationship with the idea of "treeness." Saussure wrote that the **signifier** is essentially **arbitrary** in its relationship with its **signified**. In his terms, the signifier is unmotivated – it doesn't take the sound shape that it does in relation to the signified for any particular reason. Saussure regarded **motivated** signs – such as the phenomenon of onomatopoeia or, from Peirce's perspective, **sound iconism** – as insignificant. Whereas Saussure was a pioneering linguist, Peirce was a philosopher; as such, he was concerned with signs and sign processes (semiosis) extending far beyond language and indeed, from Peirce's perspective, pervading the world.

Peirce was a friend of philosophers John Dewey and William James as well as a fellow contributor to the American school of philosophical thought called Pragmatism. (As an aside, Peirce might have been the coiner of the term "Pragmatism," but later asserted his preference for "Pragmaticism," which he famously described as "ugly enough to be safe from kidnappers" [CP 5.415].) But unlike Dewey or James, Peirce was never really accepted in academia; he never had a tenured position at a university but instead worked largely on his own.

Peirce defined a sign as "something that stands to someone for something in some respect or capacity" (CP 2.274). Buried in that definition is a triad, and, as we discussed in Chapter 2, Peirce is famous for his love of triads. To review, his best known triad is the set of sign- (or sign-vehicle) types. Peirce asserted that there are three and only three ways in which signs can stand for their objects, three "respects or capacities" – by virtue of similarity (icons), closeness or association (indexes), or some law-like generalization (symbols). That is, a sign may stand for something by resembling it or pointing to it or simply by convention (i.e., in an arbitrary or culturally constructed fashion, rather than a motivated fashion). So we see that what Saussure held to be true of "the signifier" in general – namely, its arbitrariness – Peirce instead saw as "the symbol," which is but one of three possible sign-types. Let's look now at some examples of each.

Figure 3.4 Individual icons of India are grouped together here to convey the message, "I love India." (Marish/Shutterstock)

Icons and Iconicity

Icons mean, represent, or stand for their objects by virtue of *resembling* them or sharing some common quality. All "portraits," such as photographs or paintings, are icons of the things they resemble. And many iconic relationships are more abstract than portraits. For instance, in Figure 3.4, we see a group of icons, which together convey a larger message. Having talked about icons, we need to also note that the word **iconicity** simply means a resemblance of some kind.

Indexes and Indexicality

Indexes mean, represent, or stand for their **object** by a *relationship* of closeness or contiguity. For instance, smoke indexes fire. Of course, it is only an index for someone who can actually see a plume of smoke arising out of the landscape.

In another example, a shout for help (see Figure 3.5) is an index of the shouter's presence and orientation toward getting someone's attention, but it only works if another person is in proximity and can hear the shouter. (Note that Figure 3.5 is an icon of a sign – an **imagistic** representation of a person shouting for help – even if the sign or communicative act it depicts is also indexical.) On the other hand, if you are alone in a very large and dark room and you suddenly hear a scream, it serves as

Figure 3.5 A shout for help may be indexical – if someone hears it. (Cultura RM/Alamy)

an index of the presence of at least one other person in the room. My point is to emphasize that indexes are not limited to linguistic signs. Not only linguistic shouts (indexical words like "Help!"), but even a scream, can be indexical. They both rivet the attention (Peirce CP I.369, 2.285).

Symbols and Symbolicity

Most of the signs to which a society clings most ferociously are symbols. Symbols tend to be **polysemous** (i.e., carrying many meanings). Symbols are uniquely human precisely because they embody an arbitrary or culturally conventional rule: *The sign stands for this just because it does.*

For instance, the words *water*, *agua*, and *vesi* denote something like H_2O, and no doubt speakers of English, Spanish, and Finnish, respectively, experience these words as directly reminding them of the liquid. Yet their common (denotative) **meaning** by no means forces a common sound shape in the three languages. Water is water, just because.

Are there also true symbols – **arbitrary** signs that represent their objects only by convention – *in the animal world*? Some say yes, and they thereby push us to find the uniqueness of human language in something other than the mere presence or absence of arbitrary signs in a species' communicative repertoire.

Figure 3.6 The Tunisian flag, like all national flags, includes symbols of significance to its citizens. (Dallas and John Heaton/Getty Images)

> The comparison of the use of arbitrary signs in six species (vervet monkeys, European starlings, gray parrots, bonobos, bottlenose dolphins and humans) shows that a difference between human and non-human communication is not in arbitrary, learned, voluntary, or natural signs but in the number of signs used. Language is the only natural communication system with a physically uncountable number of signs. (Luuk 2013:94)

Peirce and his great interpreter, Jakobson, located the driving force of language in symbols. And unlike Saussure, Peirce's "scrupulous attention to the indexical and iconic components of verbal symbols is intimately linked with his thesis that 'the most perfect of signs' are those in which the iconic, indexical, and symbolic characters 'are blended as equally as possible'" (Jakobson [1965] 1987:418). To compare, Saussure treated motivated, or non-arbitrary, signs as eminently ignorable, whereas indexes and icons, which are motivated signs, are central to Peirce, as well as to Jakobson and contemporary linguistic anthropologists.

A country's flag or a religious symbol (like a cross, a Star of David, or a crescent) all have both iconic and indexical elements (see Figure 3.6).

A familiar example to many is the cross, which is an *icon* of the cross on which Jesus was crucified, insofar as it resembles that cross. It is an *index* insofar as it points our attention to that original. Also, if it hangs on a necklace around someone's neck, its contiguity with the wearer is an indexical sign: That cross indexes the wearer and possibly that person's faith. To understand the **symbolicity** of "the" cross (the original cross of Jesus, which may be represented indexically and iconically by a cross on a necklace or one found on top of a church, for example), we need look no further than to the idea, belief, or conviction that this cross represents an act of individual self-sacrifice that results in divine forgiveness for others. That is, the cross is a symbol because its meanings are many, and its meanings include some that are arbitrary (i.e., culturally conventional).

CONCLUSION

In this chapter, we have looked at the historical context for the study of culture and communication by means of semiotics. We reviewed Saussure and looked more closely at Charles Peirce and his notion of "semiotic." We have seen that indexes are omnipresent in the animal world, whereas icons are somewhat less frequent. Scholars have long understood symbols as all but nonexistent outside of human communication; recently, however, some have rejected this claim. The chapter has taken us back in history and across the world, revealing that human societies have for thousands of years worried, thought, and prayed about signs but also about the very concept of a sign. Thus, to say we live in a world of signs is true not only in a biological sense, but in an ethnological (or cross-culturally comparative) sense.

Yet we have only scratched the surface of signs, and we have much yet to explore about signs in human social life. That is why we further explore many of the themes introduced here in Chapters 8 and 9. Before that, though, in Chapter 4, we turn from addressing communication in general to focusing on language in particular.

SUMMARY

After reading this chapter, you should have a good understanding of the following themes:

- Three specific kinds of signs – icons, indexes, and symbols.
- The meaning and cultural significance of metasigns.
- Sign theories throughout human history.
- Saussure's semiology versus Peirce's triads.

QUESTIONS

1. What are icons, indexes, and symbols?
2. What does a literal frame around an object (like a picture frame) provide the viewer?

3. Why is it significant that divination texts might be the oldest semiotic theories we know of or that many, if not most, ancient sign theories come from religious texts?
4. What does it mean to say that indexical meaning is context-dependent? Does the meaning of the following words change with context: "make," "like," "splash," "zoom," or "chic"?
5. What does "polysemous" mean?
6. Imagine you are given two signs (words, images, or some other form of sign). How could you tell whether one is a metasign in relation to the other?

EXERCISES

1. This exercise involves the prefix "meta-," which received attention in a story from National Public Radio, broadcast in January 2010. The narrator says at one point, "It's all quite meta – watching a movie about Los Angeles gangs while on a tour that is supposed to show riders Los Angeles gangs." Write about the communicative (social, cultural, linguistic) function of the prefix "meta-" in the line: "It's all quite meta . . ."
2. Imagine a flag outside a United States embassy in another country. (The flag's placement outdoors can help you with this exercise.) Working in groups or alone, decide the following: What elements are icons insofar as there is a one-to-one correspondence between them and something about our country? What element of this flag is an index (meaning linked inextricably with physical context)? What elements of the flag are symbolic (meaning arbitrary cultural meanings)?
3. Investigate ancient theories of signs, focusing on a particular theory that dominated a particular religious tradition at a particular time and place. From what time, place, and/or religious tradition does the sign theory come? How does it reflect that time and place? How is it like, or unlike, a semiotic tradition such as Peirce's or Saussure's?
4. View Werner Herzog's documentary film *Cave of Forgotten Dreams* (2011). Discuss how the film is a metasemiotic or metacommunicative activity. What did the filmmakers do, especially on camera, that makes the metasemiotic nature of the film clear? When you think about metacommunication that is more or less simultaneous with an act of communication (e.g., putting a frame around a sign) versus metacommunication involving a large gap in time and space (such as in this film), what thoughts come to mind about the pros and cons, dangers and advantages of metasemiosis across gaps?

ADDITIONAL RESOURCES

Bateson, Gregory. 1972. *Steps to an Ecology of Mind*. New York: Ballantine Books.

Bateson's contributions to the fields of anthropology and communication – and to our understanding of mind, culture, and language – is significant. This book includes some of his most important contributions.

Innis, Robert E., ed. 1985. *Semiotics: An Introductory Anthology*. Bloomington: Indiana University Press.

Innis provides a collection of scintillating essays representing a very broad range of semioticians and approaches to semiotics.

Urban, Greg. 1992. Semiotics and Anthropological Linguistics. In *International Encyclopedia of Language and Linguistics*, Vol. III. W. Bright, ed. Pp. 406–408. Oxford University Press.

Urban's article is a clear and concise introduction to a semiotic approach to linguistic anthropology.

4 The Structure of Language

LEARNING OBJECTIVES

After reading this chapter, you should be able to do the following:

- Identify and define the levels of linguistic structure.
- Define phonetic difference. Describe how sound variation can make either a **phonemic difference** or a stylistic difference.
- Explain "meaning" in relation to phonemes and morphemes.
- Describe the social (indexical) significance of "two ways of saying the same thing" in different varieties of English.
- Explain the social (indexical) function of switching between varying forms of second-person pronouns ("you") – for example, in Spanish, French, German, and Nepali.

Introduction

In Chapters 1 through 3, we have been exploring the nature of language – as a tool for **social action**, in speaking as a form of action, in the importance of metase-miotic reflection, semiotic ideologies (e.g., ideologies of social media and how we use them), and language ideologies (i.e., language as generator and object of value).

In this chapter, we look at language at a more granular level. Although we include a traditional view – meaning a structural linguist's view – of language, we also interweave a communicative-functional perspective on language.

To explain, very often textbooks on linguistics, culture and communication, or linguistic anthropology present readers with a hierarchy of structures, from the sounds of language (**phonetics** and **phonology**) to how words are formed through processes like adding **affixes** (prefixes and suffixes) and then to rules for joining words together into phrases and sentences (syntax). Somewhere along the way, such textbooks deal with "meaning," particularly **semantic meaning**. Finally, some textbooks describe a level of structure beyond the sentence – commonly called **discourse**, but in other contexts or **text(uality)**.

There is nothing wrong with this traditional view in and of itself. It is important, however, to recognize the range of **functions** performed at least potentially by each level: In addition to their contribution to semantic (i.e., denotative-referential) meaning, building blocks from sounds through sentences may also carry (1) social-indexical, (2) participation-managing, (3) poetic, and (4) emotional functions. (If we take "social-indexical" to be *reflecting something about the social context*, "participation-managing" is *entailing/creating some social-contextual feature*.)

Because of the importance of these functions, and because they are so rarely acknowledged in either cultural anthropology or linguistics textbooks, I introduce them here and ask you to read the remaining chapters of the book with this perspective in mind.

Levels of Linguistic Structure

I introduce this section by observing something striking: Strange things happen to words that designate levels of linguistic structure when we try to processualize them (as we discussed in Chapter 1). When we go from sound to *sounding*, we're talking about "sounding off" or how I perceive your talk ("You sound like you're from Boston!"). The word "wording" denotes something more thing-like than "using words." When we say "sentencing," we usually don't mean "making and using sentences." And what would we mean if we were to say *discoursing*? Despite all this, I really do have processes in mind when I speak of sounds, words, sentences, or discourse – but just as we did not dismiss the value of structuralism out of hand in Chapter 2, here we explore the value of envisioning levels of linguistic structure as building blocks – used in the *process* of building, but "blocks" nonetheless.

Language is compositional. We produce "strands" of language by combining the smallest building blocks into larger and larger "blocks" (see Figure 4.1) – phonemes, morphemes, words, phrases, sentences, and discourse structures, including conversations or speeches.

All languages have a repertoire of sounds and a fixed number of consonants and vowels. These sounds vary according to criteria such as these: What parts of the mouth produce them and where in the mouth are they made? (See Figure 4.2.) How are the sounds made? Are they **voiced sounds** (sounds that make the voice box buzz) or **voiceless sounds** (which are whispered)? What happens to the speaker's airflow in producing consonants? Does it stop completely, as in the case of the English consonants /p/, /t/, /k/, /b/, /d/, and /g/? Does the flow of air become constricted, producing buzzing or hissing ("fricative") sounds, like /f/ or /s/? Is it channeled through the nose ("nasals"), especially "nasal consonants" like /m/ or /n/? These questions point to just some of the many manners of **articulation** by which people produce the sounds of their individual languages.

Each language has a unique sound system. Speakers of one language may not even hear some of the sounds of an unrelated language. Or they may hear them, but not perceive them as linguistic sounds. Even if two languages share a sound, like the consonant /b/, that /b/ consonant may function differently in the context of those languages' divergent sound systems.

Step 1. We begin with the following four English phoneme "building blocks"

/g/ + /o/ + /i/ + /ŋ/

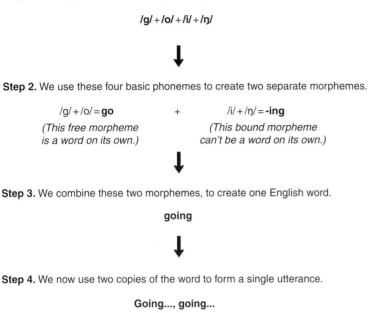

Step 2. We use these four basic phonemes to create two separate morphemes.

/g/ + /o/ = **go**   +   /i/ + /ŋ/ = **-ing**

(This free morpheme   *(This bound morpheme*
is a word on its own.)   *can't be a word on its own.)*

Step 3. We combine these two morphemes, to create one English word.

going

Step 4. We now use two copies of the word to form a single utterance.

Going..., going...

Step 5. We use that utterance to convey a specific meaning in a social context.

Going...
        going...

Figure 4.1 Compositionality: From sounds and morphemes to words and speech acts.
(Illustration Charissa Pray)

Distinctions in Linguistic Sounds: Phonemic and Non-Phonemic Differences

Sound systems enable (or force!) speakers of a language to recognize differences. And the extent and diversity of sound differences is remarkable. I share some examples of language sound diversity in the next several paragraphs. (As you read, you will notice some places where brackets are used; in others, you'll see slash marks. For more information about these technical markings, please see the Appendix of this book.)

All languages have pairs of sounds (consonants or vowels) that are produced similarly, but have the power to change a word's meaning. Other sets of sounds

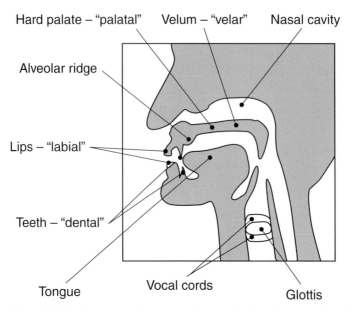

Hard palate – "palatal"　Velum – "velar"　Nasal cavity

Alveolar ridge

Lips – "labial"

Teeth – "dental"

Tongue　　Vocal cords　　Glottis

Figure 4.2 The human vocal apparatus is capable of making more kinds of sounds than we ever use, because we only learn to produce the specific sounds of the language(s) we eventually speak. (William Elford Rogers)

made with nearly identical actions of lips, tongue, teeth, and lungs show up as quite distinct waveform patterns, but pass for "the same sound" to native speakers. You can see this by looking at audio recordings of a vowel, consonant, or word using freeware like *Praat* (Mendoza-Denton 2011) or *Audacity*. For instance, English speakers learn to distinguish sounds like /b/ and /p/, which both involve the lips and a stoppage of the airflow; they are both called "stops." These kinds of sound differences exist in all languages – and in fairly unique ways in every language, some phonetic changes make a semantic difference, while others do not.

All of the different sorts of sounds made by native speakers of any language are called **phones**. In any given language, speakers experience some phones – namely, **phonemes** – as meaningful. However, we don't really experience **allophones**, at least not consciously. What do I mean by that? In trying to understand allophones and phonemes, it helps to think of them as pairs that we manipulate or switch between. Phones that change the semantic meaning of otherwise identical words are called phonemes (like the /e/ sound in "steak" in English – or the [e] sound in the word "aid" versus [ɛ], which is the vowel sound we use and hear in the name Ed – and *aid* and *Ed* are what we call **minimal pairs**). By contrast, sets of similar sounds that involve shades of acoustic (i.e., sonic) or phonetic difference that we aren't even aware of are called allophones, like the slight differences in the /t/ sound in the English words "steak" and "take." (See Figure 4.3.)

The distinctions between phones that native speaker-hearers make are never known or knowable to speaker-hearers of other languages without conscious

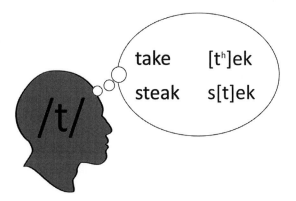

Figure 4.3 Phonemic distinction as a perceptual category. (Illustration Charissa Pray)

study. For instance, Korean speakers perceive no significant difference between /b/ and /p/, whereas English speakers use the two sounds to make different words. Thus the sound-pair /b/ versus /p/ constitutes a difference of two phonemes in English, but not Korean (Finegan 2007:111–112).

Let's say an English speaker tells us, "I said *pat* him on the head, not *bat* him on the head!" We know that /p/ and /b/ are different phonemes in English, so replacing one with the other creates a different semantic meaning – and likely a different outcome! The two distinct words "pat" and "bat" are a minimal pair, words that are identical except for the two sounds occurring in the same position. (In this case, the phonemic variants /p/ and /b/ both occur at the beginning of the word.)

Speakers of all languages also alter sounds in ways that do not appear to matter to them, and every language has its separate set of sounds that include close phonetic pairs that do or do not alter word meaning. For example, English speakers actually produce at least two /p/ sounds that, objectively speaking, are quite different. The two different forms – [pʰ] (which is an aspirated "p" – i.e., a "p" followed by a puff of air) and [p] (an unaspirated "p") – are chameleon-like variables, meaning they change "color" depending on their phonetic environment. (You can read more about aspirated and unaspirated sounds in the Appendix.) For another example, when you say "pat" [pʰæt] and "spat" [spæt], the difference in the /p/ sounds is likely not obvious to you. But try saying each word in front of a lighted candle, and you'll find that [pʰ] (an aspirated "p") blows the candle out, while [p] (an unaspirated "p") does not. (Incidentally, the vowel æ is pronounced like the "a" in words like paddle, lamp, and spat.)

In some languages, "phonemic lengthening" affects semantic meaning; in other languages it does not. As an English speaker, you may "stretch out" (lengthen) either the "uh" or the "m" in the pseudo-word "uhm" as an indication that you are thinking and not yet ready to speak. But whether or not you lengthen a Finnish vowel or consonant affects semantic meaning significantly. For instance, *ja* (pronounced "yah" or "ya") means 'and', while *jaa* means 'share'.

Sound Variation as Pure Social Index

In language, whatever bits and pieces are not already "busy" distinguishing words or sentences from each other by serving a denotative function – that is, those that go unclaimed by conscious structure – are either subject to less conscious rules or *are available for stylistic use* (i.e., for communicating emotional or social-indexical meanings). For example, in **standard** American English, the two sounds /d/ and /th- [ð, as in ðæt "that"]/ exemplify differences that make a distinction in semantic meaning. The evidence of their "phonemic" contrast is their contrastive role in a minimal pair, which refers to two words that differ minimally (i.e., in which only two closely related sounds occur in the word, such as "data" [dæta] versus "that, uh" [ðæta]). As we shall see, this contrast, which is phonemic in standard American English, is a class-linked variable in New York City dialects.

The relatively new field of sociophonetics, associated with Penelope Eckert and her students, is discovering the sociocultural meanings produced by micro-alterations in the pronunciation of individual vowels. In Eckert's research (2000) in a high school in the United States, variant pronunciations appear to index affiliation with one of two major divisions among students – either "jocks" or "burnouts." Because individual students shift their pronunciation from situation to situation, the variant pronunciations can thus be said to index their relative force of identification with a particular group or role, a force that varies across situations. The pronunciation of individual sounds, therefore, is a communicative act; it is a matter of practice (as we discussed in Chapter 2).

Non-Phonemic Sound Variation: Emotion, Stance, or Contextualization Cue

Nasalization of vowels is phonemic in some languages, and thus – like other sound features – is committed to the task of distinguishing one word from another in terms of its semantic (denotational-referential) meaning. In other languages, like English, nasalization is not tied up with referential distinction, but may be used, for example, to signal irony (sarcasm) or a negative evaluation of someone. Nasalization may also be part of a derogatory mimicry of some speaker (Vaux et al. 2007:338).

The performance of irony involves some degree of emotion. Other ways of voicing our vowels also serve emotional functions. "Cry-breaks" heard both in country-western singing and in ritual weeping or lamenting are vocal icons of crying – they are *like* crying, yet not quite the same as crying (Feld and Fox 1994; Urban 1988). A final special voicing of vowels is called "creaky voice." It can indicate many things about the speaker, including emotion as well as social indexicality (for example, age – creaky voice seems increasingly common among young speakers of Finnish).

Phonation: Variable Voice Qualities

How do various voice qualities pertain to communication, let alone culture? In fact, they pertain to both. People are aware of voice quality. For example, they might ask if a particular Malaysian healer's voice is "beautiful" and whether it "rings out" (Laderman 1987:298–299), because the aesthetic quality is essential to the bomoh's healing power. Similarly, cultural beliefs of the Warao people in Venezuela include criteria for determining what kind of voice used by women in lamenting the dead makes for an authentic, effective lament.

"Timbre" refers to **voice quality** or the quality of sound made by various musical instruments (Feld et al. 2004). What linguistic anthropologist Charles Briggs calls the "wailing timbre" *typically* associated with lamenting contrasts with the bright ("operatic voice") timbre of one lament that Briggs recorded. When he played the recording to a group of Warao listeners two years after making it, the performance was laughed at. Listeners said the voice of that woman strongly indicated she had not been feeling sadness as she should have been (Briggs 1993:936–938).

Sound Symbolism or Iconism

In this section, I present three examples of sound symbolism – relational attitudes in the Kiksht language, various stereotyped voices in the Bangla language, and a variety of stances in communities of speakers around the world.

Sound Variation as Index of Social Attitude

The Kiksht language was originally spoken in Oregon, but apparently became extinct in 2012 when the last fluent speaker of Kiksht died. Nonetheless, this language provides an interesting example of indicators that have the kind of diminutivizing or augmentativizing functions that we first discussed in Chapter 2 using Spanish examples. Those examples are simple in terms of their form (morphology, discussed later in this chapter) because they are suffixes.

In Kiksht, the sequence of sounds used to index affection and dislike for someone have sound shapes that are icons of those diminutive (endearing) and augmentative (pejorative) functions. And what makes the example somewhat challenging to understand is that the sounds used for those functions are not glued together like *i-t-o* in Spanish to form a suffix (*-ito*). Kiksht diminutivizing and augmentativizing indexes are individual sounds spread *across* a word. We could say they have become unglued from each other.

The forms of augmentative language index "repulsiveness to speaker," while diminutive forms index objects that are viewed as subtle or endearing (Silverstein [1981] 2001:389). Just as Mohawk and Spanish morphology makes it possible to index a speaker's feelings toward a referent, Kiksht morphology does the same thing. In Mohawk, this is accomplished by a mandatory choice between two different third-person feminine prefixes. In Spanish, speakers choose among totally optional diminutive and augmentative suffixes. In Kiksht, choice among relatively diminutive and relatively augmentative forms indexes speakers' evaluations of both human and nonhuman referents.

In addition to permitting a two-way marking of feeling toward referents via augmentative and diminutive morphology, Kiksht also provides a neutral option or options. The particular aspects of Kiksht morphology that make it possible to index neutral as well as positive or negative emotional **stances** toward a referent are extremely complex. The importance of the issue, as Michael Silverstein argues ([1981] 2001), is that certain features of Kiksht morphology used for indexing emotional stance help explain something Silverstein experienced when interviewing a native speaker. The native speaker uttered a word with augmentative morphology, but when Silverstein asked her to repeat it, she was unable to. Instead she produced the neutral form. It appears that this form might be subliminally experienced as non-indexing. In fact, some cross-cultural evidence points to a shift, in many languages, toward indexically neutral (or non-indexing) forms (Bender 2008; Halliburton 2005; Keane 2003).

Peirce/Piercing Our Consciousness: Nasalization as Sound Symbolism and Acoustic Power

Linguist and India specialist Edward Dimock explores sound symbolism in Bangla, arguing that onomatopoeias are icons believed to represent some referent more directly than less marked forms of language (1989:52). He uses the nasalized vowel [æ̃] as an example. (Note that the æ vowel is the vowel in the English word "paddle," although it is nasalized as the tilde on top indicates.) In relation to sound symbolism in the Bangla language, Dimock (1989:66) writes

> All [sound-]symbolic forms with /æ̃/ as the base vowel indicate something decidedly unpleasant, either in the nature of the thing indicated or in its effect upon the speaker. Thus, /kæ̃ṭkæ̃ṭ/ indicates a color or combination of colors that is extremely harsh, or a shrewish, loud-voiced woman, /ṭæ̃kṭæ̃k/ something annoying or vexing, /pæcpæc/ thick, distasteful mud or dirt, /pæ̃npæ̃n/ a child wheedling or crying for a long time, etc. The effect of any of these forms can be heightened by [increasing the] nasalization.

My experience of language, and particularly **sound iconism**, in rural Bangladeshi discourse, echoes Dimock's. A young man who lived near me in a large multi-family compound was mystified as to why I would record everyday speech and interaction. He laughingly described my corpus to his family as a bunch of children "doing kæ̃kæ̃." The effect of his remark was to sum up all natural speech – particularly the complaints he knew were my focus – as irritating whinings (Wilce 1998:126) of the sort Bangladeshis associate with children, acts of complaining, and some kinds of spirits. (There are at least three kinds of spirits recognized in Bangladesh – *jinn* is a class of spirits recognized in Islam, while *bhut* and *rāksmos* are local, non-Islamic spirits, inhabiting trees, and attracted to blood.)

Nasalization can act as an index of yet another seemingly different way of speaking – reciting the Qur'an and calling Muslims to prayer. Nelson (2001) writes that "one of the most obvious characteristics of Qur'anic recitation is its nasal quality. This is not to be attributed to custom, aesthetics, or natural voice quality... but to the rules of [recitation, which are called] *tajwīd*. The effect of *gunnah* [(nasalization) and related vocal practices]... is to prolong the duration as well as to change timbre [voice quality]" of each sound, particularly vowels (2001:22).

So it seems that complaints, children, spirits – and even, at a different level, calls to prayer – share a common phonetic index in Bangla because they are somehow structurally homologous in a sound aesthetic that is both Bangladeshi and unconscious (Sapir 1927). What might this aesthetic be, and what is its integrating value? Calls to prayer, children, and spirits share an ability to transgress the privacy of the ear and consciousness – to enter, to share, and yet not share the listener-interlocutor's identity. Monsur Musa, once the Director General of the Bangla Academy (the Bangladeshi government's official language organization), affirms that whenever *jinn*, *bhut*, or *rāksmos* (three sorts of spirits) are animated in the folktale performances of grandparents and so forth, their voices are nasalized (Musa, personal communication, 1996). It could be no accident that Abu Ishaque's (1955) novelistic portrayal of the *jinn/bhut's* voice shares this trait with a 1992 performance by a male Bangladeshi Muslim possession-medium (Wilce 1998:127). Nor is this unrelated to the agreement by a number of interviewees from Matlab and Dhaka in 1996 that a nasalized vowel is disagreeable relative to an oral vowel. In sum, it is no accident that the call to prayer (with nasalization prescribed by tradition), the whining of children, the persistent demands of the *jinn* in Ishaque's novel, and the Bangla lexemic representations for complaining, nagging, whining, and insistent crying (*ghẽnghẽn*, *pyæ̃npyæ̃n*) all achieve their self-indexing or attention-getting function by a combination of nasalization with other homologous phonetic features (W. Beeman, personal communication, August 1995).

Non-Phonemic Creaky Voice and Other Phonatory Variations

Using the so-called creaky voice (or "vocal fry" – easily found on YouTube) involves not only manipulating symbols in Peirce's sense of the term but also physically engaging listeners and forming a *vocal* icon of a *nonvocal* state, such as misery. Brown and Levinson (1987) propose that the whispery creak is associated universally with misery or commiseration, because its acoustic character (see Figure 4.4) involves a very low level of vocal energy. It is a short logical leap to infer that this makes it iconic of misery (1987:119, 267f.). (Interestingly, it is because creaky vowels are produced with low energy that the left column of Figure 4.4 is very light.)

Brown and Levinson's claim turns out to be anything but universal. Creaky voice may have this iconic meaning in Dravidian and Mayan languages where they did

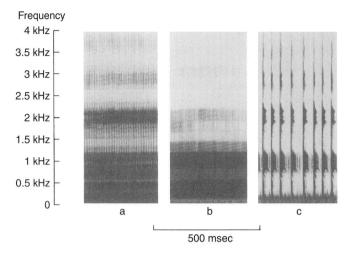

Figure 4.4 Spectrograms of vowels, showing three forms of vocalization – full (regular), whispered, and low energy voice. (Laver 1980)

their fieldwork. The link between creaky voice and suffering also fits the perspective of the Amazonian Shokleng, for whom the creaky voice is found in everyday speech but is also the typical or unmarked vocal quality in ritual wailing (Urban 1985: 311).

In any case, only in a very few languages are creaky vowels phonemic – i.e., changing the meaning of words. That tiny handful includes the source language for Figure 4.4 (Burmese-Myanmar, or Pali-Myanmar). It is because creaky voice is *not* phonemic that its common occurrence in many other languages – including Finnish (Ogden 2003) and Bangla (Dimock 1989, Wilce 1998) – can have an iconic, indexical, or "stylistic" meaning. The most recent linguistic anthropological work on creaky voice is the fascinating work of Norma Mendoza-Denton (2011), who describes the use of creaky voice to index in a very complex manner a hardcore and tough Chicano gangster male persona – a far cry from suffering and weakness!

Put simply, use of the creaky voice may provide a familiar signal. Still, conventions are not abstract governors of behavior. Hence, over and above the conventionality of these vocal gestures, their availability and local social history do condition the significance of their use. This semiotic fact potentiates something even more interesting – the ability of actors to invoke, play with, and deviate from convention – if there is a convention at all (Mendoza-Denton 2011: 265–266).

Morphology: Building Words

As we continue our exploration of the structure of language, we move now from the most basic level, sound, to the next level, morphology.

Morphology might be a word you are familiar with from disciplines other than linguistic anthropology. In biology, it refers to the shape of a plant or animal or of some part thereof. In relation to language, the word means two rather different things: word "shape" (i.e., the rules for building words out of smaller units of meaning) and also the study of those phenomena.

The key principle here is that words, but also word "bits," carry meaning. Some languages have words consisting of many meaningful bits, while others allow only one meaning-unit in a word. We call these meaning-units **morphemes.** They may be **free morphemes**, which are whole words. Or they may be **bound morphemes** – word roots, stems, and word bits like prefixes and suffixes that never occur on their own. Examples of bound morphemes specific to English are the plural suffix /-s/ and the past-tense suffix /-ed/.

Note that bound morphemes can *become* free, as in the case of "-ish" according to some accounts (Bochnak and Csipak 2014; Morris 1998), and free morphemes like "going to" can become bound, as in "gonna" – a process called **grammaticalization** (Hopper and Traugott 2003:3)

All morphemes carry meaning, although sometimes it is a functional or grammatical meaning.

The Responsiveness of Morphemes to Sound Environment

Different languages have different word-building rules or different outcomes when they squeeze two or more morphemes together to form a word. Languages such as Turkish maintain pretty watertight boundaries between the various morphemes used to build complex words. On the other hand, the boundaries of morphemes that English speakers stick together to make words are porous; the sounds that make up morphemes shift when juxtaposed to each other. The same sorts of rules that cause phonemes to change their shape also influence the shape of morphemes. When morphemes change to fit their sound environment, the resultant variant forms are called **allomorphs.**

When the English word /in/ is a preposition (as in "in this textbook"), it is a free morpheme. However, when the English word-bit /in-/ is a prefix, it is a bound morpheme with the function of flipping or negating the semantic meaning of a word or root (as in "inflexible").

When it is a prefix, /in-/ is pronounced differently depending on the sound that follows it. It becomes im- before /p/ and /b/ sounds, like "impossible" (ɪmpɑsəbl). It becomes iŋ- before /k/ and /g/ sounds, like "incredible" (ɪŋkrɛdbl). And /in-/ keeps its basic form (in-) before vowels, like "inevitable" (ɪnɛvɪtəbl).

Morphology and Emotion

Many Euro-Americans commonly think, in relation to language and emotion, that emotion resides in words that denote or label feelings. In actuality, almost every feature or dimension of language can signal or carry emotion.

The word "mood" is interestingly ambiguous. Linguists use **mood** (and **modality**) to refer to markers on verbs that signal different stances. Some languages have quite a number of mood/modality distinctions, each with its own formal features, often just a difference of morphemes. Linguistic anthropologist Niko Besnier (1990:424) points out the great range of such distinctions in the world's 6,000 or so languages:

> Many categories commonly associated with inflectional morphology can also carry affective [emotional] meaning; for example: mood (e.g., variations between conditionals and indicatives in Romance languages) . . . and case marking (e.g., agentive noun phrases marked for ergative, oblique, or genitive case in Samoan).

Morphological Variation as Social Index

Just as we found in relation to social (or sociolinguistic) variation in the production of individual sounds like [d] and [ð] (the sound represented as "th-" in the word "that"), the pronunciation of morphemes can vary according to social situation or one's "social address" (gender, age, or class). One oft-studied variable is that between "-ing" and "in-." *Standard* pronunciation of the suffix spelled "-ing" [which appears as -ɪŋ in the International Phonetic Alphabet] in the word "jumping" (IPA, *jʌmpiŋ*) contrasts with the *non-standard* pronunciation "jumpin'" (IPA *jʌmpin* with the suffix appearing as -in). Sociolinguist Peter Trudgill found that male versus female speakers and working-class versus middle-class speakers are systematically more or less likely to use the informal -in suffix. (For more about IPA, see the Appendix.)

Note that switching from the first to the second pronunciation of the suffix (from [-ɪŋ] to [-in]) does not involve *dropping* a sound. Phonetically, the words are the same "length," so jʌmpin (jumpin) is not *missing* a sound or "letter." Rather, it ends with the sound /n/ rather than the sound /ŋ /, which is a single symbol in the International Phonetic Alphabet. The IPA does not use "ng" to represent the sound the English letters "ng" make in words like "sing" for two reasons: because "ng" in English sounds very different in natural pronunciation of "then go," and because it is preferable for the sake of scientific analysis that every IPA character represents one and only one sound.

Syntax: Building Phrases and Sentences

As we saw in Figure 4.1, languages work on the principle of **compositionality** – the smallest units (sounds) fit together to make meaningful units (morphemes), morphemes join together to form words, words join to make phrases, and strings of phrases make sentences. The structure of phrases and sentences – especially the *ordering* of words to make phrases and of phrases to make clauses and sentences – is called **syntax**. (As you probably know, complex sentences typically consist of multiple **clauses** – dependent clauses ["When it rains"] cannot stand on their own, and independent clauses ["it pours"] could be sentences standing alone.)

To study syntax is to study phrase and sentence structure. Like phonology and morphology, syntax is important to students of culture and communication because of the *social* value attached to syntactic (grammatical) variation.

Defining and Illustrating Syntax

Languages tend to have preferences for the ordering of sentence pieces, like subject (if there is one), object (if there is one) and verb. This particular order is often abbreviated as SOV, and it appears to be the most common order among the world's languages. (We discuss this further in Chapter 6.) But for now, consider this: Whatever word order is dominant (at least in languages like English), it can be altered in what we call "poetic license." Departing from the typical word order can serve the purpose of parallelism – for instance, vaulting a word that is needed for a rhyme pattern to the end of the sentence. In his poem *The Jabberwocky*, Lewis Carroll (which was Charles L. Dodgson's pseudonym) plays with many features in English, including its typical word order. Consider this line where the subject comes at the end of the sentence rather than occupying its typical sentence-initial position.

> All mimsy were the borogoves

Is there a "semiotics of syntax"? Indeed, there is an understood iconicity between the order of clauses in a complex sentence that involves, say, listing activities and the order of the events they represent. When someone says, "I got up late, threw some clothes on, and rushed to the store," we understand that the order of these verb phrases or implicit clauses as **representations** of the real world *is* the precise order of the events that occurred in that world.

Syntax and Emotion

Besnier (1990:425) asserts that "many syntactic features are exploited for affective purposes." He then goes on to list some of the many. There are grammatical ways "to assign blame" or engage in the socio-emotional act of shaming someone (Lo and Fung 2012). In Japanese, construing an event by means of a "separate passive construction" represents the event as having had "an adverse effect on the grammatical patient" (Besnier 1990:425). Finnish has a particular "impersonal" construction – a grammatical structure that, as in some passive constructions, lacks any mention of the subject or agent; it can be used to elicit empathy from those to whom the user of the construction is speaking (Ruusuvuori 2005).

Participation-Organizing Function of Syntax

How might the different syntactic structures (grammars, especially word order, as in Subject-Object-Verb versus Subject-Verb-Object) interact with other factors to influence how the give and take of conversational turns unfolds? Might "overlap" be more common in conversations in some languages, say Italian, compared to others, like German? In fact, some evidence points to that very thing. While being cautious about making overly broad claims, Schegloff, Ochs, and Thompson (1996:28–32) argue that there are strong reasons for overlap or interruption to occur in a language like Italian, in which more of the semantic-meaning-punch is front-loaded, than in one like German, where it is back-loaded. They first admit that matters are somewhat complicated in German sentences, which often have two verbs. However, they point out that the one which expresses "the semantic heart of the verbal expression may occur in final position" (1996:29), thus more meaning-loss would occur in German than in Italian, where the main-point-carrying-word (the main verb) can certainly occur earlier in the sentence (1996:28–32).

Meaning: Semantic and Pragmatic

In exploring the meanings we find in language, we must consider both semantic and pragmatic meanings.

Semantic Meaning and Semantic Relations

Semantic meaning is that dimension of meaning that we think of as stable across contexts. It is the kind of meaning we find in dictionaries – denotative, referential meaning. Later in this chapter, we encounter a pioneering attempt in the eighteenth century to categorize semantic relations – in the context of semantic parallelism.

Pragmatic Meaning

The question "What does this mean?" can represent at least two sorts of inquiry. The first involves a kind of decoding – matching each word and every grammatical connection to its "sense." For example, we decode by considering the word "stifling" in the context of these two utterances: "It is really stifling in here with everything closed up," and "The boss creates a stifling atmosphere instead of a creative one." We can find at least these two senses of "stifling" in any good dictionary.

The second type of inquiry involves finding what "here" refers to (in the phrase "in here" in the first example). This can be challenging if you are reading the sentence out of context, but easy if the first utterance is being addressed to you and you are sitting next to a closed window, with this factual proximity being apparent to the speaker. This second kind of inquiry can be answered in terms of "pragmatic" meaning. The **context** for "It's stifling in here" helps us imagine what the speaker was *doing* by saying it. The pragmatic meaning of an utterance is what that utterance accomplishes.

Deictics

The word **deictics** refers to linguistic indexes. They straddle the semantic–pragmatic divide as well as the divide between *language as a system* that to some extent transcends context and *language as a toolkit* for performing actions in or upon a particular context.

Here we pay particular attention to spatial and temporal deictics that tend (at least in Indo-European languages) to come in pairs, like here/there, now/then, and this/that. Such words/word-pairs have one foot in grammatical structure and the other in the unfolding context of language-in-interaction. We have deictic adverbs ("here," "now") and deictic verbs ("come" and "go," and "bring" and "take"). Languages as diverse as Finnish and Yucatec Mayan have a large number of variant forms meaning something like "here" or something like "there" (Sidnell 1999).

Pronominal indexes ("I," "you," and "we") are examples in English, but in order to imagine the importance of deictics, you must either think of older forms of English or of another language altogether. For example, in Yucatec Mayan, powerful men can use "we" to mean "I"; they can also use forms of "here" that are more egocentric than the forms available to the men who work for them (Hanks 1996).

Textuality, Poetic Structure, and Parallelism

In the preceding sections, we have seen how the structure of language – the stuff of "linguistics" – is hard to separate from the social and emotion functions of signs in general and of individual linguistic structures in particular. To grasp those indexical and emotion functions, we need only remind ourselves that we have value judgments about speech, for example, about variant pairs like "jumping" (jʌmpiŋ) versus "jumpin" (jʌmpin). The chapter has also offered examples of the emotionally expressive function of grammatical constructions, like Japanese passive voice.

We turn now to yet another function served by phonological, morphological, and syntactic structures – the poetic function (one among Roman Jakobson's [1990] six functions of language, which I acknowledge as an indirect inspiration for the following discussion).

Parallelism is the defining principle of a broad range of genres, including political oratory and ritual speech. Yet it may not come to mind when we hear the words "poetry" or "poetics." The term parallelism signifies the juxtaposition of linguistic elements that share some feature. These elements can be sounds, (semantic) meaning-units, or grammatical structures. In fact, parallelism is probably found at every level of linguistic structure, from sounds to syntax and semantics. And as we shall see, parallelism may occur at more than one structural level simultaneously. In fact, grammatical and semantic parallelism often co-occur.

If parallelism entails the juxtaposition of linguistic elements sharing some feature, the prototypical example is *pairing*. Consecutive lines that rhyme are parallelistic. "Format tying" in children's arguments, as discussed in Chapter 1, is another name for parallelism; it involves the juxtaposition of paired utterances like Deniecey's "An that happened last year," followed by Terri's retort, "That happened *this* year." Terri repeats Deniecey's utterance almost verbatim.

The preceding example shows how parallelism involves repetition *with variation*. A famous musical example is Franz Josef Haydn's *Surprise Symphony* (Symphony No. 94). In the Second Movement, Haydn introduces a theme. He then repeats it more quietly. By this time, the audience "knows" what notes to expect; in particular, they "know" the *final* note on which the theme ends. And yes, Haydn gives the audience the note they were expecting, but repeats it, suddenly much louder, giving the symphony its name. Listen to just the first 35 seconds of the "Surprise Symphony" (www.youtube.com/watch?v=lLjwkamp3lI) to hear how its peaceful and oh-so-quiet opening bars lull the audience almost to sleep, only to have Haydn wake them with a start. All parallelism involves some repetition of structures, but also *play* with linguistic structure. What good is structure (in music or language) if you can't play with it?

Note that listeners encounter several variations quite apart from, and before, the "surprise" (a loud note played by all members of the orchestra). Look at the score (www.gardenofpraise.com/key21bj.htm) two measures at a time. We can call the first measure pattern A and the second pattern B.

What is the cultural significance of such playful poetic structure? Anthropologists, folklorists, and others have frequently encountered parallelism in ritual contexts. In fact, the **speech variety** that some Indonesian islanders call "speaking in pairs" is but another way of saying "ritual speech" or "the speech of the ancestors" (Fox 1988; 1989). We could thus view parallelism as a marker of the unusual. After all, how common are rituals in the full sense of the word? Or we could view parallelism as imparting to everyday talk something of the *quality* of ritual. I suggest you keep this latter view in mind as the discussion of parallelism continues. In any case, "Parallelism is a marvelous vehicle of literary expression – an esthetically pleasing and engaging device" (Berlin 1979:43).

Let's look now at some specific aspects of poetic structure.

Phonological Parallelism

Phonological parallelism involves pair-wise similarity-and-contrast between sound segments – single sounds, rhythmic or metrical structures, and longer segments like intonation.

Parallelism Involving Single Sound Segments

English speakers are quite accustomed to the poetic function making use of sounds, especially with rhyme. Yet it also makes sense to look at larger or longer sound patterns like the intonation of successive phrases or sentences in oral listing, such as a politician's listing of the promises she or he has kept or of the opponent's broken promises. We start, though, with the poetic use of single sounds or sound segments.

Rhyme and Alliteration

Rhyme involves the pairing of word-final sounds, as in Samuel Coleridge's famous poem *Kubla Khan*, with rhyming pairs like "rills ... hills," "cover ... lover," and "seething ... breathing." In some traditions, **alliteration** involves pairing of lines, with each of the two lines beginning with words that begin with the same sound. In Karelian folklore, however, alliteration is much more intensive, with long strings of words beginning with the same sound. We hear (and see) intense alliteration in the famous early lines of the Finnish epic, *The Kalevala*, as collected and crafted into Finland's national epic by Elias Lönnrot (1835). (See Figure 4.5.) Here is the oft-repeated three-word line that invokes the Finnish culture-hero – *Vaka vanha Väinämöinen* ("Väinämöinen old and steadfast") (Ramnarine 2003:55). Indeed intense alliteration pervades the oral tradition underlying this foundational literary work.

   Richard Nixon's one-time vice president, Spiro Agnew, did not do much for the standing of alliteration through his infamous contributions – "nattering nabobs of negativism" (Lewis 2010) and "the hopeless, hysterical hypochondriacs of history" (Halmari 2011). Whereas some forms of parallelism add power to political rhetoric (see Kornblut 2006; see also Silverstein 2003a on the Gettysburg Address), Agnew's alliteration became the butt of jokes instead.

Suprasegmentals

The term **suprasegmentals** refers to phonetic units – syllables, words, or strings of words – that are longer than single sounds. Not only do linguistic rules govern many aspects of suprasegmentals, but they are also crucial to the poetics of language.

Meter, Rhythm, and Length of Longer Speech Segments

Poetic meter may involve patterns of stressed and unstressed syllables, instead of repeating the vowel or consonant at the end of the final word in a poetic line (i.e., rhyme). In Yemeni Arabic poetry, however, syllable "weight" is the basis of meter.

> Not every syllable [in sung poetry in Yemen] is assigned to a single note; rather, often a syllable has to be stretched across several notes depending on the length of the melody (in other words, there are more notes than syllables). However, usually a long vowel is stretched, as in the above example, over two notes (ya-a), whereas a shorter vowel is held for only one (wa), so that there is a rough equivalence between musical time and syllabic quantity (or weight). (Caton 1990:83)

Figure 4.5 One of the many depictions of Finnish folk hero Väinämöinen, a primary figure from the nation's epic work, *The Kalevala*. (Heritage Images/Getty Images)

The line from *The Kalevala*, quoted on the previous page, exemplifies not only alliteration but the pervasiveness in many Finnic folklore genres of "trochaic tetrameter," groups of four lines, each beginning with a stressed syllable – or, more accurately, "eight syllables in alternating lifts (metrically stressed positions) and falls (metrically unstressed positions) invariably opening with a lift" (Frog and Stepanova 2011:199) – a very strong metric tradition in the region indeed. In this modern rendition (www.youtube.com/watch?v=A8UfdehDqm4), listen for the pattern of stressed (1, 3, 5 . . .) and unstressed (2, 4, 6 . . .) syllables.

Intonational Parallelism

Phonic or phonological parallelism can involve single sound segments or suprasegmental features like intonation and meter. It is useful to think of intonation and meter in relation to their counterparts in music – namely, melody and rhythm. The musical term "theme and variations" denotes a musical form of parallelism in which a melodic theme or motif (like the notes G-G-G-E^b in the opening motif of Beethoven's Fifth Symphony) is repeated, but with twists and turns. Traditions of written poetry meant to stand alone lack full-blown melody; this contrasts with epic poems that were performed orally, and perhaps semi-musically, for centuries before being written down. "Intonation" denotes the semi-melodic ups-and-downs of an utterance. In American English, in a natural conversation in which we happen to tick off a list of, say, five items, the first four may well rise in pitch, while the last falls. The first four form an intonational (and typically morphological) pattern that we call parallelistic.

As with other forms of parallelism, the intonational type can play a role in ritual. Urban (1985) describes ritual wailing in several social groups living in Amerindian central Brazil, and he is able to position their ritual wailing on a continuum. At one end, we find fully melodic/musical lamentation and, at the other, lamentation is characterized by conversational intonation.

> Shokleng wailing involves spoken words, and thus is more speech-like, less perfectly regular in musical terms. Yet it makes use of a distinctive "sing-song" intonation involving a number of tonal peaks. Typically, pitch rises immediately to the highest tone from an initial glide, then drops back down, then up again, with the second tone being slightly lower than the first, and so forth, in gradual descent to the end of the line. (Urban 1985:388)

Morphological Parallelism: The Verbal-Art Function of Morphology

Up to this point, we have been discussing parallelism in sound and sounds. In that context, I introduced the example of verbalizing a list of items in American English that we intend to buy at a grocery store and falling into a pattern of intonational parallelism. The items in our list, however, are likely to be similar to each other morphologically as well. We might list "banana-s, apple-s, cucumber-s, and egg-s." Each of the four items is a noun, and each is marked with the pluralizing suffix /-s/. Not only that, but because banana, apple, cucumber, and egg all end with **voiced sounds**, the pronunciation of the suffix is consistently /-z/. Thus, this example involves morphological parallelism. All forms of parallelism involve whole or partial repetition; morphological parallelism involves the repetition of morphemes (i.e., words and smaller units of meaning such as a plural marker). For our purposes, a string of nouns – words belonging to the **lexical** category "noun" – is an example of morphological parallelism.

In *Jabberwocky*, Lewis Carroll plays not only with English syntax, as we saw previously, but with its English lexicon. However, Carroll grounds his play, his artistry – and makes it understandable – by conforming to the rules of English in many ways, holding phonotactic, inflectional- and derivational-morphological, and syntactic structures steady even as he either wreaks havoc on, or adds boldly to, the lexicon.

> 'Twas brillig, and the slithy toves
>   Did gyre and gimble in the wabe:
> All mimsy were the borogoves,
>   And the mome raths outgrabe.
>
> (from *Through the Looking-Glass and What Alice Found There*, 1872)

Because Carroll retains a lot of standard English morphology – the pluralizing "-s" suffix, for example – he signals to his readers that the otherwise nonsensical terms "toves" and "borogoves" are *nouns* (precisely what we saw in relation to the items in the grocery list). Actually, Carroll's retention of syntactic rules plays a key role in the recognizability of "toves" and "borogoves" as nouns: they occur in phrasal units that begin with the definite article (with or without an intervening adjective like "slith-y," involving a typical adjectival suffix). 'Toves' and 'borogoves' manifest phonological parallelism, which is a result of his arbitrary creation of two rhyming words. At the same time, Carroll does as other English poets have done, exploiting the two instances of the plural suffix – morphological parallelism – to add to the length of the rhyming syllables.

Examples from Religious and Political Oratory

Parallelism in general, and morphological parallelism in particular, are at their most intense in ritual oratory. The ritual that occasions the oratory may be religious or political.

Indeed, the "religious" and the "political" are often interwoven in ritual. The Gettysburg Address is a compelling example. (See Figure 4.6.) Lincoln himself uses words like "consecrate" and "everlasting" that evoke the sacredness of the occasion. Among the structural features that define Lincoln's address is morphological parallelism. It begins with three past forms – "brought forth," followed by two past participles, "[a nation that was] conceived . . . and dedicated," and ends with three future forms introduced by "shall" ("shall not have died in vain," "shall have a new birth," "shall not perish.")

Those who speak the languages of the Eastern Indonesian archipelago have for generations performed rituals using "the speech of the ancestors" – a linguistic register or **style** defined by parallelism. Again, among its several forms, we find morphological parallelism in the speech of the ancestors. Anthropologist James J. Fox (1989) describes this in one of his many works on the eastern Indonesian Rotinese language. It seems clear that the sacredness of the ritual "chants" that Fox analyzes depends completely on parallelism of the semantic and morphological type. Fox analyzes a chanted narrative poem in which adjacent lines may contain pairs of synonymous verbs, but also pairs of the same verbs in a different form (Fox 2014:112).

De neda | masa-nenedak	Recall, do continually recall
Ma ndele | mafa-ndendelek	And remember, do continually remember

The first verb in each line of the sample couplet (the verb that precedes the slash mark) is a regular (non-reduplicated) verb form. The second verb in each line is "partially reduplicated." (Words involving two syllables with the second being a full reduplication of the first include "papa," "mama," and "bah-bah.")

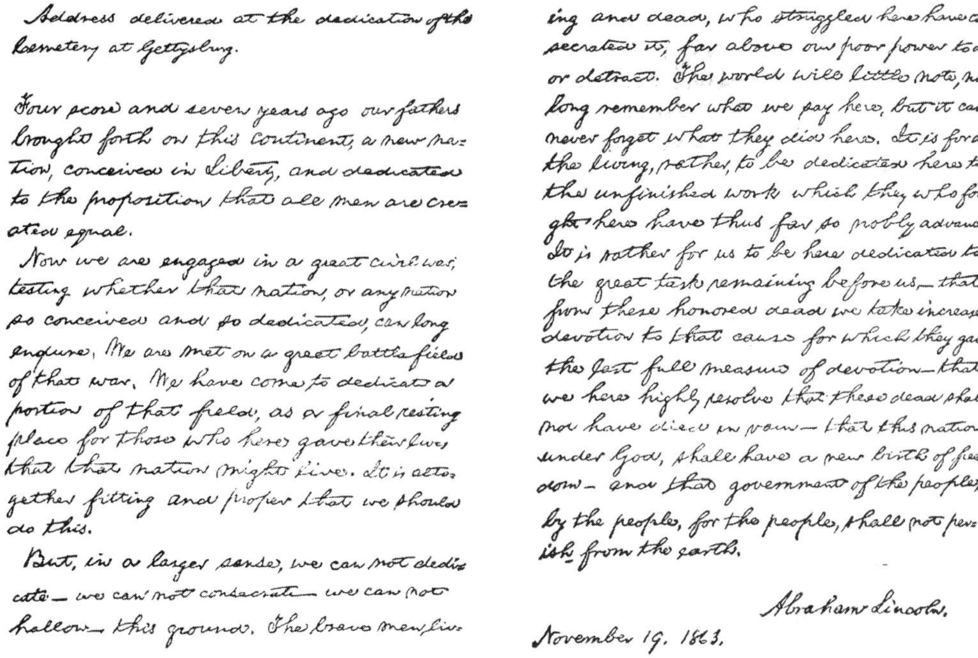

Address delivered at the dedication of the Cemetery at Gettysburg.

Four score and seven years ago our fathers brought forth on this continent, a new nation, conceived in Liberty, and dedicated to the proposition that all men are created equal.

Now we are engaged in a great civil war, testing whether that nation, or any nation so conceived and so dedicated, can long endure. We are met on a great battle-field of that war. We have come to dedicate a portion of that field, as a final resting place for those who here gave their lives that that nation might live. It is altogether fitting and proper that we should do this.

But, in a larger sense, we can not dedicate — we can not consecrate — we can not hallow — this ground. The brave men, living and dead, who struggled here have consecrated it, far above our poor power to add or detract. The world will little note, nor long remember what we say here, but it can never forget what they did here. It is for us the living, rather, to be dedicated here to the unfinished work which they who fought here have thus far so nobly advanced. It is rather for us to be here dedicated to the great task remaining before us — that from these honored dead we take increased devotion to that cause for which they gave the last full measure of devotion — that we here highly resolve that these dead shall not have died in vain — that this nation, under God, shall have a new birth of freedom — and that government of the people, by the people, for the people, shall not perish from the earth.

Abraham Lincoln.

November 19, 1863.

Figure 4.6 President Abraham Lincoln's 1863 Gettysburg Address used parallelism and other structural features in ways that continue to inspire. (Archive Photos/Getty Images)

That second verb contains the simple form plus an extra syllable, and that extra syllable is a repetition of one syllable of the simple verb. The couplet thus contains four verbs in all. Each is translated as an imperative – *neda* and *ndele* are the simple forms corresponding to "recall" and "remember," while [*masa-*] *nenedak* and [*mafa-*] *ndendelek* are the "partially reduplicated" versions of the same verbs. *Nenedak* is not a simple repetition of the root *neda*; it contains the root, but doubles its first syllable *ne*. Likewise, *ndendelek* contains the root *ndele*, but also an "extra" *nde*, and thus a doubling of the first syllable of the root verb.

Note that the couplet actually involves not only the morphological parallelism produced by pre-copying the first syllable of the two verbs that we translated as recall and remember, but also semantic parallelism. The verb translated as "remember" echoes the meaning of its predecessor, "recall." The two are synonyms. So the repetition *within* each line exemplifies morphological parallelism, while the repetition across the two lines involves semantic meaning.

Fox writes that this couplet exemplifies the elaborate linguistic forms used in Rotinese ritual: "Such a distinctively styled expression can only occur in ritual language" (2014:112). Both reduplication and its cultural importance to speakers of Rotinese may seem strange to us. European languages have few reduplicated forms, have no contemporary process by which to form such verbs, and lack an explicit cultural concept such as "the speech of the ancestors," let alone the idea that our ancestors "spoke in pairs." Linguistic anthropology, however, involves the comparative study of different ways of speaking. What is not consciously important to *our* understanding of ritual and ritual speech is *very* important on the island of Roti.

Syntactic Parallelism

Syntax is word order, and syntactic parallelism involves the repetition of a group of words (i.e., in phrases and sentences). It is common for pairs of lines to manifest syntactic, semantic, and intonational parallelism (which we discuss later in this chapter). For example, a grocery list is a simple example of parallelism – all the items are nouns, many of them plural. When we listen or read for structure or features that make discourse cohere, we are paying attention to listing patterns.

The Declaration of Independence

The American Declaration of Independence is an oft-analyzed example of written American political rhetoric and of poetic structure beyond individual words or sentences.

Let us take a closer look. Near the very beginning of the document, we encounter the first of several lists. Readers are tipped off that the authors of the Declaration are about to provide a list by these words: "To prove this, let Facts be submitted to a candid world."

Listing almost always involves parallelism of a syntactic sort in addition to the forms we have already found in lists – intonational and morphological. In what follows, we see the kind of list that the phrase "let Facts be submitted" introduces, and I have formatted this text as a bulleted list to make it stand out as such.

- He has refused his Assent to Laws, the most wholesome and necessary for the public good.
- He has forbidden his Governors to pass Laws of immediate and pressing importance, unless suspended in their operation till his Assent should be obtained; and when so suspended, he has utterly neglected to attend to them.
- He has refused to pass other Laws for the accommodation of large districts of people, unless those people would relinquish the right of Representation in the Legislature, a right inestimable to them and formidable to tyrants only.
- He has called together legislative bodies at places unusual, uncomfortable, and distant from the depository of their Public Records, for the sole purpose of fatiguing them into compliance with his measures.
- He has dissolved Representative Houses repeatedly, for opposing with manly firmness his invasions on the rights of the people.

Immediately after the "He has _____-d us" list comes the "For _____-ing us" list, which includes these parallel lines:

- For depriving us, in many cases, of the benefits of Trial by Jury:
- For transporting us beyond Seas to be tried for pretended offences:

Parallelism manifests the poetic function of language – but not only so. In Chapter 1, we encountered Goodwin and Goodwin's (1987) three examples of what they call format tying, which clearly involves parallelism. However, that form of parallelism emerges turn-over-turn in conversation rather than from within a poem, a piece of political oratory, or a ritual text. It thus demonstrates that participants in talk build on or even borrow whole phrases from the person who last spoke. This kind of parallelism helps organize participation, just as the freedom within conversation for an utterance to emerge with its particular structure as it will. Format tying does index mutual involvement and engagement, even if that engagement is conflictual.

Semantic Parallelism

The modern Western study of parallelism began in the context of biblical studies with the pioneering work of Anglican bishop, grammarian, and Oxford professor of poetry, Robert Lowth. He designated three distinct semantic relations, which in his area of interest meant three forms of semantic parallelism – synonymous, antithetical, and synthetic.

The Hebrew Psalms: Psalm 1

Following Lowth (Lowth and Gregory [1787] 1829), we find elaborate examples of semantic parallelism in the Hebrew Psalms, for example, in the first Psalm. (I am using the New American Standard translation of the Bible, as found at http://biblehub.com/nasb/psalms/1.htm.)

Parallelism typically involves pair-wise relations. In the first verse of Psalm 1, however, we see triple synonyms – "the wicked," which is reasonably synonymous with "sinners" and "scoffers."

> [1] How blessed is the man who does not walk in the counsel of the wicked,
>> Nor stand in the path of sinners,
>> Nor sit in the seat of scoffers!
> [2] But his delight is in the law of the LORD,
>> And in His law he meditates day and night.
> [3] He will be like a tree firmly planted by streams of water,
>> Which yields its fruit in its season
>> And its leaf does not wither;
>> And in whatever he does, he prospers.
> [4] The wicked are not so,

But they are like chaff which the wind drives away.
[5] Therefore the wicked will not stand in the judgment,
    Nor sinners in the assembly of the righteous.
[6] For the LORD knows the way of the righteous,
    But the way of the wicked will perish.

A complex poetic structure involving semantic relations exists between verses 2 and 3 on the one hand and the verses surrounding them (verse 1, then verses 4–6) on the other. The Psalm begins and ends with a focus on "the wicked," as though two bookends surrounded the symbolic heart of the Psalm in which "the righteous" are described (vv. 2–3).

The Union of Semantic and Pragmatic Meaning, Structures, and Parallelism

I close by taking our consideration of parallelism one step further – by asking whether there is a pragmatic counterpart to semantic parallelism.

The answer is yes – for two reasons or in two senses, the first being the most obvious. Pragmatic parallelism is of course possible because users of language do string together chains of promises, threats, complaints, commands, and so on. What Greg Urban (2001:119–128) calls "the **Litany** of Complaint" section of the Declaration of Independence can be analyzed in terms of semantic and grammatical parallelism. But each complaint is just that – a complaint. Each repetition of the grammatical form "He has _____-ed us" or the form "For _____-ing us" is a social act, indeed part of a dangerous revolutionary act.

The second sense in which there is indeed a pragmatic parallelism relies on our seeing a text as a whole, be it a ritual or a powerful speech that we rarely think of as a ritual text. Each repetition of "He has____" is like one beat of a drum. The "Litany of Complaint" is a series of drumbeats, and in some sense we can say that the beats get louder as the series emerges. Reading or hearing the series of figurative beats, together with the climactic "declaration [small-d] of independence" in the last lines of the Declaration (big-D) is like listening to Ravel's *Bolero* or participating in a shamanic ritual. A shamanic soul-calling ritual may or may not involve drumming, but it will always be moving toward a climax. The whole, not only the parts, serves a function. Whole texts of the sort we are considering have a pragmatic function; yet to understand it, we must focus on the parts. It is the fusion of utterances into chains or musical scores that makes ritual discourse *do* what it does.

CONCLUSION

This chapter has described language in a way that both reflects and challenges traditional linguistic thought. I have described language as a series of nesting structures, from the smallest (sounds) through the largest (text-poetics), and this captures both the conventionality and the unconventional nature of the chapter, as do other features, such as playing with the semantic–pragmatic divide.

Language must be studied for its communicative functions. We must understand communicating as conveying messages built of small and large semantic meaning units. But we must also grasp linguistic communication as a mode of *social* action. And we must recognize "events" of communication (consisting of texts) as acts whose *force* depends on the degree to which they consist of parts that make up a whole, beats that make up a rhythm, individual voices that make up a chorus.

SUMMARY

This chapter focuses on the following themes with which you should be familiar:

- Language can be thought of as a hierarchical series of nesting structures.
- These structures are tied to functions – each, for example, providing for the possibility of parallelism.
- Parallelism is the juxtaposition of linguistic elements that share some feature, be it a feature of sound (phonological parallelism), internal word structure (morphological parallelism), grammar (syntactic parallelism), or semantic meaning (semantic parallelism).
- The poetic function, defined in terms of parallelism, is crucial to sociocultural function (i.e., ritual).

QUESTIONS

1. What are the levels of linguistic structure? Name and define them.
2. What kind of difference at the sound level translates into a difference in semantic meaning? What do we call the relationship between a pair of similar sounds that works as follows? When you replace one sound with the other in an otherwise identical word (like replacing /b/ with /p/ in the words "bat" versus "pat" in English), you change its semantic meaning.
3. Does sound length change semantic meaning in Finnish? What about English?
4. Certain sound variations are already "busy." What are the non-busy kinds of sound variation available for? Name an example in English.
5. Explain how switching between two related phonemes produces two words with different meanings. What is the difference between phonemes and morphemes?
6. Name examples of the social significance (indexicality) of "two ways of saying the same thing" in English. First, provide a case involving two forms or pronunciations of a single morpheme (e.g., a suffix). Second, provide a case of two grammatical rules operating in two dialects or sociolects of English. (Suggestion:

Go to www.youtube.com/watch?v=0mSstSG0O9U, move the slider to about 2:15, and listen to what the man selling boots says about size eight and a half. You can't use this example in your answer, but reviewing it might help you come up with another example.)

EXERCISES

1. List all the things that speakers of American English do with their mouths and with sounds for effect or for stylistic reasons. Among those, find at least one case in which doing the same thing with the sound(s) would change the dictionary (i.e., semantic, denotational, referential) meaning of the word. Do not use examples from this chapter.
2. Analyze these lines from *The Jabberwocky*, indicating which "part of speech" (lexical class) each word represents:

    'Twas brillig, and the slithy toves
      Did gyre and gimble in the wabe:
    All mimsy were the borogoves,
      And the mome raths outgrabe.

3. Do you speak another language well enough to have noticed how much conversational overlap occurs in that language? Can you contrast it with the prevalence of overlap between speakers of yet another language, like your native tongue?
4. What exactly is the similarity between Haydn's "Surprise Symphony" and poetry written in the age of rhyme or ritual speech (including great political oratory)? Are "surprises" common?
5. Look at five rhyming poems in English. Are there lines that do not fit in with any others, that do not share the rhyme scheme with other lines, or that cap off the poem with words made up of sounds that are a surprise, not a continuation of the pattern of parallelism?
6. Try the same exercise with two great political speeches. Analyze what sorts of parallelism they involve, and look for surprises.

ADDITIONAL RESOURCES

Fabb, Nigel. 1997. *Linguistics and Literature*. Oxford and Malden, MA: Blackwell Publishers.

> *Like Jakobson before him, Fabb effectively demonstrates the relevance of linguistics to works of literature.*

Finegan, Edward. 2008. *Language: Its Structure and Use*. Boston: Thomson/Wadsworth.

> *If you wish to ground your understanding of linguistic anthropology in linguistics, Finegan's introductory textbook is one of the best, and certainly most accessible, to turn to.*

Jakobson, Roman. 1987. *Language in Literature*. Cambridge, MA and London: The Belnap Press of Harvard University Press.

Roman Jakobson's influence on a broad range of disciplines – linguistic anthropology, linguistics, poetics, semiotics, and Russian literature (to name but a few) – is profound. This book brings together many of Jakobson's most important contributions.

5 Culture, Society, Communication, and Language Evolving

LEARNING OBJECTIVES

After reading this chapter, you should be able to do the following:

- List the kinds of evidence scientists invoke to explain the origin of language.
- Explain how language development helped our human ancestors post-hunt more than during a hunt.
- Discuss the role of narrative in human evolution and the evolutionary importance of **recursivity** in narrative.
- Describe the changes in human vocal anatomy and the advantages and disadvantages of these changes.
- Discuss the usefulness of framing as a model for understanding communication in contemporary humans and in nonhuman animals.

Introduction

In Chapter 4, we looked at fully modern language quite apart from its evolution. Now, in Chapter 5, we explore the evolution of communicative systems, with a specific focus on language. And whereas previous chapters have focused almost exclusively on human communication, in this chapter, I situate our species in the midst of our relatives, both close and distant.

Most anthropologists regard evolution by natural selection as a foundational idea. In this chapter, we look at language as an evolutionary feature of humans. In the process, we explore the origins of human language, the benefits and risks to its development, and its distinguishing features that may have bolstered our development by facilitating complex social interactions and complex thought. What becomes clear as we explore these ideas is that modern human language and the modern human mind, in fact, evolved together.

Although contemporary linguistic anthropology focuses little attention on evolution per se, broader anthropological and semiotic approaches to culture and communication explore all forms of animal communication that result from **evolutionary processes**. Thus, I provide relevant examples of animal communication as part of our discussion here.

Figure 5.1 Common ravens have demonstrated intelligence through their impressive problem-solving and communication skills. (Photo by author)

Communicative Systems Evolving

Language is a capacity common to all members of the species *Homo sapiens*. This capacity is built into all of our brains, and it reflects our evolutionary heritage, particularly the semiotic systems of our forebears, including mammals like cetaceans (whales, dolphins, and porpoises) and **primates** (from the most primitive prosimians to monkeys, and especially apes).

Thus, although language reflects and requires a fully human brain, neuroscientists looking at primate brains, and even birds' brains, see traces of the communicative systems that preceded full-fledged language. For example, the brains of ravens (see Figure 5.1) have evolved in ways that facilitate their ability to learn complex communication systems (Emery and Clayton 2004; Reber et al. 2016).

Evolution is a biological process involving genes whose manifestations include anatomy and physiology and even complex behavioral capacities – with feedback loops such that, for example, human sociality is both a product and a driver of evolution.

Language is one such capacity. It has emerged out of evolutionary processes – not fully formed as a result of a single genetic mutation, but gradually emergent, building at each step upon the semiotic systems of our ancestors. Genes drive human development in the womb and throughout life. Tiny shifts in the bodily structures of our **hominid** ancestors – in their brains, throats, and tongues – reflect tiny genetic changes. (Note that the family Hominidae includes humans and all of the other great apes.) But how do we know anything with certainty about the evolution of something intangible – the language-able brain, which, unlike cranial bones, does not fossilize?

Forms of Evidence

For linguistic anthropologists, it is crucial to focus less on the brains of isolated ancient speakers and more on **languaging**, which is a co-achievement of inter-locutors. Of course, this kind of interaction does not fossilize. Nor do the brains that helped produce language and interaction. However, brain cases of our ancestors did fossilize, and on some rare occasions the inner surface of those brain cases also fossilized (Schwartz et al. 2004), which has given us some glimpses of evolutionary processes at work.

However, given the limits of human fossil evidence for brain function, we focus more on visible similarities and differences between humans and our evolutionary kin, especially primates. Thus, we make presumptions that the evolutionary path from animal communication to human communication via language constitutes relevant evidence.

Comparative studies of animals like monkeys and chimps – with each other *and* with us – are, in fact, evolutionary studies. For instance, we recognize the utility of comparing, say, humans with great apes, both at the gross and fine levels of anatomy. Looking at physical evidence on the *gross* level can involve comparisons of chimp and human vocal anatomy. It can even involve looking at fossils of ancient hominid brain cases, sometimes with traces of the brain's external folds and creases remaining – reflections of the lines and grooves ("sulci" and "gyri") marking divisions of ancient brains – their **structure** and thus, indirectly, their **functions**.

Comparing *fine* levels of anatomy in human and some primate brains can include looking at genetic evidence. Paleoanthropologists like Daniel Lieberman (2007), for instance, ask how important for the evolution of language is the presence or absence of specific genes, like the FOXP2 gene. Neuroscientists as well as anthropologists are interested in the workings of this gene; among other things, they study the comparative workings of bird and human versions of the FOXP2 gene (Haesler et al. 2007).

Comparing the presence or absence of **mirror neurons** is another relevant area of study, and it can result in lively debates about the relationship of such structures to something called "Theory of Mind" (which we discuss later in this chapter). Mirror neurons (Richardson and Keuck 2002) are a class of brain cells first dis-covered in macaques and now known to be in most primates. They are found in the prefrontal (or visuomotor) cortex of the primate brain (Holmes and Spence 2005). This class of neurons is very special in that they activate or "fire" both when primates (including humans) *see* another member of its species doing something and when the primates perform such actions themselves.

Comparative studies of anatomy are not the only form of evidence we can examine though. We also study archaeological remains, including three-dimensional objects such as stone tools and two-dimensional phenomena such as cave paintings, for evidence of the evolution of language. These fascinating works by our ancestors can be quite convincingly described as symbolic in nature. And some anthropologists find the presence of symbolic artifacts in the archaeological record – especially the way they seem to explode onto the scene around 60,000 to 30,000 years ago – a likely sign that their producers already spoke a fully modern form of language. It is worth noting this is by no means settled science at this point.

Yet another kind of evidence comes from studies that treat contemporary human foraging societies (hunter-gatherers) as stand-ins for proto-human populations. Evolutionary anthropologists who invoke this "ethnographic analogy" envision present-day hunter-gatherers living much as our common hunter-gatherer ancestors did. The dangers of thus projecting from a largely mysterious past to the present is obvious, although many archaeologists argue that there is some value in ethnographic analogies. (Both sides of this argument are well presented by anthropologist Holly Martelle Hayter [(1994) 2011].) Despite the risks of this approach, carefully conceived comparisons can, in fact, generate some useful models – for example, hypotheses as to how and why our ancestors communicated with each other.

Let me explain. Many evolutionary neuroscientists consider language as a complex form of behavior. As you know, linguistic anthropologists prefer to consider speech as a form of **social action**. Hence, if we contemplate whether our first language-using ancestors (roughly 50,000 years ago) told stories – and we think they did – then we must ask what sorts of *actions* those stories might have performed. This leads us to hypothesize likely benefits of storytelling to early human groups, benefits that must have been matters of life and death. For instance, early stories must have increased the chances that story-listeners would have success in hunting and gathering, as anthropologist and evolutionary psychologist Michelle Scalise Sugiyama, who is a prominent advocate of this model, has shown (1996, 2001, 2011).

Insights from Semiotics

Pondering evolution, as we have been doing here, always entails pondering continuities and discontinuities, ancient inheritances and deviations from long-gone ancestors. Thus, we consider both, largely from a semiotic perspective.

"Signs" are the stuff of semiotics. Keep in mind, however, that in this book we usually focus not on individual signs, but on sign *systems*. Matters of causation, or more complex principles of organization that govern systems, are also the stuff of

Figure 5.2 Vervet monkey gives a specific alarm call to signal the presence of a snake. (De Agostini Picture Library/Getty Images)

semiotics, leading us to ask what causes – or, more accurately, what complex phenomena – influenced and still influence the shape of communicative systems.

The old fights over "nature versus nurture" endure to some extent in anthropology. However, an emerging consensus sees the *interplay* of nature and nurture as the proper focus of science. Language is an evolved communicative system, with its roots in primate communication. The brain modifications that make our species what it is – language-capable – likewise build on primate brain features. That's why scientists carrying out some of the most interesting work on the interplay of nature (specifically, evolution) and nurture (i.e., development) give their field the shorthand name "evo-devo" (Pennisi and Roush 1997).

Even the brains of primates rather distantly related to humans, such as vervet monkeys (see Figure 5.2), equip these monkeys to communicate in a way that includes some arbitrariness in indexing danger, and that indexing behavior has a pseudo-referential function. That is, vervets are known to make three distinct alarm calls, indexing the presence of snakes, cheetahs, and eagles.

The sound shape of each of these vervet calls is arbitrarily connected to their indexical objects (i.e., the particular animal threat). Moreover, vervets are born with an ability to use these three signals in a crude manner, but their brains also enable them to refine this innate ability with experience over time.

We can say here, following Richardson and Keuck (2002:499) as well as the evo-devo group, that "ontogeny [the development of an individual] recapitulates phylogeny [the evolutionary development of *Homo sapiens* and others]." We must note that the originators of the expression – Haeckel and Lankester (1883) – proposed a stronger form of this theory that is often rejected today, whereas Richardson and Keuck's (2002) modified form is more acceptable to scholars now. And we can expand this notion, with Ingold (2001), to say that human children undergo a single developmental process that combines social, cultural, and biological dimensions.

In animals, from birds and dolphins to humans, there is a profoundly interesting mix of imitation and creativity. Song imitation in songbirds, for example, appears to be regulated by the bird version of the FOXP2 gene (Haesler et al. 2007). And creativity in dolphins has been studied by both Bateson (1972) and Herman (2012). In fact, Herman claims that dolphins have not only the *capacity* to imitate but a *concept* of imitation. The closer one gets to humans genetically, the greater the degree of creativity that we find in imitation.

Arbib (2011) locates the roots of human language-based communication in ape **gestures**, some of which were learned, and in the evolution of the brain, particularly mirror neurons. Simple imitation apparently governed the older human Oldowan tool culture (approximately 2.6 to 1.4 million years ago) and came with all of the costs of inflexibility (e.g., the opportunity cost of the absence of creativity). The more recent Acheulian tool culture (McKee et al. 2015:23 [Table 1.4]) shows signs of deepening and more creative imitation. And the emergence of anatomically modern *Homo sapiens* around 100,000 years ago (McKee et al. 2015:352) includes an "explosion" of human cultural diversity (Arbib 2011:259). The bottom line is that it was essential for human brains to develop highly complex imitative capacity, along with a burgeoning capacity for creativity. Only this would explain the evolution of language, which is both crucial to cultural transmission processes across generations and highly creative.

The modern human ability to generate an infinite number of possible sentences based on a flexible and recursive set of grammatical rules is often referred to in the literature on language in its evolutionary context as "productivity." It is in the very nature of our most common and defining mode of communication – face-to-face conversation – to move between the poles of relatively long and predictable chunks (like tired old ways of saying things) and the apparent freedom we have when improvising and perhaps inventing new ways of saying things (Sawyer 2001).

What language scholars call "conversation" reflects not only the interplay of predictable and creative but also the prelinguistic give-and-take of proto-conversation in infants that has its roots in the evolution of our species

(Stern 1985) – an important example of evo-devo. Human infants are not yet capable of speech but are capable nonetheless of communing and communicating with others. Infants and parents engage in prelinguistic forms of communication that have been described as dance-like (Malloch and Trevarthen 2009).

The capacity to **synchronize** or at least tap into the same sense of time, once developed in infancy, continues into later life, becoming the ability to engage, which Schutz (1962–1966) describes as "making music together." The ability to feel with the other must be shared by parents and children. It must also depend on the physicality of acoustic resonance (Pickering 2015) – the vibration of sound – while producing what child psychologists like Feldman (2007) and psychoanalysts like Coburn (2001) refer to as "emotional resonance." This is what my generation used to refer to as sharing a "vibe" [vibration, resonance], and others might call "being in tune" with each other.

From Biosemiotics to Manipulated Signs: The Evolution of Culture and Communication

In this section, we cover a range of topics pertaining to evolution – specifically the evolution of systems of communication as well as culture and what led up to it (protoculture). I address the evolution of "animal semiotics" or communication in nonhuman animals. In doing so, I attend to the evolution of the three sign modes, iconicity (for example, in facial expressions), indexicality (which, in animals in the wild, does *not* include pointing), and symbolicity (which is confined to human communication). Symbolicity is particularly relevant to language as it has evolved in humans.

Later in this section, I narrow our focus to human language – the evolution of human vocal anatomy and the features of language that make it unique among semiotic systems, including conscious (neocortical) control, compositionality, referentiality, and narrative. Along the way, I consider "Theory of Mind" (ToM) in both apes and humans, how deceit is related to ToM, and why ToM in humans might have been important in the evolution of language.

The Animal World and the Evolution of Sign Systems

Examining the characteristics of sign modes in animal communication that are analogous to those in that of humans should lay a foundation for our exploration of the evolution of language. Biological anthropologists have excelled in studying primate communication, particularly in the wild – especially Seyfarth, Cheney, and Marler's studies of monkey troops in east Africa (1980a, 1980b). But anthropologist Gregory Bateson (1972) did more than anyone else to theorize commonalities between human language and the communicative systems of infrahuman species. Key to his model is the concept of **metacommunication**, which we discussed in

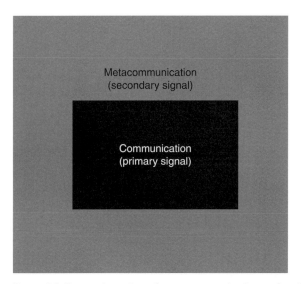

Figure 5.3 Bateson's notion of metacommunication as framing (Bateson 1972:272) as illustrated by the present author.

Chapter 3. In Figure 5.3, I evoke the work of Bateson (1972) in demonstrating the metacommunication, or framing, performed through both animal and human facial expressions.

The Evolution of Sign Modes: Iconicity

Let us consider the evolutionary history of sign modes, starting with iconicity. If we think only of intentional representations, or intentional mimicry, we will find few icons in the wild, apart from our closest cousins, our fellow apes. However, *genetically* driven mimicry abounds in the biological world. Indeed, all genetic reproduction involves the replication or copying of DNA, and all life involves iconic relationships between DNA and RNA. There are also many fascinating instances in which natural selection results in mimicry, such as the evolution of camouflage.

On a more abstract level, iconicity is displayed in large mammals – such as foxes and gorillas. As you see in Figure 5.4, facial expressions are **framing devices**.

Moving from the top row toward the bottom represents shifts from greater to lesser emotional intensity – from anger, to fear, to play. This intensity is expressed by the degree to which the mouth is open and teeth are showing – most open for anger to the least for play. The teeth are framed by the lips and the rest of the face. The teeth are the primary signal – "I'm a scary dude!" – while the various faces and the displays that those faces achieve via facial muscles carry **metasignals**, such as "I'm showing myself to be scary, but *this* 'scary dude' display *is play!*"

Our species – anatomically modern *Homo sapiens* – has a dynamic ability not only to use and recognize "frames" (a rather static-sounding noun), but to keep up with a "context [that] scrolls" (Lindstrom 1992). The ever-shifting context of

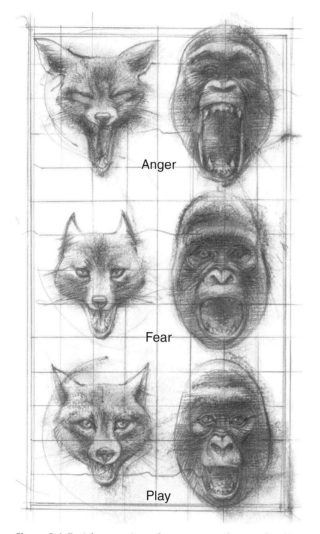

Anger

Fear

Play

Figure 5.4 Facial expressions, from anger to fear to play (Brown 1994)

talk-in-interaction requires not static frames but a continuous process of moment-to-moment framing. That is, it requires a continuous production of **contextualization cues** (Gumperz 1982). These are "conventions" that do not just reflect something inert that we call **context**; instead, they both reflect the context into which you might fit an utterance and also remake the very context of talk (Gumperz 1996; Maynard and Heritage 2005).

When talk-in-interaction is face-to-face (be it on Skype, FaceTime, or in **embodied** or physical co-presence), "the interaction" involves making and interpreting facial expressions. The whole human face becomes the frame surrounding and helping us interpret such things as upwardly curving lips: If we see the eyes "twinkle" and the muscles around the eyes flex, we know at some level that the smile is "genuine." That much is a biological universal. Yet cross-cultural differences exist, for example, in reading the duration of a smile: Japanese people are more sensitive than Americans to rapidly fading smiles – which play into "attachment-related anxiety" according to a study by Ishii and colleagues (2011).

Trouble occurs in the evolved human brain, however, when "normal" frames – such as "she is looking at me and moving her lips, and I hear something that must be her talk" – break down. For neuroscientist Timothy Crow (2000), the evolution of the two split-and-yet-in-contact hemispheres of the brain not only makes us human but also makes the basic frame-confusion we call "schizophrenia" possible. In particular, Crow argues that the failure of one brain hemisphere or the other to become dominant makes it possible for roughly one percent of all people on the planet to confuse voices produced in the outside world (such as the one produced by "she who is looking at me and moving her lips") and one's inner voice or thoughts. Crow also cites some evidence that another disorder of brain development – autism – sometimes involves a difficulty in learning to use "I" and "you," whose meaning constantly shifts in the give-and-take of conversation. (One moment "I" means me, but in the next moment I must recognize the "I" that I just heard coming from someone else who a moment ago was "you" to my "I." That sign system is complex enough to make it almost miraculous that any of us manages within it.) The challenges posed by autism and schizophrenia relate to pragmatic and **semantic meaning**, to words and syntax, and the social context of their use.

As we recall from Chapter 4, words are composed of smaller chunks of meaning (like "-er," "-or," and "pre-"), and those chunks in turn are composed of individual sounds. From the evolutionary perspective we are exploring now, you may wonder how a system like language developed in which larger units (sentences and phrases) are composed of smaller units (words and sounds). This universal trait of human language, **compositionality** (see Figure 4.1), can also be defined thus: "The meaning of an expression is a monotonic function of the meaning of its parts and the way they are put together" (Cann 1993:4). That is, linguistic expressions mean what they do as a direct ("monotonic") reflection of the meanings of their parts – unless the expression is an idiom like "kicking the bucket"!

By contrast, the compositionality of signs does not seem to occur in even our closest relatives, the bonobos (cousins to chimpanzees) or in other highly intelligent mammals like cetaceans (dolphins and whales). Why compositionality evolved in, and gives structure to, human language but no animal communication systems (at least not to the same extent, by any means) remains a mystery. Evolutionary scientists often speak of "selective pressures" – the pressures of natural selection, imposing benefits or costs on individuals (e.g. individual humans) who have or lack a trait such as the ability to use fully compositional language. It would appear that a mix of biological and cultural pressures rewarded compositionality (Smith and Kirby 2012).

Indexicality in Animal and Human Sign Systems

Humans and animals produce numerous indexical signs, many of which can – even among humans – be unintentional and unconscious. We know from studying a variety of animals that sign systems can rely on various senses – the olfactory (pheromones, scent marking), visual (male bird displays), auditory (alarm calls), and sensorimotor (mating dances). We all smell, and we all have a unique timbre or **voice** print that enables others to identify us even before we say anything of substance.

And we point – at least humans do. We often hear that "pointing" is a useful synonym for "indexing." Animals, however, do not literally point. They manage to "index" without an index finger. For instance, excited bees reporting back to their hive index the direction of their sweet find by the orientation of their "honey dance" (Hurford 2008).

As we saw in Chapter 2, many vertebrate species produce alarm calls, including birds like chickadees and many groups of primates (e.g., monkeys). Very recent research confirms what Seyfarth and Cheney discovered in the 1970s:

> Numerous animal studies have shown that vocal signals alone can be
> sufficient to elicit appropriate responses from listeners in the absence of
> the natural events that normally elicit them (Seyfarth et al. 1980a, 1980b;
> Macedonia and Evans 1993; Evans and Marler 1995; Zuberbühler et al. 1997;
> Zuberbühler 2001; Manser et al. 2001; Templeton et al. 2005). It has
> become customary to refer to such signals as "functionally referential",
> provided they are produced in context-specific ways and elicit specific
> adaptive responses in listeners. (Cäsar et al. 2012:405)

The "referential" meaning of an utterance or sentence is what it talks about. From my point of view, full-blown referential meaning does not exist outside of human language. However, animal sign systems, like vervet monkeys' three-way alarm call system that differentially signal the presence of three common predators, do *function* something like the referential utterances of humans.

Human and Infrahuman Multisensory Communication

As Levinson and Holler (2014) argue, spoken language occurs not independently, but in a broader communicative context that is multimodal or multi-channel. When gestures accompany speech, as they do in face-to-face communication, a shared environment typically becomes a kind of whiteboard. For example, to archaeologists in field schools, dirt is more than something in which to dig; they may use it to trace meaningful patterns with a trowel (Goodwin 1994).

Human communication indeed evolved in layers, consisting of the sorts of modes mentioned previously, over perhaps a million years. Human pointing by using the index finger is related both to ancient precedent and to the use of full-blown language by modern *Homo sapiens*. Indexicality does appear in ape gestures, though apes in the wild do not use their index fingers to point. We can draw a contrast between language and gesture, despite their co-evolution and co-occurrence in human communication. In language, **deictics** (which we discussed in Chapter 4) form a large category, much larger than one gestural form like using the index finger to point. Deictics are linguistic indexes. Like all indexes, they are signs that draw attention – often to themselves.

We might think of pointing gestures and all indexical signs as behaviors manifesting the activity of individual minds. As we have seen, however, indexes can be produced quite unintentionally – which is to describe the evolution of language not as a device of use to minds conceived of in a hyper-individualistic way, but as a social tool capable of highly specific cultural performance. As Schilbach et al. (2010) describe, human minds are created by and "for sharing," indexical signs initiate such sharing or "joint attention," and they thereby "recruit reward-related neuro-circuitry." We are thus hard-wired to get something rewarding out of having our attention riveted to something through indexes embedded in social interaction with our fellow humans. Pointing gestures, as Levinson and Holler (2014:3) argue, lead humans quite automatically to seek out in the shared environment something relevant to what the speaker-and-pointer is saying.

> Pointing is thus an extremely powerful device, not because it accurately denotes (as Wittgenstein 1969:Paragraph 33 noted) a point at, say, pieces of paper could be indicating the colour, the shape or even the number, but because it invites the recipient to locate a referent of mutual interest (a social process that recruits reward-related neurocircuitry in humans). (Schilbach et al. 2010)

Having explored the connections between animal and human communication systems, we turn now to the distinct physiological features of *Homo sapiens* that enabled our development of language.

The Evolution of Brain and Vocal Apparatus

"Evidence from seemingly unrelated disciplines suggests that the specialized anatomy and neural mechanisms that confer fully human speech, language, and cognitive ability reached their present state sometime between 100,000 and 50,000 years ago" (Lieberman and McCarthy 2007:15). In order to speak, and specifically to sound like any contemporary human being in producing the whole range of speech sounds that we make, certain changes had to occur in the vocal tract. Looking at our ancestors' faces (see Figure 5.5) – from chimps all the way down to Neanderthals and early examples of anatomically modern *Homo sapiens*'– we see … well, a lot of face, meaning a bit of a snout (they were "prognathous"). Our ancestors' necks were much shorter than ours, and their tongues too. Modern humans' jaws have pulled back, and our tongues have "dropped," so that the root of the tongue is part way down the throat (the pharynx).

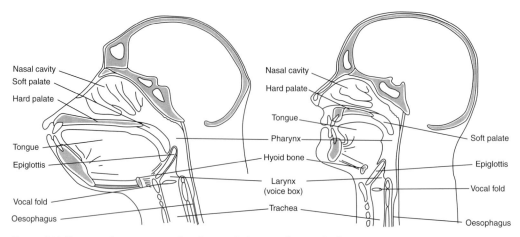

Figure 5.5 Comparative anatomy, showing evolutionary changes in face structure.

In thinking about how language must have conferred some evolutionary (competitive, selective) advantage, we can be emotionally struck by how marvelous language is. In fact, we can get (or more accurately, language can get us) all choked up. This is literally true: We use our throats for eating and breathing, as do other mammals; but we also use our throats for speaking, a task that requires a lowering of the tongue, and that means we are vulnerable to choking to death.

Continuing on, we explore the interconnectedness of the physiological, linguistic, and musical.

The Evolution from Instinct to Language

A number of scholars have argued that music and language evolved together in our hominid ancestors (Botha 2009; Brown 2001; Falk 2009; Mithen 2005; van der Schyff 2013; Van Puyvelde and Franco 2015). Previous generations of thinkers tried to strictly segregate music as emotional and language as referential. However, examples such as Karelian lament, which include "heightened and intermediary forms of crying, singing, and speaking," help blur the distinction (Tolbert 2001b:84–85).

I argue that *indexicality* is the most primitive of Peirce's three sign-types or modes. Tolbert, by contrast, asserts the primordiality of *iconicity*, at least in the early phases of our hominid ancestors' evolving use of the voice. Our ancestors no doubt used calls, some of which were, as Tolbert says, "emotion calls" that had an unquestionable indexical link with inner states (2001b:89–90). Whatever it was in our evolution that allowed early hominids (or perhaps more strictly, early *Homo sapiens*) to manipulate (i.e., produce icons of) indexical calls was a crucial evolutionary step.

> [T]o the possessor of a social mind, the voice could now be interpreted ambiguously as both an intentionally modeled emotion call and as an unintentional index of an internal state; furthermore, a socially aware being

> would know that others could interpret one's own vocal utterances in this way. This double-edged interpretive possibility was not possible before crossing the symbolic threshold, when an indexical sign would have been taken at face value. (Tolbert 2001a:460)

This means that a kind of fall from "Eden" occurred, involving the loss of the absolute trustworthiness of human communication. Henceforth, even icons and indexes came under the control of consciousness and its social manifestation – culture. Compare the following statement from linguistic anthropologist Gregory Urban (2002:238):

> For once crying operates as metasignal, the larynx and the vocal cords become the targets of neocortical [conscious or semi-conscious] manipulation of an otherwise instinctively controlled vocal apparatus. The transition from instinct to culture, in this area, occurs in the transition from signal to metasignal.

Our unique human form of communication – namely, language – could emerge in its full form only under the control of the neocortex or higher brain. In this way, the evolution of language concurrently mirrors the evolution of culture.

The Evolution of Culture from Protoculture

Culture has evolved. It is fairly safe to say that it exists only in our species. That means that only *Homo sapiens'* behavior predominantly reflects "social transmission" rather than genetic transmission. Yet surely our capacity for transmitting culture relies mainly on language, and neither language nor culture could exist without our highly evolved brains. Moreover, as with every product of evolution, some form of culture or some aspect of our *capacity* for culture must have pre-existed full-blown culture.

As is seen among humans, many vertebrate species acquire their full behavioral repertoires only through some learning that builds on a genetic platform. Baby vervet monkeys show *some* ability to produce alarm calls appropriately (i.e., coinciding with the appearance of eagles, snakes, or leopards). Still, their hardwiring fails to fully equip them to consistently recognize and produce alarm calls. The young make mistakes, but their skill at alarm calls increases as they mature.

Learning per se, however, is not the same as "traditional transmission," or transmission of behavioral patterns through verbal direction or elaborate narratives, including myths. There must be a link between learning through trial-and-error and full-blown culture as a learned behavioral complex. We call that mediating link **protoculture** (Price 1973).

Protoculture involves "learned habits" that "may be socially transmitted, even in the absence of speech" (Hallowell 1968:219, as cited by Price 1973:209). For some decades, scientists have carefully observed a beach-loving troop of Japanese macaques (a monkey species, *Macaca fuscata*). Why do the macaques stay on their

Figure 5.6 Japanese macaque shows learned food-washing behavior. (Cyril Ruoso, Minden Pictures/Getty Images)

bit of sandy real estate where scientists can continue observing them? The answer is that the scientists provide them with food – sweet potatoes. In 1953, a juvenile female monkey named Imo (Japanese for "yam") apparently tiring of sweet potatoes à la mud, took hers to a stream and washed it off. (See Figure 5.6.) What makes that accident of fate or individual experimentation so interesting is that the washing caught on.

By 1983, 46 out of 57 members of the troop were habitual washers. Although this "catching on" involved no teaching nor language, let alone storytelling, it was one step above mere trial-and-error because the learning was inherently social. That is, it involved monkeys watching one other monkey and eventually whole groups of monkeys. The early adopters were not infants (the subjects of many studies of primate learning), but Imo's juvenile peers, followed later by adults (McGrew 1998:312). Writing more generally, McGrew claims that these Japanese monkeys "show innovation, dissemination, standardization, durability, diffusion, and tradition in both subsistence and nonsubsistence activities, as revealed by decades of longitudinal study" (1998:301).

Figure 5.7 We have learned much from Jane Goodall's 55-year study of endangered chimpanzees' social and family life. (Michael Nichols/National Geographic/Getty Images)

Full-blown language and culture, then, evolved along with our brains, specifically the increasing signals by the neocortex or higher and newer ("more evolved") brain. Language is both the product of evolution and yet unique, quite different from its precedents in the animal, especially primate, world – although readers can certainly find arguments that run counter to this idea (e.g., Proust (2016)).

As we have seen, humans share brain features with other **primates**. And exploring these shared features helps us understand the protocultural links to human cultural behavior and practice. Let's look now at another link that helps flesh out this evolutionary perspective. That link involves mirror neurons, which some claim are the biological basis for intersubjectivity and **Theory of Mind** (often referred to as "ToM"), the ability to imagine another's perspective as separate from one's own. (Incidentally, the term "Theory of Mind" can be misleading: It is important to understand that ToM is a psychological ability, not a scientific theory.)

So what sort of evidence is there that apes have ToM? Oddly enough, the key answer may lie in their advanced capacity for deception. The most compelling examples in the scientific record come from primatologists led by Jane Goodall (1986) who worked with *Pan troglodytes* (chimpanzees) in Gombe Stream National Park in Tanzania. (See Figure 5.7.)

Of particular interest are stories of a chimp that the scientists named Figan (Byrne and Whiten 1990). As an adolescent, Figan learned to suppress his excitement at finding bananas (left by the scientists) and thus learned how to eat his share of them without competition from chimps who would have been signaled by the sounds of food-excitement. Figan also developed the art of heading in precisely the wrong direction to find bananas, hooting all the while in the manner common to food-excitement – only to double back quietly to the true site after misleading his troop. Byrne, Whiten, and Goodall call this Figan's "lie" (Byrne and Whiten 1990:89).

How does Figan's "lie" amount to evidence of ToM, and how is it also evidence relevant to the evolution of language? Figan demonstrated ToM by being aware that his fellows had different perceptions than he had – being aware, for example, that he knew where the day's supply of bananas was and others perhaps did not. Second, Figan's capacity to tell "lies" amounts to an ability to use signals in some way other than "literally." (In fact, lying might be the first evolutionary step toward metaphor.) Finally, for young Figan to suppress his excitement calls required conscious effort, great strain, and remarkable self-control. So we see that Figan – and presumably chimps as a species – demonstrated reflexive awareness of his signals *and* their effects.

Interestingly, we know that although great apes (like chimpanzees) manifest ToM, monkeys do not. Apes are genetically and behaviorally much closer to humans than are monkeys. Then too, we must assume that chimpanzees' higher capacity for deceiving reflects brain size and brain "contents" (i.e., the development of certain parts of the brain beyond that of monkeys' brains). In other words, we are comparing the evolution of ToM in primate species along a continuum of related-ness-to-Homo-sapiens, a continuum understood to reflect millions of years of cognitive development as apes evolved separately from monkeys.

This is somewhat similar to comparing the development of, say, 5-year-old human children with that of human 2-year-olds. In doing so, we are invoking behavior (in growing human children *over time* and in apes versus monkeys in *real time*) as evidence supporting models of evolution of brain and communication.

Comparing children and their development of ToM over time with that of chimps – *and* observing that chimps, but not monkeys, have ToM – is a good example of linking "evo" and "devo" together in an evo-devo approach. That is, such arguments reflect the understanding that individual development (ontogeny) recapitulates the evolution of populations or species (phylogeny). If we accept this premise, we are then led to infer something about primate-hominid evolution *from* the ontogenetic trajectory or developmental progress of human children: that children's gradual acquisition of ToM *reflects* the evolution of ToM in higher primates.

One final note on the evolution of perspective taking or ToM: Psychologist Brian MacWhinney (2005) argues that, as language and brain co-evolved, increasingly complex forms of perspective taking arose. Grammar, then, emerged as a means of supporting accurate tracking and switching of perspective. The idea that grammar emerged in evolutionary time in part because a grammatical brain capacity helps one have a perspective-taking brain capacity is a very important claim in relation to the connections between language and mind, which we explore in more detail in Chapter 6.

Narrative

As we have seen, the development of culture out of protoculture is intertwined with the evolution of complex human perspective taking. Now we look at how language development has evolved more broadly out of the need for structured ways to share knowledge.

By using language to build narratives, our species shares knowledge – conveying information, creating meaning, and deepening relationships, to name just a few of its functions (Ochs and Capps 2001). In this section, I describe characteristics of language that support narrative and discuss why narrative may have developed in pre-historical human groups, especially narrative that "lent itself ideally to transmitting fitness-enhancing knowledge" (Francis 2012:270), or knowledge that enhances individual and group survival – where to find animal herds, how various animals behave, and where the best plants are for gathering.

Narrative and Recursivity: Structured Creativity in (Evolved) Grammar

Recursivity is the phenomenon, shared by all natural human languages, wherein a structure like a sentence can be built out of two "sentences" (really a combining of independent and sometimes dependent clauses). Linguists represent recursivity thus:

S → S + S (A sentence can consist of a sentence plus a sentence.)

One model for the evolution of language centers on the hypothesis that selective pressure (the pressure of natural selection) favored individuals who could make use of the "recursive" capacity of language. This makes sense, they argue, because the recursive capacity allowed our ancestors to tell mini-stories in an efficient and highly specific manner. Thus, recursive rules are rules for generating a structure that embeds shorter sentences within the longer sentence. It takes time and effort to say, "The carcass is under the tree. The tree has purple leaves." Recursivity allows the two sentences to be fused into one shorter one: "The carcass is under the tree *that* has purple leaves." Note that, in place of "the tree" or "it," the new sentence has the **relative pronoun** "that," which enables us to embed the second clause as a kind of modifier or delimiter of "the tree" introduced in the first (main) clause.

As Original "Motive" for Evolution of Language

What function did recursivity-equipped language serve for our ancestors that provided a benefit adequate to overcoming its evolutionary costs (e.g., the increased risk of choking)? As we discussed earlier in this chapter, the idea that language arose to facilitate human social actions, like telling a story, is central to a linguistic anthropological perspective on the evolution of language. Sometime within the last 100,000 years, early modern *Homo sapiens* developed the ability to tell stories that were useful to subsistence. (See Figure 5.7.) Some have argued that our capacity

Figure 5.8 Early people may have begun developing language to help coordinate their actions after a hunt. (Mauricio Anton/Science Photo Library)

for language evolved to facilitate hunting. However, since coordinating actions during a hunt would require stealth that could best be facilitated by gesture, another explanation is more likely. It might well have been the narrative capacity of language that facilitated and coordinated communal actions *after* the hunt. "We need language more to tell stories than to direct actions" (Jerison 1976:101). Bruner later wrote, "The structure of human grammar might have arisen out of the proto-linguistic push to narrate" (1990:138).

Norbert Francis (2012: 283, citing Scalise Sugiyama 2005), who specializes in linguistics and bilingual and multicultural education, further contributes to this perspective:

> even prior to the emergence of language, it is hard to conceive of archaic humans without at very least a basic platform of pre-narrative ability consisting in the capacity to cognize temporally coherent event sequences. The evolution of basic proto-language ability would suffice to propel this nascent narrative capacity forward.

CONCLUSION

In previous chapters of this book, I describe signs and sign systems, especially language. In this chapter, I offer a portrait of the evolution of human language from the animal sign systems that preceded it. Those predecessor systems included iconic and indexical signs, but this chapter argues that symbolicity is a function of human language alone. The evolution of language required changes in the brain and the vocal tract. Over at least a million years, protolanguage emerged along with primitive music and, along with protoculture, became the foundation for contemporary human language and culture.

In the face of various theories about which function of language was beneficial enough to outweigh the risk that some vocal tract changes posed to individual survival (e.g., choking), I argue that language emerged not from the need for gestures during the hunt but for protonarrative after the hunt. One possible scenario would involve strings of utterances telling where the kill could be found. In this scenario, such utterances would have benefited from the evolution of efficient (even energy-saving) recursive sentences.

In the next chapter, Chapter 6, we revisit the terrain covered in Chapter 4, but now emphasizing cross-linguistic diversity and evidence for that global semiotic variation correlating with significant diversity in our experiences of the world.

SUMMARY

In this chapter we explored the origins and evolutionary benefits of human language and its features. After reading it, you should be familiar with the following ideas:

- Human evolution from ancestors, and human language from animal communication systems.
- Natural selection operating on language, with benefits in survival and reproductive success that language provides.
- The changes in brain and vocal tract necessary to the emergence of *Homo sapiens* as a user of language.
- How icons, indexes, and symbols evolved.
- Examples of protoculture and how it differs from culture.
- The advantage inherent in narrative-capable language and narrative-capable *Homo sapiens*.

QUESTIONS

1. There are many studies, and many kinds of studies, of the evolution of language. What characteristics make a small minority of these the most relevant to a linguistic anthropological perspective?
2. Not all introductions to the subject "culture and communication" take a linguistic anthropological perspective, and not all introductory texts in linguistic anthropology take a semiotic perspective. How does it affect your learning from this chapter to have both a semiotic and linguistic anthropological perspective combined here?

3. Name a historical example of research and academic writing that addressed animal communication but that has contributed conceptual models to linguistic anthropology.

4. How does the concept "Theory of Mind" lend itself to universalist and particularist or relativist perspectives on language, mind, and social interaction?

5. In defining culture, how important is the requirement that it be passed down to the next generation via tradition (i.e., traditional transmission)? How important is it, specifically, in relation to the notion of protoculture?

EXERCISES

1. Review the short video about camouflage at www.youtube.com/watch?v=KLESZStQqZY. How does camouflage boost an animal's chances of surviving and living long enough to pass on its genes?

2. Review the short video at www.wildfilmhistory.org/film/241/clip/418/Macaques+wash+their+sweet+potatoes.html. Is it showing culture or protoculture? What is the means of transmission? How complex is the level of imitation involved in macaque (monkey) behavior and its transmission?

ADDITIONAL RESOURCES

Bowie, Jill. 2008. Proto-discourse and the emergence of compositionality. *Interaction Studies* 9(1):18–33.

> *Bowie offers an unusual approach to the compositionality model of the evolution of human language. Its uniqueness – its focus on discourse (and not as a level of linguistic structure but a mode of interaction) – makes it a particularly useful contribution to the intersection of linguistic and biological anthropology.*

Chow, Cecilia P., Jude F. Mitchell, and Cory T. Miller. 2015. Vocal Turn-Taking in a Non-Human Primate Is Learned during Ontogeny. *Proceedings of the Royal Society of London B: Biological Sciences* 282(1807):20150069.

> *This article is particularly welcome to all who have an interest in conversation and its structure – turn-taking – and the relationship of that apparently modern human structure to its forebears.*

Fitch, Tecumseh. 2010. *The Evolution of Language*. Cambridge University Press.

> *Fitch's book is one of the most important contributions to the study of the evolution of language as our uniquely human mode of communication.*

Haworth, Karen. 2006. Upper Paleolithic art, autism, and cognitive style: Implications for the evolution of language. *Semiotica* 162(1–4):129.

> *Although somewhat speculative – and what specific claims about our ancestors are not? – Haworth's article is also evocative and challenges our thinking about the mind and what is cognitively "normal."*

Steels, Luc. 2012. Interactions between cultural, social and biological explanations for language evolution. *Physics of Life Reviews* 9(1):5–8.

> *For many who study human evolution, it is crucial to treat the evolution of society/culture/ language, as both* sui generis *(a thing unto itself) and interconnected with the hard (or hard science) facts of biological evolution. Steels' argument explains this and shows why it is important.*

6 Diverse Languages and Perspectives: Communication, Expression, and Mind

LEARNING OBJECTIVES

After reading this chapter, you should be able to do the following:

- List the three levels of language whose influence on cognition has been studied.
- Define linguistic relativity and Whorfian effects, and provide reasons to avoid referring to either as the Sapir–Whorf hypothesis.
- Explain two key differences in the studies of "thinking for speaking" and "imaging in iron."
- Explain whether the contrast between "thinking for speaking" and "imaging in iron" calls linguistic relativity into question.

Introduction

This chapter explores the tremendous diversity we find when we look cross-culturally at language and other systems of communication. Here we revisit centuries-old arguments about the relationship between language and culture as well as newer arguments about language and ways of perceiving the world and about language and forms of **social action**.

The chapter expands beyond older views of language as a mediator of cognition and action, instead exploring the broader "**semiotic mediation** of culture" (Mertz and Parmentier 1985). We start with that broad approach to the power of semiotic or nonlinguistic communicative systems and then explore linguistic diversity specifically.

Communicative Diversity

In comparing the nonlinguistic communicative or semiotic forms that social groups use and that profoundly shape their shared cultural lives, we find at least as much diversity as we do in comparing languages around the world. We see a striking diversity of semiotic structures, semiotic practices, and **metasemiotic** models. And we find that the *relationships* among diverse communicative means or **modalities** differ as well.

Figure 6.1 The hebu mataro rattle is important for use in curing rituals in Venezuela. (Dale A. Olsen)

For example, Farnell (1995) discovered that a sign language called "Plains Indian Sign Talk" was not only used between tribes in the Great Plains region of the United States, but it was part and parcel of *all* speaking. "For the Assiniboine [or Nakota, living in northern Montana], speech acts are at once vocal and manual" (Farnell 1995:1, 4), meaning that words and gestures are used simultaneously, rather than for separate purposes. This highly developed **gestural** system has traditionally been of special importance in "the storytelling traditions [that] provide the focus for [Farnell's] study" (1995:4).

Music, in both its **structure** and its communicative **function**, offers more examples of nonlinguistic cross-cultural variation. Music is also accompanied by communicative signs of other sorts, and the combinations themselves vary. For instance, among the Kaluli or Bosavi of Papua New Guinea, a certain melodic pattern is associated with not only a bird species (the muni bird or Beautiful Fruit Dove), but also a myth that explains how a boy turned into a muni bird; the myth also communicates cultural expectations about food sharing between boys and their older sisters (Feld 1990). Among pre-conversion (pre-missionization) Kaluli, grief was played out socially through various semiotic **media** – dancing, singing, weeping, and burning of the dancers (Schieffelin 1976).

As another example, the Warao people of Venezuela have long relied on *wisidatu* **shamans** (**ritual specialists**) for healing of all sorts of illnesses. In shamanic curing rituals, we find multiple sign modalities. There is music, including the rhythmic playing of rattles (see Figure 6.1), as well as the visual evidence of the presence of *hebu* (diseases/spirits) in the spark those rattles produce (because they contain crystals, understood as the bodies of *hebu*), all accompanied by singing of lyrics sometimes in everyday speech but often in a special shamanic register. The "crystals are bodies of particular *hebu* that reside in the rattle, and each stone is named and accorded a kin term" (Briggs 1996:196).

Finally, we can understand the embodied process of healing itself as another sign system – providing evidence of the effectiveness of healing rituals among the Yolmo wa ('Yolmo people'), a Tibetan group living in Nepal (Desjarlais 1996).

In quite a few societies, people have understood what we might categorize as musical, including phenomena like *resonance* (e.g., the way one vibrating string might set off vibrations in another string on, say, a guitar) or "echoes," as related to human speech and human interconnection. In Nepal, Yolmo wa like Mheme (a Buddhist *lama* or priest) understand that how people talked about him while he was alive, but particularly after he had died, is a kind of echo (Desjarlais 2000, 2003) or resonance. This resonance involves iconicity. In the echo, as an example, a series of "like sounds" follows an original sound. An object with an innate frequency – again, a string in a piano or guitar – is "forced" to "vibrate when another nearby object begins to vibrate at a frequency equal to or close to its own" (Thygesen 2008:64). And various cultural systems have regarded that completely impersonal sign system involving two inanimate objects that are attuned to each other as an **icon** of the kind of connection or communion that human beings are capable of experiencing with others – e.g., in group therapy (Thygesen 2008) or in a crying circle during a Finnish-Karelian lament course (Wilce 2011a, 2011b; Wilce and Fenigsen 2015).

One way of summing up the previous paragraphs is by invoking *metaphor*, a kind of iconicity as culturally perceived. Metaphors compare two classes of object, each class occupying a different *semantic domain* or area of meaning. We are especially interested in metaphors that are **metasemiotic** or **metacommunicative**, comparing one sign relationship to another. The comparison makes sense at a profound, perhaps even unconscious, level – or at least it makes deep sense from a particular cultural vantage point. These metacommunicative metaphors (or **tropes**) make deep sense because they arise from the depths of one's culture. As oft-voiced and reinforced visions of perceived links between different sign relationships – string to string, person to person – these tropes profoundly influence our experience of the world (Whorf [1939] 1956).

Keith Basso described the workings of metacommunicative tropes like epitomization and metaphor in his analysis of Western Apache "joking imitations of The Whiteman" (Basso 1979). Performances of these joking imitations involve several significant and signifying dimensions – a safe space (a friend's house), embodied acts, and discourse. Basso (1979:46) describes how a jokester (J) "ambushes" an unsuspecting friend (L) who is unlucky enough to knock on J's door one evening, with Basso presumably already inside the home of J and his wife K.

SETTING: The living room of an Apache home at Cibecue [Arizona].
PARTICIPANTS: J, a cowboy (age 40+); K, his wife (age 37); four of their children (ages 4–12); L, a clan "brother" of J (age 35+).
SCENE: It is a hot, clear evening in mid-July, and J and K have just finished a meal. J is seated on a chair, repairing a bridle. K is washing dishes. Their children play quietly

on the floor. L is not yet present. J starts to speak . . . but is interrupted by a knock on the door. He rises, answers the knock, and finds L standing outside.

J: Hello, my friend! How you doing? How you feeling, L? You feeling good?

[J now turns in the direction of K and addresses her.]

J: Look who here, everybody! Look who just come in. Sure, it's my Indian friend, L. Pretty good all right!

[J slaps L on the shoulder and, looking him directly in the eyes, seizes his hand and pumps it wildly up and down.]

The scene Basso describes is full of humor – and danger. But much of it would be lost on anyone unfamiliar with what Apaches regard as "living right" versus being foolish. J's behavior is offensive – or it would be if a humorous frame for interpreting his behavior were not available. In this case, what makes the series of offenses somewhat *less* offensive is the understanding that J is engaged in a particular genre or speech activity – a "joking imitation of The Whiteman" (Basso 1979). J's violent pumping of L's hand represents an Apache perception of white politicians who visit Indian country just long enough to shake hands at election time. The direct eye-to-eye gaze and the personal questions – "How are you? How are you feeling? You feeling good?" – are considered grossly intrusive at best, and at worst, "dangerous" in this Western Apache context. Note, however, the cultural particularity of the joking performance, with its particular synthesis of semiotic modalities: It offends on several levels – long and intensive body contact, inappropriate visual connection, and overly probing speech.

As potentially offensive as this kind of joking may be, what exactly makes it dangerous? Basso explains that, "Sometimes . . . the butts of jokes do not play along." That is, they misread the joker's behavior as being his (the joker's) own, rather than as parodying The Whiteman. "When this happens . . . the consequences can be explosive" (Basso 1979:43). And what makes the joking worth the risk of angering or alienating a friend? Basso's Western Apache friends believe that dangerous joking performances can help to sustain and even deepen a friendship. They might describe such acts of speaking as being like chewing on a tough hide to soften and stretch it (Basso 1979:67). This metaphoric revelation, based on an ethnographic approach to acts of speaking, is a compelling example of culturally particular metacommunication. It shows us two manifestations of linguistic relativity that other treatments of relativity tend to ignore: First, it is clearly a case of communicative behavior whose appropriateness is unique to that cultural setting. Second, it is a case of a local metaphor (friendship is like leather) for the communicative behavior in question.

Linguistic Diversity and Diverse Experiences of the World

To complement the broader *communicative* diversity we have just been exploring, we now turn our attention specifically to the diversity of language. The sum total of the world's languages represents a cornucopia overflowing with variety. And we find this variety at every level of linguistic structure, every stratum of discourse practice (ways of speaking and writing and of doing things via our speaking and writing).

Later in this section, we probe arguments for the reality of **Whorfian effects** – that is, the kind of influence Whorf and others argued that language has on individual and shared ways of thinking, understanding, and experiencing. In that discussion, we explore three levels at which language might exert such influence. That discussion reflects the work of Lucy (1996), who first proposed a triad of approaches to the issue of linguistic relativity, each based on a different level of language. We can frame these three approaches as questions:

- What might the cognitive effect be of merely "having a natural language or not," which Lucy (1996:38) calls "semiotic relativity"?
- How might the basic and contrastive linguistic structures encountered in various languages influence their speakers' thoughts and experiences?
- In what ways can cultural patterns of language use be associated with cultural patterns of thought?

First, Though, a Research Concern

Before we dive into these questions, however, a prefatory note is in order – regarding experimental approaches to assessing the potential impact of communicative structures, or practices, on the mind.

First, it is important to know that not all linguistic anthropologists find "positivist" or experimental methods appropriate to understanding natural language use and its relationship to natural manifestations of thought or perspective. Positivism holds that "the basic scientific method is the same in both the natural and social sciences" (Kincaid 1998), so there is always a neat way to distinguish between independent and dependent variables.

Along these lines, some linguistic anthropologists, such as Lucy (1996) and Danziger (2005, 2010, 2011), *are* convinced that a positivist hypothesis-testing model of linguistic relativity is appropriate. These researchers take care to design experiments involving a clear distinction between the nature of both the independent and the dependent variable.

For instance, if the independent variable is the native language of the experimental subject (e.g., Hopi or English), the dependent variable must involve a task whose performance does not involve speaking or writing. In what follows, we examine tests of the relative degree to which subjects have acquired a **Theory of Mind** (ToM) – the ability to imagine (or to have a "theory" about the contents of) other minds, which I introduced in Chapter 5. In these cases, the independent variable is the *level* of language that subjects have acquired. Using a *verbal* ToM test would be inappropriate in this case, because it would confuse the relationships between the two kinds of variables.

Fortunately, many studies distinguish appropriately between independent and dependent variables by letting having or lacking language remain the independent variable – allowing children at different ages, for instance, to point to something rather than speaking. Imagine two pairs of children, ages 2 or 3 versus 5. They sit at a table with two cups and one marble. The marble is under the cup on the left when both children are in the room. One child leaves. The marble is moved. The child who remains is asked what cup the child who left will say the marble is under.

The younger children, with less language development, cannot imagine the child who left would falsely believe the marble never moved. By contrast, typical 5-year-olds *can* imagine other minds having (false) knowledge different from their own (i.e., they *can* have ToM.)

It is important to not have either age group perform linguistically. That would be circular – choosing two sets of children based on their primitive versus advanced language skills and then having them demonstrate those skills. The **false belief test**, by contrast, tests the hypothesis that primitive language skills are associated with underdeveloped ToM.

Having clarified this research concern, we now examine each of Lucy's three questions about linguistic relativity.

Having or Not Having a Language, and Points Between

John Lucy (1997:292) refers to the most basic level of possible differences – the difference between having and lacking any language – as the engine of semiotic relativity. As you will recall, this is the first of his three approaches to linguistic relativity.

Cognitive scientists and primatologists interested in cognition have intensely studied great apes in captivity. In order to gauge these apes' *potential* to acquire language, researchers have taught individuals and families of apes American Sign Language or some other invented sign system involving, for example, the manipulation and grouping of colored plastic shapes. Some of these experiments have witnessed important breakthroughs and revelations of unexpected capabilities, such as the great apes' creative and independent production of new "sentences."

Despite some successes, these studies are not well suited to investigating the cognitive effects of language per se. Any language effects are so tangled up with differences between species, particularly in relation to species-specific brain differences, that the ability of these experimental interventions to tell us what we want to know is severely limited. When it comes to investigations of the level of linguistic development in children and adults, studies of deaf persons – those whose acquisition of language is delayed because they are born into environments in which no one uses sign language – have been particularly common, and most promising.

In the preceding paragraphs, I portray the scope of variation in terms of "having language," emphasizing studies (e.g., Schick et al. 2007) that have taken as their

Figure 6.2 Mother of deaf infant models communication through signing. (JGI, Jamie Grill/Getty Images)

independent variable the degree and timing of language acquisition in children, rather than simply studying two groups, one "with language" (as though they had completed their language acquisition – in relation to what?) and the other "without any" language.

Laura Ahearn (2012) has demonstrated the utility, for linguistic anthropologists, of studies that compare prelinguistic children with children who have already acquired a language. For Ahearn as well as myself, natural experiments involving human children are more interesting than those involving apes in captivity. By "natural experiments," I mean those in which crucial differences in children's language acquisition are because of natural circumstances. The majority of these studies involve children who were born deaf. (See Figure 6.2.) One such set of experiments involves the natural circumstance of choices that hearing parents of deaf children make: Some parents do not, or choose not to, use sign language. Some related studies – like that of Pyers and Senghas (2009), summarized in this chapter – examine language development across the life span of sign language users.

A large and indeed growing number of studies have linked the development of linguistic capacities to the development of Theory of Mind (introduced in Chapter 5). ToM is our capacity to imagine that others have minds that are separate and different from our own, with different perspectives and knowledge. The link between ToM and linguistic development has sometimes been studied in the context of persons on an atypical path to that development – particularly deaf persons who for various reasons experienced a delay in the full development of language. Pyers and Senghas (2009) studied adult speakers of Nicaraguan Sign Language (NSL), which is a fairly new language, unavailable in full form to adults in the first cohort of learners. The first forms in the evolution of a language for Nicaraguan deaf people comprised barely more than a system of **gestures**. That system, if it truly qualifies as such, was what "Generation 1" spoke. A minority of Generation 1 eventually learned the far more developed system known as NSL, as did their children. Those adults and children comprised the second cohort, Generation 2. The group that learned the first, gestural, system represented only 50 or so users. The second cohort comprised more than 1,000 users. Pyers and Senghas administered false belief tests to those in the first cohort who had not learned the more developed form of NSL as well as to those in either cohort who had learned that form, whether as children (in the case of the second cohort) or as adults (in the case of some in the first cohort). NSL users of the more complete linguistic variety scored higher on ToM tests than the non-NSL group. As the authors point out, even adults with two or more decades of social experience had difficulty acquiring the social-cognitive ability to accurately imagine other minds and others' knowledge.

Some related studies have involved administering false belief or ToM tests to *children* with delayed versus "normal" language acquisition (de Villiers and de Villiers 2012). Such studies of the acquisition of ToM and language in children have focused on the *level* of language acquisition. Research questions have included the degree to which study participants have learned "mental-state verbs" like "think" and "know" (Pyers and Senghas 2009). Other researchers have found that the key sorts of verbs to learn are not mental-state verbs but metacommunicative verbs that take a **complement clause** (the following two italicized **clauses** being examples) – says *that she will come*, promises *that he will* ... (de Villiers and de Villiers 2012).

Some studies of ToM in children have compared the relative impact of acquiring verbs (be they mental-state or metacommunicative verbs) with acquisition of complex grammar. These studies have found the latter more closely associated with advanced levels of ToM (Levrez et al. 2012). Others (Rakhlin et al. 2011) studied children's storytelling and the use of psychological verbs – which is surely one contributor to children's ability to *talk about* others' mental states – and complex grammar in those stories. They specifically compared whether grammatical complexity or the ability to use mental-state verbs had a greater impact on false belief test success. Rakhlin et al. found that the ability to use psychological verbs did much less for children's ToM than their ability to use complex grammar, particularly those complex linguistic structures that help one *refer to* or *talk about* others' perceptions, knowledge, and beliefs – namely, complement clauses. Complement clauses use "that" to introduce minimal sentences or clauses like "that she would come" in a full sentence like, "She promised that she would come." Another complement clause would be "that we hate this movie," as in "He knows [a psychological or mental-state verb] that we hate this movie." The role of complement clauses in Whorfian effects is described by Lee (1997).

More than their scores on a test of knowledge of mental-state verbs, children's general and specific grammatical abilities help explain their abilities to imagine other minds (i.e., their ToM). In a complicating twist, however, children's general grammatical abilities *along with a well-developed vocabulary* seem to have the greatest impact on ToM development, especially among deaf children (Levrez et al. 2012).

Linguistic Structure

The world's 6,000 or so languages share many features. In other ways, however, diversity reigns. And that diversity is found at every level of linguistic structure, in every category of linguistic practice, and in the kinds of **multimodal communication** or **semiotic multimodality** (i.e., the range of *types* of signs such as gesture, language, and artifacts) in which language plays a role. So let's consider some of the wealth of cross-linguistic differences as examples of Lee's second of three approaches to linguistic relativity.

Phonological Diversity

As we discussed in Chapter 4, the smallest building blocks of language are sounds (**phones**, phonological units). Each language has a **sound system**. The range of variation in sound systems is impressive, starting with the number of sounds that native speakers of a given language recognize as distinct (i.e., the number of distinct **phonemes**). Polynesian languages have relatively few, while Khoisan languages (spoken in southern Africa and famous for their "click" consonants) have many. (South African singer Miriam Makeba, a Xhosa speaker, made these famous in *Qongqothwane*, "The Click Song.") Linguists categorize sounds according to how and where in the mouth they are produced or *articulated* – thus, according to the **manner of articulation** and **place of articulation**. Some languages use clicks in forming words; others have borrowed click sounds (Irvine and Gal 2000).

Rules for combining sounds (**phonotactic rules** or "constraints") vary widely, too. From an English speaker's perspective, words in Slavic languages can have strikingly long consonant clusters, such as the noun *pstros*. Not only sound length but other sound (phonetic) features may be referentially uncommitted. For instance, when we speak of **prosody** (voice quality, speech tempo, and pitch or **intonation** patterns), we typically mean stylistically variable prosodic features. Prosody can thus be available to constitute speech **registers**, like the Wolof griot and noble speech that we discuss in Chapter 9.

As mentioned earlier, speakers of some languages use clicks phonemically. In other languages, clicks are used not to form words but to communicate in other ways – in making kissing sounds, producing odd little shaming utterances (like "tsk tsk tsk"), or in the sound some use to encourage a horse to speed up. The "fricative voice gesture" in Korean is a particularly interesting example of a phonetic shift that reflects important cultural models (Harkness 2011:104–105).

If you visit South Korea and happen upon men drinking soju there, you may well hear the sound that men traditionally produce after a gulp of the bitter alcohol. In case you aren't able to visit Korea, you can watch this video (www.youtube.com/watch?v=tSnSMbqTLjQ) in which an American-sounding young man offers a lesson in soju drinking. You will notice that he comments on several acts in the overall act sequence, but when (just before the video ends) he and his Korean friend make the traditional fricative vocal gesture, no one comments. Yet commentary on this sound is central to the recent linguistic-ethnographic work of Harkness (2013).

> Although non-native speakers and heritage learners of Korean often comment on this sound, native Korean speakers, for the most part, are not immediately aware of the sound's distinctiveness to outsiders. In my interviews with Korean informants, there was a fairly clear division among groups as to how recognizable the sound was as a segment (or dimension) of prosodic speech. Often, its gestural function did not seem noteworthy upon reflection.

The issue for Harkness and his Korean consultants is not whether the fricative vocal gesture is a distinct phoneme, nor is it the way the sound or "gesture" might add up to a bit of grammatical meaning. It is to those bits – called **morphemes** – that we now turn.

Morphological Diversity

As you remember from Chapter 4, putting phonemes together into words brings us to the next level of structure – **morphology**. As in their phonological systems, languages vary in their morphology (their morphological systems) too. Let me give some examples. English has very few of the sorts of suffixes and prefixes by which other languages anchor words in context (markers of person, gender, **tense-aspect**, mode, honor). Mexicano (also known as Nahuatl or modern Aztecan) has a complex morphological system for marking honor. Spanish has a rich tense-aspect system. Finnish has no definite or indefinite articles and no gender distinction in its third-person pronouns.

And let me give a more detailed comparative example of morphological differences. Whereas English has ways of marking three noun **cases** – a noun's subjecthood (**nominative** case), objecthood (**accusative** case), and possessorship (genitive case) – Finnish has sixteen active cases and another half-dozen that are rarely used. These include various *locative* cases, cases that refer to or index location or movement in space – such as the *adessive* ('on top of', -*lla* or -*llä*, depending on the phonetic context, meaning the preceding sounds in the word to which the case suffix is added), and *inessive* ('inside of', -*ssa* or -*ssä*, again dependent on the phonetic context) – as well as non-locative cases like the *translative* (-*ksi*, underlined in the Finnish sentence below) that marks change of state or "becoming."

Hän haluaa lääkäriksi. (IPA version: Hæn haluaa læækæriksi.)
Literal translation – S/he wants doctor-TRANS
Idiomatic translation – S/he wants to become a doctor.

Perhaps this will give you some idea of the variety of ways that different languages form parts of words and whole words – and then use them to convey meanings that native speakers take for granted and non-native speakers might struggle to learn, given how different the meanings that can be expressed in different languages are. That is what Sapir meant when he wrote that "the worlds in which different societies live are distinct worlds, not merely the same world with different labels attached" (Sapir 1929:162). We talk more about the great linguistic anthropologist Edward Sapir later in this chapter.

Syntactic Diversity

And then there are all of the different ways that languages string words together to make phrases and phrases to make sentences – the processes we call "syntactic." In other words, **syntax** refers to the rules that, in any language, govern how units are strung together into sentences. (Later in this chapter, we deal with language-specific sets of rules for stringing sentences together to form larger discourse units.)

Global syntactic variation includes variation in the ordering of words or, more accurately, "constituents" like verbs, their objects, and their subjects. Probably a majority of the world's languages distinguish between two classes of subjects – true agents (subjects of transitive clauses – those that require direct objects, words that refer to "undergoers" of the verb's action) and other subjects (subjects of intransitive clauses – those that may not have a direct object).

Some tend to order their sentences (or transitive clauses) thus – Subject-Object-Verb – while English and others prefer Subject-Verb-Object. This is called "basic constituent order," which is more accurate than "word order," since subjects, verbs, and objects may each be multi-word constructions (phrases). Subjects and objects are "noun phrases," not necessarily single words (nouns). Likewise verbs are better called "verb phrases." Constituent or word order is highly variable in languages that mark the grammatical function of nouns with *case*. For example, in Latin, since nouns carry their *case suffixes* with them, subjects can come last or first in a sentence or be in the middle.

In any given language, variation in that language's constituent order indexes special or poetic speech. Lewis Carroll's delightfully nonsensical poem *Jabberwocky* (Figure 6.3) – published as part of his novel, *Through the Looking Glass* (1872) – provides a useful example.

See how each of the following lines from *Jabberwocky* has a different constituent order (shown in parentheses).

(i) He took his vorpal sword in hand (SVO)
(ii) Long time the manxome foe he sought (OSV)

Figure 6.3 Lewis Carroll's Jabberwock was as fantastic and intriguing as the unfamiliar words Carroll used to tell this poetic tale. (Bettmann/Getty Images)

(iii) So rested he by the Tumtum tree (VS_)

(iv) And stood awhile in thought (V__)

Note that clauses (iii) and (iv) are intransitive (i.e., have no grammatical object or direct object, also known as the semantic "patient" or "undergoer": Duranti 1997:192–193).

All three nouns in the *Jabberwocky* lines above – sword, foe, and tree – are what we call "count nouns." It turns out that languages do important work when they draw the line, wherever they do, between so-called *count nouns* and *mass nouns*. In English, it is grammatically correct to say "three buckets," but not "three airs." We can say "six grains," but not "six salts." Moreover, English *requires* plural marking on a large number of nouns (count nouns like grasshoppers, glasses, or goats), whereas Lucy writes, "Yucatec speakers *optionally* signal plural for a comparatively *small* number of lexical nouns" (1997:297). He continues,

> Whereas English numerals often directly modify their associated nouns (e.g. one candle), Yucatec numerals must always be accompanied by a form referred to as a numeral classifier which provides essential information needed to count the

referent [e.g. *un-tz'iit kib* 'one long thin wax (i.e. one candle)']. The classifiers reflect the fact that all lexical nouns in Yucatec are semantically unspecified as to essential unit. (Where our pattern is like the Maya, we use the functional equivalent of a classifier ourselves: a cube of sugar). (Lucy 1997:297–298)

As we will see later, Lucy argues that the way nouns and numeral classifiers work together in Yucatec – separating out all but the substance (wax) from the noun word – engenders in Yucatec speakers a cognitive orientation toward, or focus on, substance more than shape. The argument rests on the idea that, in any noun phrase, the noun as "head" of the phrase is more salient than other parts of the phrase. A noun phrase in this case consists of morphemes that denote number (singular or plural), numeral classifiers, and nouns themselves. Note that the English equivalent of numeral classifiers are separate words like "cube" (in Lucy's example) or "loaves" or "gallons" that we must use in counting bread or water.

Diverse Patterns of Language Use

Language *use* encompasses many things, for example, "linguistic indirection" (discussed in Chapter 9). Here we focus on literacy – the ability to read and write, or at least to read (Schieffelin 2000). As you will recall, this section relates to Lucy's third and final approach to linguistic relativity. We are truly talking here about acquiring literacy – actually multiliteracy, the ability to read (but not necessarily write) in several languages. As we shall see, it is quite possible to be literate – say, in Arabic – in such a way as to be able to read, but without understanding, and not write.

Linguistic anthropologist Laura Ahearn's (2012) review of studies relevant to the Whorfian or *cognitive effects* of certain *ways of using language* is very helpful, particularly her review of the groundbreaking sociocognitive research of Scribner and Cole (1981) on multiliteracy among the Vai of Sierra Leone. Vai adults are often triliterate – acquiring Arabic, English, and Vai literacies each by different means and for different purposes.

> English is the official script of political and economic institutions operating on a national scale; Arabic is the script of religious practice and learning [for the purpose of chanting, without understanding], Vai script serves the bulk of personal and public needs in the villages for information preservation and communication between individuals living in different locales. (Scribner and Cole 1981:77–78)

Given that learning Arabic involves huge amounts of rote memorization, it is no surprise that acquiring that form of literacy is associated with high performance on memory tasks relative to, for example, those who are literate not in Arabic but in Vai. Vai writing does not include word breaks, and thus learning to read and write in Vai is unique not only for functional reasons – Vai is used, for example, in

Figure 6.4 Coyote is seen in different ways in the stories of various Native American tribes, often as crafty and intelligent and as a character to learn lessons from. (Danita Delimont/Getty Images).

writing personal letters – but also because learning involves discerning where one word stops and the next starts (Scribner and Cole 1981).

In addition to Ahearn, other anthropologists have made fascinating contributions to our understanding of literacy. The cognitive effects of writing and of learning to write have been studied often. In fact, studies of literacy since the work of Goody and Watt (1963) have defined cognition rather narrowly, certainly excluding feelings in a perpetuation of the old trend in Western thought to distinguish mind from **body** as well as cognition from emotion. More recent studies of literacy-in-use by anthropologists like Besnier (1995), by contrast, have shone a light on the kinds of feelings that writing – such as writing personal letters – can channel.

When we speak of specific uses of language, we are in the realm of language as a mode of action and of specific linguistic practices as modes of specific kinds of social action. Such practices, quite often locally recognized and named, are called *discourse genres*. These genres – narratives, long jokes, and others – rely on language, but also on other semiotic systems to do what they do. For instance, many Native American tribes have Coyote stories, and they may or may not share the nonlinguistic context (namely, the agricultural cycle) that determines that winter is the time of year when performing these stories is both permitted and encouraged. (See Figure 6.4.)

In a very different kind of narrative genre from Coyote stories, Capps and Ochs found evidence in their study of panic disorder (which focused on a participant named Meg) that telling stories was a means of developing or reinforcing personal theories about emotions in relation to the world and to who or what has the ability to act upon the world. As the researchers discovered, it was "in their storytelling interactions [that] Meg and Beth construct a view of the world in which people are victims of their own and others' uncontrollable emotions and the actions they inspire" (Capps and Ochs 1995:165).

> We can track on a linguistic plane how Meg's narratives construct theories of a world in which emotions creep up on, invade, and sometimes overwhelm the present rather than being contained at a distance. In this sense, agoraphobia can be seen as an outcome of theories individuals develop as they act and interact with others in the world. (Capps and Ochs 1995:21–22)

Meg's storytelling **style**, which she appears to be passing on to her daughter, seems to constantly reorient mother and daughter to experiencing themselves as victims. And the style includes a "grammar of helplessness" (Capps and Ochs 1995:66) in which Meg's "I" is never quite in charge.

The three examples in the preceding section – Vai multiliteracy, seasonal Coyote stories, and stories in relation to helplessness – all illustrate Sapir's assertion that the languages we speak differ not superficially but deeply, leading us to inhabit "distinct worlds." Moreover, these are all examples of linguistic relativity that derive from cross-cultural differences in *language use* – examples rarely found, say, in cultural anthropology textbooks.

Schooled Language, Literacy, and Mind

Although linguistic anthropologist John Lucy proposed the three approaches to the study of Whorfian effects (**linguistic relativity**) that we have been exploring in the previous sections – having or lacking language, linguistic structure, and language use – he also cautions us against seeing the three as easily separable. "Patterns of use," Lucy argues, play a key role "in mediating structural relativity," but "variation in usage might have effects in its own right" (1996:38). Lucy is on similar ground when he discusses "how linguistic structure and discursive function interact dialectically in conjunction with language" (1996:38).

Let me illustrate the overlap between Lucy's three loci (areas) for the study of Whorfian effects. The levels of children's language acquisition are often measured in structural terms. That is, their language acquisition is described in terms of when they learn words and the rules for word-building (including, in English, knowing and using exceptions to rules, like "children" instead of "childs"). But structure and rules governing structure are *inseparable* from rules of language use-in-context: Structure + Use = Pragmatics.

Although examples of the inseparability of structure and use can be found in all languages, the case of Mohawk language-in-use is particularly interesting. Mohawk is a Northern Iroquoian language whose remaining speakers live in New York, Ontario, and Quebec. The language has developed two pronoun-prefixes (prefixes which do the job that pronouns like "she," "you," or "I" do in English); both can be used to refer to a woman who is neither speaking nor being addressed. These pronoun-like bits of language are "third-person." In some circumstances, the two forms, *ye-* and *ka-*, make a distinction that is referential. That is, the forms can distinguish women by age category, old or young. Just as often, however, they distinguish positive or negative feelings toward the woman. The latter function is indexical and not referential. *Saying* something like "I don't like that woman" would amount to explicit reference to one's feelings, but *ye-* and *ka-* simply perform, point to, or indicate those feelings (Bonvillain 2003). The two-way morphological distinction – the two prefixes – that is available to speakers of Mohawk can be used for pragmatic and not just referential meaning. This represents a choice that speakers of Mohawk must all make, almost constantly – the choice between indexing positive and negative feelings – but only in relation to third-person feminine referents like women who are neither speaker nor addressee, not in relation to male referents!

In another example of the inseparability of language structure and use, Spanish provides its speakers with a range of suffixes – such as *-ita/o and -iña/o* – called **diminutive** and another range (e.g., *-ón/a*, *-azo/a*) called **augmentative**. Although in some cases these may "diminish" or "augment" the *size* of the object or the *person* referred to (the **referent**), these suffixes are very commonly used to index a speaker's *feelings* (diminutive = dearness, positive feeling) toward the referent. However, whereas using one of the two Mohawk prefixes whenever one must speak about a woman is an unavoidable choice, adding Spanish diminutive or augmentative suffixes is completely optional. For Whorf, it is precisely what is "compulsory" in a given language that exercises the greatest influence on speakers' "worldviews."

The fact that one language provides one range of options from which to choose in conveying either referential or pragmatic meaning, whereas a second language provides a very different range of options, may have some impact on thought. As linguist Wallace Chafe (1997) argues in relation to Mohawk, its speakers *must* think differently from speakers of languages that lack a two-way distinction for referring to women one likes or dislikes, i.e., a two-way indexical distinction. Speakers of Mohawk, English, or any other language *must* each think differently, because of the difference in choices imposed upon their awareness by their language.

So Chafe asserts that there is a strong correlation between habits of thinking and of speaking. As we move on to discuss the relationship between structure and genre, I want to stress that the studies just reviewed confirm our sense that trying to distinguish linguistic structure from practice is problematic. Instead, we find evidence indicating that discourse practice, or ways of using language, may *always* rely on linguistic structures. Those structures represent choices – optional or obligatory – that speakers must make in *languaging*, or "committing acts of language."

The Long History of Arguments over Language and Mind

The cross-linguistic diversity that we've just been looking at is not uninteresting, nor of merely exotic interest, nor of interest purely on its own. Since the eighteenth century, scholars who have contemplated cross-linguistic diversity have tried to connect the particularity of languages with unique "worldviews."

Wilhelm von Humboldt did much to advance scholarly thinking about language and *worldview*, a concept for which Humboldt used the term *Weltansicht* but others, perhaps more commonly, use *Weltanschauung*. European speculations about the influence of language on worldview were mostly confined to European languages and to the romantic-nationalist movement that gave rise to the modern nation-states of Europe. Humboldt and others thought that a (European) language mapped neatly onto the geographic space occupied by a (European) nation-state. Such thinking is still apparent in popular, scholarly, and policy discourse today.

Some readers will perceive that what I am talking about is the so-called Sapir–Whorf hypothesis. If you are aware of this term, you may know that many scholars object to it, on several grounds. First, it removes the *Weltanschaung* or worldview concept from its history of use, divorcing Sapir and Whorf from one of their sources of inspiration, Johann Gottfried von Herder (whose work *Ursprung der Sprache* [Origin of Language] was actually the topic of Edward Sapir's master's thesis) and from Sapir's mentor, Franz Boas. (See Figure 6.5.) Second, it falsely implies that Sapir and Whorf collaborated and co-published. Third, it projects onto the work of two twentieth-century anthropologists a particular model of science – a hypothesis-testing model – that we don't really see in either Sapir's or Whorf's writings. Further, Whorf – a chemical engineer by his Yale training and profession (i.e., not a professional researcher) – did not use the term "worldview" in his best-known article, although he admittedly used closely related terms. Finally, like Sapir and Boas before him, he focused on Native American languages, particularly Hopi; he was by no means myopically focused on European languages.

In comparison with the Sapir–Whorf hypothesis, the term "linguistic relativity" is less objectionable, and I use it henceforth. **Linguistic relativity** is the claim that language stands between us and our world and works like a lens or a filter to influence our experience of the world. It is probably best considered an axiom than a hypothesis. As such, we should judge it "on the basis of the extent to which it leads to productive questions about talk and social action" (Hill and Mannheim 1992:386).

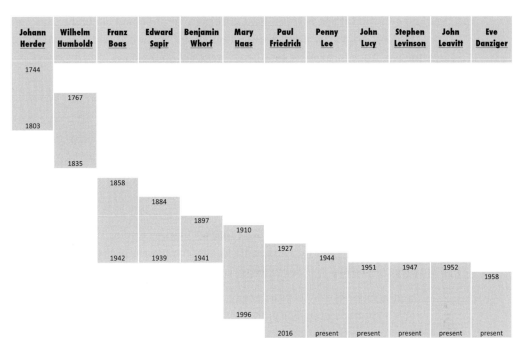

Figure 6.5 It is interesting to note when important contributors to the development of linguistic relativity lived in relation to each other and how this may have affected their ideas. (Illustration by author)

Habitual Thought Reflecting Obligatory Grammatical Categories

Although there are good reasons for not referring to the ideas that passed from Humboldt, through Boas and Sapir, to Whorf as a scientific hypothesis, extremely interesting "hypothesis testing" has in fact since been carried out by John Lucy, among others. The hypothesis is that linguistic relativity – the effects of language on thought or experience – should be apparent whether we look at linguistic structure, language in use, or simply having or not having a language (Ahearn 2012; Lucy 1996).

Lucy himself has studied Yucatec Mayan. In a series of experiments, he compared the cognitive preferences of Yucatec and English speakers living in Chicago. The two "languages contrast in the way they treat numerals and this contrast derives from a deep underlying difference between [them]" (Coward 1993:xii). Lucy's findings indicate that *linguistic structures* appear to influence their speakers' perceptions.

What I have called "cognitive preferences" arise in Lucy's experiments "involving classifying triads of certain test objects (i.e., 'Is item X more like A or more like B?')." In such experiments,

> speakers were shown a small cardboard box of the type used for holding cassette tapes and asked whether it was more like a small plastic box of roughly the

> same size and shape or more like a small piece of cardboard about the size of a
> half-dollar. English speakers consistently matched on the basis of shape and chose
> the box. Yucatec speakers consistently matched on the basis of material and
> chose the small piece of cardboard. (Lucy 1996:50–51)

The stripping of any reference to shape from the noun word, leaving it to focus on material or substance alone, is what – according to Lucy – prepares Yucatec speakers to choose material over shape in classifying objects as similar or different.

A Different Take on Linguistic Relativity

Linguistic anthropologist Paul Friedrich follows Sapir as well as Sapir's sources in searching for the aesthetic rather than the purely cognitive effects of language. And by language he means, especially, poetic language.

> The deeper levels of Boas's excitement about language were, I feel, aesthetic, just
> as his finest book in cultural anthropology was Primitive Art . . . In Cassirer and,
> later, in Suzanne Langer [1895–] we see a tendency to resolve the conflict
> between reason and emotion, the universal and the unique, through a philosophy
> of aesthetic form. (Friedrich 1986:10)

How might this focus on the aesthetic rather than the purely cognitive apply in our lives? Here's one possible example. Many readers may have grown up in, or joined, religious groups that function not only in the same language as its members usually speak, but in the same form of language with few modifications. For those of us for whom that is true, the idea of religious language being chanted, not spoken – and indeed of "having" a "religious language" that is distinct from the one we speak, read, or perhaps even understand – is quite a foreign idea. However, for another sizable portion of readers, the sacred has a particular sound to it, and that is the sound of a sacred language. This group of readers may have regularly participated in religious rituals that involve the ancient Sanskrit of the Vedas, Church Slavonic, Latin, or Classical Arabic. In addition to these languages – which have, or have had at one time, global reach – there are several thousand indigenous languages that for their speakers have always represented the very sound of the sacred.

For Friedrich, the experience of devout participants in rituals involving the sacred sounds of Sanskrit, Latin, or Arabic (sacred to Hinduism, Catholicism, and Islam, respectively) represents a particular cultural and experiential understanding of sound, meaning, and the sacred. For these participants, the beauty of the chanted language is itself the ultimate way of conveying the heart of the religion (Friedrich 1986). Whether it is a syllable (like *Om*), "wild" poetic images designed to jolt a shaman's patient out of torpor and entice the wandering soul back to the body (Desjarlais 1996), or a certain poetic patterning, Friedrich argues that the aesthetics of certain linguistic forms "shapes the imagination" (1986:43). The particular aesthetics invoked in ritual probably always involves the *sounds* of language, for example, in Hinduism, which in many of its forms involves "soteriological experience of the divine through sound" (Coward 1993:xii).

New Research

In this chapter, we have seen that the idea of linguistic relativity long predates Sapir and Whorf. That punctures one myth related to the so-called Sapir–Whorf hypothesis – that the idea of linguistic relativity dated from an early twentieth-century collaboration.

We have also challenged a companion myth – that all interesting research on linguistic relativity turned out to be a bust and ceased in the 1950s. This impression comes from my reading of cultural anthropology textbooks, which tend to reduce linguistic relativity to claims about isolated words, rather than looking at any of the three areas of research this chapter covers. They also tend to cite outdated research and make unsubstantiated claims about how "most modern scholars are skeptical about" linguistic relativity (Bailey and Peoples 2013:55).

In fact, we have been examining work that has appeared much more recently and, in the sections that follow, we continue discussing recent material that is extremely important to understand. All in all, we find here a convincing case for the current interest in, and dynamic scientific testing of, linguistic relativity.

Color Categorizing Colors Perception

Psycholinguist Li Hai Tan and his colleagues (2008) put the question about linguistic relativity to the test in a way that goes well beyond previous studies. They used fMRI (functional magnetic resonance imaging, a technique that enables scientists to study the differential activation of various portions of the brain) to look for how and where experimental subjects' brains make "perceptual decisions" when subjected to a color discrimination task.

A first experiment gave Tan et al. relatively strong assurance that some familiar colors are easy to name quickly while other colors, despite being familiar, are harder to name. A second experiment – which was the subject of their article (Tan et al. 2008) – involved watching brain activity stimulated by a different task: The task was not to name colors, but to get a glimpse (for 100 microseconds) of two colors and rapidly decide whether they were the same or different. Tan et al. hypothesized that "certain neural circuits" that are activated by the color decision task would be circuits associated with both word finding (language tasks in the brain) and color perception. They found that "perceptual discrimination of colors" activates not only areas of the brain known to be involved in color identification (identification without necessarily naming or using language in any way) but also other brain areas relevant to language processes. Tan et al. concluded that "[l]anguage appears to affect neural activity patterns activated in the course of color perception" (2008:4007).

Color perception has long been an issue in debates over linguistic relativity, and it is an example of a topic that cultural anthropology textbooks tend to address by drawing on outdated sources. Work by Tan and colleagues is exciting because it uncovers links between parts of the brain devoted to language on the one hand and color perception on the other – a very "high-tech" test of linguistic relativity. As we shall see, this is far from the only topic of research on linguistic relativity that is much more recent than the aforementioned textbooks imply.

Thinking for Speaking

Approaching research in a very different way, linguist and psychologist Dan Slobin carried out a series of studies (1996) that also contribute significantly to our understanding of linguistic relativity. He took a unique approach to the question of how and when linguistic structure might shape mental activity. The "when" in this case is in the specific instance of "thinking for speaking," and one grammatical category – verb aspect – that corresponds roughly with the "how." The technical linguistic term **aspect** refers to ways of encoding *the temporal nature of events* – not when they occurred relative to a moment of speaking (which is "tense"), but what sorts of features define a particular event. In a language rich in aspectual distinctions, the morphology of a given verb can indicate, for example, whether an action is ongoing or completed and whether it has an inherent end-in-view-from-the-start perspective.

Slobin recruited children to participate in an experiment involving two pictures. These children were speakers of four languages – English, Spanish, Hebrew, and German. They were told that, after viewing two pictures (Figures 6.6a and 6.6b), they would be asked to tell the story of the actions they perceived in those pictures. Slobin wondered whether "their stories [might] differ consistently, depending on the language" they spoke. He predicted that a particular structural difference between the four languages – the number and kinds of aspectual categories that those languages require speakers to use – would lead some children to make relatively fine distinctions between actions involving the characters in the pictures (a boy, a dog, an owl, and some bees).

One might say that the two pictures together tell a story. But it's not a story until it's told – through the perspective of the teller and his or her language. Events can be described "from within." That is, the ongoing-ness of an event can be a matter of perspective. Even though fine linguistic distinctions are not built into these two pictures, they capture events in such a way that speakers of the language with the greatest number of aspectual distinctions among the four – Spanish – should have been able to use a number of those distinctions.

As Slobin predicted – based on grammatical differences between the languages in the experiment and, clearly, not on any features of the two pictures – English speakers were habituated "to verbally express whether an event is in progress, … Spanish speakers to note whether it has been completed; … and Hebrew speakers

Figure 6.6a Story-board borrowed from Mercer Meyer's wordless picture book, *Frog, Where Are You?* (Dial Press, 1969). (Adapted from Slobin 1996:72)

Figure 6.6b Story-board borrowed from Mercer Meyer's wordless picture book, *Frog, Where Are You?* (Dial Press, 1969). (Adapted from Slobin 1996:73)

[to be] indifferent to conceiving of events as durative or bounded in time" (1996:88).

So what was the owl doing in the two pictures? It was seeing. In the following two sentences – the owl saw that the boy fell, and the owl saw that the dog ran – note how much Spanish grammar this 5-year-old boy has already internalized:

Indeed, in Spanish the seeing is perfective **(PFV)** in the first instance, imperfective **(IPFV)** in the second:

(a) El búho vio   que el niño se cayó
     the owl saw-PFV   that the boy fell-PFV

(b)   El búho veía   que el perro corría.

       the owl saw-IPFV   that the dog ran-IPFV

This will be evident to Spanish-speaking readers, as it is to Spanish-speaking preschoolers in our study ... Yet do English-speakers sense that seeing can be perfective or imperfective? (Slobin 1996:74)

What this proved to Slobin was that a particular task – "thinking for speaking," that is, looking at the two pictures while engaging in a kind of thinking that was focused on preparing to tell "the story" that the pictures "contained" – was the real place where obligatory grammatical categories that differ from language to language in fact connect to habitual patterns of thought. Slobin thus concludes that this connection is the locus of linguistic relativity.

> I am convinced, however, that the events of this little picture book are experienced differently by speakers of different languages – in the process of making a verbalized story out of them. I propose that the grammaticized categories that are most susceptible to [source-language] influence have something important in common: they cannot be experienced directly in our perceptual, sensorimotor, and practical dealings with the world ...
> It seems that once our minds have been trained in taking particular points of view for the purposes of speaking, it is exceptionally difficult for us to be retrained. (Slobin 1996:88)

Thinking for Speaking versus Thinking in Images

Does Slobin prove that the languages we speak – particularly, the specific linguistic structures that both offer us choices and also constrain our choices – influence thought? Not if "thought" also includes a kind of mental planning like that required to shape a hot metal object into something like a horseshoe. Keller and Keller (1996) argue that such thinking – which they call "imaging in iron" – has to be imagistic.

Structural features of blacksmiths' language are relatively unimportant to their practice or production. This argument rests on what Keller and Keller see as a sharp distinction between "declarative knowledge" and "skill," especially motor skill. But it is just this sort of distinction that "practice theory" (see Chapter 2) tries to overcome.

Other Sign Modalities, Experience, Emotion, and Thought

In this book, I address all human communication, including gesture, and not just language. Unfortunately, from my perspective, research on linguistic relativity has treated language and cognition as though emotion were not part of cognition, and gesture were not intimately linked with language. Thus, in this section, we examine the relationships between gesture, communication, and cognition (broadly defined). We look at gesture as a mode within communication *and* gesture as communication itself. The connections between the broad concept of language and gesture as embodied communication within language carry implications for the roles of multimodal language in individual and group experience.

We begin by exploring embodied action as metaphor and cognitive aid. Metaphor – which cognitive linguists treat first and foremost as a mental phenomenon, even if they agree that it is manifested linguistically – may have a relationship with emotion, including depression. Meier and Robinson (2005) broaden the semiotic context in which we view language and metaphor, however, and stress the role of action or "nonverbal cues" (Waxer 1974) as *enactment* of metaphor. This is based on their review of evidence that depressed participants in one study "had a more declined (i.e., lowered) head tilt in comparison with nondepressed participants" (2005:246, citing Waxer [e.g., 1974]). Then, Meier and Robinson (2006:451) argue that "negative affect in general, and depressive symptoms in particular, appear to bias selective attention in a direction that favors lower regions of physical space." In fact, the expression "feeling down" may be reinforced by looking down as an embodied habit (Meier and Robinson 2005:252).

I want to continue along this path for a moment, looking both at human multimodal communication (certainly with gesture as part of it) and at subjectivity, experience, and cognition. To begin, let us visit those areas of the world where improvised crying songs – laments – still live something of a social life. There we can ask: Which comes first, the emotion or the expression – pressing a handkerchief to the cheek, rocking, sad singing, crying or "cry breaks" in song, raising one's arms together?

The answer may well be that neither comes first, but it is clear from my interviews with lamenters (Wilce 2011a, 2011b) that these kinds of actions or expressions do play a role in helping lamenters enter into a grief that is with-and-for-others who are gathered at, say, a funeral.

As we have seen in relation to language more broadly, gestures that are embedded in cultural contexts of performance do play a role in molding experience along lines that are socially expected. We could even say that gesture is a profoundly social and cultural modality of communication with a role in obtaining culturally desirable inner states.

At the same time, I want to explore evidence of the *cognitive* role of gesture and indeed its potential relationship to particular activities in particular parts of the brain. Like "self-talk" aimed at self-regulation or self-comfort, gesture can represent a means for us to communicate with ourselves as well as others. Our gestures may help us think of the right words in a given context, help the brain focus spatially, or even "help speakers to package spatial information into units appropriate for speaking" (Alibali 2005:318).

> The act of gesturing influences the **representations** and processes that take place in the gesturer's mind. If this is the case, then producing gestures may actually influence the course of spatial reasoning and problem solving. Thus, a

complete account of the processes involved in spatial reasoning will require understanding the potential contributions of gesture (and body movements more generally) to spatial cognitive activity. (Alibali 2005:318)

Cognitive and developmental psychologist Martha Alibali and her research team (Alibali et al. 2004) recruited experimental participants for "a problem-solving task" specifically focused on predicting from instructions how a complex set of gears would move. They were asked to say how the movement of one gear would affect the movement of another. Some participants were allowed to gesture as they answered, while a second group was not. The gesturing group "tended to use depictive strategies in which they modeled the movement of each individual gear (usually in gestures) in an effort to infer the direction of movement of the target gear" (Alibali 2005:320). Those who were prevented from gesturing, by contrast, tried to answer by appealing to abstract rules – a less effective strategy than answering by modeling and describing the direction of gear movement. "Producing gestures appeared to help solvers mentally represent the actions of the gears, and therefore promoted use of depictive strategies" (Alibali 2005:320, summarizing Alibali et al. 2004).

Do these studies raise questions about the sharp distinction Keller and Keller (1996:118) make between "declarative knowledge" and "skill"?

Experience Narratives Predating Experience: Power, Story, Mind

As I wrote in Chapter 1, "An anthropology of 'culture' without a clear vision of 'society' can miss the social distribution of power and wealth." The linguistic relativity that we focus on in this chapter is typically associated with culture – and with cultural anthropology. However, relationships between language and mind are relationships of power. We see this, for example, in the power of certain fairly fixed "narratives" or plot structures to shape experience. One example is the experience of getting treatment for post-traumatic stress disorder (PTSD).

According to anthropologist Alan Young, there is a certain way of talking about one's life, actions, and feelings that makes it more likely that one will receive a diagnosis of PTSD – at least in the US Veterans Administration (VA) psychiatric facility where Young carried out ethnographic research (1995).

Like patients who visit the VA facility, diagnosticians there drew on very stable ways of narrating the patients' characters, strengths, flaws, and psychiatric condition. This became clear as Young analyzed "a series of diagnostic sessions" (Young 1995:145) involving potential PTSD cases that led him to believe that "in practice, the structure of [clinicians' narratives about candidates for diagnosis with PTSD] exists prior to their content." Describing the clinicians' interviews with patients that preceded the diagnostic team meetings, Young claims that, "even before an interviewer has begun to collect his statements, the organization of his account is already in place, embedded in the composition and clustering of the questions making up his protocols" (1995:169).

The very fact that such ethnographic findings are so rarely discussed in relation to linguistic relativity is, I think, a very good reason to introduce Young's work into the discussion in this chapter. The decades-long debates and discoveries related to linguistic relativity and the kind of critical medical anthropology for which Alan Young is known (which we discuss further in Chapter 12) shed light on each other. Any effect of language on habitual patterns of thoughts is at least potentially a reflection of **social structure**, organization, or stratification.

A Final Thought

One of the best-kept secrets in the social sciences is that linguistic relativity continues to be a vital area for research. Some of that research follows a positivist, hypothesis-testing, or experimental model (Lewis 2009), and some follows a post-positivist model, as Enfield (2015:207) describes:

> New lines of work must reconsider the idea of linguistic relativity by exploring the range of available interpretations of the key terms: in particular, "language" beyond reference, "thought" beyond nonsocial processing, and "reality" beyond brute, nonsocial facts.

The bottom line for linguistic anthropology is this: Whatever we may think of older work on the topic or of our intellectual predecessors who carried out such work, our subfield would not be what it is apart from the conviction that language plays an active role in mediating between us and the social and natural world.

CONCLUSION

This chapter elaborates on questions about mind, experience, and expression. Older approaches to linguistic relativity treated "languages" as independent variables and forms and habits of thought as dependent variables subject to the influence of those languages (Hopi, English, and so on). The linguistic diversity that mattered to those intellectual forebears was countable: Count the languages of the world, and you will have accounted for all the drivers of cognitive or perceptual diversity.

By contrast, such contemporary linguistic anthropologists as Duranti locate diversity within the societies that speak any given language – that is, they focus on sociolinguistic diversity – and they look to **social activities** like assigning responsibility for an action as the hot sites of human sociocultural diversity influenced by sociolinguistic diversity.

In keeping with these newer trends, Chapters 8 and 9 explore various ways of studying sociolinguistic diversity, including semiotic models, and Chapter 11 resumes the study of "mediation" from a new perspective. However, before we move to these fascinating explorations, we look in Chapter 7 at the sorts of methods that linguistic anthropologists use to collect and analyze data – starting with the question: What constitutes "data" for our linguistic anthropology tribe?

SUMMARY

After reading this chapter, you should have a good understanding of the following themes:

- The centrality of linguistic relativity, as a powerful way of affirming the role of language in human life, to linguistic anthropology.
- The power of linguistic diversity as it pertains to the semiotic mediation of culture.
- The complexity of what is sometimes reduced to "the Sapir–Whorf hypothesis."
- The different semiotic dimensions that can influence cognition and be studied as such.
- The new neuroscientific turn in research related to linguistic relativity.

QUESTIONS

1. What is linguistic relativity? What exactly did Sapir or Whorf stand for?
2. What intellectual ancestors most influenced Sapir and Whorf? When and where do we find predecessors of linguistic relativity?
3. What are some of the more recent approaches to questions of language, mind, experience, and expression?
4. What are the three ways of testing for Whorfian effects discussed in this chapter?

EXERCISES

1. Demonstrate your ability to discern between appropriate and inappropriate uses of the concept of linguistic relativity. Find videos of statements about "Others" and their Other languages that "lack a word for" this or that.
2. Guess how many languages are spoken in your state, province, or country. Then look up your area in the *Ethnologue* (Lewis 2009) to see the number given there. Then describe the problems with this model of languages as distinct countable items and whether the *Ethnologue*'s goals could be accomplished if it were to speak of "languaging" instead of languages. Could the book even be written in that case?
3. This is an exercise in the aspect markers of Hopi verb morphological analysis, (Trask 1995:62), which is borrowed from Ottenheimer (2012:33, who in turn borrowed the dataset from Trask). First, review the ten Hopi words in the following list.

Hopi

1. tíri he gives a start	6. tiŕírita he is trembling
2. wíwa he stumbles	7. wiwáwata he is hobbling along
3. kʷíla he takes a step forward	8. kʷilálata he walks forward
4. ʔími it makes a bang	9. ʔimímita it is thundering
5. ngáro his teeth strike something	10. ngarórota he is chewing on something

Then, working together in groups, answer the following questions:

- What type of **affix** (prefix, suffix, or infix) is shown in entries 6–10? What is its form? (There are three things to note here.) What is its approximate meaning in English?
- Given /róya/ 'it makes a turn', what would be the most likely form for 'it is rotating'?
- Given /ripípita/ 'it is sparkling', what would be the most likely form for 'it flashes'?

ADDITIONAL RESOURCES

Chafe, Wallace. 2000. Loci of Diversity and Convergence in Thought and Language. In *Explorations in Linguistic Relativity*. M. Pütz and M. H. Verspoor, eds. Pp. 101–124. Amsterdam: John Benjamins.

Here Chafe makes the same convincing argument for the linguistic relativity of richly indexical third-person gender pronouns in Northern Iroquoian languages that he made in an earlier version of this article. That importance is, at least in part, their exemplification of a grammaticalized view of gender very different from any in European languages.

Duranti, Alessandro. 1997. *Linguistic Anthropology*. Cambridge University Press.

Duranti makes a powerful case for updating linguistic relativity by reference to the internal diversity of speech communities, including for example, the unequal distribution of grammatical forms in the Western Samoan community in which he did fieldwork.

Webster, Anthony K. 2015. Why the World Doesn't Sound the Same in Any Language and Why That Might Matter: A Review of the Language Hoax: Why the World Looks the Same in Any Language. By John H. McWhorter. Oxford University Press. 2014. *Journal of Linguistic Anthropology* 25(1):87–104.

Webster's article is indeed a book review, but goes much further, updating our model of linguistic relative-ity, giving it a "sonic" twist and drawing in particular on his intimate knowledge of Navajo poets, poetry, and poetics.

7 Researching Communication and Culture as a Linguistic Anthropologist

LEARNING OBJECTIVES

After reading this chapter, you should be able to do the following:

- Understand linguistic anthropology methods you might use in a project's data collection stage.
- Grasp the meaning of **naturally occurring** interactions.
- Summarize three valid approaches to **transcribing** discourse.
- Establish which analytic methods are appropriate to data you might collect.

Introduction

In previous chapters, I have introduced *perspectives* on the world that characterize linguistic anthropology. That includes the questions that interest us and the issues that motivate us.

But *how* exactly do anthropologists interested in the intersection of culture and communication do what we do? What methods do we use? How is it that we can call what we do "methodical"? And how might newcomers to our field – perhaps you – start studies of your own?

This chapter provides a behind-the-scenes look at linguistic anthropological research – from planning and design, to methods of collecting data appropriate to our discipline, to methods of analyzing data, and to preparing and delivering presentations and publications or finding other ways to circulate your results. This chapter builds on what might appear to be "merely" theoretical. It builds, in particular, on the idea that speech is a form of social action – and that languages are cultural products and filters through which we encounter the world. These are not – or not *just* – "hypotheses," but guidelines that inform our research.

It is important to state here that linguistic anthropology is a science. Specifically, it is one of the "human sciences" (Keller 2016). Therefore, *interpretation* plays a role along with what is typically called *analysis* in the so-called "hard" sciences. You will see examples of this interpretive research throughout this chapter.

Why should anyone conduct research in the various ways laid out in this chapter? What we've talked about in Chapters 1 through 6 provides the answer: *We conduct linguistic anthropological research because we are interested in social action and therefore are interested in ways and moments of speaking. We conduct research because language is not a pseudo-tool that merely refers to things in the world without doing anything to them. Instead, language is a real tool that does all kinds of things in the world. That is what we seek to learn ever more about through research.*

Preparing to "Do" Research

Before we go out into the field to begin a particular research project, we must, of course, carefully plan that project. And to plan, we must first understand some research basics: What methods are available to us, what theoretical considerations inform those methods, how can we operationalize the questions we seek to answer, and how can we know if a natural research setting will yield valid results. The information in this section describes some of these basics.

Range of Methods

Let's talk first about the wide array of research methods that linguistic anthropologists often use, depending on the goals of any particular research project. We may:

- conduct ethnographies of communication (Hymes 1972) and study communicative ecologies (Shoaps 2009).
- engage in ethnographic or anthropological discourse analysis (Philips 2013) or an ethnographic form of **conversation analysis** (Clemente 2015; Goodwin 1990).
- examine the role and structure of discourse in ritual – uncovering, among other things, **ethnopoetic** patterning (Hymes 1981; Silverstein 2003a);
- analyze visible as well as audible communication, including **gestures** (Goodwin 1979; Haviland 2004; Kendon 1997; Matoesian 2005) and also sign languages (Farnell 1995; LeMaster 2006; Senghas and Monaghan 2002).
- study variation across class and situation in communities whose languages have been called pidgins and creoles, keeping language ideologies constantly in view (Fenigsen 1999, 2005, 2007).
- elicit language ideologies, specifically in the context of "matched guise" experiments (Bilaniuk 2003; Lambert 1975).
- study fine differences between high school peer groups by combining ethnographic and close phonetic analysis in a field called sociophonetics (Hay and Drager 2007).
- collect and analyze materials from others or in the public domain, including audiovisual materials – YouTube videos, speeches or sermons on iTunes, radio broadcasts, and podcasts – as well as existing written texts – newspaper articles (Lo and Kim 2011), blog posts (Doostdar 2004), archives of missionaries' letters to

supporters and literacy materials developed in recently missionized communities (Schieffelin 2000), and the published transcripts of other scholars.

Additionally, linguistic anthropologists and others have uncovered interesting things that people do with their bodies. Some examples: Sign language relies exclusively on visible bodily movements. Oral language is the product of the human vocal mechanism (all parts of our mouths, nasal cavity, and vocal cords). And writing is, in fact, as physical as gesturing. Human communication, in short, is embodied. That's why the study of many communicative practices requires video recording for analysis.

But before we can decide what method or methods will best serve our research goals, we need to understand the theoretical underpinning they rely on.

Ethnomethodology

Many linguistic anthropologists are influenced by a theoretical approach called **ethnomethodology**, which is really a meta-theory or "grand" theory. Sociologist Harold Garfinkel (1967) founded ethnomethodology as a school of thought related to **phenomenology**, and this ethnographic method, in conjunction with Erving Goffman's work (1964, [1959] 1973, 1981), inspired conversation analysis.

Ethnomethodology tells us there are no "givens" in such things as interaction. Instead, we improvise. The theory is called *ethno*methodology because its key assumption is that people (in Greek, *ethnos*) are essentially social actors who come up with guesses – or theories – about what is going on between themselves and their interlocutors: How you respond to something I have just said tells me your theory about my utterance.

With that understanding about how interaction works, linguistic anthropologists are committed to finding out and giving priority to what social actors *think* they're doing together by looking at what they *are* doing. So we carry out our research not by asking these social actors what they're thinking, but instead by *analyzing what they do* – especially what they do *by saying*. That means we can conduct this kind of analysis not just for face-to-face interactions that we, as researchers, are present for, but also for video clips and other kinds of secondary sources.

As you have undoubtedly gathered, ethnomethodology assumes that meaning is not static, let alone kept in a lockbox. Indeed, in order to interact successfully, speakers must constantly be sending **metasignals**, interpretive cues that Gumperz (1982) calls "contextualization cues" – "the subtle, minute-to-minute pragmatic signals that permit speakers to make assessments and convey their intentions" (Mertz and Yovel 2000). Each interlocutor constantly signals guesses about what the other means. Here's an example. You are at home eating at the dinner table with your partner, and you are sitting by a window. Your partner says, "Geez, it's hot." You signal a guess at what your partner was getting at and open the window that is within your reach. Your partner may then say, "No, I wasn't hinting about the window, I was ..." (fill in the blank). The timing, pitch patterns, and grammatical structures that characterize each instance of what Goodwin (1979) calls a conversational "turn-at-talk" are all potential contextualization cues, signals as to when it's time for a switch in speakers or – crucially – what one thinks the other means. (Compare Goffman's phrase, "turn at talking," 1964:135–136).

As just one example of the kind of detail that linguistic anthropologists analyze in the research process, these metasignals include intonational cues. (The term **intonation** denotes speech melody, the ups and downs of pitch across words in a phrase or utterance.) For example, a falling pitch pattern might signal that a speaker is approaching a moment to stop talking and await a response. Conversation analysts refer to such an action-filled moment (of talk combined with falling intonation) as a "transition-relevant place."

Hopefully this brief overview of ethnomethodology gives you a sense not only of its importance as meta-theory but also of the fine level of detail that linguistic anthropological research involves.

Operationalizing

Before we can set out to collect and then analyze the fine level of detail we've just been discussing, we need to think about how we can define what it is we seek to study in a way that makes it identifiable, measurable, and understandable. In other words, we need to **operationalize** what we plan to study.

Operationalizing involves defining a phenomenon in which we are interested so that we can, through some "operation" or systematic application of criteria, determine whether or not some thing or process is an example of that phenomenon. If we don't make the effort to do this as part of our preparation, we may have only a fuzzy understanding of our research results – and we may be able to convey to others only a fuzzy impression of our conclusions.

Let me give an example. Linguistic anthropologists find the *questions* – especially those concerning power – raised by philosopher and social theorist Michel Foucault, one of the twentieth century's greatest minds, to be compelling. Yet his vague use of the term "discourse" (Foucault 1990) is less so – because he never operationalizes the term. (See Chapter 4 for more about the term discourse.)

On the surface, it appears that Foucault is interested in the same phenomenon – discourse – as are linguistic anthropologists. Yet Foucault's use of discourse in phrases like "a discourse like that of clinical medicine, or political economy, or Natural History" ([1969] 1972:72) or "the discourses on madness" ([1969] 1972:33) is hard to pin down. Hence, it is often difficult to know exactly what Foucault means when he uses the term.

As anthropologist of language and medicine Joel Kuipers (1989:105) points out:

> [T]he crux of the problem [with Foucault's approach] seems to lie in his notion of context (e.g., Foucault 1972[1969]:97), combined with his unwillingness

> to link systematically what he calls a formulation (a situated, individually authored utterance) with a statement (a repeatable, "circulatable," decontextualized semiotic modality that transcends actual situations of use (1972[1969]:107).

Linguistic anthropologists, who are generally not positivists, do not take the notion of operationalizing variables or concepts as far as some who study language, like quantitative sociolinguists. However, I do embrace simple and straightforward attempts to make my research data and analysis accessible for rethinking by other anthropologists – which is what operationalization is about. Let me provide examples from others' work.

Charles Antaki, whose work sometimes falls under the rubric of language and social psychology, has argued for viewing "self-disclosure as a situated interactional practice" – which is both the title of his article and an indication of his embrace of ethnomethodology. To ask, "What, then, is 'self-disclosure'?" is to request that it be operationalized. And that he does: "First, the phenomenon is operationalized: here, most usually into a set of statements about a person's life" (Antaki et al. 2005:182).

In another example, Paul Kockelman writes about "stance," which he defines as our "orientations to [expressed] states of affairs." Stance may consist, for example, of "epistemic" orientation. Epistemic stance is "operationalized in terms of complement-taking predicates" (Kockelman 2004:127). Complement clauses are those beginning with "that" in an introductory sense: "I doubt (or I believe) *that* dolphins are smart." These structures can be chased down and counted using software that corpus linguist Doug Biber has written (Biber and Reppen 1998). Analyzing these structures requires turning them into useful variables, and that requires operationalization.

Natural, Naturalistic, and Naturally Occurring Discourse

We need to look at one additional question related to our research preparation, one that is both theoretically as well as methodologically interesting: What is the meaning of "naturalness" in a research **context**?

As you might imagine, "naturally occurring" interactions are the ideal phenomena, or data, for linguistic anthropologists to study – since our goal is to learn ever more about language as a real tool that does all kinds of work "in the real world." However, we must be careful in making claims that this or that instance or type of speech is "natural," either as an intrinsic quality or in relation to other instances or types of discourse.

So what makes a particular instance of discourse "natural"? We might consider whether it reflects any or all of the following four characteristics, which are adapted from Fenigsen and Wilce's four "authenticities" (2015):

- Common patterns of language socialization and thus a cultural tradition of discourse.
- **Style** and content that reflect cultural values.

Figure 7.1 Does this interview by an African anthropologist in Benin qualify as naturalistic research? (Godong/Getty Images)

- Whatever traits are necessary in a particular genre or type of discourse to render it effective in a particular, culturally conceived setting or occasion.
- An accurate reflection of a speaker's inner self.

Linguistic anthropologists strive to find, observe, record, participate in, describe, and analyze events that are naturalistic or naturally occurring – even as we recognize the problems with declaring any communicative event, or any type of communicative event, as natural. Hence, on a practical level, the term "naturalistic" means simply "as natural as it gets" – despite the presence of a researcher and of necessary recording equipment. (See Figure 7.1.)

Can Interviews Be Naturalistic?

For some scholars, "naturally occurring" excludes interviews that are arranged, directed, and controlled by researchers. For myself and others (De Fina and Perrino 2011), interviews that "spin out of control" can be fortuitous rather than problematic. During my fieldwork in rural Bangladesh, it was impossible for me as a man to interview a woman alone (just as it was impossible for a woman to walk from her home to the bazaar on her own). The mandatory presence of other adults during interviews that I thought of as focusing on a particular woman easily led to the transformation of *my* "interview" – a concept totally foreign to poor rural women in Bangladesh anyway – into a freewheeling conversation involving other people as well. Likewise, my attempts to interview rural Bangladeshis apparently suffering from schizophrenia inevitably became fascinating multi-party interactions. The bottom line is that it is usually a good thing when interviews change in ways the interviewer can't control. When "interviewees" become *participants* in talk that they and their co-participants control, the event can hardly avoid being a "natural" reflection of local culture.

Despite our skepticism about the naturalness of formal interviews, though, we linguistic anthropologists do conduct them. Moreoever, our interviews do differ from those conducted by cultural anthropologists and others. For example, we often ask interviewees about *language use and users*, recognizing that cultural notions about various forms of language and their speakers constitute what to us is an extremely important category – namely, language ideologies. We may ask people about speech and speakers explicitly, exploiting the ability of language both to convey referential meaning and to refer to itself.

However, being able to ask questions and receive answers about anything – acts of explicit reference – is only part of the value of interviewing. Linguistic anthropologists are also unique in how we *use* interview data. As with any other sort of data we collect, we use interview data to understand not just in *what* people say but *how* they speak. This is precisely where concerns arise about just how "natural" interview-talk is: Do people speak "naturally" in interview contexts? Here again is where our "losing control" of an interview situation becomes valuable. In exercising *their* control, interviewees may choose not only their own topics but also their own ways of speaking.

Inducing or Simulating Naturalness

You will recall that, for our research purposes, the term naturalistic means "as natural as it gets." I want to introduce other ways that researchers appear to stretch the concept of "natural," but with a goal of getting interviewees to speak or think more naturally.

Sociolinguistics is a discipline with some affinity to linguistic anthropology. One prominent quantitative sociolinguist, William Labov, thought up a number of ways to break out of the formality of "the interview situation," and he is famous for a series of ingenious experiments he conducted in 1960s New York City. Labov designed these experiments to reveal correlations between the socioeconomic class of speakers of New York English and the sociolinguistic variety that they spoke. (We'll discuss **sociolects** more in Chapters 8 and 9.)

Labov's formal elicitations included handing New Yorkers lists of "minimal pairs" (introduced in Chapter 4). He then asked his "informants" (whom anthropologists now prefer to call "consultants" or "interviewees") to read pairs of words that, at least in the standard sociolect, differ only in having or lacking an /r/ sound after a vowel. Examples would be *draw* and *drawer*. For some Eastern seaboard English speakers, the two words are pronounced identically. Labov describes various strategies he invented to "avoid … the self-consciousness of formal elicitations" (1972:xiii).

One of Labov's strategies for rendering the interview situation more natural was to ask interviewees what came to be known as the "danger of death" question: "Have you ever been in a situation where you thought you were in serious danger of being killed – where you thought to yourself, 'This is it'?" (1972:93). If the interviewee says yes, Labov writes, "Often he becomes involved in the narration to the extent that he seems to be reliving the critical moment, and signs of emotional tension appear." Labov had been interviewing a man he called Eddie, who

> had been quite reserved and careful in his replies. He had given no examples of casual or spontaneous speech until this topic [a time in which he was in danger of dying] was reached. Within a few short sentences, a sudden and dramatic shift in his style took place. Eddie began to speak, we might say, in his "natural" fashion. (1972:93)

Other researchers who are more centrally located in linguistic anthropology (as opposed to quantitative sociolinguistics) have also used Labov's "danger of death" method. During her decades of linguistic anthropological research in the Malinche volcano region of Mexico, linguistic anthropologist Jane Hill (1995b) recalls an instance when she was interviewing Don Gabriel, a man well known to her. Hill asked him about a time *he* had nearly died, and Don Gabriel said he had such a story, but it was about his son, who had in fact been killed. This led to a poignant story, whose layers of meaning Hill was obligated to uncover, honoring Don Gabriel's son and the older man's grief as well as her academic interest in stories.

Labov's methods for injecting a kind of naturalness into the interview situation have real potential, sometimes tapped by linguistic anthropologists. Most of us, however, prefer to wait until narratives arise quite on their own, as they do in interpersonal conversations and storytelling sessions in many communities around the world.

One last point about "naturalness" in the research context: Because of our commitment to **ethnography**, particularly the ethnography of communication, many linguistic anthropologists regard context as highly important. And that includes both the *linguistic* context of stories (what is said before and after the main story) and the *situational* context (any differences between what is happening socially in the run-up to the conversational narrative and what happens afterward). So part of preserving naturalness is to retain the whole context of the discourse in the research that we do.

Doing Linguistic Anthropology and Related Forms of Research

In the previous section, we gave thoughtful consideration to several aspects of preparing to "do" research. Now let's talk more directly about what actually happens "in the field."

We begin by addressing the most basic presumption and commitment we bring with us to the field: Linguistic anthropologists, like some other social scientists, avoid making judgments – either moral (*Is what "they" are doing "right"?*) or intellectual (*Does this grammatical form, communicative activity, or cultural idea or practice make sense?*).

This is crucial to all of the research we do – and it is crucial from when we first get started on a project until we are disseminating the results of our research.

Getting Started, Getting Acquainted

Just as we enter our field community or particular communicative event without judgment, we also make no presumption about what we will find there. We try to suspend or "bracket" prior ideas we might have, for instance, about "tradition" or "traditionality." In my fieldwork in Finland, for example, I suspend any musings about whether or not there is such a thing as a pure or unchanging lament tradition, a right and a wrong way to lament, or who might be a better or worse group of lamenters.

We then start the research process by listening and observing. (See Figure 7.2.) Many follow the advice of Charles Briggs (1984) and postpone asking questions – especially conducting formal **interviews** – until we have some observation-based

Figure 7.2 Anthropologist Robert Desjarlais talks informally with two men in a Nepali bazaar. (Photography by Robert Desjarlais, Nepal, 2011)

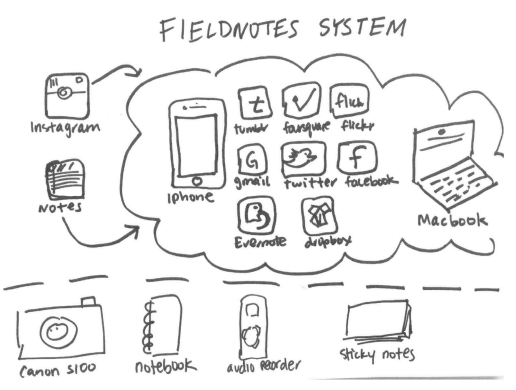

Figure 7.3 Cultural sociologist Tricia Wang shows components of a fieldnote system she used in 2011 as part of her live fieldnotes practice. Of course, her system continues to evolve as technical tools also evolve and change, sometimes leading to new fieldwork capabilities. (Illustration by Tricia Wang)

idea of how people learn in the field community we will be researching. This involves observing as mostly passive participants. It still qualifies as **participant observation**, with the special twist for linguistic anthropologists that we focus on participating in the activities of daily life that are most communicative and learning how communication works in our research setting – often by joining in the very activities we are studying in this new community.

At this early stage in our research, we often refrain from making audio or video recordings, but we do find time each day – better yet, several times each day – to write rich fieldnotes. In my fieldnotes, for instance, I describe event settings, chance encounters, and what is happening in my adopted family or community. I especially jot down as much as I can remember about naturally occurring talk I've witnessed, particularly such talk as interests me for particular reasons (such as hypotheses I'm exploring). These notes, which are typically written just for ourselves, are useful not only in initial stages of research but throughout a project. Each of us develops a system that works for us, perhaps starting with handwritten notes or typing informally into a notebook or laptop, and then choosing ways to store these data so they are accessible for later use. (See Figure 7.3.)

Incidentally, one sort of fieldnote that is very important to me is the kind I write when I am recording what could be an overwhelming amount of video data. In that circumstance, I jot down notes about important topics being discussed, along with a time code from the video camcorder so I can easily find what I want to focus on later.

Sometimes, though, we have to begin a research project in a different way, depending on the constraints of the specific situation. The rule of "passive participation first, active later," for instance, did not apply to my first days of fieldwork in Finland (in 2003) – because of requirements set by the group of people engaged in "reviving lament" that I wanted to study. Even before I met them, the leaders of the lament course that I had requested to view decided that if they were to allow me to be present and to video record any part of the course, then I would have to participate in it fully. Thus, I not only observed, listened, and recorded, but was also an active participant – being silent when appropriate, but also combining weeping, words, and melody (which is what defines lament) when it was my turn to do so.

Recording Communication, Focusing on Events

A basic part of doing fieldwork involves recording the events of the communicative acts and practices we are studying. As I have stressed, the recording stage typically, though, starts only after you have immersed yourself in the life of the community as a participant observer and then have later shifted, at least partly, toward more active participation.

I need to include a brief aside here: For many researchers (such as American anthropologists affiliated with universities or hospitals), getting approval from our institution's Human Subjects Protection Committee or Institutional Review Board (IRB) must, of course, be done before going out into the field and participating in the community, let alone starting to record. Since receiving that approval is done before beginning our field study, we are then able to read our IRB-approved Informed Consent statements to, and receive permission from, those participating in our research at the beginning of the research project. My point here is to mention that sometimes consent is recorded using audio or video equipment, before recording our interviews. In other cases, our participants provide consent by signing a document ahead of time.

If recording video is at all possible, linguistic anthropologists prefer, and sometimes absolutely rely on, having such recordings. (See Figure 7.4.) In most of the fieldwork I conduct now, I use two or three video cameras and at least one device that records audio. (I do this because I've learned the hard way that having just one backup device is not always adequate: I've even had three devices fail, despite checking their batteries before recording an event!)

When I talk about using video cameras, lately that has meant using "still" cameras that record high-definition video. So, two or three "superzoom point and

Figure 7.4 Video recording this Chinese wedding tea ceremony allows gathering many kinds of data beyond just the speech acts involved. (PhotoAlto/James Hardy/Getty Images)

shoot" cameras off the shelf are now my all-in-one devices. I then use a high-quality digital audio recorder and sometimes my cell phone (in voice memo mode) as my audio devices. In many of the situations I record, the point of using multiple cameras is to capture action from various angles. It is sometimes necessary to use at least two cameras simply to capture all of the people in a room.

With so many technical considerations in the background, how do we record events in a way that we aren't disrupting naturally occurring interaction *or* seeming too detached from it? I can't really answer, except to say it's a people skill that we likely develop with experience. I *can* say that, as I keep trying for that balance, I also invite my "field friends and neighbors" to give me feedback about how I am coming across to their community – and hope they will be willing to do so.

It is worth noting that even though video recording is ideal because it allows us to capture embodied actions and interactions as well as speech, there are times when audio recording is more appropriate. To respect gender norms in rural Bangladesh, for instance, I might record only audio when interviewing a woman. On the rare occasions when I interview children, I prefer to use audio only. In other interview situations, I decide on a case-by-case basis how to proceed.

I must admit that sometimes, having decided to use only audio, I have stopped an interview "mid-stream" to ask permission to record video because, for example, my interviewee is so gesturally expressive. One instance of that occurred during my fieldwork in Finland. The video that I began shooting half-way through an interview is among the most memorable field recordings I have, largely because the woman I was interviewing was acting out, in oral (and aural) and visible ways, her stereotype of her own Finnish people.

Leaving the Field, Saying Goodbye

And what happens when the recording is done? In the next section, we explore transforming these recorded data in useable formats by transcribing them. But before turning to that important topic, it is worth talking briefly about how we end the fieldwork part of a research project.

I want to make clear that what we call fieldwork can vary in several notable ways. It can involve several months of living within a community in some other part of the world. Or it can mean traveling from home daily to a geographically near but culturally distant community. Sometimes fieldwork involves a single encounter of whatever length; other times, our research involves returning to the same community several times over, perhaps, a period of years. Nonetheless, ending any fieldwork experience is something to do with awareness and with respect for the people we have been working with.

Part of that respect involves addressing the expectations of those we have been working with. We often find our field folks anxious to hear what we have learned from them. Particularly when our anthropological projects are **applied** (see Chapter 12), we need to build feedback to the community into our fieldwork design and to let folks know from the beginning what we will share with them at the end. It is worth noting, though, that it is always challenging to find an appropriate balance between saying too much and too little about "what I have learned" in a way that is meaningful to our field communities, so it is important to not "overpromise" what we'll be able to share.

Quite apart from the "business end" of wrapping up fieldwork, there is also the personal. In the course of doing fieldwork – spending time with people, inviting them to share information with us, even living in their homes and families sometimes – we do develop relationships, ones that can be viewed in different ways by those involved. All of this is important to be aware of, so appropriate goodbyes can be shared.

My experiences with ending fieldwork have been varied. Sometimes, to be honest, leaving the field has been a relief – particularly when it has meant rejoining my family after a long absence. Sometimes it has involved explaining why I cannot fulfill the wishes of others, for instance, to provide them copies of recordings or transcripts that would not be appropriate for me to share. In a more extreme case, I had to say no to a young man's request for help in leaving Bangladesh (he begged me to take him to the United States and to pay him to be my personal servant because he so badly wanted "out" of his living situation at the time).

On the other hand, leaving both Bangladesh and Finland, my two longest-term fieldwork sites, has involved saying goodbye to people I treasure, including two who died not long after I left. I still feel the loss – as well as gratitude – for the fieldwork opportunities that made it possible for me to get to know them in the first place.

Transcribing the Results

Turning audio and video recordings into data for analysis is an essential part of linguistic anthropological research. In this section, I discuss the transcribing process, provide two transcript examples, and discuss ways to confirm the accuracy and completeness of our transcripts.

In a sense, the real data of linguistic anthropologists will always remain our original sources, whether that be a handwritten letter in an archive or, more commonly, a video recording of some kind of human interaction in which language plays a major role. Linguistic anthropologists expect to return again and again not only to the transcripts we make but also to the original instance of discourse as well.

Despite the abiding importance of original recordings, though, the process of transcribing them is absolutely crucial. By itself, playing a recording for an audience is inadequate. Doing so cannot persuade an audience of any argument you might want to make. We make an argument – or we might say, we put forward a theory of what is going on in our data and why that is important – by reprocessing the data in some way. A transcript is thus a theory (Ochs 1979) – not a "grand" theory like **structuralism**, **materialism**, or phenomenology – but a theory that follows participants' own models (their use of their own "ethnomethods") of what they are doing in our recording, for example.

I also want to mention here that in addition to using word-processing software to prepare hard copies or digital copies of transcripts, when the aim is to present one's data and analysis to an audience – say, at a conference – it has become common for linguistic anthropologists to use presentation software. Specifically, we use such software because it enables us to combine video clips and transcripts for use together. Such a combination is especially important if our data, analysis, and argument include crucial visual as well as audible acts.

Basic Decisions in Transcribing

At the heart of linguistic anthropologists' understanding of human **social activity** – especially "speech in interaction" (Heath 1978:2; Levinson and Holler 2014) – is the conviction that interlocutors give each other metasigns that lead to tentative interpretations based on those signs. Those interpretations might be, "I guess it's my turn to say something," or "You seem to want me to answer a question (or close a window, etc.)." But if we are to look for *evidence* of such metasignals, we must transcribe at least some of the common features of those metasignals.

Figure 7.5 Making audio recordings of what research subjects say is important, as is capturing how they say it, what they sound like, and many other aspects of audible speech acts. (Jana Fortier)

Thus, as we sit down to transcribe, we are faced with choices – even if we are working with audio only (see Figure 7.5) and are thus spared some of the complexities of working with video. These choices, again, reflect the fact that preparing a transcript is preparing an argument or making a "little theory" of a communicative event.

For linguistic anthropologists, or at least those who treat speech-in-use *as* meaning, not just as a "conduit" of meaning (Reddy 1979), representing recorded speech as though it were prose, using paragraphs, is often inadequate. There are several reasons why one would want to transcribe speech-as-action in lines, something like a poem, instead. One motivation would be to capture the metasignals that each interlocutor picks up from the other, thereby gaining the ability to make good guesses about the interactive and **pragmatic** dimensions of talk as it flows. Another motivation is to capture the natural poetics of speech, its rhythms and pauses, and the ways that the speech is parallelistically organized (as we saw in

Chapter 4) – because the poetics of everyday speaking can signal not only *inter-actionally* relevant information but *denotationally* relevant information too.

So the issue at hand is that the speakers, the social actors we record, are sending all sorts of signs intended to help those with whom they are speaking to understand the context in which they speak. One of the signs we pay attention to, for instance, is when speakers take micro-breaks. There happens for a very basic reason: Human beings must breathe. Thus we must transcribe in such a way as to include those breaks.

As we discover when we are extremely excited about something and want to tell about it, it can be tricky to use our lungs for two purposes at once – breathing and speaking. In some recorded events of speaking, you can hear marked in-breaths. An example of that is sobbing speech (i.e., in lament). The stream of speech is thus broken at regular intervals. The spaces between those intervals are called breath units. Neither breaths nor what comes between breaths is random. Rather, the words and phrases that come between breaths have a coherence, an affinity for each other that is marked by the timing of breaths. We often take breaths as we bring a syntactic unit to completion. The same is true with intonation, the melodic pattern of a spoken phrase or utterance. Like breath groups, "intonation units" (Chafe 1993) tend to follow predictable patterns. Intonation units are clusters of words whose affinity for each other – whose integrity or unit-wise existence, whose belonging together – shows up in mini-melodies.

Let's look at two transcripts to see how this works. One is a lament performance from my fieldwork in Bangladesh that demonstrates theoretically driven line breaks. The next is from linguist anthropologist Sabina Perrino's (2002) work with healers and patients in Senegal and its inclusion of nonverbal communicative acts as well as line breaks that indicate conversation dynamics. Together these examples demonstrate common practices of data collection and analysis within linguistic anthropology.

Latifa's Lament

The following represents an extremely small excerpt from a long performance of a lament by a young Bangladeshi woman I call "Latifa," which is a pseudonym (adapted from Wilce 2009a). By the way, using pseudonyms is standard practice in ethnography – to protect the privacy of field folks. I need to mention, however, that at least one well-respected anthropologist suggests that using pseudonyms may provide a false sense of security to both **ethnographer** and so-called research subjects (Scheper-Hughes 2000).

Latifa's lament is very easy to break into lines because it is punctuated regularly with sobbing in-breaths. In the transcript, you see these in-breaths represented thus: •hh. (This way of representing signs occurring in natural interaction comes from conversation analysis, which has developed an elaborate and broadly agreed-upon set of transcription conventions [Seedhouse 2004].)

Latifa's sobs correspond quite closely to portions of her lament melody and the syntactic units of her lament as discourse. As you look at this transcript, you see that I broke line 74 into parts (a) and (b), despite the fact that 74a does not end with a sobbing in-breath; I did this simply because the line was too long to fit as such on the page you are now reading. The two half-lines are marked as "latching" with each other by the equal signs (=) at the ends or beginnings of lines. (Whereas the concept of latching is usually used for the close-but-not-quite overlapping lines of two interlocutors, I use it here to show that there was no pause between the two half-lines.)

72	*amare ni ghorer bahir korlo bun* •hh	They have cast me from the house •hh
73	*bun go o o* •hh	sister – sister, •hh
74a	*amare diye pagol koiya* =	By calling me "mad" =
74b	*= koite dilo na go* •hh	= they prevented me from speaking! •hh

What advantages come from transcribing the preceding excerpt from Latifa's lament as I did? I assert that even these few short lines show the natural poetics of speech, its rhythms and pauses, and the ways that the speech is parallelistically organized. But do they, in fact, show anything of the sort? I argue that the line breaks I have incorporated into my transcript clearly reflect the reality of Latifa's speech-song. That is, the breath and tone groups – words occurring between sobs – are forms of organization she clearly, though not consciously, used.

And why is the poetic organization I show here particularly important? Two reasons stand out. First, what I am calling the poetic organization of Latifa's lament makes it like other laments or traditional lament performances (in the positive sense of *performance* discussed in Chapter 10) around the world. Second, Latifa "performed" her lament for her kin, who debated the value of her performance even as she spoke/sang it – and ultimately they banned her from lamenting. The value of Latifa's lament might have hinged in part, whether consciously or unconsciously, on an achievement of locally conceived poetics. Its controversy, however, pertained to the genre of protest laments (Caraveli 1986; Ch'en and Greenbaum 1998) upon which she drew. (The most relevant account of protest lament is no doubt that of the social anthropologist Veena Das [1996]).

The form of my transcript, then, reflects not just my idea of Latifa's performance, but the very features over which her audience (her family) debated. That audience eventually turned on Latifa and stopped her lamenting (Wilce 2009a).

Healers in Senegal

This second example, adapted from Perrino (2002), involves the greeting phase of an encounter between a patient and a traditional healer in Senegal. (I analyze a longer portion of the greeting phase in Chapter 8.) I include a brief portion here to show the range of possibilities at hand when we transcribe discourse.

TABLE 7.1 Brief transcript excerpt of greeting phase of healing encounter with a Wolof *sérīñ* (Perrino 2002)

Participant	Line	First line: Wolof Second line: English	VISIBLE behavior TRANSCRIBER'S COMMENTS
Sérīñ	4	(0.31)Waaw = Yes	{*SÉRĪÑ* GAZES UP AGAIN AT THE PATIENT AND THEN RETURNS HIS GAZE DOWNWARD A MOMENT LATER}
Patient	5	= Siñaañ waay = ' = Oh, Siñaañ = '	[[PATIENT SHAKES HEALER'S HAND]]
Sérīñ	6	= Na nga def? '= How are you doing?' [	
Patient	7	Siñaañ [	

Sérīñ	8	Sa yaram jàmm
		    'Peace be upon your health'
		      [	

Patient	9	Siñaañ	{PATIENT REGRASPS HEALER'S HAND}

The greeting phase of a Senegalese Wolof (West African) encounter with a *marabout* or *sérīñ* is crucial to the encounter as a whole and the hoped-for experience of healing. Studying healing encounters ethnographically, as Perrino does, provides evidence of the local cultural importance of the greeting ritual. In fact, the way Perrino joins two sorts of evidence – close analysis of the encounter as talk-in-interaction, plus **contextualizing** ethnographic evidence from interviews – typifies best methods in linguistic anthropology (Philips 2013).

As you read the brief transcript here (see Table 7.1), take special note of the beginnings and endings of numbered "lines." In particular, note the use of the equal sign (=) signifying latching and the right-facing bracket ([ ) signifying overlap. Let me explain these terms a bit more.

Latching is the phenomenon in which the words of a new speaker bump up against those of the previous speaker, or interactant, without a perceptible gap or overlap. Latching is signaled in the transcript by the equal sign.

In **overlap**, two speakers are talking at the same time, but not "talking over" one another completely. Overlap is signified by brackets between lines (see connecting line 7 with 8). The bracket's placement indicates the precise point in the previous speaker's words (e.g., the ending of line 7) at which line 8 begins to overlap. Here the sérīñ "speaks over" just the half-word *añ*, which is the last syllable of the sérīñ's surname. (Siñaañ is the last name of the sérīñ, or traditional healer.)

Figure 7.6 In documenting the previously undescribed Eibela language in Papua New Guinea, anthropologist Grant Aiton (left) plays an audio recording for his main consultant, Stalon Sapai, and asks for his commentary. (Courtesy Grant Aiton)

Playback Interviews: Collaborative Transcription

When we make field recordings in languages in which we are not fluent, we often rely on the help of native speakers, sometimes even participants in the events we recorded, in transcribing. (See Figure 7.6.) This is sometimes called a "playback interview," and the first use of the term appears to be Witmer's (1973). However the term came into being, its relevance to linguistic anthropologists' fieldwork is certainly clear today.

Linguistic anthropologist Bambi Schieffelin has helped develop ways of studying "language socialization" – the joint process of acquiring a language and acquiring insider's knowledge of culture. Schieffelin provides us with explicit descriptions of the methods she used from the outset of her fieldwork with the Kaluli people of Papua New Guinea. In the passage that follows, Schieffelin describes the collaborative process of transcribing communicative events involving children and caregivers. The process involved not only clarifying exactly what was said in the recorded event but also receiving comments on the event, so that Schieffelin was simultaneously creating an accurate record of a particular interaction and gaining insider's perspectives on its significance. She writes:

> As soon as possible after completing the recording of a given sample, I would transcribe the audiotapes with the assistance of the primary caregiver (among the

Kaluli, the child's mother). This initial transcription process includes integrating the contextual notes with the speech as a first step in the development of the annotated transcript. During the transcription time, I could discuss the recorded interactions in order to gain a greater understanding of and generate further questions about recurring interaction patterns from which I could eventually describe the Kaluli classification of speech acts and speech events. (Schiefflin 1979:79)

Analytic Methods: The Search for Patterns

The following sections cover analytic frameworks involving an eye toward emergent patterns. Dynamics of conversational interactions may be found and analyzed through conversation analysis, while the tradition of ethnopoetics seeks to uncover repeating patterns across genres. Comparing patterns occurring between genres in one society, or in related genres across societies, may provide particular insight about how language articulates with and reflects the social structures across cultures.

Inductive Search for Patterns: Collections of Cases in Conversation Analysis

Conversation analysis (CA) involves a search for the systematic organization of **conversations** in general and of what I would call particular **genres** of conversation, such as institutional or medical interactions. It is an inductive method for uncovering practices, such as recurring moves in conversation – often occurring in pairs called "adjacency pairs" (e.g., openings or closings) (Schegloff and Sacks 1973) – pairs made up of "first-" and "second-pair parts" (Duranti 1997:250ff.). The norms that apply to unmarked or basic conversations carry over into marked, as in institutional, genres of talk-in-interaction, with some systematic divergences.

For example, any particular example of medical talk – like an instance of practitioner–patient interaction (which is often confused with the more inclusive category of medical discourse [Wilce 2009b]) – includes multiple examples of practices of the sort that conversation analysts collect. These add up to "collections of openings, explanations, physical examinations, diagnostic announcements or other sequences" (Goodwin 1990).

CA analyzes a broad array of practices of a particular type (i.e., collections) with an eye to finding the expected and the unexpected, the preferred and the dispreferred. The example that follows shows an instance of a preferred response (2a) to an invitation (1a) and a dispreferred response (2b), which is italicized here.

(1a) SYLVIA: You are certainly invited.
(2a) RACHEL: Thank you, I'll be there!
(2b) *RACHEL: Well, uhm, gee, I'll have to check my calendar.*

Figure 7.7 Conversations between doctors and patients can take many forms. In discussing a diagnosis of HIV, this Vietnamese doctor talks very directly to the 27-year-old patient before him. (Chau Doan/LightRocket/Getty Images)

In this example, response (2b) falls in a "response-to-invitation" but "deviant case" (i.e., an example of a dispreferred conversational move). Its deviance is marked "locally" by Rachel through her hemming and hawing (*well*, *uhm*, and *gee*) that signal the main part of the dispreferred response in which Rachel does not accept the invitation outright. (We discuss this example in greater detail in Chapter 8.) Maynard and Heritage (2005:430) emphasize the importance of analyzing such "departures from an interactional regularity, or what is known as 'deviant case analysis,' which allows researchers to validate empirical findings and discern larger patterns in which a practice helps achieve particular **social actions**." They provide a useful example. They note a preference for "shrouding bad news and exposing good news" in the diagnostic announcement phase of medical encounters, but with the deviant case found in medical encounters in an HIV clinic. There, the deviant "norm" was to be quite blunt in announcing to patients their HIV-positive status. (See Figure 7.7.) This bluntness accomplished something that is consistent with the reasons underlying the preferred pattern (shrouding bad news and highlighting good news): The blunt announcement "was meant to prompt the discussion of dreaded issues associated with HIV and AIDS" (2005:430).

CA provides a rigorous method for finding patternment (Whorf [1939] 1956) in naturally occurring talk. It is not by any means, however, the only such method.

Those who look for textual patterns in discourse they regard as poetic – which does not refer to "poetry" as we in the West typically think, as something completely marginal to all that is important in "our culture" – have their own ways of uncovering parallelism in particular and patternment in general.

Ethnopoetics and the Search for Textual Patterns

The search for textual patterns in the ethnopoetic tradition is a search for various forms of **parallelism**. Sometimes it is useful to track parallelism between linguistic forms across turns. That is, we might trace examples of one speaker borrowing another's words from one turn to the next – "format tying" (Goodwin 1990). However, it is more common for linguistic anthropologists and their scholarly kin who study parallelism to examine it within long stretches of talk (or writing, as we have seen in the Declaration of Independence) that represents a single voice. This voice is typically that of a ritual leader (Lincoln at Gettysburg, [Silverstein 2003a]) or of a performer of traditional forms of verbal art, such as storytelling (Hymes 1981).

Carrying out an ethnopoetic analysis requires familiarity with the kinds of linguistic units that might be involved. As we saw in Chapter 4, these units range from the smallest (e.g., word-final sounds in parallel lines, which we call *rhyme*) to the largest (parallelism between lines in a long text, for instance, a stretch of discourse like the Declaration of Independence). Being able to recognize **deictics** often helps us to uncover text-level parallelism.

In one analysis of the sort of parallelism that hinges on a series of contrasting deictics, I (Wilce 2008) trace how a psychiatrist uses contrasting deictic pairs in an unfolding construction of biomedicine as enlightened and tradition as benighted. In this brief excerpt from a longer conversation, note that "D" indicates the doctor and "B" indicates the patient and her family (especially the patient's brother, whom the psychiatrist addresses as "you"):

142 D: *Before*, by amulets and charms
143 D: the way you provided treatment –
144 B: Mhm
145 D: The first time . . .
146 D: *This* second time,
147 D: you are pursuing treatment on *this line*

The long example from which the excerpt comes involves a Bangladeshi family who had brought an actively psychotic member to the capital city, Dhaka, in search of biomedical treatment, having already tried traditional forms of medicine for the woman. This transcript comes alive only when we recognize the crucial role played by deictic pairs, which become "emblems of identity" (Silverstein 2004:630), particularly in the linguistic usage of the psychiatrist.

How does this come about? First, deictic usage has a center that is typically the speaker's perspective. Second, if one speaker dominates deictic usage, she might impose her perspective on her interlocutors. That would be an example in which the story told by turn-taking in the discourse we examine here (the "interactional text" that emerges from that discourse) influences the story told by the referential language in the discourse event under consideration. The methodological point I am making is this: It is extremely useful to uncover and analyze the specifics of deictic use. This particular discourse event exemplifies that point, as we uncover how the psychiatrist uses a long series of deictic pairs to construct sharp contrasts between herself and her interlocutors and between biomedicine as enlightened and tradition as benighted.

Qualitative Analysis

This chapter and, for that matter, this whole textbook reflects my preference, and that of most linguistic anthropologists, for qualitative over quantitative research. The reasons for this are subtle, but important – and worth explaining here.

The nature of ethnography, as many of my colleagues practice it, emphasizes intense research relationships with relatively few interviewees. And, in our subfield in particular, that intensity carries over into our approach to analysis: Everything from transcription to follow-up interviews to various methods of analysis takes an immense amount of time. So why, you may wonder, do linguistic anthropologists favor such labor-intensive methods? The answer is that we use qualitative approaches because of their inherent advantages for the kind of science that linguistic anthropology is.

Although there are times when we use basic quantitative methods, we generally find that "thick description" (Geertz 1973) *befits research on beings who, after all, have agency and subjectivity that linguistic anthropologists value and embrace.* To create a "thick description," we interview real people and then create transcripts of the locally grounded words these people use to describe and act upon their worlds. In other words, we use "experience-near" descriptive language as opposed to "experience-distant theorizing," in psychoanalyst Heinz Kohut's ([1977] 2012:303) famous terms. And that descriptive language helps us learn, from real people, how they construct meaning in their lives.

Fortunately, we now have qualitative analysis software that can help discover the rich patterns in our data that we so value, as I have just explained. Not many linguistic anthropologists are yet using these tools, perhaps out of a strong distrust of anything appearing to be reductionist. However, I do use this software in ways that I don't believe fall into those categories or traps.

In the sections that follow, we look at qualitative methods generally – methods that might or might not be enhanced by computer-aided analysis. We first compare communicative actions, by which I mean two kinds of discourse analysis (comparing examples of a single speech genre, and comparing across genres). Then the results are re-analyzed in relation to a body of data reflecting insight from ethnography defined as broadly as is typical among sociocultural anthropologists. I borrow this "two-plus-one" analytic approach from Susan Philips (2013), as I explain in the following section.

Comparing Communicative Actions

In 2013, the *Journal of Linguistic Anthropology* launched what is intended to be a series of articles on analytic methods in our subfield. Linguistic anthropologist and Polynesianist Susan Philips authored the first of these articles. In it, she proposes a complex form of comparative analysis as central to linguistic anthropology – two ways of comparing discourse to discourse, combined with a third analytic step that transforms the two-way initial analysis into **ethnographic discourse analysis**.

In the following quote, Philips (2013:83) explains why an anthropologist should devote time and effort to the analysis of discourse.

> Whether our analysis focuses on the functions of ergative case markers in Samoan fonos (Duranti 1994) or the representations of gender in stories about La Llorona (Mathews 1992), we compare and contrast units of interaction: e.g., fonos (a type of meeting) with each other or stories with each other, or fonos with classroom encounters. We do this in order to make claims both about what all instances of a unit have in common, and about how they differ and vary. Thus comparison of units of interaction is methodologically at the heart of anthropological discourse analysis. When we recognize such units as researchers, it is because we have been taught to do so by the people whose communication we are studying, and because we draw upon our human cognitive ability to create and recognize units of discourse that are also units of interaction and units of culture.

Clearly, to linguistic anthropologists, language is not individual behavior (like the behavior of a lone wolf). Instead, it is action – and units of interaction. As such, the units of discourse that we study are also units of culture.

Speech Genres: Comparing and Contrasting Recorded Examples

Philips collected two large bodies of recordings of courtroom discourse – in Tucson, Arizona, and in the Polynesian Kingdom of Tonga. After every event-example in the two very different places, Philips (2013:89) discussed the proceedings with one or more local experts, in a kind of debriefing:

> ... a common practice for linguistic anthropologists who want to know what the people they recorded, as well as others, thought was going on in the material they recorded. An influential innovation in this tradition was Fred Erickson's sharing of videotapes with people he had recorded to get their reactions to the material. (Erickson and Shultz 1982)

As another example, one of the speech genres I studied in Bangladesh was divination, or "diviner's talk." At least in that country, divination involves a kind of inspired guessing about problems from lost cows to curses. Rural Bangladeshi

Muslims who practice divination go through an elaborate process that enables the diviner to eventually make a pronouncement of results. My focus, however, was less on this process and more on analyzing the pronouncements. In doing so, I compared a dozen recordings of encounters with a diviner in rural Bangladesh, which revealed the pattern of his discourse. The following is a partial list of the elements I identified in the dozen divinations I analyzed (Wilce 2001):

1. The Pronouncement Proper
   - Identify the sorcerers.
   - Identify the sorcerers' aim.
   - Enumerate the evil charms deployed against the victim, including those that are somehow fed to the victim and those sent toward the victim by air or breath.
   - Describe sorcery-related symptoms, typically one or more of the following: a burning sensation, abdominal pain, and/or a "hot" mood.
2. The Diviner Invites Confirmation from Clients
3. The Clients Respond
4. Final Stage
   - Write a protective text.
   - Insert text into metal amulet.

It was the comparative analysis of recorded divination encounters that enabled me to compile this list of steps in the divination process. (Incidentally, I then asked myself what methodological step might come next: Follow-up interviews with all participants [or only some]? Playback interviews? Conducting a playback interview with a cultural expert was crucial to a re-analysis of the data that eventually resulted in a second publication [Wilce 2006].)

Comparing One Genre to Another

In a second step in the process of comparing genres, we might collect three bodies of data – for instance, from university lectures and study groups, laments and shamanic chants, and encounters between patients and traditional healers versus biomedical doctors. For example, Philips has compared the use of honorifics – linguistic forms locally understood to be ranked according to the degree of honor their use entails – across three Tongan speech genres (church services, village-level meetings [*fonos*], and Magistrate Court proceedings). (Interestingly, Tongan language ideologies represent the sort of honorifics paid to judges in Tongan courts as relatively lower than another set of honorifics to pay deference to God and Jesus in prayer.)

Bringing It Together: Ethnographic Discourse Analysis

As adumbrated in the preceding section, Philips (2013:93) does a fine job of outlining ethnographic discourse analysis as a whole.

One is, however, never confined to one's transcripts, to the smaller subset of texts that are an analytical focus at a given point in time. No analysis of transcripts ever rests on the transcripts alone. Here I have distinguished understandings that come from a given transcript of a recording of a unit of analysis, understandings that come from comparing interactional units with each other, understandings that come from direct participation in the lives of the people one is living among, and understandings that come from other systematic methods of data collection and analysis.

We have talked in this chapter about a series of research methods used in linguistic anthropology – participant observation, recording naturally occurring discourse, conducting playback interviews on these recordings, repeating these steps across discourse genres, and conducting more interviews to elicit local models of genres, speech in general, the place of speaking in a larger model of communication, and so on. Here, Philips neatly summarizes these methods, uniting them into a whole.

CONCLUSION

Scholars from many academic disciplines study human communication. Even human linguistic communication is the focus of many fields of scholarship. This chapter has offered an overview of the methods of linguistic anthropology and our approaches to human interaction, especially face-to-face linguistic interaction.

This study of human linguistic communication starts with theory, meaning specific models of language and interaction built up over a century, some of which are specialized enough to come with their own methods, including methods of transcription. In contrast with the great twentieth-century scholar Michel Foucault (1990), linguistic anthropologists focus on discourse – not "discourses" – and analyze one example at a time. Often starting with recording, we capture relatively natural instances or events of discourse. We apply our particular models of talk and other communicative modalities to the task of transcribing and then to further stages of analysis (with transcribing itself as the first stage). Our models (theories) and methods represent linguistic anthropology's attempts to uncover the social and cultural significance of particular events and then to compare events or to connect single events into chains, according to their history or their order of occurrence.

Other chapters of this book, particularly the next one (Chapter 8), take this one step further, showing how linguistic anthropologists apply our analyses to the big questions confronting social sciences in general, and anthropology in particular.

SUMMARY

This chapter focuses on the following themes with which you should now be familiar:

- Linguistic anthropologists use a broad range of methods applied to naturally occurring language.
- These methods share much in common, reflecting the field as that branch of anthropology concerned with language-in-use as a form of cultural practice.
- Linguistic anthropologists are broadly concerned with forms of embodied communication.
- The methods overlap with those of sociocultural anthropologists.

QUESTIONS

1. How do linguistic anthropologists go about their work? What research methods do they use?
2. What methods do linguistic anthropologists have in common with **sociocultural anthropology**, and which methods are unique to linguistic anthropology?
3. What is participant observation, and why should it precede interviewing?
4. What truly deserves to be called "naturally occurring interaction," and why do linguistic anthropologists prioritize recording and analyzing such interactions?
5. Define "playback interview." How does it reveal the key methodological preference of linguistic anthropologists in terms of which method(s) should come first and which should come later?
6. How do linguistic anthropologists find what they are looking for – namely, patterns between and among signs, and between signs and society?

EXERCISES

1. Choose one written text that was originally delivered orally from the following list: President Lincoln's second inaugural address, President Kennedy's inaugural address, President Reagan's "Tear Down This Wall" speech, or Dr. Martin Luther King's "I Have a Dream" speech. Carry out an analysis of its parallelism, focusing on deictics.
2. Choose a short segment of verbal dialogue to use in creating a whole transcript. Create the transcript in the following stages, and show the transcript in each of these stages. (This is adapted from an exercise by Sable Schwab.)
   - Record a verbal action.
   - Write out the verbal interaction like a script.
   - Determine lines. No line can be longer than a literal typed line (on a screen or a printed line) or a handwritten line on an 8.5" x 11" piece of paper.

- Add symbols such as latching (=) and note pauses longer than a second.
- Number the lines.
- Listen again to check.

3. The following link takes you to resources on anthropological methods, collected by Russell Bernard and sponsored by the American Anthropological Association: www.americananthro.org/LearnAndTeach/ResourceDetail.aspx?ItemNumber= 1465

   From the extensive list of links on this page, click on one of the following, and watch the associated video:
   - "Designing a Research Question"
   - "What is Sensitive Interviewing?"
   - "Gabriela Pérez Báez, Curator of Linguistics"

   After watching the video, reflect on what you learned from it, and also reflect on its perspective. In what ways is it similar to and different from the perspective I take in this chapter and in the book as a whole?

ADDITIONAL RESOURCES

De Fina, Anna, and Sabina M. Perrino. 2011. Introduction: Interviews Vs. "Natural" Contexts: A False Dilemma. *Language in Society* 40(1):1–11.

   De Fina and Perrino assemble a set of essays that make a compelling case for treating interviews as "natural" in their own way – an argument with important implications for linguistic anthropological methods.

Desjarlais, Robert. 2000. Echoes of a Yolmo Buddhist's Life, in Death. *Cultural Anthropology* 15(2):260–293.

   Desjarlais' article makes it clear that, when anthropologists record, transcribe, and publish life history interviews, the repercussions are not only academic. Especially in his case – publishing the life history of a Tibetan Buddhist lama in Nepal – the repercussions affect the future life of the lama's soul.

Duranti, Alessandro. 1997. *Linguistic Anthropology*. Cambridge University Press.

   Chapter 5 of Duranti's textbook on transcription methods is a classic in the field.

Kroskrity, Paul. 1993. Exceptionally Instructive Individuals in the Tewa Speech Community. In *Language, History, and Identity: Ethnolinguistic Studies of the Arizona Tewa*. P. Kroskrity, ed. Pp. 109–142. Tucson: University of Arizona Press.

   Kroskrity explores what he calls "lingual life histories" – a method that I believe is underutilized.

Modan, Gabriella. 2016. Writing the Relationship: Ethnographer–Informant Interactions in the New Media Era. *Journal of Linguistic Anthropology* 26(1):98-107.

   Those anthropologists working in the environment of "the new media" face many challenges. Modan's article offers a unique sort and degree of help along this new frontier.

8   Human Social Semiotics

Introduction

In this chapter, we explore how the nature of signs and their workings – particularly indexes/indexicality and icons/iconicity – help to create the sociocultural realities we inhabit.

Here we revisit the two kinds of indexicality we first discussed in Chapter 2 and the important role they play in the contexts of communication. We also build on the preliminary discussions of iconicity in previous chapters and explore **diagrammatic iconicity** as a key concept in the analysis of ritual communication.

Next in this chapter, we move on to **multimodality,** which is the complex nature of most instances of human communication, often involving layers of signs, including those that are visible as well as audible. Finally, we discuss cultural reflections on signs and their workings, with an emphasis on cultural metaphors for aspects of communication and communicators.

In Chapter 9, which follows, we continue building on these themes.

Language as Social Action, Communication as Culture

Linguistic anthropologists approach language and communication in a very particular way, which sets us apart from linguists, cultural anthropologists, and those in communication studies, among others. Linguistic anthropologists agree that language is a cultural resource and that speaking and communicating in general are forms of **social action** (Duranti 1997:1).

This chapter addresses the question of how communication, particularly discourse, constitutes society (i.e., the social order) and culture. By discourse, I mean language-in-use, in both face-to-face and mediated interaction. Discursive communication (re)constitutes or (re)creates the social order. The importance of interaction via **new media** reflects what we mean by a changing "social order," with international borders and populations both shifting in new, rapid, grand, and unpredictable ways. (We explore these topics in more detail in Chapter 11.)

Indexes, Indexicality, and Indexicalities

By now, you are familiar with icons and symbols as well as both indexes and indexicality. Indexicality is the property or properties of being an index – immediacy, context-bounded-ness, or pointing-ness. Here I argue that it is useful to distinguish two **indexicalities**, or ways in which indexical signs relate to their context.

Two Kinds of Indexes: Two Relationships to Context

Starting in the 1970s, Michael Silverstein distinguished two relationships between linguistic signs and their contexts, with both relationships being indexical. Speech may be *appropriate to context*, thus reflecting or "presupposing" it. Or it may be *effective in its context* and thus be said to entail or create its context (Silverstein 2003b).

Let us start with categories of linguistic signs that exemplify the first sort of relationship to context. "This" and "that" are examples of a subset of deictics or indexicals that grammar books call "demonstratives" or "demonstrative pronouns." Their meaning depends on a pre-existing context shared by speaker and addressee – speech roles that are among the most common of deictic or indexicals across all languages. In many languages, speech role deictics reflect relative degrees of respect. That is, speaker and addressee may exchange different "speech levels" or degrees of honorification. (We discuss this again in relation to the *priyayi* of Java later in this chapter.) Even when these linguistic "pointers" are accompanied by pointing **gestures**, the composite sign succeeds at meaning something only when speaker and addressee share either a physical context or a discourse context. I must either *see* what a speaker is pointing to or *understand* what a storyteller or a novelist "points" back to by saying "this" or "that." (Example: "At that time, your grandfather was but a boy.")

In the latter circumstance, I must understand a particular moment in "discourse time." The same sort of "rule" applies to speech in which "this" and "that" are used, not spatially but contextually (as in the previous example).

These demonstratives do not change the nonverbal context; pointing to "that" rock does not move or transform it.

Other indexes of the presupposing or reflecting sort are more complex. They include whole repertoires of behavior that is "appropriate to context" (Silverstein 2003b). Imagine you are seated in a room with several rows of chairs and an empty, elevated chair in the front of the room. Suddenly a person in a black robe enters, someone says, "All rise!" and you and others in the room stand up. A few minutes later, you move up to the person now seated in the elevated chair, and you say "Your honor," before giving a particular kind of speech. Standing up on cue and prefacing your speech with the term "Your Honor" – these are presupposing indexes. Their relation to the context – a courtroom, of course – is one of appropriateness-to-*that*-context.

In contrast to "this," whose meaning-in-use we can discern if we share with the one who speaks and who perhaps gestures to a physical/visual context, the meaning (or **referent**) of the English pronoun "we" is not necessarily knowable merely by looking around at a physical/visual context. Imagine persons A, B, and C in a room. Person A says "We know why we are here." Person A might be looking at Person B in saying this, and that would be good evidence of who "we" includes, though we might want more evidence to be sure. Even if we look at Person C (or A, or B), we still cannot know who is included when A says "we." In almost every instance of its use, "we" creates its own referent. It is only by the act of uttering this linguistic sign that some "we" comes into existence. Typically, when speakers are somewhere together, sharing a spatial context, it is nonlinguistic signs like the direction in which the speaker gazes that clarifies who "we" is. In fact this gaze, together with utterance of "we," contributes to the context-creating moment.

I have alluded to complex signs that are indexes of the **presupposing** or "reflecting" sort. Likewise, indexes that function creatively – as "effective in context" (Silverstein 2003b) – can be far more complex than a single pronoun word like "we." Let's say that you and your friend both speak two languages – Homespeak and Schoolspeak – fluently. By Homespeak, I mean the language variety you learned at home, from infancy. You only learned to speak the other language variety, which I have dubbed Schoolspeak, comfortably during your time together at an elite university. Imagine that both you and your friend are speaking Homespeak. Suddenly one of you switches to Schoolspeak. You have performed an act of "code-switching" as do, for instance, the Tewa people in Arizona whose switching between Tewa, Hopi, and English I introduced in Chapter 1.

This important concept in linguistic anthropology denotes changing your linguistic variety in the middle of a speech event. When we are not careful to avoid objectifying thing-like terms, "codes" can be what we call "languages" – or "sociolects" or "registers" – which we introduce in detail later in this chapter. A community need not be multilingual to harbor lots of code-switching. Every speaker and every "speech community" (discussed in Chapter 9) speaks in multiple forms, including forms associated with home versus a far-away university.

What would happen if a third person were listening and observing when you and your friend "code-switched"? She might well notice that your change of code corresponded to a change in your conversational topic to something related to your shared university experience. In those circumstances, switching back to Homespeak would then "creatively index" your life back at home. (The preceding paragraph is an adaptation of Blom and Gumperz 1972.)

Now it gets more complicated, because every indexical act in human interaction both reflects and creates context. Every index is both "appropriate to" and "effective in" context, though sometimes more one than the other. Think of conversational turns-at-talk, for example. (We introduced turn-taking in Chapters 2 and 4 and discussed the analysis of turns-at-talk in Chapter 7.) Turn-taking is a more or less commonsense term; we all know enough about the give-and-take of conversation to know how to take turns.

Think about this, however: Every turn reflects what has already been said and also anticipates – and creates a slot or preface for – what will be said next.

(1a) SYLVIA: You are certainly invited.
(2a) RACHEL: Thank you, I'll be there!

Line (1a) reflects what has passed between Sylvia and Rachel – a context-of-talk to which we have no access, but which we can presume. At the same time, by taking a turn-at-talk that entails an invitation, Sylvia shapes Rachel's turn. Line (1a) makes a certain class of response relevant for Rachel to provide in line (2a). This is not to say that line (2a) is completely predetermined by line (1a). Not at all. Line (2b) is also valid. Line (2b) is a turn-at-talk that is relevant to line (1b). It falls in the category of "response," even though the hemming and hawing may creatively index a future act that does not involve accepting the invitation.

(1b) SYLVIA: You are certainly invited.
(2b) RACHEL: Well, uhm, gee, I'll have to check my calendar.

Things proceed as they normally do in conversational interaction as long as line 1x (an invitation like that in 1a or 1b) is followed by something you can interpret as a response. If Rachel, on the other hand, were to (a) say nothing at all, (b) turn and run away from Sylvia, or (c) choke and fall over dead, we would know that we were not in the realm of ordinary conversational give-and-take. Those who make it their work to analyze conversation would refer to acts (a) and (b) as dispreferred responses (if they are responses at all), while act (c) is presumably not a response of any kind.

Pygmalion/My Fair Lady

The plot or overall trajectory of the George Bernard Shaw play *Pygmalion* (which became the Broadway play *My Fair Lady* and later the film of the same name) aptly illustrates creative indexicality.

Figure 8.1 In *My Fair Lady*, Professor Higgins decides to change Eliza Doolittle's life completely, simply by changing her speech. (Museum of the City of New York/Getty Images)

Protagonist Eliza Doolittle, when she first meets Professor Henry Higgins (see Figure 8.1), speaks a form of English sometimes called Cockney. Higgins tells a colleague that her speech condemns her to a life "in the gutter," but wagers with his colleague that he can remake her, even pass her off as a lady. Higgins indicates this feat would result only and entirely from transforming Eliza's speech. After much hard work and suffering at Higgins' direction, Eliza does in fact learn to speak and act "like a lady."

Indeed this form of action, which involves Eliza's use not only of language but other cultural sign systems or semiotic modalities, is a fine example of a semiotic register. This transformation is passed off as the effect of Eliza's new **sociolect**. Sociolects are ways of speaking that people think of as pointing to our **social address** (i.e., the variables that "locate" us in social space, like gender, class, and ethnicity). According to this notion of social address, a person has various "attributes determining social address or 'place' in a community (theoretically on a par with class, race, age) and also determining a distinctive relation to linguistic variation (e.g., pronunciation patterns or orientation toward **standard** grammar)" (Eckert and McConnell-Ginet 1992:465).

Pygmalion/My Fair Lady would be just an amusing story if it were not replicated, with much effort and suffering, every day, at least in the United States. If I want to rid myself of a stigmatizing "lect," for instance, I could hire an expensive dialect coach who helps actors learn to say their lines in the language variety appropriate to the dramatic part they must play.

Acquiring a new sociolect in this expensive way entails what Pierre Bourdieu (1991) describes as an exchange of one kind of **capital** (i.e., money) for another – cultural or symbolic capital. Cultural capital is the sort of prestige attached to "having *culture*" in the sense associated with the pronunciation *culcha*. Some scholarship in the field of language and society seems to presume that our ways of speaking merely *reflect* our social address. For example Labov's (1968) article is titled, "The Reflections of Social Processes in Linguistic Structure." But regular folks know that indexes are creative or *effective* in context and not just *appropriate* to context – that acquiring new ways of speaking can open social doors for them. If not, they would not expend time, energy, or even money on "improving" their sociolect to enhance their status.

In the previous section, we learned that indexical dimensions of language use are either appropriate-to-context or effective-in-context and that most are both. "Being polite," for example, may be "what one does" in a particular setting but may also earn the polite speaker some sort of "points."

In the rest of the chapter, we explore some of the many ways in which social indexicality works. In particular, we are interested in the creative, context-renewing, context-transforming, socially effective and transformative dimensions of indexical communication.

Iconicity in Human Communication

Having further explored indexical relationships in communication, we shift focus in the next sections to different forms of iconicity and the roles they play in communication. We also revisit themes developed by Peirce about the function or characteristics of iconism. In so doing, these sections clarify the ways that changes in sound as well as imagery and syntax build communicative relationships.

Sound Iconism

In Chapter 4, I introduced the notion of "**sound iconism**," often called "sound symbolism" (Jakobson [1987] 2002). There are no pure icons in the human world, since iconicity is an arbitrary, culturally filtered perception, and arbitrariness is a defining feature of symbols, not icons. Sound iconism really entails cultural evaluations of linguistic sounds. The kinds of iconicity involved in these cultural practices of sound include both of the vowel modifications that make the vowel seem harsh to native speakers, such as **nasalized** vowels in Bangladeshis' perspective, discussed in Chapter 4.

Also in Chapter 4, we encountered an example (from the Kiksht language) of the simultaneous modification of several sounds occurring throughout words that *index* a speaker's attitude toward a person being talked about. We saw that the total effect of these modifications is to sonically capture endearment/positive feelings (diminutive) versus negative evaluations/feelings (augmentative).

It turns out that there are not just two attitude-indexing forms (diminutive for positive feelings and augmentative for negative) in the Kiksht language. Instead, there are six forms whose *indexical* value varies stepwise from very positive (or small) to very negative (or big). And it is no accident that, as a speaker shifts from augmentative to diminutive, his or her vowels shift from a mouth-wide-open "ah" to a relatively closed-mouth "eh" sound. (From here on, I will use IPA symbols to show "ah" as [a] and "eh" as [ɛ]; see the Appendix for more information.) When I say this change in sound is "no accident," I mean the sound–meaning relationship is "motivated" or *iconic*: Open equals big, closed equals small. We can also say that [a] indexes dislike and [ɛ] affection. Indexicality and iconicity merge in these Kiksht sound changes.

As far as I know, there are no languages in the world in which diminutives belittle and augmentatives inflate the importance of a referent. Instead, diminutives are "grammaticalized" means of expressing positive feelings, even for deities. I know of no examples in which an augmentative ending shows respect for a "big" referent (e.g., God).

The labels "sound iconism" and "sound symbolism" are both appropriate for their own reasons – and indexicality is at work here too! Let's say I am a Kiksht speaker and use an augmentative while talking about a person. Such a use, or speech act, "says" nothing about that person (denotatively) but indexes him or her and my feelings toward him or her. Second, as I have shown, the sound shifts on which I must draw in order to index my feelings are themselves iconic. My act of indexing involves the iconic relationship between the size or relative openness of the mouth in producing [a] versus [ɛ] and in the "size" and feeling indexed by the forms that use [a] and [ɛ].

Finally, the label "sound symbolism" fits the Bangla nasalization example and the much more complex Kiksht example. Why is that? Because the perception and evaluation of sound contrasts in both cases is arbitrary, cultural, and thus symbolic.

Two Kinds of Icon

Charles Peirce said there are two types of icon: images and diagrams. Metaphors are **imagistic icons**, meaning word pictures that highlight resemblance or similarity. For example, in a metaphor used throughout a long, socially significant meeting in Bangladesh, a rural Bangladeshi community was depicted as a sick person (Wilce 1996). In this case, the image – this verbal image of the sick person – resembled the

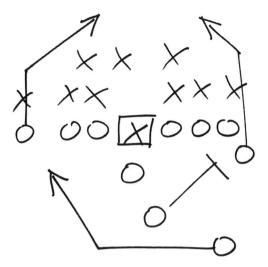

Figure 8.2 A schematic representation of a football play as an example of diagrammatic iconicity. (skodonnell/Getty Images)

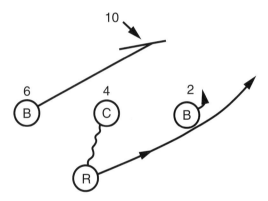

Figure 8.3 Diagrammatic icon of a long-slant or off-tackle drive from an older style of football. (Wilce 1923:103)

depicted (the community) insofar as the community was said to share the sick person's deviance or pathology.

On the other hand, a "diagram" (again, in its technical semiotic sense) or diagrammatic icon, can be quite schematic. Circles and arrows might serve as a sketch of a football play (Figures 8.2 and 8.3), but the sketcher does not try to make any element resemble an actual football player. The point is that the arrows show the relationships between the players moving on the field.

Diagrammatic iconicity turns up in surprising places in language – namely, in syntax. Syntax is, in the view of many linguists, the defining phenomenon of language. Surprisingly, a kind of iconicity lies at the core of syntax. A clear example is our expectation that the order of events in certain compound sentences will mirror the order of events in the world to which the speaker refers. If I say,

"I'm going to the store, then I'm coming back," my listener will understand the two parts of my outing to occur in the order in which my sentence presents them. The relation between the two clauses in the sentence is a diagram of the events as they will take place in the world.

Why would diagrammatic iconicity interest anthropologists and other social scientists? The chief reason is that it plays a key role in ritual, as we explore in the next section.

Social Action and Cultural Meanings in Emergent Textual Structure

As you are aware, I have taken care in this book to distinguish between the concepts of society and culture. At the same time, we have talked about the concept of culture being necessary to defining human society. The metaphor I have used is that a common or shared culture (a set of concepts, practices, products) serves as a kind of glue for the society that "owns" it, holding that society together.

Rituals can be understood as activities occurring at the intersection of society and culture. Rituals are shared *communicative* or *semiotic* activities that reinforce social bonds. The *patterning* of signs from the beginning to the end of a ritual is itself a crucially important sign. And linguistic signs are perhaps paramount among several types common to ritual. Ritual sign patterns bespeak, correspond to, embody, or constitute cultural concepts like "God is here," "We are a nation," "Our nation is eternal," or "Healing occurs in social encounters like that between healer and patient." Each concept pertains to social cohesion, and each is culture-*in-linguistic-form*. Each of the propositions in the previous sentence presupposes *local* or *unique* cultural concepts. After all, concepts like "god," "nation," and "healing" come to us in culturally variable forms, despite having somewhat recognizable core features. Moreover, the sign patterns crucial to making such cultural concepts real to ritual participants share much cross-culturally. **Parallelism** (Silverstein 2003a) is both the most widespread of such pattern-types and the easiest to comprehend (see Chapter 4).

The previous paragraph reflects one of the three lessons that Silverstein (2004) says linguistic anthropologists have learned in recent decades about the relationship between language, culture, and society. His article "'Cultural' Concepts and the Language–Culture Nexus" neatly packages those lessons. Here I focus on the first lesson Silverstein presents: Talk-in-interaction *evokes* sociocultural concepts. Turning this around, I could say that people express and reinforce their key cultural concepts in **emergent** textual patterns (i.e., in patterns that make discourse cohere, hang together, and make sense). This "sense" may not be altogether conscious. The specific cultural concepts that emerge particularly in **ritual** discourse might be named therein. The American concept of freedom or independence, for example, becomes explicit at the climax of the Declaration of Independence. Just as often, however, talk-in-interaction does not name cultural concepts but only represents them in a figural way.

It is unnecessary for ritual texts to make direct reference to the cultural concepts they convey. What is common to all such instances is *not* direct reference to cultural ideas and values. What *is* universal is the "figural," "textual," or "poetic form of discourse" that embodies cultural concepts. It is ritual communication whose emergent form is especially likely to convey concepts central to a community. Often, it is in the path traced over "textual time" – via "movement" within the "text," or **intratextual movement** – particularly when that movement involves a kind of acceleration, intensification, or (figuratively speaking) crescendo. That dramatic intratextual movement toward a crescendo is aptly illustrated in the Declaration of Independence, which is the first of two examples that we examine here.

The Emergent Structure of the Declaration of Independence

The significance of structure – and particularly parallelism – in the study of linguistic communication is by now familiar to readers. We find parallelism of all varieties described in Chapter 4, appearing with the greatest intensity in ritual communication. The authors of the Declaration of Independence debated it orally and hammered it into powerful prose (see Figure 8.4). Since then, it has circulated in written (as well as oral) form. How does a written document exemplify ritual communication? Where is the ritual setting? Where is the assembly of text producers and audience, caught up together in ritual "effervescence" or conscious and intensified sociality, communality?

Communication need not be face-to-face, though it must entail circulation of some sort. Revolutionary discourse and even particular wording circulated among the Founders before they signed the document in its final form. And crucially, copies of the document circulated among the thirteen colonies. This circulation spread the document's most memorable phrases, enabling them to penetrate deeply into American English and especially the register of American political rhetoric. It also gave the leaders of each colony time to debate and eventually approve the document themselves.

The ritual nature of the Declaration reaches maximum clarity at its climax, in the words *"we therefore … declare."* As we learned in Chapter 1 and will see again in Chapter 10, such statements are referred to as **performative** – magical, powerful, efficacious words that *do* what they may superficially appear to talk about. There was no "declaring" to refer to before the act of declaration, which the whole document but particularly the climactic utterance *"we … declare"* brought about. There was no declaring, no independence, and no United States of America. This makes the Declaration something like a naming ceremony, like christenings in some Christian churches or other kinds of naming ceremonies around the world. How is that? Baby christenings create social persons through their performative language. Likewise, the Declaration "brought forth a new nation," as Lincoln said 87 years after the signing.

Parallelism characterizes the Declaration from the outset. After *"We hold these truths to be self-evident,"* a series of statements follow, each beginning with *"that"* – the most famous being *"that all men [sic] are created equal."* Parallelism

Figure 8.4 The drafters of the Declaration of Independence used parallelism to great advantage. (Rischgitz/Getty Images)

intensifies in the middle section, which Greg Urban (2001) calls "the **Litany** of Complaint." The litany is a list of *"facts* [being] *submitted to a candid world."* It begins with *"He* [the King of Great Britain] *has refused … he has forbidden … he has refused …"* The text then introduces the victims of the King's actions as "the people/People" (as in *"invasions on the rights of the people"*). Finally, in the climax of the Litany comes a series of pronominal references that denote the same group referred to as "the People" – namely, "us" and "our": *"He has combined with others to subject* us *to a jurisdiction foreign to* our *constitution."*

The grammatical structure repeated in this subsection refers to the victims with the first-person plural pronouns "us" and "our" – **accusative** and genitive case, object and possessive pronouns, respectively. This means pronouns that are *not* "we" (i.e., not **nominative** case), which denotes the grammatical *subjects* of sentences. See Chapter 6 for a discussion of cases like nominative and accusative.

At this point in the Declaration of Independence, the "He has ____ed us" series switches for a time to "For _____ing us," such as *"For transporting us beyond Seas to be tried for pretended offences."* As a brief departure from the pattern that precedes and succeeds it, the "For _____ing us" section exemplifies the variation that must occur within repetition in order for parallelism to have the power that it does.

> *He has plundered* our *seas,*
> *ravaged* our *Coasts,*
> *burnt* our *towns,*
> *and destroyed the lives of* our *people.*

A very important switch of pronominal **case** occurs as the text approaches its climax – from "us" and "our" to "we" (first-person plural *nominative* case). A section full of "we" pronouns following the Litany culminates in the ultimate "we" – the act of declaration itself. We can refer to this final section leading to the declaration as the "justification section." Here the framers tell the *"candid world"* addressed earlier in the text everything they have tried, short of an all-out war for independence.

> *We have petitioned . . .*

> *We have warned,*

However, the need for "we" – and indeed the relatively new, and certainly modern, "we" as in *"we the People"* – is clearest where it is used to greatest effect:

> *We*, therefore, the Representatives of the United States of America . . . do, in the Name, and by the Authority of the good People of these Colonies, solemnly *publish* and *declare*, that these United Colonies are, and of Right ought to be Free and Independent States.

Crucially, the climax of the text contains two performative verbs. By that I mean "verbs of speaking" or "metapragmatic verbs" – those which name an act of speaking or "discoursing." Those verbs are "publish" and "declare." "We ... declare" is the very act that gives the text its name. That climactic act is backed up, however, by another performative or speech act – the framers pledge or promise to support the declaration with their very lives.

Readers (or hearers) of the Declaration easily grasp one cultural concept – the signatories' willingness to commit themselves to making the independent United States a reality. A different, perhaps broader but surely more subtle, cultural concept is to be found in no particular word or sentence but in the intratextual movement from *us*-ness to *we*-ness, victimhood to assertion. It is also, however, a movement from a factual disunity or multiplicity (of the colonies) to a united entity indexed by the pronoun "we." The disparate populations of the various colonies could suffer separately as so many "us"'s," but it is only a unified "we" that can index a subject united-in-independence.

The Declaration of Independence exemplifies diagrammatic iconicity. This type of iconicity involves one *pattern* (or "diagram," consisting of sign-vehicles, signs) resembling another *pattern* (consisting of sign-*objects* in the world).

The diagram in the Declaration as a text starts with propositions (e.g., individual complaints), and then builds to groups of propositions such as the Litany and the climax. Finally, if you were to read or listen to the Declaration, in that real time of being with the text you would experience movement between the *us*-laden Litany and the *we*-filled climax. What *makes* this diagrammatic iconicity, however, is that the pattern we're calling intratextual movement becomes an icon of the "real-world" movement or change (in this case, toward independence) that the ritual text serves to bring about.

Ritual speech helps to power transformation, and diagrammatic iconicity involves linguistic sign patterns (or intratextual movement) that resemble transformations beyond the text. Keep in mind that, to anthropologists, *transformation* – not repetition, let alone "empty" repetition – defines ritual. ("Beyond the text" means in the cosmos or at least the "real world.") The transformation caused by the original publication of the Declaration involved the relationship *among* the American colonies and *between* the colonies and Great Britain.

Encounters with Sérĩñ in Senegal

The previous example – a written discourse whose access to an audience depended (and still depends) on its circulation as a document – challenges our notion of ritual and ritual language in one set of ways. This second example, which I introduced in Chapter 7 and discuss here in more detail, involves an encounter between a patient and a traditional healer. We give particular attention to the greeting phase of that encounter (Perrino 2002).

In some ways, this second example is more easily recognizable as a ritual than was the first example. Yet it also challenges our ideas of ritual. Referring to an encounter between a traditional healer and his patient (see Figure 8.5) as a *ritual* encounter is not surprising. As you read the transcript below and notice its repetitiousness, you may think, "Ahah! This is ritual as I know it – repetitious to the point of being silly." On the other hand, the greeting phase of a Senegalese Wolof (West African) encounter with a *marabout* or *sërĩñ* (see Chapter 7) may challenge those who, like me, expect to find the transformative ritual activity occurring some time *after* the greeting phase. Here, the transformation *begins with* that initial greeting phase. In fact, the healing outcome hinges on the intimacy that is first achieved in the greeting. Admittedly, a prolonged greeting seems not only strange but also, as a ritual, disappointing. Still, we should remind ourselves of the first lesson linguistic anthropologists have learned about the relationship between language, society, and culture: If we are looking for cultural concepts in language, we ought to look at the *structure* of discourse, especially in ritual settings.

Studying healing encounters ethnographically, as linguistic anthropologist Sabina Perrino has, provides evidence apart from the transcript discussed here for the local cultural importance of the greeting ritual. In fact, the way Perrino joins two sorts of evidence – the close analysis of encounters with healers as a particular type or genre of talk-in-interaction, plus **contextualizing** ethnographic evidence from interviews – typifies the best methods in linguistic anthropology. (Chapter 7 discusses these methods in detail.)

Figure 8.5 A traditional marabout has the power to influence healing outcomes. Here, Senegalese President Abdoulaye Wade (*right*) meets with his marabout Serigne Saliou Mbacke. (SEYLLOU/AFP/ Getty Images)

As you read the transcript that follows, take special note of the beginnings and endings of numbered "lines." Watch for latching (=) – the phenomenon in which the words of a new speaker bump up against those of the previous speaker or interactant without perceptible gap or overlap. Watch also for overlap, which is signified by brackets between lines (e.g., connecting "line" 7 with 8). (You will remember that latching and overlap are introduced and defined in Chapter 7.)

I place the word "lines" in quotation marks because, in other circumstances, linguistic anthropologists have reasons to make "a line" a literal line of transcribed speech – dividing discourse such that each literal line of transcribed words receives its own line number (see Wilce 2008:104–106). Perrino chooses to include comments within the "line" idea. That means that "line" 9, for example, takes up eleven lines on the page.

Why pay such attention to overlapping and latching, as Perrino does in her original analysis? Their importance lies in what they represent, as two dimensions of diagrammatic iconicity. Of what are they iconic? Answering that question unlocks the puzzle of how *the structure of this greeting encounter and the way it is transcribed* reveal something important. True, both the encounter and the transcription are likely to be foreign to most Western readers. Yet they reveal a cultural concept that is important for Wolof Muslims who visit traditional healers (see Table 8.1). And **transcribing** an event in such a way that it reveals

TABLE 8.1 Transcript of greeting phase of healing encounter with a Wolof *sérīñ* (Perrino 2002)

Participant	Line	First line: Wolof Second line: English	VISIBLE BEHAVIOR TRANSCRIBER'S COMMENTS
Patient	1	1 *Salaam Maalekum!* 'Peace be upon you!'	{WITH HIS SHOES REMOVED, THE PATIENT KNOCKS ON THE EDGE OF THE DOOR, THEN ENTERS THE HUT BAREFOOT. HE APPROACHES THE *SÉRĪÑ*, WHO IS SEATED ON THE FLOOR; THE *SÉRĪÑ*, IN TURN, GLANCES UP.} [[Arabic expression]]
Sérīñ	2a	(0.22) *Maalekum Salaam!* 'Upon you be peace!'	{THE *SÉRĪÑ'S* GAZE RETURNS TO THE PAGES OF THE BOOK ON HIS LAP AS HE UTTERS THIS ARABIC EXPRESSION.} [[Arabic expression]]
	2b	2b (0.99) *Bissimillah!* In the name of Allah '(0.99) Welcome!'	[[Arabic expression]]
Patient	3	(0.44) Ah- gó- góor gi! '(0.44) Ah, nice to see you here!'	
Sérīñ	4	(0.31)Waaw = Yes	{THE *SÉRĪÑ* GAZES UP AGAIN AT THE PATIENT AND THEN RETURNS HIS GAZE DOWNWARD A MOMENT LATER.}
Sérīñ	6	= Na nga def? '= How are you doing?' [	
Patient	7	Siñaañ [	

Sérīñ	8	Sa yaram jàmm
		    'Peace be upon your health'
		      [	

Patient	9	Siñaañ	{THE PATIENT STARTS TO ROLL HIS RIGHT HAND BACK TOWARD HIM AND REGRASPS THE HEALER'S HAND BY WRAPPING HIS FINGERS AROUND HIS THUMB AND THE BACK OF THE HEALER'S HAND. THE HEALER FOLLOWS HIS LEAD AND DOES THE SAME.}
Sérīñ	10	Sa yaram jàmm 'Peace be upon your health' [	
Patient	11	Jàmm rekke Siñaañ 'Peace be upon you, Siñaañ' [	{BOTH THE PATIENT AND THE *SÉRĪÑ* RECLASP HANDS IN A REGULAR HANDSHAKE FASHION.}
Sérīñ	12	Jàmm rekey 'Peace be upon you'	

TABLE 8.1 (*cont.*)			
Participant	Line	First line: Wolof Second line: English	VISIBLE BEHAVIOR TRANSCRIBER'S COMMENTS
Patient	13	= Naka wa kĕr gi? '= How is your household here doing?' [	{THE *SÉRĪÑ* IS THE FIRST TO WITHDRAW HIS HAND, WHILE THE PATIENT LEAVES HIS HAND OUTSTRETCHED FOR A MOMENT, THEN RETRACTS IT.}
Sérīñ	14	Sa yaram jàmm 'Peace be upon your health'	

the heart of the text *and* the culture of its producers is the point of transcription in linguistic anthropology.

What is going on here? As Perrino argues, this greeting phase is key to the ritual healing encounter. But why all this overlap and latching? Why should we attend closely to it? How could these equal signs and brackets signal anything meaningful to the Wolof participants in this healing encounter? Perrino argues that "the multi-modal texture [of the ritual greeting phase of the encounter] helps establish for the participants a semiotically palpable sense of connection" (Perrino 2002:239). *And without that sense of connection or "intimacy," no healing is believed possible –* certainly an important cultural concept. Note that the intimacy required between healer and patient is what we might call "conversational intimacy." To return to Perrino's words:

> The recurrent latching and overlap create the impression of a seamless dialogue between the **voices**. The relative lack of temporal separation between the turns comes to signify a relative lack of interpersonal separation between the speech participants; that is, this pattern helps project a sense of interpersonal intimacy. (2002:234)

Clearly, this is a case of iconicity – a culturally felt resemblance between a concrete textual *pattern* and a relatively abstract cultural value or form of experience. The exchange of words from one speaker's mouth to another becomes an icon of intimacy as the interlocutors' turns meet and sometimes "kiss" in what is technically called latching, or meet and overlap slightly. The iconicity here is *diagrammatic*.

Yet the two parties in the interaction are not co-equal. Like turns-at-talk by the two interlocutors, symmetry and asymmetry meet and "kiss" in healing encounters. Only the *sérīñ* quotes the Qur'an. Most of the Arabic words (borrowed into Wolof) are the *sérīñ*'s. And on top of all of the linguistic signs of asymmetry and symmetry, one more thing proceeds from the *sérīñ's* mouth: As the healer chants Qur'anic verses, he "invests his saliva with" the words. He then casts it upon the patient and sometimes massages it into the problematic **body** part.

We know all of this because of the ethnographic work accompanying the analysis of the primary, **naturally occurring** event – the healing encounter. Beyond words exchanged in it, there are "publicly circulating metadiscourses … that stress the need for intimacy between healer and patient" (Perrino 2002:234).

As **ethnographers**, linguistic anthropologists collect and analyze these naturally occurring metadiscourses. However, like Perrino, they also engage in what have come to be called "playback interviews" in which a recording is made of either participants in an original recording that captures their interaction or a cultural consultant. In either case, the goal is to elicit and record metacommunicative commentary on the original event.

Perrino played recordings of Wolof greeting rituals that occurred in Senegal as part of healing encounters to a Senegalese man – Mamadou Sow – living in the United States. As he listened to

> the overlap and latching of this initial greetings phase[,] he remarked that the initial greetings seemed "melodious and harmonious," and added that the greeting event was "like a braid," in the sense of braided hair. He stated that this was a "real" encounter between a Senegalese traditional healer and a patient and stressed that greetings must be this way; otherwise, the healing therapy is less likely to be effective. (Perrino 2002:239)

Senegalese healing encounters work as rituals in no small part because of sign-complexes or patterns of signs that powerfully convey the cultural concept of *healing intimacy*. This example obviously features structure that is "emergent" in two senses. By emergent, I first mean not planned but improvised. But second, emergent means what comes out of complexity. The example I used (in Chapter 1) to introduce this sense was that of termites, and what they are capable of – building huge mounds – because they live in societies. The "intimate" structure of the Senegalese healing ritual is emergent in that second sense, too. The structure reflects the complexity we see when discourse is embedded in interaction. It is that interactive structure of discourse that subtly but powerfully reconfirms Wolof cultural knowledge that encounters must be "conversationally" intimate in order to heal.

In both the Declaration of Independence and the greeting exchanges between Senegalese healers and patients, cultural concepts arise not in explicit referential speech, but in discourse structure. The Declaration does not refer to the moment when a new "we" is born. Instead, the movement in the text from an active "he" and a suffering "us," to an agentive "we," brings this new sociocultural reality to life. Likewise, no phrase even vaguely like "the necessity of conversational healing intimacy" ever appears in Senegalese healing encounters. But whether it is an overarching "crescendo" of political assertiveness (in the Declaration) or the "braiding" (or harmonizing) of pairs of utterances exchanged along with the intertwined fingers of a handshake and "Qur'anic saliva," one key lesson in social semiotics is that we ignore the *form* of linguistic communication – and the contribution of that form to social action and cultural meaning – at our peril.

This second example demonstrates Silverstein's (2004) assertion that the language–culture nexus often involves the conveying of cultural lessons not in the referential content alone, but in the poetic or textual patterning of discourse, particularly in ritual context. It exemplifies the textual-cosmic link we have been calling diagrammatic iconicity. The repeated close calls or near collisions between the healer's and the patient's utterances (i.e., the sign-to-sign relationship) is an icon of the desired relationship between patient and healer. And that relationship is culturally projected as a crucial prerequisite or even as part of the process of healing.

Evoking Sociocultural Concepts

The two examples just presented are "indexical icons." That means that, not only do the sign patterns *resemble* the desired "cosmic" outcome of the ritual and its text, but they also point to that outcome. The "we" pronouns found in the climax of the Declaration of Independence draw listeners in to themselves, into the experience of *we*-ness. Put differently, they do not just presuppose the existence of a citizenry with enough solidarity to refer to itself as "we" but help *create* that new American "we."

These two texts illustrate one more facet of interpersonally and culturally meaningful exchanges or productions of signs that is very important to understand – the "intentionality" of such texts, discursive productions, or sign patterns. In the West, it is common to understand the meaning of speech as a straightforward reflection of an inward psychological intention. We in the West confuse the speaker's intention with *the* meaning of speech. But intention need not mean the conscious, personal, and psychologically grounded goals of speakers. In phenomenological thought, going back to one of its progenitors, Edmund Husserl, "intention" is orientation (1931, [1913] 1970). A toddler *faces* a wall. The wall is the object of her gaze, her orientation, and *in that sense*, her intention. Is she planning to scale it? go around it? paint on it? None of those conscious personal intentions necessarily apply to her act of facing the wall. (See the discussion of intentionality in Chapter 1, especially Figures 1.9a and 1.9b.)

Did Thomas Jefferson and other contributors to the Declaration have a conscious intention to write a document declaring their independence, declaring war in some sense on Great Britain? Probably. But even so, intentionality as orientation is a far larger phenomenon than such individual goals as we or Jefferson might have (had). The larger phenomenological intention is always present. Sometimes intentionality in this larger phenomenological sense involves goals or ends consciously linked to means, but not always. We can imagine Jefferson struggling to get every word right, vis-à-vis his goal. It seems unlikely, by contrast, that *marabout* healers and their patients time their utterances consciously so as to achieve either no overlap (latching, which lacks any gap) or minimal overlap.

The point here is that rituals *intend* or *orient towards* something on a plane that is transcendent. On that plane are such hopes as finding forgiveness, divine aid, healing, or making history with "firm reliance on the Protection of Divine

Providence" (as the Declaration says). Rituals "intend" such things regardless of whether they *state* the goal. Ritual actors "intend" such things whether or not they are conscious of the goal, let alone have a plan to accomplish it. In clarifying intentionality-as-orientation, we have contributed yet another reason not to imagine linguistic meaning as a conduit through which thoughts that do not yet have linguistic form eventually flow, or as an instrument just for denotative-referential communication, rather than a sort of all-purpose tool for performing all sorts of acts in speech (so-called speech acts).

Symbolicity

Symbols mean, represent, or stand for their objects by means of an **arbitrary** or culturally conventional rule. The sign stands for this just because it does. "Water" means water despite having no resemblance to it. (See Figure 8.6.) The English noun doesn't *sound* like water, as we may think "bubble-bubble" or "splash" do. Nor is water an act of pointing, as are words like "this" or "that," "here" or "there." One can say "water" all one wants in the middle of the desert, but it doesn't make water suddenly appear. Most words are symbols, which in semiotics means they stand for their objects only in a cultural or arbitrary way. However, words like "water" rarely feel arbitrary to speakers of a language. Rather, they tend to feel somehow like *natural* signs of something.

Symbolic meaning is related very closely to denotational meaning. What a word denotes is to be found, for example, in dictionaries. And we can think of those as giant cultural rule books arbitrarily linking certain words with other words that we consider to be the true meaning of the original word. Saussure would have said, quite rightly, that dictionaries arbitrarily link a sound shape with a denotation. The problem, as we shall see, is that the common Western understanding of language (our dominant language ideology) tells us that denotation or referring is *the* **function** of language.

I do need to mention that "connotation" is generally a useless term in the careful analysis of linguistic communication, despite the fact that "denotation" is quite useful. It is misleading to define "indexical meaning" as "connotative." It may seem tiresome that we must learn new terms when we learn a new science – terms like "index," "indexical," and "indexicality" in linguistic anthropology or "hemor-rhage" and "ischemic attack" in medicine. However, learning such terms is in fact basic to the study of any science.

I close this section with a perspective on the power of the symbol, particularly in language. This comes from the great interpreter of Charles Peirce, the philosopher of language and literature, Roman Jakobson: "The prevalently symbolic signs are the only ones which through their possession of general meaning are able to form propositions, whereas 'icons and indices assert nothing.'" Jakobson goes on to associate icons with "past experience" and indexes with "present experience." By contrast,

Figure 8.6 Seeing or hearing a drop of water does nothing to explain why water is called water. (Derek Croucher/Getty Images)

> The being of a symbol consists in the real fact that something surely will be experienced if certain conditions be satisfied. Namely, it will influence the thought and conduct of its interpreter ... The value of a symbol is that it serves to make thought and conduct rational and enables us to predict the future ... But [wrote Peirce] a general law [i.e., a symbol] cannot be fully realized. It is a potentiality and its mode of being is *esse in futuro* [being in the future]." (Jakobson 1965:36-37, citing Peirce 1960:360)

Multimodal Semiotic Registers: Situation-Based Communicative Forms

I make a fundamental distinction between **sociolects** and **registers** (which we will explore more fully in Chapter 9). In the section below, we discuss registers as a semiotic phenomenon, often being experienced and evaluated as multimodal.

Let us consider a very simple case as our first example – the nuts and bolts of written wedding invitations. Several semiotic forms add up to create this register or situation-based semiotic form:

- A certain kind of language.
- Certain fonts, certain paper type.
- A similarity to other sorts of formal invitations on nice card stock.
- A contrast with shopping lists, text messages, tweets.

Now let us consider a more complex register example.

Honorific Registers: The Example of Javanese

Registers, their use, and their emergence or development – the processes called **enregisterment** (Wilce 2008) – are particularly important to linguistic anthropologists. Their importance lies in the way they bridge culturally stereotyped situations (a clinical encounter with a biomedical practitioner, a church service, or some other such widely recognizable and often explicitly labeled cultural event) with stereotyped social fractions or groups associated with certain activities. Think, for example, of doctors, preachers, or other categories of social actors associated not only with activities but also with value or status, who are familiar in and to communities around the world. For students familiar with Euro-American cultures and categories, I offer here a register associated with a cultural context and social identities that are quite unfamiliar, unlike the wedding invitation example. Following Fajans (2014), learning to "familiarize the exotic" is one of the hallmarks of anthropology, along with "exoticizing the familiar" (i.e., "our own" sociocultural lives).

For some time before the period of Dutch colonial rule over what is now Indonesia, the island of Java was home to kings whose power was conceived of as both political and semi-divine. The person of the king was the powerful center of the royal court, which was the center of the king's dominion. The royal court thus housed the highest power and the highest levels of exemplary behavior. Those who served in the Javanese royal court were the king's *priyayi* (a word deriving from a Sanskrit root denoting closeness or dearness).

These kingdoms collapsed under the pressure of Dutch hegemony in the nineteenth century. Yet, to this day, many Javanese people regard the descendants of the *priyayi* as the ideal speakers of the complex Javanese language and the keepers of the most respectful forms thereof. The highest or most polite "speech level" (or register) achieves politeness in part by tamping down signs of one's individuality and emotion (following Judith Irvine 1990). Crucially, however, the linguistic element is only part of the honorific register.

> Politeness ... is expressed by the Javanese in their gestures as well as through their speech. A complicated etiquette dictates the way a person sits, stands, directs his eyes, holds his hands, points, greets people, laughs, walks, dresses, and so on. There is a close association between the rigor with which the etiquette of movement is observed and the degree of refinement in speech. The more polite a person's language, the more elaborate are his other behavioral patterns; the more informal his speech, the more relaxed and simplified his gestures. (Poedjosoedarmo 1968)

This, of course, is just one example of honorific registers. To read about another example – the register traditionally required in laments that were once commonly performed at funerals in what today is southwestern Russia, home to Finnic peoples such as Karelians (see Wilce and Fenigsen 2015).

Two Sorts of Action and Indexicality: To Refer or Not Refer

Before we leave the subject of politeness indexicals, it is important to recognize another dimension, another dividing line setting apart one new set of indexes from another. This dimension is the referential versus nonreferential. You might say, "Wait, don't all uses of language involve referring to something?" Actually, the answer is no. That is, not all linguistic or semiotic features – not all "pronunciation" features of an English utterance, for example – refer to anything, even though they *mean*. Meaning is much broader than reference.

Silverstein makes a four-way distinction between indexical forms (1976:36). This distinction involves two axes – the presupposing versus the creative and, what is new to our discussion here, the referential versus the nonreferential. Code-switching, discussed earlier in this chapter, is significant. It bears meaning. And "codes" include dialects, sociolects, and registers. It means something to switch from a dialect or sociolect in which I might say "Pahk yah cah in Hahvid Yahd" to one in which I say "Park your car in Harvard Yard." But the meaning in the switch is not referential. The switch is a "pure index."

Now, instead of a switch between two ways of pronouncing the "Harvard parking" utterance, let's imagine two speakers talking about the same thing at the same time, a couple of blocks away from each other. Their contrasting sets of phonetic ("accent" or dialect) features index contrasting identities. Or, as I would prefer, uttering the two different pronunciations involves two different degrees – or ways – of identifying "with Boston" or "as Bostonians." One of the two speakers might proudly identify as a Bostonian or even someone from "Southie," a working-class Boston neighborhood (Nagy and Irwin 2010). The other might choose not to openly identify in the same way, despite being from Boston. (For more information about sociolinguistic variability in American English, see the educational video *American Tongues* [Kolker and Alvarez 1988].)

What other examples are there of "nonreferential" meaning-making? "Being polite" is a mostly nonreferential sort of *action*. Now it is true that talking *about* something is also an action, but that action is simply what we call "referring." The silly sentence taught to Eliza Doolittle in *My Fair Lady* – "The rain in Spain falls mainly on the plain" – would appear to accomplish nothing but pure reference. The whole point of teaching it to Eliza, however, was to enable her to perform a nonreferential semiotic act. That act was to pronounce the silly sentence just as Henry Higgins would. Linguistic anthropologists sometimes call such Higgins-style an "elite-aspiring" pronunciation (such that the vowels in the sentence are pure vowels rather than dipthongs – see Appendix).

Oddly enough, although the conflicting dimensions that we have been exploring are another two forms of indexicality (referential and nonreferential), they appear to our ears and our minds as icons. Higgins' way of characterizing speech like Eliza's reflects his opinion of speakers like her: Higgins's insults pertain to Eliza's supposed lack of oral control. And that in turn pertains (iconically) to a lack of upper-middle-class moral control or self-discipline. It is this sort of perceived and projected iconicity to which we turn in Chapter 9, where we discuss "iconization." For now, we explore **semiotic ideologies** of the sort that surely undergirded Henry Higgins' attitudes toward Eliza's original sociolect and his goal of getting her to substitute a sociolect more like his for that old way of speaking.

Metasemiotics: Semiotic Ideologies, Pragmatic Metaphors

Semiotics, as you know by now, encompasses the breadth of communication and signs, even transcending the human. A semiotic ideology, however, is uniquely human and, in fact, very socioculturally particular. Ideas about not only language but the way the body produces language are common to most sociocultural groups around the world. The same can be said of "pragmatic metaphors" in which, for example, "wrong" semantic markers of "number" often carry an "entailed" or "creative" social indexical (i.e. "pragmatic") act of making "the addressee count for more than one social individual" (Bourdieu 1991:86.)

Ideas of body and language often have a central role in how we imagine communicative forms (i.e., forms of semiotic activity) and communicators (groups of social actors). Groups of social actors are valued or devalued to the extent that their communicative practices are valued or devalued. Not surprisingly, the part of the body that is most salient in semiotic ideologies is the mouth. People who "have class" and those who "lack class," for example, may be defined vis-à-vis ideas of how they use their mouths.

Mouth

Language is a "technique of the body" (Mauss 1973). Linguistic, especially phonetic, competence is a bodily technique in which one's whole relation to the social world, and one's whole socially informed relation to the world, are expressed.

> [The way the mouth is used in speech] is an element in an *overall way of using the mouth* (in talking but also in eating, drinking, laughing, etc.) and therefore a component of the bodily *hexis* [class-linked ways of using the body] . . . Thus, in the case of the lower classes articulatory **style** is quite clearly part of a relation to the body that is dominated by the refusal of "airs and graces" (i.e., the refusal of stylization and the imposition of form) and by the valorization of virility – one aspect of a more general disposition to appreciate what is "natural." (Bourdieu 1991:86)

TABLE 8.2 Two mouths in French. (Adapted from Bourdieu 1977:661)

Expressions containing *la bouche*	Expressions containing *la gueule*
faire la petite bouche [pick and choose]	*'s'en mettre plein la gueule,'* [stuffing oneself with food and drink]
faire la bouche fine [be fastidious]	*casser la gueule* [smash]
bouche en coeur [simper]	*fort en gueule* [loud-mouthed]

Could it be that different populations, different social groups, have *different mouths*? It's highly unlikely. And yet, at least in French, it is possible to speak of human voices using two distinct, highly value-laden, words – *la bouche* and *la geuele*. Pierre Bourdieu considered the two French words to neatly represent two lifestyles, two ways of being in the world, two ways of using the body, and of course the mouth in particular. His evidence was a set of idiomatic expressions containing the two contrastive words.

> The opposition between the working class relation to language and the bourgeois relation is crystallized with particularly clarity in various French idioms which make use of one or the other of two words for the mouth: *la bouche*, feminine, dainty, distinguished, and *la gueule*, which is typically masculine insofar as it is often used to sum up the whole male body. (Bourdieu 1977:661)

Table 8.2 helps us see at a glance the differing values associated with *la bouche* and *la gueule*. "From the standpoint of the dominated classes, the values of culture and refinement appear as feminine, and identifying with the dominant class, in one's speech for example, entails accepting a way of using the body which is seen as effeminate ('putting on airs and graces,' 'la-di-da,...' (Bourdieu 1977:661).

Voice

The more specific the claim about gendered speech, the more likely it is to have some empirical underpinning. The average pitch level of human voices is a good place to start. Women's voices are higher pitched than men's, but the ranges overlap. Manipulations of "F0" (baseline vocal pitch) can serve purposes metaphorically designable as "voice" – "frantic voice," "enthusiastic voice," "sexy voice," voices that are ambiguous as to gender orientation (Corwin 2007).

A claim about a local case of gender and *voice* may be easier to substantiate than one about *language*, which is a much broader semiotic category. There is a rich literature treating "voice" as a metaphor whose meaning is akin to sociolect, or in other cases, register (Agha 2005; Bakhtin [1975] 1981, 1984a, 1984b, 1986; Kroskrity 1993; Tedlock 1983). Within this literature, Jane Hill's (1995b) work stands out for its refusal to distinguish between embodied vocal practices and metaphoric social "voice." Despite its value and relevance to themes I have taken up in this chapter, this important literature is not addressed here. Instead, I encourage you to review Chapters 2, 3, and 4.

CONCLUSION

The groundwork for this chapter was laid in Chapter 6, which explores linguistic diversity and its potential effects. In this chapter, we have examined *sociolinguistic* diversity, and we have demonstrated the utility of a semiotic approach to human communication, particularly in and through language.

With this chapter (Chapter 8), the book takes an important turn, fulfilling the promises I made at the start of the book – to treat language as a cultural resource and speaking as a form of social action (Duranti 1997:1–2).

The next chapter takes this theme a step further, exploring the benefits of processualizing the apparent "thingy" nouns commonly used to designate different sign-types (icon, index, and symbol), with a particular emphasis on the process of iconization.

SUMMARY

In this chapter, we examined how various functions of language influence and reinforce social structures and relationships. You should now be familiar with the following concepts:

- The distinction between presupposing and creative indexes, the latter exemplified in *Pygmalion/My Fair Lady*.
- The distinction between referential and nonreferential indexes.
- The two kinds of iconicity and the special role that diagrammatic iconicity plays in ritual.
- Symbolicity as the uniquely human sign mode, building on iconicity and indexicality.

QUESTIONS

1. Define "diagrammatic iconicity" and "imagistic iconicity." What is the difference?
2. What are the two "icons of intimacy" that Perrino says are crucial to the efficacy of a healing encounter between patient and *sérìñ*?
3. How do sets of words in Spanish, French, German, or Nepali that mean roughly the same as the English word "you" participate in the grammar of those languages (i.e., in a system that to some extent transcends context) and at the same time participate in language as a toolkit for performing actions in or upon a particular context?

EXERCISES

1. What I call "Homespeak" and "Schoolspeak" correspond to two words in Norwegian – *Ranamal* and *Bokmal* – described by Blom and Gumperz (1972). One of

these is associated with the scholarly life and other facets of life in Oslo, the national capital. Write a review of their article focusing on "metaphoric code-switching."

2. Look at the section in this chapter titled "The Emergent Structure of the Declaration of Independence," which describes the verb "publish" and its importance in the Declaration of Independence. Then look up "publish" in the *Oxford English Dictionary*, paying particular attention to older meanings. How does that historical context help explain how "publish" can serve as a synonym for "declare," and specifically as a "verb of speaking"? Describe in a nutshell what the OED entry tells you about the shift in the meaning of "publish."

3. The forerunners of "playback interviews" are many, including:

   • Schieffelin's involvement as a co-transcriber of participants in her recordings of caregiver–child interactions (1979).

   • Fred Erickson's sharing of videotapes with people he had recorded to get their reactions to the material (Erickson and Shultz 1982).

   • Briggs' (1996:211) use of two recorders to accomplish precisely what is meant by playback interviews in recent methodological writings – playing back one recording (e.g., a tape of a naturally occurring event) in order to make another (recording a consultant's comments on the first tape).

   Trace this history, and write a synthesis focusing on the evolution of methods in a social science like linguistic anthropology.

ADDITIONAL RESOURCES

Agha, Asif. 2007. *Language and Social Relations*. Cambridge University Press.

Agha's 2007 book deals very well with the complexities of registers and the ideologies that surround and undergird them.

Agha, Asif, and Frog, eds. 2015. *Registers of Communication*. Helsinki: Suomalaisen Kirjallisuuden Seura (Finnish Literature Society).

In a sense, this is a follow-up to Agha's 2007 book, with the advantage of presenting a broad range of on-the-ground examples of registers.

Bender, Margaret. 2012. Changing Sacred Registers in Cherokee in the 19th and Early 20th Centuries. In *Register: Intersections of Language, Context and Communication*. Frog and K. Koski, eds. Pp. 24–33. Helsinki: Folklore Studies, Department of Philosophy, History, Culture and Art Studies, University of Helsinki.

Bender's work on the semiotics of sacred Cherokee medicinal texts in the nineteenth and twentieth centuries is a fine example of the intersection of linguistic, semiotic, and medical anthropology.

9 Communicative Enactment and Transmission of Society and Culture

LEARNING OBJECTIVES

After reading this chapter, you should be able to do the following:

- State the similarities and differences between "speech communities" and "language communities" as "organizations of diversity."
- List the reasons linguistic anthropologists use terms like "languaging," "language socialization," and "iconization."
- Describe what distinguishes genres from registers.
- Explain what makes the anthropological use of the term "socialization" different from the popular use of the word.
- Describe the relationship of language, culture, and society in the context of language socialization.

Introduction

This chapter builds on the introduction to human social semiotics in Chapter 8. I now explore how indexical relationships come to appear as iconic. We then turn toward communicative forms in sociocultural context, addressing the following questions: What happens if we start an analysis of culture and communication using social "fractions," by which I mean parts of societies defined by demographic characteristics like gender and ethnicity? What happens, on the other hand, if we start such an analysis with activities and the settings for those activities, or with communicative forms, especially registers and genres?

Finally, I introduce "language socialization" as the process by which communicative forms are transmitted to novices (especially children), such that they learn to act – especially to engage in communicative activities – in ways that are appropriate to their society (and the "fraction" to which they belong) and its culture (rules and norms).

Iconization

By now, you are familiar with the terms **icon** and even **iconicity**. Here, however, I introduce a new concept – **iconization**.

From the Preface onward, we have considered the advantages of using words that remind us that human life – which is always social and cultural and which constantly involves communication – is filled with *processes* that we misunderstand as *things*. For instance, I have pointed to some disadvantages in using "language," which sounds like a thing, when "languaging" might be more accurate. More generally, I have advocated processual terms such as "discoursing" and "identification" in our discussions about communication.

To understand iconization, we must realize that it starts with indexes. In particular, its raw material is the indexical relationships between groups of people and speech patterns associated with them. Iconization treats those phenomena as iconic. Certain markers of sociolect – such as the use of "ain't" or the practice of dropping "r"s at the ends of words – are subject to critical awareness. Linguist William Labov dubbed these "sociolinguistic stereotypes" (1972). To the extent that there is a statistical association between "ain't" and speakers who belong to a certain **social address** (e.g., a socioeconomic class), the relationship is indexical. Likewise with r-dropping in American English, which might be statistically associated with speakers of the dialects spoken along the Atlantic seaboard.

Statistical associations are always contingent, never absolute. In fact, these speech patterns only *point* to the social group that we think of as using these specific patterns. They are not *bound as some sort of essence* to such a group. But iconization takes that pointer – that contingent, statistical, "maybe" sort of relationship or association between speech and speakers – and turns it into an icon. The speech becomes the *essence* of the group.

Judith Irvine and Susan Gal pioneered studies of iconization. They describe iconization as involving

> a transformation of the sign relationship between linguistic features (or varieties) and the social images with which they are linked. Linguistic features that index social groups or activities appear to be iconic representations of them, as if a linguistic feature somehow depicted or displayed a social group's inherent nature or essence. (Irvine and Gal 2000:37)

Iconization is pervasive in human linguistic communication, especially in metalanguage. I am speaking in particular about **language ideologies**, which are cultural notions of linguistic varieties and their speakers. To say these ideologies are pervasive is to say that speaking about others' language and our own is commonplace. However, what concerns us here is this: Not only is talk about language common, but reflections on others' languages commonly represent them as iconic of others' essences: "They" speak as "they" do because "they" are what "they" are – such are the iconizing foundations of language ideologies.

What would it be like to speak in some *other* way about language forms, ours and those of others? We might instead recognize that speech forms are unequally distributed in a community and thus belong "more or less" – *not* absolutely – to

Figure 9.1 The multilingual welcome sign on a Scottish pub is an icon of local and global social diversity. (Lonely Planet/Getty Images)

individuals and subgroups. (See Figure 9.1.) Thus, it would make little sense to speak about any whole group having a particular essence. We might also reflect out loud, in speaking about our speech and that of others, that we speak differently *in different situations* – again throwing general and essentializing representations into doubt. (Essentializing representations of culture treat it as an "essence" distributed equally among all members of a society.)

Table 9.1 provides a systematic, step-by-step description of the process of iconization, from the initial existence of some indexical pattern to its final transformation into an icon.

As Irvine and Gal (2000) make clear, iconization is very real and concrete – and seems always to be destructive. In particular, they show what a destructive role iconization has played as an instrument of imperialism.

> [Languages using clicks] have drawn the attention of many visitors and newcomers to southern Africa over the centuries. Many early European observers compared them with animal noises (Kolben 1731:32, as cited by Irvine and Gal 2000:40). To these observers and the European readers of their reports, such iconic comparisons suggested that the speakers of languages with clicks were in

	Interpretation of indexical pattern	Type of interpretation
TABLE 9.1 Interpretation of indexical pattern		
1.	Social group A may be statistically more likely than B to use linguistic variety X.	*a sociolinguistic "fact"*
2.	Thus X is a loose index of A.	*an interpretation of this "fact" as an index*
3.	But B makes X an icon of A.	*the process of iconization*
4.	That is, B claims that X reflects the very essence of A.	*other-iconizing*
5.	Or A claims that Y reflects the essence of A.	*self-iconizing*

some way subhuman or degraded, to a degree corresponding to the proportion of clicks in their consonant repertoires. (Irvine and Gal 2000:40)

Having outlined how the process of iconization simplifies the complex relationship between groups of people and their ways of speaking – with the risk of this being a destructive process – we now examine related semiotic **functions** of communicative activities.

Performing Social Variation: Communicative Patterns as Indexes

Let me start by acknowledging that the following section, introducing technical terms for how we perform social variation (**sociolects** including **dialects**, **registers**, and **genres**), is challenging. Yet understanding these terms and their uses can help us recognize and evaluate some of the biases and misconceptions that affect us as individuals and groups.

In this section, we distinguish ways of speaking from stereotypes (i.e., speakers' models of others' speech) that appear to cultural insiders to truly capture social characteristics like gender (e.g., male or having masculinity [Butler 2013]), class (e.g., working class [Bourdieu 1977]), or place of origin (e.g., New England, northeastern United States) – yet we then stitch speech forms and models of those forms back together in describing sociolects. (By the way, linguist Samuel Levin apparently coined the term "sociolect" in the context of asserting the legitimacy of Southern speech, purportedly including "the Negro dialect" [Lane 1967:1; Levin 1965:116–117].)

In the section after that, we contrast "genres" – popularly named communicative activities, things we do with words and other signs (e.g., prayer) – with "registers," which are usually described as the words and other signs we use to perform genres or the various signs that people in a certain role have mastered because they are masters of that role. For instance, think of experts in social etiquette whose behavior – ways of holding the **body** or bowing (Mauss 1973), along with specific speech behavior (Errington 1988; Poedjosoedarmo 1968) – is regarded as the epitome of politeness. Or consider health practitioners whose specialist status is confirmed by using certain tools of the trade like a stethoscope and a set of technical terms and even grammatical forms (Wilce 2008) that define what scholars of medical communication call "medicalese" – a term whose academic use goes back to at least Waife (1958).

Starting with Social Fractions: Sociolectal Variation

When trying to describe speech varieties, we begin with **social fractions** – any division within a community, such as gender, class, age – and describe ways of speaking associated with it. The term "social fractions" has, by the way, been used at least since Bataille (1979).

Variation Contained: Communities Defined vis-à-vis Linguistic Variation

From the outset, this book has not only contemplated diversity but embraced it. After all, anthropology can be defined as the study of human diversity – from our origins until now, and from "here" (wherever "here" is for you) to "there" (again, the demonstrative has meaning only in a context, and your location can be the context). In fact, I have argued that – whatever it might mean (and we have seen how hard it is to define) – "culture" is not a population, let alone one that is homogeneous, but rather an "organization of diversity" (Wallace 1952).

"Speech communities" are good examples of these "organizations of diversity" – communities defined by how they encompass, embrace, and to some degree follow norms. In relation to speech communities, these "norms" can include the use of multiple semiotic forms, especially linguistic varieties – multiple "dialects," "sociolects," "registers," or "languages." (Keep in mind that none of the words in quotes are concrete objects stable enough to be put under our microscope as "things.") To belong to, or participate in, a speech community is to have some command of these multiple forms or practices. It was precisely the conviction that linguistic diversity in communities could be studied scientifically that led to the emergence of sociolinguistics. Linguistic anthropologists certainly share that conviction.

Scholars of language and society have distinguished these speech communities from "language communities," starting in the 1960s (Crissman 1967; Fischer 1961; Kloss 1966) until now (Silverstein 2015). In fact, Silverstein (1996:129) wrote:

> Communities must be differentiated according to the type of linguistic phenomena we are investigating. [A] *speech community* [is] based on . . . "rules of use" in short – of who, normatively, communicates in which ways to whom on what occasions, [while the term] *language community*, [is] definable for a population manifesting regularity of usage based on allegiance to norms of denotational code [a particular language].

Silverstein goes on to provide an example (1996:129):

> [T]he kind of bilingual individual in question is a member of two language communities; perhaps there is a single speech community in which the two languages involved bear a regular "register" relationship . . .

In the first quotation from Silverstein's (1996) article, he provides a very standard definition of a speech community – a multilingual group with norms governing how, when, and with whom people speak what linguistic variety. To his definition of a speech community – already a complex notion – Silverstein then adds the concept of "register." What does that addition do? What does it signify?

We live in an era of "globalization," and in a Eurocentric way, we think of ourselves as though (flipping Bruno Latour's [1993] title) "we [Euro-Americans?] *had always* been modern." At least more modern than the Other. Notice that I opened this paragraph by invoking "*an* era of globalization" – not *the* era. Globalizing processes have always been with "us," and that "us" is far more encompassing than it appears from a Eurocentric perspective.

The early nineteenth century, in which the British were cementing their reign (the Raj) over India, represents one previous era of globalization. The British inherited a situation in which Indian elites were bilingual in, say, Bangla, used for most purposes (Cohn 1985:296); and Persian (used in the royal court, 1985:277). However, the British soon helped establish "Hindustani" (now known as Urdu) as "the language of command" (1985:276–329).

Here was one speech community that, like others, involved norms of fluency in, and appropriate – and stratified – uses of, registers. These registers, in the context of speech communities, have been recognized and called such by, for example, Irvine (1990), vis-à-vis noble speech and griot speech – not two distinct "languages" (if there be such things) but two ideologically loaded forms of Wolof.

Linguistic anthropologist Susan Gal defines the distinction between speech communities and language communities *in Europe*:

> Migrant and diasporic populations in Europe are part of European speech communities in that they interact with speakers of languages and linguistic varieties spoken in Europe and can decipher the indexical signals provided by many kinds of multilingual and multi-varietal speakers. But their sense of linguistic correctness, their orientation to a [language] . . . and its literary norms, also links them to other regions where there are speakers of the named languages they use. Often they are linked to more than one such centre of linguistic norms located outside of Europe, for instance to language communities consisting of Hindi, Urdu, Indonesian, Turkish or Yoruba speakers. (2006:172)

As we move on, please keep in mind the discussion of these two forms of diversity, "contained" within and serving to actively define communities. It is an example of inverting our commonsense understanding of language – as though language differences merely reflected sociocultural differences. Here communicative practices do far more than passively reflecting pre-existing forms of social stratification, or pre-existing "identities." True, norms governing diverse ways of speaking play a clearer and more explicit role in defining "speech communities" than "language communities." This is a reflection of the fact that we more easily sense that we are speaking of an activity when we invoke the word "speech" than we invoke the concept of "language." The truth here is that it is useful to recognize the already-objectified or reified notion of "language(s)" used in scholars' discourse about language communities. In fact, as Gal mentions, popular discourse on "languages" also objectifies them. Not only scholars, but most members of language communities, think about them as fixed, stable, solid, named, and geographically centered in particular places.

The processual reality behind the ideologically constituted popular idea of "our language" is clear in these two passages from the article by Gal cited earlier, with which I close this section of the chapter:

> We must conceptualise publics as reliant on inter-discursive links across occasions of talk, and often across languages. (2006:166)

> Indirect links among certain European populations exist by virtue of the fact that they orient to the same centres of (non-European) linguistic correctness: Moslem populations from Turkey who live in Belgium and Germany, for instance, rely on the importation of Turkish teachers and clerics. North African Moslems resident in Paris or Berlin are connected to Bosnians, as well as to practising Moslems elsewhere in the world, through Koranic schools and their associated Arabic linguistic rituals. (2006:172)

You will encounter these concepts in more detail in Chapter 11.

Language, Communication, and Gender

Social scientists have typically treated gender as one box, class as another, and so on. It is important, however, to recognize their interplay. Do "women" and "men" speak differently? (See Figure 9.2.) And why would the words "women" and "men" be in quote marks? If we can presume the reality of anything, surely it would be the biological difference between women and men, right? Wrong, perhaps. Framing the question thus – Do women speak differently than men? – stifles other questions, such as how different might the speech of different groups of men in a particular society be. It stifles the kinds of questions anthropologists love to ask: Are ideas about gender, gendered practices in general, and gendered speech practices, *universal*? Or are all of these simply *variables* when we look at them cross-culturally (Eckert and McConnell-Ginet 2003)?

Asking whether women's speech differs from men's also ignores the question of language ideologies. People in fact do universally embrace, and at least sometimes talk about, ideas about languages (or *forms of language*) and the people associated with them. Such concepts of language *reflect and perpetuate social categories and thus*

Figure 9.2 Do women and men communicate differently? (leungchopan/Shutterstock)

social hierarchies. The idea that "women speak in one way, and men speak in another" is already an ideology. Its status as an ideology becomes even clearer when differing value is associated with this or that way of speaking. Oddly – or perhaps not so – we find that every society tends to have its own characterization of gendered speech, such as "women are polite" or "women are verbally aggressive," yet societies embracing the former may, in fact, value assertiveness over politeness, while societies embracing the latter might value politeness most highly. What is going on here? It seems that valued speech patterns – regardless of what those are – tend to be associated with men, while stigmatized patterns are associated with women (Eckert and McConnell-Ginet 1992; Keenan 1974).

Do such ideologies apply to all men in any given society, or to all women? Isn't there something "real" underlying these ideologies of language and gender? That is, aren't there "really" empirical differences in language varieties that are regarded as "gendered"? What we *do* know is that women and men in the same society may have very different ideologies of language and gender. In Javanese (Indonesian) society, for example, men and women might agree that women are more polite to men than men are to women, yet they are likely to differ as to why or what it means: Smith-Hefner (1988) finds that Javanese women interpret their own greater politeness as a sign of greater refinement, while men consider women's deference to them as men's just deserts.

There are some exceptions, such as relatively egalitarian societies like the Kuna of Panama (Sherzer 1987). And besides the huge variation across societies, it is also true that within societies there is often a large gap between empirical differences in gendered speech and the language ideologies that accompany them. And yet, it is probably safe to say that women's speech in every society reflects, at least to some extent, their relative vulnerability vis-à-vis men.

Class

This section encourages you to think of social fractions first and then to ask how linguistic varieties are connected to them. Labov's work fits very well into this category. The studies that best exemplify those that start with social class and then ask how "sociolinguistic variables" are distributed across class lines are Labov's experiments in New York City. Labov (1972) discovered in the 1960s that New Yorkers shared a common (albeit new, since the end of World War II) attitude toward pronunciation variables like the /r/ in words like "floor." He found that New Yorkers stigmatized r-dropping. This means that New Yorkers shared with outsiders some disdain for their own speech. And among New Yorkers, the lower middle classes were most likely to regard their own speech patterns as incorrect. In New York City, and possibly other East Coast speech communities, so-called "r-less" sociolects of English may still be stigmatizing. In the words of Pierre Bourdieu, speakers of such a sociolect lack "social capital" (1991). The stakes involve power and prestige, on the one hand, and *shame* – not as a private feeling, but as an experience of "the loss of a social bond" (Scheff 2000) – on the other. Dominant language ideologies represent speaking or speech behavior as a matter of taste, or even having or lacking "culcha" (OED Online 2016). This pronunciation does not index the anthropologist's concept of "culture." Rather, it reminds us of the German concept of *Kultur*. And New Yorkers may well answer questions about someone's level of "culcha" by mentioning class-linked pronunciation variables.

What Labov's argument overlooks, however, is that ways of speech do not merely reflect but also help *constitute* class. One cannot conceive of class in Labov's New York City, or in London, apart from an array of signs including linguistic signs. Moreover, working-class New Yorkers do not pay large sums of money for lessons in "accent reduction" (Lippi-Green 1997) for nothing. They strongly believe, as did Professor Henry Higgins in the musical film *My Fair Lady*, that one can improve one's class status by "improving" one's speech.

Nationality

Myths about "culture" and "communication" in relation to specific nationalities are also common. Non-Italians who speak of Italians, for example, as "a culture" (rather than as a society or nationality) may invoke the supposed Italian predilection for using ample **gestures** while speaking. They might even translate that into a judgment about Italians' "emotionality." Some nationalities and national languages have come to be associated with emotion (French? Italian?) and others with cool rationality (German? English?). What is clear is that we are dealing here with ideologies. What is unclear is their factual basis. But the latter seldom matters to the former.

Race and Ethnicity

Anthropologists have collected a great deal of evidence demonstrating that "race" is not a biological reality. In fact, there is more biological (especially genetic) diversity *within* so-called races than there is between them. Nonetheless, you and I probably embrace "race" as a reality (consciously or not), rather than as a social construct.

We also tend to have a poor understanding of ethnicity – what it is and what it is not. Because we tend to (mis)use the word "culture" to denote a population, we are likely to have little room in our minds for "ethnic groups."

And yet, amid this confusion, race and ethnicity are constructs that can be played with. Rampton has described interethnic adolescent peer groups in London whose members play with each other's languages. A working-class white boy in such a group may imitate his Anglo-Jamaican friend's English dialect in order to intimidate a teacher (Rampton 1995). Likewise in the United States, a Korean-American university student may infuse his mostly "Mainstream American English" with **lexical** bits from "African American Vernacular English" in the process of "actively [defying] dominant characterizations of Asian men as nonmasculine and passive" (Chun 2001:61). (See Figure 9.3.) Such playing with difference could help

Figure 9.3 Stereotypes of Asian men do not fit well with individuals' identities. (mmac72/Getty Images).

undermine or at least blur old ethnic boundaries and construct "new ethnicities" founded on the embrace of difference and diversity – resisting the old and inventing a new "cultural politics" (Rampton 1995, citing Hall 1988).

As the previous sections show, sociolects – patterns of communication that are popularly believed to characterize social groups – serve as indexes of those groups while also reinforcing dominant ideologies of language. Moving forward, we examine the social implications of other indexical forms and patterns of communication.

Communicative Forms, Cultural Activities, and Social Situations

In the previous section, we explored what happens when researchers start with a concept of a social fraction, and then link such fractions to communicative forms. In this section, we start with communicative forms and explore how they constitute social fractions, making them appear real.

Here we consider genres and registers, contrasting them with sociolects. As our first case study, we take up Irvine's analysis of Senegalese (West African) Wolof speech associated with griots and nobles. She uses her ethnographic case study of these speech forms to illumine the difference between registers and sociolects. Then we turn our attention to my work in Finland and that of Michelle Rosaldo in the Philippines – to understand the role of direct and indirect speech in conveying deference and indexing social organization.

Sociolects versus Registers: Wolof Griot Speech and Noble Speech

We focus here on two sorts of affective (emotional or unemotional) registers (Irvine 1990; 1998). Irvine makes a strong case for considering these two speech varieties to be registers, not sociolects. Registers are associated with a *practice* (and indirectly with a group), whereas sociolects or social dialects are associated more stably with a social (i.e., demographic) fraction. Irvine's ethnographic work in Senegal focuses on the emotional speech of Wolof griots. Here "griot" denotes a group of praise-singers and storytellers descended from slaves. In the Senegalese caste system, griots contrast with the "nobles," descendants of local slave owners. "Nobles" often hire griots to speak emotionally on their behalf. Yet, as Irvine demonstrates, the affect-laden **speech variety** (or "performance form") is *not a sociolect* restricted to griots. Rather, such speech constitutes a *register* available to nobles too (Irvine 1990). In fact, anyone who engages in *praise* or thanks must use the so-called griot speech (register).

Let me explain a bit about griot and noble speech – called *waxu gewel* and *waxu géér*, respectively. Griots are bards, known for praise-singing and other forms of highly emotional expression – though it is not simple "self-expression," since griots are understood to be performing *someone else's* feelings. Griots' highly emotional speech style contributes to ranking them below nobles.

The relationship between these two social fractions and the semiotic forms that Wolof people associate with them has far more than local relevance. In the skilled hands of Judith Irvine, it becomes a brilliant example of language and "the political economy." The political economy is the system determining control over power and wealth. In her classic 1989 article, "When Talk Isn't Cheap: Language and Political Economy," Irvine argues that language is not just a tool for *thinking* or *talking about* economic exchanges. Rather, linguistic signs and acts of speaking actually enter into local economies. Crucial to this argument is her construal of griot and noble speech as two very different forms of verbal *labor*. The "praise speech" nobles pay griots to produce as expressions of *the nobles' feelings* is a form of what sociologist Arlie Hochschild (1979:569) has called *emotion work*, defining it as labor in which "feelings are **commoditized**." Besides this speech, griots do other forms of hard physical labor. And though you might not think of bardic labor as demanding, the physical energy with which griots perform emotion is an icon of their status as descendants of slaves who still perform hard labor. Their patrons sit quietly, impassively, and listen (Irvine 1989:258–260) as their emotions are performed.

Stillness is an icon or index not only of the nobles' status as those who do not *need* to do physical labor – those for whom *others* work hard. It is also iconic of the nobles' essence. Irvine explains that

> Wolof nobles rationalize their claim to superiority over lower ranks in terms of sangfroid and restraint; perhaps more surprisingly, nobles and griots actually *agree* that nobles' restraint and griots' energy reflects what they "are made of," so to speak. Nobles are stable because they are of the earth. They lack the dangerous, passionate dynamism of griots, for of the four constitutive elements – earth, air, fire, and water – the stable earth predominates in them. (Wilce 2009b:102–103, citing Irvine 1990:133 and 153)

This is a local model of iconicity, a metasemiotic model: Wolof villagers understand each others' speech, **embodied** performance, and habitual levels of emotionality to be the very image (sonic and visual) of constitutional differences.

The following section, on direct and indirect speech, might seem a sudden departure from our focus on communicative forms that constitute social fractions. It is not. My exploration of indirect speech is, rather, a continuation of my description of griot performance. What could be more indirect than performing someone else's emotions?

Direct versus Indirect Speech

One of the most fascinating discoveries made by linguistic anthropologists and **ethnographers** of communication is the variation in the extent to which different societies value so-called direct or indirect communication and in what circumstances. There has been controversy in my tribe – linguistic anthropologists – as to whether indirection is a universal sign of politeness. Still more heated is our debate over whether indirection is universally a reflection of power differential plus social distance on the one hand and intimacy on the other (Brown and Levinson 1987).

Brenneis (1987) argues that a history of plantation agriculture is the matrix out of which at least some of the pervasive practices of indirection arise. Brenneis asserts that indirection is actually four distinct phenomena, or four dimensions within which communication can be situated as relatively direct or indirect. The first involves *what is said* and *how* – obscuring meaning through the use of metaphor, aphorism, or even a sudden collapse of one's normal vocabulary by a factor of ten, so that if one word in normal speech denotes one thing, a word in altered speech can denote ten. For a fascinating example of this collapse – a register shift that signals the presence of "in-laws" among the Australian Indigenous speech community called Dyirbal – see the work of Dixon (1972) and Silverstein's later interpretation of it ([1981] 2001).

Brenneis's second type of indirection, centered around "voice," appears in the everyday practice of quoting others' speech and in ritual events such as trance-possession: *Who is actually speaking* becomes unclear (e.g., Wilce 1998:54–57).

His third form of indirectness renders the question of *intended recipient or audience* unclear. In singing funeral laments – wailing songs apparently for the dead – in Karelia, one could not use the personal name or kin term of the deceased, and a one-word kin term like "mother" was traditionally replaced by a longer phrase or "circumlocution" (E. Stepanova 2012). Although "you who bore me/brought me into this world" obviously indicates one's mother, some of the substitutions were mysterious to the majority of villagers who were not experts in the "lament language" (E. Stepanova 2012:257).

In *event-centered* indirection, Brenneis's fourth form, one event masks another underlying event. Outsiders might think Karelian wailing, led by an expert lamenter (see Figure 9.4), was all about personal grief, when in fact lamenting was locally understood to honor distant ancestors and lesser deities and to form a kind of path that the recently deceased soul could follow into the realm of those beings (Honko 1974; E. Stepanova 2012; Tolbert 1988). Additionally, events of ironic speech, declarations of false praise or respect, and various forms of humor all appear to be one thing while in fact being another (Bakhtin [1975] 1981, 1984a, 1984b).

We are now seeing a global trend to replace elaborate traditions of indirection with straightforward communication. I relate this point by summarizing a relevant and well-known 1973 article by Michelle Rosaldo. She and her work are worth citing here not only for their direct relevance to the discussion in this section but more generally for several reasons. Her death in 1981 following an accidental fall in the mountains of Luzon, Philippines – home of the Ilongot people – was a blow to anthropology because it cut short the life and career of one of the most promising ethnographers of the 1970s. Rosaldo was just 37 when she died. She contributed in

Figure 9.4 Karelian "cry women" were professional lamenters who performed important functions, particularly at funerals. (Photo by Väinö Kaukonen, Finno-Ugric picture collection, The National Board of Antiquities, Finland. [SUK475:249])

important ways to linguistic anthropology – especially through her posthumously published (Rosaldo 1982) critique of John Searle's (1969) "intentionalist" approach to "speech acts." (By "intentionalism" I mean the idea that the meaning of utterances proceeds from the speaker's intentions, mind, thoughts, etc. – i.e., the dominant view in Western societies and their cultural systems.) Note, too, that the 1973 Rosaldo article summarized below was published in *Language in Society*, an important journal in linguistic anthropology, sociolinguistics, and related fields. Although it is ironic that Searle and Rosaldo shared an interest in discursive "indirection" or "indirect speech," we who study culture and communication appreciate Michelle Rosaldo's fine ethnographic ear and theoretical sophistication.

Finally, the death of Michelle Rosaldo is important to anthropology insofar as it elicited a moving and classic essay by her bereaved husband, Renato Rosaldo. The essay is famous as an exemplar of postmodern anthropology, given how "self-reflexive" it is vis-à-vis the meaning of grief for the author (Renato Rosaldo) and the people whom he and Michelle studied – the Ilongot (Rosaldo 1984).

Even in 1973 when Michelle Rosaldo's well-known article was published, change was coming to the Ilongot people. The transformation was making its way up from the lowlands, where Christian missionization had made great inroads, to the more traditional highlands. In recent centuries in Europe, dominant language ideologies embraced the idea of direct unflowery speech, even locating it at the heart of a democratic social order (Bauman and Briggs 2003). By contrast, when newly introduced to the Ilongot people, such direct speech had very different associations. Straight speech indexed a new militaristic and hierarchical social organization, as Rosaldo (1973:195) explains:

> Allusive styles ... may be used by individuals to disguise their private interests, but they also may emerge in a social order based more on persuasion than compulsion, a world in which the complexity of individual intentions is recognized as more important than any simple set of privileges or rules. So, for the Ilongots, "crooked" speech has been linked to an egalitarian ethos; and the new "straight" or direct kind of oratory is associated ... with Christianity but [also] with a radical shift in people's conceptions of the nature of human relationships, and a new, and increasingly authoritarian idea of social life.

Elsewhere in the article cited above, Rosaldo expands on what she calls an "increasingly authoritarian idea of social life." The settlement and **social structure** of the newly Christianized Ilongot differs radically from traditional social structure. Each *barrio* or village had a "captain," and every captain had "his men" (1973:195).

The preceding section sheds light on some of the ways that social organization is constituted in and through language. In it, we explore the social functions of register and how they can reflect and reinforce differences between groups of people. Moving on, we consider similar implications for another category useful in the ethnographic description of sociolinguistic variety – the genre. In thus moving on, we shift our attention from the relationship(s) between speech varieties and social fractions (producer, key *participants*) to the link between communicative forms and *forms of participation*.

Communicative Genres: Cultural Activities and Participant Structures

Genres are communicative activities. People often recognize these activities, giving them a genre label – emailing, praying, storytelling, lamenting, "talking smack," or "hurled speech." As activities, genres have typical ways of organizing participation. That is, they have a defined set of actors or roles and widely accepted models of how each actor participates.

To help us transcend our tendency to think of genres only as "thing-y" communication types, in the way our English teachers talked about them (as categories such as written prose or poetry), it is helpful to consider some examples in which the themes of activity and participation are too obvious to ignore.

The first examples are culturally close to home – slapstick comedy and protests. What does slapstick involve? Generally, a couple of men, some conversation between them, and physical activities like a pratfall (Craine 2013). Protests are political activities that involve marching and the shouting of calls like "The people united shall never be defeated!" Genres, then, involve stereotyped actions and participant structures – pairs of men co-performing comedy, crowds of people united in producing chants (Bucholtz 2011).

Moving farther from at least my home, we look at wedding poetry in Yemen to help us understand genres as categories of activity, with some of that activity being linguistic and some involving bodily posture and so on. Yemeni tribal wedding poetry (*bālah*) involves men only, and men dancing. There is literally an inner circle of men dancing and improvising lines of poetry that must fit with the lines produced by one's predecessor. In order to participate in this genre of improvisatory poetry, a man – say, a young man – must "break through into performance," both figuratively and literally. Dell Hymes, who coined the phrase ([1975] 1981), used it figuratively; he spoke of a "breakthrough" as in a shift in style, a shift from mere recital to full-on performance. (Here performance is defined as action in the presence of and with accountability to an audience for *how* the performer communicates, rather than just for *what* is being said.)

I understand this as a literal breakthrough as well. In Yemen, being a good adult Muslim means being a good tribesman, which means being judged as a dancer, a poet, and a rifleman. One moment of "trial" for a young Yemeni man is the moment at which he inserts himself into the inner circle and produces a poetic couplet or two. The literal breaking into the center of wedding poetry performance might here become a figurative breakthrough into adulthood.

Clearly, understanding linguistic genres in the performance context can involve layer upon layer of different communicative forms or modalities. Gaining such understanding takes linguistic anthropologists like Steve Caton a long time (2006) – he's had many years of engagement with Yemeni tribesmen. But once we understand that linguistic anthropologists strive for this sort of understanding as an ethnographic gold standard, we can identify with his investment.

Linguistic anthropologist William Hanks illustrates genres – even discourse genres – as forms of socially meaningful and often physical as well as verbal activity. This he illustrates with the Mayan discourse genre known as "hurled speech." Performing this genre requires three women, two within a walled domestic compound and a third woman who happens to pass by on her way to the market. That third woman will be dressed up, thus fulfilling a local stereotype that only adulterers dress up to go to market. The two women inside the domestic compound are more verbally active than the third. The genre/act that they perform requires a fine sense of spatial awareness and of timing. They – Woman A, the "instigator" or "thrower," and Woman B, the "pivot" or faux addressee – must also align their bodies just right in relation to Woman C, the "target" or passerby. Women A and B must then produce the speech of innuendo that their roles assign to them at just the right moment so the passerby will hear. This genre entails a "discrepancy between speech physically directed to one party [i.e., by the direction of the thrower's gaze] but intended for another." Hanks further explains that "A addresses B with words really intended for C, and B play-acts C, responding as she thinks C would respond if A's innuendos were correct" (1996:260). "The genre requires the collusion of the pivot in order to achieve completeness … a joint production" (1996:263).

> The same kind of attack would be unthinkable were the target a Maya man, since none of these dominant values apply, and indeed any man who would stand leaning on his wall talking with a neighbor while watching the street would himself be vulnerable to criticism. The entire relationship to lived space is different for me and therefore gendered in a strong sense. (Hanks 1996:263)

Distinguishing Genre, Register, and Sociolect

The term "dialect" is more familiar to many people than "sociolect." Yet you know by now that sociolects are ways of speaking that point to what Eckert and McConnell-Ginet (1992) call a speaker's **social address** (i.e., where they can be "located" in relationship to variables like gender, class, and ethnicity). According to Agha (2007:135), a dialect is a special case of sociolect that is understood to indicate only the speaker's geographic origin or "extended residence, and the like."

It is my conviction that there are probably no direct associations between ways of speaking and types of "social address" – a term that is, for our purposes, synonymous with social fraction. Rather, the relationships between social and linguistic forms of variation *seem* real only because they have the weight of culture behind them. These apparent relationships are cultural understandings of speech and speakers. As cultural understandings or models, their truth seems completely persuasive. People rarely question the origin and function of such models.

Sociolects tend to color the speech and gesture of social actors all the time, or so it is commonly assumed. This sets sociolects apart from genre and register, which characterize an individual's communication more narrowly (i.e., when that individual is participating in a certain activity or performing as a certain persona). I may speak in a working-class version of a New York City *sociolect* pretty much all of the time, based on where, when, and how I grew up. But most people use their professional *registers* only at work rather than with their children or partners. (On the other hand, I know of two students who complained about a teacher who purportedly "always speaks like a teacher," by which they meant in a condescending way.)

As another example, even if I speak in a particular sociolect, I also engage in various speech activities with their own structures of expectation and participation. In tucking my 5-year-old into bed at night, I might tell him one of the folktales collected by the brothers Grimm, from memory, starting with "Once upon a time …" Or I might read one of Kipling's "Just So" stories, starting with "Once upon a time, oh my Best Beloved"). In doing so, I cue my son that what I am about to perform may include the voices of talking animals.

Genres and Registers Intertwining: A Historical Example

How does a register come into being? Let us consider the development of "medicalese" – a register of English discourse from eighteenth-century Scotland. (It is interesting to note that similar events of "enregisterment," meaning the "birth" and circulation of registers – related in this case to English medicalese – occurred in France and Germany around the same time.) Crucially, this rather unified way of writing (even more than speaking) – this medicalese – emerged via several important genres. We can assign priority to the clinical chart note, since other genres were at least purportedly derived from these ostensibly empirical written records of interaction with particular patients. Among these other genres were:

- the case history, which Freud later turned into an art, fusing fictional-narrative and scientific features (Berkenkotter 2008; Freud 2003);
- the scientific article, especially those published in the *Edinburgh Medical Journal* (Atkinson 1992);
- the medical textbook and the medical atlas (Wilce 2008:93–94 and 2009c: 203)

Genre as a linguistic category conveys norms of participation and inclusion within an activity. Unlike "speech events" or speech event types,

> it is of the very nature of genre to be recognizable outside of such primary contexts. Thus a curing chant may be performed in another context for entertainment, for the pleasure afforded by the chanter's display of virtuosity, or in still another as pedagogical demonstration in the instruction of a novice curer. (Bauman 1999:84)

It is crucial to recognize another defining feature of genres – they orient the audiences (or "publics") that they help create to receive the work (visual art, verbal art, etc.) in a certain, culturally approved, way (Bauman 1999:84; Marsilli-Vargas 2014:44). They are thus classical framing devices, illustrated in Figures 3.1a, 3.1b, and 5.3, all of which show us how *framing is metacommunicating* (Bateson 1972:177–193).

Several genres may be "used" to constitute a register. Registers form at the intersection of patterns of linguistic usage and patterns of ideology. Ideologically, they are believed to iconically index social distinctions and ways of communicating between speakers regarded as appropriate. These phenomena, along with sociolects and their associated ideologies, are conveyed through social actors in order to socialize new members of a group.

How All of the Above Is Transmitted: Language Socialization

We commonly use the word "socializing" to mean talking, gabbing, chatting, and so on. Social scientists reserve the term for a very different use – transmitting culture, passing on the skills needed to participate in a community, bringing up a child to know how to act properly in the range of contexts in which he or she can expect to participate. "To socialize" in the technical sense is a transitive verb, whereas the verbs talk, gab, and chat are intransitive. Therefore, using "socialize" in its technical sense, we socialize *someone*, and as a result he or she is "socialized" – just as feeding, kissing, or dressing a baby results in the baby being fed, kissed, dressed. We don't "gab (or talk, or gossip) someone," nor does gabbing result in someone "being gabbed." As Duranti (1997:59) points out, "We cannot use intransitive verbs in passive sentences."

Socialization is thus the transmission of the *theoretical* (ideas/ideologies) and *practical knowledge* (skills) necessary to being a competent participant in a society.

What then is *"language* socialization"? Among the most important skills transmitted from experts to novices are communicative skills. We call the transmission of communicative and particularly linguistic skills "language socialization."

Language socialization is the term that Ochs and Schieffelin codified, in a series of important works, within linguistic anthropology to denote a crucial dimension of the process of socializing novices – *passing on (transmitting, teaching) and picking up (learning) how to use language appropriately in a given community*. The notion of language socialization that Schieffelin and Ochs developed "concerns *two major areas of socialization: socialization through the use of language and socialization to use language*" (1986:163, emphasis added).

We teach novices to talk in certain ways – picture young children just learning the language – or languages! – spoken at home and in other settings to which they are exposed. Or imagine new members of a religious group who must learn to pray or "testify" in a particular way.

Allowing your imagination to zoom in a bit, picture a little boy in his first year or two of life being surrounded by talkative adults and children. Beginning in babyhood and extending through later childhood, this boy hears and observes thousands of hours of interaction. He sees how gifts are given and hears what is said along with the giving. He hears how verbal discipline is administered, how prayer (or argument, etc.) is conducted. He sees how his community acts and hears (if his community uses oral, as opposed to sign, language), what they do with speech in particular. All of this means that the little boy you are imagining is immersed in *culture*. (See Figure 9.5.) He is expected to learn cultural lessons through all of the events we have been imagining. In prayer, argument, and dozens of other activities, people enact cultural meaning(s) in and through the use of language.

*All language socialization practices reflect cultural models of persons, acts and modes of action, accomplishments, and "**agency** ... the socioculturally mediated capacity to act"* (Ahearn 2001:112). Cultural models of personhood are traditionally transmitted ideas or models of what human beings – and, for our purposes, especially children – are like. In Samoa, adults regard children as being born rude and blunt. The first word that Samoans expect to hear, and thus *do* hear, from all children (at roughly 2 years of age) is *tae*, 'Eat shit!' (Ochs and Schieffelin 1984: 296). Thus,

Figure 9.5 Young Jewish boy takes in his cultural heritage directly and indirectly, from infancy on. (Peter Guttman/Getty Images)

caregivers have to direct children to engage in more polite speech. By contrast, adults in the Papua New Guinean region of Mount Bosavi start from the opposite assumption – that children are born "soft" and must be "hardened." They must be taught to speak assertively. The following examples from a Bosavi- (or Kaluli-) speaking mother exemplify *socialization to use language* in the way that Kaluli people consider important. They *explicitly* model for their children what to say and how, more generally, to *demand* (e.g., food, from siblings): "'Whose is it?' – say like that!" and "'Is it yours?' – say like that!" (Ochs and Schieffelin 1984:292).

To return to the two-part definition of language socialization offered by Schieffelin and Ochs (1986), the Kaluli example just cited involves socialization *to* the use of language – that is, socialization to use language in particular ways. This is the mode of language socialization that we recognize most easily. Think of all of the occasions when – as a small child or even a university student – someone suggested, or commanded, that you say something or speak in a certain way:

- "Say 'thank you'!"
- "Say 'please'!"
- "Stop talking like that, or I'll wash your mouth out with soap!"

The second facet of language socialization involves socialization *through* the use of language. If the first mode involves *transmitting linguistic culture*, the second involves *transmitting culture linguistically*. Examples of this second mode are both more common and a bit more difficult to conceptualize than examples of the first. Children hear their parents use polite language to some and direct or blunt language to others. They hear their parents interacting with their children and with each other in ways that index gender relations. And in these situations children absorb ways of using language. This happens without any explicit metalinguistic reference, i.e., without anyone saying "Speak like this."

In its role as the *medium* of socialization – socialization through the use of language – language is in the background. Some instances of this form of socialization focus explicitly on cultural norms, or norms of good behavior, while the linguistic form of a parent's speech to a wayward child sinks in deeply, despite the fact that it is not the focus on the parent's utterance. That is, children internalize their parents' speech patterns. Linguist Patricia Clancy (1986) visited the home of a young Japanese boy and recorded his interactions with his mother and with Clancy. The mother referred to Clancy, by the way, as the child's "big sister." The mother tried to get her son to share a plate of cookies. Importantly, she did so indirectly, using hints or attributing speech to the silent Clancy – "Big sister says_____." Clancy argues that this ventriloquation (Bakhtin 1981:199; Cooren 2012; Leppänen 2015; Tannen 2010) – the ventriloquist-like act of the mother throwing her **voice** through the mouth of Clancy toward her son – teaches children to make guesses as to what others are feeling but are too polite to say. This, she says, amounts to a lesson in empathy. As the boy failed to respond to such indirect strategies, his mother used increasingly direct commands. An American mother in the same time period (1986) might have simply issued an order to her son: "Share those cookies!" In both cases, these children are learning that their communities permit the issuing of direct commands when needed.

Skills and Means of Transmission: Culture as Structures of Communication

In this textbook, we are dealing with "communication," a broader category than "language." Communication includes embodied **semiosis**. For example, how babies are held, and specifically in what direction – toward the caregiver's chest or toward the broader social world (of kin, in particular) – is a very important facet of what is typically called language socialization. However, this might be more accurately labeled "the cultural semiotics of socialization."

Research in this field has, from the outset, attended to the embodied dimensions of socializing infants – with an early emphasis on the way in which infants are carried, whether facing inward toward the caregiver or outward (Ochs and Schieffelin 1984). An incident from my fieldwork in Bangladesh comes to mind. I was living in a compound of some six households and seventy people, a situation that offered many opportunities to see the sorts of practices that helped define human life across the life span. One day a young woman was walking near my hut, carrying her sister's child – facing outward – while the aunt pronounced the proper kin term designating each person they encountered. The direction in which she held her niece had a substantive connection to the task of growing up as a Bengali and thereby being oriented not so much to one's own needs and feelings as to one's extended family. The "**language game**" (Wittgenstein 1958:section 23) that the aunt played with her niece crucially involved physically orienting the child to her family while introducing her to what seemed to me a quite complex set of kin terms that every Bengali knows. Speech and intercorporeal **attunement** (mutual awareness of and sensitivity to others in the immediate environment, body sensing body) went hand in hand.

CONCLUSION

In this chapter, we have focused on the plethora of **social activities** that people engage in using language, the social-indexical significance of language varieties (sociolects, genres, and registers), and the categories or social fractions that language helps create.

Think of this chapter as expanding on the theme of "identification with …" or "identification as …" that we have earlier discussed. To say that various ways of speaking can index something is to say that some speech variety can be used to linguistically identify with some person, some group, some style, and so on.

As we have discussed, language is always enacted or produced materially. It never dwells solely in the symbolic realm (often thought of as immaterial). As we have seen in Chapter 8, in France at least, people can think about class by invoking one of "two mouths" – by thinking about the mouth in ways that stand in for class (Bourdieu 1977). Of course, the **embodiment** of language goes far beyond the mouth. Taking the theme of embodiment further, we address in this chapter the physical voice and various ways of altering it in speaking. We enlarge the scope of what we mean by the embodiment of language far more when we think of honorific registers that work like the highest of the Javanese "speech levels," meaning linguistic forms always accompanied by ways of holding or moving the body.

We can carry the theme of embodiment still further. We always encounter culture (like language) in some material embodiment (Urban 2001). In order to travel across time, culture must be reproduced. This process is entangled with biological reproduction. Think again about children. Just when their bodies – and especially, for our purposes, their *brains* – are growing most quickly, so grow the expectations of caregivers around the world about children's appropriate participation in society. Biological, social, and cultural reproduction are processes that happen simultaneously, as Ingold (1991) writes.

This chapter has demonstrated in many ways – and more intentionally and explicitly than have other sources – that processes of identification and socialization occur in large part *in and through language*.

SUMMARY

In this chapter, we focused on the following themes with which you should be familiar:

- The shift to process-oriented ways of speaking about key dimensions of language, society, and culture.
- How we can transcend the thing-like appearance of "speech communities" and "language communities."
- The relationship between, and definitions of, terms that capture different perspectives on speaking and ways of speaking – genres, sociolects, and registers.
- The relationship between forms of language and social fractions (gender, class, race, and ethnicity).
- The significance of research on culturally variable forms of language socialization.
- The embodiment and/or materiality of all language and communication.

QUESTIONS

1. What is the difference between a genre and a register? Give one example that involves both.
2. What steps does iconization consist of? Name an example of self-iconization and one of iconization by some Other (those of another class or ethnic group, for example).
3. What is the problem with saying Speech Variety A indexes Social Fraction X, without taking language ideologies into account?
4. What is an example of a multimodal semiotic register (other than those described in this textbook or in your classes)?
5. From the point of view of sociology or **social anthropology**, why is it useful to be able to make the distinction that the terms "sociolect" and "register" allow us to make?
6. Why do traditional (highland) Ilongots experience "crooked speech" as respectful of others – for example, others who are involved in a marriage negotiation event lasting several days?
7. What is the technical, social scientific use of the verb "socialize"? How is it different from the common use of the same verb? Why is it important to distinguish between the two and to recognize that only one is a transitive verb?

EXERCISES

1. Listen to the following radio segment (www.npr.org/2012/07/05/156325909/ceo-ruffles-lawmakers-by-using-their-first-names). Find and name two interpretations

of indexicality. Then find and name passages when Member of Parliament Teresa Pearce stresses that the context should determine how one addresses another or, by contrast, that Mr. Diamond was trying to do something in or to the context by the way he addressed others.

2. Find websites in English that discuss holding babies facing outward. What stance do they take regarding this practice?

3. Look for a YouTube video that exemplifies a particular way of speaking reserved for special settings or practices (i.e., a register, used in several genres). You might, for example, find a religious service, if and only if there is a single register in use across several genres. Transcribe a few lines from each genre to illustrate the continuity of register.

4. To explore attitudes versus ideologies, first read Wilce 2009b:115–116. Then explain one advantage that the phrase "language ideologies" has over the phrase "language attitudes." Also, what is the author's context? What is his discipline? What kind of relationship between the author's discipline and Lambert's discipline (Lambert 1975; Lambert et al. 1960) do these pages hint at?

5. Read the article *A Face in the Crowd* at http://azdailysun.com/a-face-in-the-crowd/image_eff17b09-55a1-5eb4-b5bf-6e7287cabca6.html. What is at stake for the three Cody family members in wearing masks of their graduating senior's face? Identity shift? Identification with? Something different?

6. Why does it make sense to call the following websites examples of identification rather than identity?
   - *Ich Bin Ein Berliner* (www.youtube.com/watch?v=56V6r2dpYH8)
   - *Today, We're All Haitians* (http://kristof.blogs.nytimes.com/2010/01/13/today-were-all-haitians/)
   - *Today, We Are All Norwegians* (http://arbiteronline.com/2011/07/25/today-we-are-all-norwegians/)
   - *Today, We Are All American Sikhs* (www.cnn.com/2012/08/06/opinion/kaur-sikhs/index.html)

7. Watch the 1991 film, *The Doctor*. Although this piece of dramatic fiction focuses more on a doctor's personality than his use, for example, of "medicalese," it is a moving critique of a certain kind of communication or communicative insensitivity. Listen for his use of medicalese (commonly called medical "jargon"), especially in interacting with patients.

ADDITIONAL RESOURCES

Agha, Asif. 2007. *Language and Social Relations*. Cambridge University Press.

Agha presents the relationships between sociolects, registers, and the social structures to which they relate in a very useful – and highly sophisticated – way.

Berkenkotter, Carol. 2008. *Patient Tales: Case Histories and the Uses of Narrative in Psychiatry*. Charleston: University of South Carolina Press.

This is the best source I know for rich case studies of genres that, from the perspective of linguistic anthropology and this chapter in particular, have combined to foster enregisterment – in this case, the enregisterment of medical and especially psychiatric English.

Ingold, Tim. 1991. Becoming Persons: Consciousness and Sociality in Human Evolution. *Cultural Dynamics* 4(3):355–378.

Ingold is perhaps the most holistically balanced anthropologist at work today – that is, one of the best role models to be found for anthropological models of human growth, culture, society, and communication.

10 Cultures of Performance and the Performance of Culture

LEARNING OBJECTIVES

After reading this chapter, you should be able to do the following:

- Understand the overlap and distinctions between performance and performativity.
- Describe under what circumstances performativity is related to ritual.
- Explain how performativity is related to "magic."
- Understand how the field of folklore studies is related to culture and communication.
- Know what the poetics of performance does and does not mean.
- Understand the centrality of parallelism to performance.

Introduction

In Chapter 10, we explore what folklorist and linguistic anthropologist Richard Bauman (1975) calls "verbal art as performance." As he puts it,

> It is part of the essence of performance that it offers to the participants a special enhancement of experience, bringing with it a heightened intensity of communicative interaction which binds the audience to the performer in a way that is specific to performance as a mode of communication. (Bauman 1975:305)

For our purposes, we may define "art" as an intensification of the ordinary into memorable, inspiring, transforming discourse. Perhaps we could say that performance involves just being ourselves, only more so!

However, I find being ourselves (i.e., being "authentic") a problematic category. So I might find it more accurate to say that performance involves "just *doing* what is culturally or situationally 'being ourselves.'" In other words, being ourselves is "the presentation of self in everyday life" (Goffman [1959] 1973). (Also see Sacks [1984] on "doing 'being ordinary.'") Rather than affirming a model of human **social action** as authentic or inauthentic, in this book I take the perspective that there are, in fact, multiple **authenticities** (Fenigsen and Wilce 2015; cf. Wilce and Fenigsen 2016).

I do believe **verbal art** can be universally characterized in terms of an intensification of the ordinary. Nonetheless, local **language ideologies** are important in relation to verbal art as performance. Woolard (1998a:1) points out that, "Ideologies of language are not about language alone. Rather, they envision and enact ties of language to identity, to aesthetics, to morality, and to epistemology." In my view, Woolard's list can be extended thus: Language ideologies are about relations between language and the cosmos, about the role of language in how the universe works.

Performativity and Its Kin: A History in and beyond Anthropology

I have just invoked the cosmos and its relationship to language. The remainder of this chapter should make it clear that two concepts help a great deal in understanding that relationship – **performance** and **performativity**. Naturally, the chapter concerns itself with the ethnographic context in which these two phenomena come together. I believe it will help us get off on the right foot in our journey toward understanding *performance* in ethnographic context if we start with the history of its twin, *performativity*.

At least since the early work of Bronislaw Malinowski – a founding father of anthropology who made important contributions to culture and communication – anthropologists have been developing ideas that are very similar to the idea of "performativity." In 1923, as a relatively young anthropologist, Malinowski argued that in "primitive" societies, language served as a mode of action (1923:315). In particular, he argued that language performs its active role by creating a positive social atmosphere.

By 1935, in *Coral Gardens and Their Magic*, Malinowski had rejected his earlier association of speech as action with so-called primitive societies

> as if the theoretical uses of words in modern philosophic and scientific writing were completely detached from their pragmatic sources. This was an error, and a serious error at that. Between the savage use of words and the most abstract and theoretical one there is only a difference of degree. (1935:58)

In the same book, Malinowski's description of the power of speech foreshadows what contemporary feminist thinker Judith Butler (2013) writes about performativity. The power of magical (or, in contemporary words, "performative") speech in Malinowski's thinking both derives from and helps create its context. For him, magical speech is never reducible to any individual, whether speaker or addressee. Rather, "the magic . . . is throughout an impersonal verbal act" (1935:318).

Neither Malinowski nor any other anthropologist coined the term "performativity." Rather, it was invented and developed by four major philosophers – John L. Austin, John Searle, Jacques Derrida, and Judith Butler. In *How to Do Things with Words* (1962), Austin invented the term "performative" for utterances that actually *perform* the very actions to which they only appear to refer. Searle (1969) dubbed not only explicit performative utterances but all utterances "speech acts," and he located the meaning of speech acts in the personal intentions of their speakers. (See the discussion of "intentionalism" in Chapter 9.) Many linguistic anthropologists, however, side with Derrida (1977) and Butler, who reject this intentionalist interpretation of Austin. Among those anthropologists rejecting intentionalism, Michelle Rosaldo (discussed in Chapter 9) is one of the best known. This stance should shed some light on the attitudes of linguistic anthropologists toward Searle, performativity, and speech acts.

Note the similarity between the following passage from Butler's book *Excitable Speech: A Politics of the Performative* and Malinowski's *Coral Gardens and Their Magic*:

> In this sense, an "act" is not a momentary happening, but a certain nexus
> of temporal horizons, the condensation of an *iterability* that exceeds the
> moment it occasions. The possibility for a speech act to resignify a prior context
> depends, in part, upon the gap between the originating context or intention
> by which an utterance is animated and the effects it produces. (Butler 2013:14,
> emphasis added)

We return to the idea of iterability shortly. For now, note that Austin's book introducing the idea of performative utterances, *How to Do Things with Words*, included some eleven invocations of heterosexual marriage. Yet it was only decades later that Judith Butler introduced the idea that at the very heart of language is its role in constituting gender and sexuality. To speak of "constituting" such realities is to say they are performative. Together with Jacques Derrida, Butler rejected Searle's notion of speech acts as reflections of individual intention.

What defines language, according to Derrida and Butler, is its quotability, repeatability, or iterability. And this iterability is central to Butler's performative theory of gender – performatives are significant (and signifying) because they repeat past utterances. Gendering, as in the gendering of "girl" babies, is an act with profound results. The key example of gendering that Butler offers her readers consists of a doctor "who receives [a newborn] child and pronounces 'It's a girl.' Butler calls this "being 'girled.'" Performativity is key to gender insofar as such acts of gendering entail "a long string of interpellations [those sometimes violent acts by which someone is inserted into a prefabricated role] by which the baby is transitively girled: gender is ritualistically repeated" (Butler 2013:49).

Performance and Performativity

Folklore, as we shall see, has become one academic venue for the study of **performance**. Yet, if asked what folklore is, few Americans or Europeans would approximate Dan Ben-Amos's explanation that "folklore is artistic communication in small groups" or recognize it as a "scholarly construct," let alone see it as a

symbolic construct that is "energized by the dynamic processes of traditionaliza-
tion, ideology, social thought, and the artfulness of everyday life" (1971:13).

Instead, most Americans and Europeans would cite something from a book
containing versions of the folktales collected by the famous brothers Jacob and
Wilhelm Grimm, rather than thinking of a performance they had seen. The Grimm
brothers' stories are, to us, now timeless **texts** (Bauman and Briggs 2003). They
have undergone "entextualization." In other words, those who originally produced
them (in this case, the Grimm brothers) built into them structures that make them
memorable. They built in patterns that make the stories appear not as talk
grounded in context whose meaning is thus fleeting, but as "text" that can circulate
with an apparent timelessness. Unlike our common uses of the word text today, in
many scholarly domains it means, following Hanks (1989), a coherent set of signs.
Or following Bauman and Briggs (1990:74–75), text means discourse that is fashioned in such a way as to be memorable, lifted out of context and quoted.

Bauman was at least partially responsible for shifting the focus of folklorists from
texts toward performance. That shift has many ramifications. For example, we might
think of "Coyote and the Birds" (Wiget 1987), a culturally important narrative told
among some indigenous groups of the American Southwest. Yes, Native peoples of the
Southwest have told many versions of the story. However, one of the most obvious
and important of the ramifications of the shift to an emphasis on performance is
to question the assumption that these many tellings of the "Coyote and the Birds"
story are manifestations of a single and true source-text. Instead, Bauman suggests
that each performance of such stories must be examined on its own. Bauman's
definition of performance has influenced generations of scholars studying performances in various cultural contexts: "Performance involves on the part of the performer
an assumption of accountability to an audience for the way in which communication
is carried out, above and beyond its **referential** content" (1975:293).

Especially if you are reading this book as your first exposure to linguistic anthropology, it can be hard to grasp the distinction between *performance* and *performativity*. When we think of achieving success in verbally performing for an audience,
we are thinking about performance. Performance is about skill. Often the recognition it garners goes to an individual. Performativity, on the other hand, is another
word for "magic" – meaning powerful, ritual, transformative acts. (See Figure 10.1.)
In both cases, "audiences" are important, and they play a more active role than we
may typically imagine (Duranti and Brenneis 1986).

The acts of ritual discourse that we call "performatives" are often named, and
their names may be forms of the name for the ritual – the priest's baptizing words in
the context of a baptism ritual, a public official's christening utterance in a ritual
naming of a ship, a pastor's marriage pronouncement in the context of a wedding.
One becomes an Evangelical, a member of the Church of the Latter Day Saints
(LDS), or a Muslim through performative acts. Individuals who join Evangelical and
LDS groups are expected to testify. The more they tell the story of their conversion,
or of "what God is doing in my life," the deeper their own faith becomes, as Peter

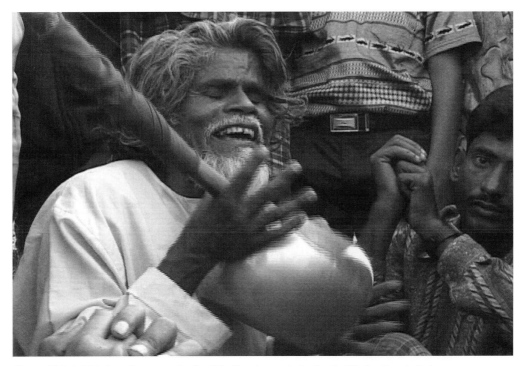

Figure 10.1 A fakir (an often unorthodox Muslim devotee) singing in Dhaka, Bangladesh. (Photo by author)

Stromberg and many others argue. Linguistic anthropologists like Crapanzano (2000) and Keane (2007) provide useful overviews of the semiotic ideologies at work in evangelical Protestantism. See also the various edited collections on the anthropology of Christianity, particularly those by Robbins and Bialecki (Bialecki et al. 2008; Robbins 2001, 2004, 2014).

In the early 1980s, Stromberg studied Evangelicals like a man he calls Jim in a church in California. The more he listened to the way Jim and others spoke – apparently about a past event we can call his conversion experience – the more Stromberg's assumptions about language and experience were challenged.

> Jim's conversion narrative is not only or even primarily an account of events from the past, it is a creation of a particular situation in the moment of its telling. The way to look at Jim's conversion, I have come to see, is not as something that occurred in the past and is now "told about" in the conversion narrative. Rather, the conversion narrative itself is a central element of the conversion. (Stromberg 1993:3)

Jim's speech, in other words, was performative – one medium through which Jim has been, and continues to be, transformed. Jim gave Stromberg his personal testimony of conversion in an interview, and Evangelical and LDS groups often encourage and set aside time for this "speech **genre**" in their church meetings (Stromberg 1993:3).

Figure 10.2 A *bomoh* is a traditional Malaysian healer who works with people facing all kinds of illnesses. (Saeed Khan/AFP/Getty Images)

Let's look at performative acts from another perspective. A judge who says "I declare this case dismissed" or "I sentence the defendant to life" may have an unpleasant voice, may stumble over his words, or have some sort of garment malfunction during his or her utterance. But those features – features of performance – pale in comparison to the *effect* of the judge's words. And if I were to stand up and say to the judge, "Bravo, well done," or even, "False!" – not only would my behavior be deviant, but it might lead to incarceration or a psychiatric examination. Such are performative acts. They are neither true nor false, nor must the voice that delivers such acts be beautiful.

The voice of one engaged in performance, by contrast, might indeed be subject to a norm or expectation of beauty. The very beautiful *bunyi* 'sound' of a successful Malaysian *bomoh* traditional healer (see Figure 10.2) – his voice and its quality – may reflect a background in performance in the narrow sense. Medical anthropologist Carol Laderman describes one such *bomoh* (Pak Daud) as having cultivated a fine vocal aesthetic during his youthful role performing in the traditional Malay romantic operas. The successful *bomoh*'s voice is beautiful, sweet, and melodious. Laderman (1987:299) writes that "the word 'bunyi' [encompasses, all at once] the concepts of sound, melody, meaning, content, [and] purport." Successful here means efficacious – magical, powerful, and thus curative. Laderman can be taken to mean that features of **voice quality** (**phonation** or phonatory features) carry almost as much "meaning" as does a *bomoh*'s articulateness in voicing words that carry denotative-**referential** meaning.

This presents a problem to any account of *performance* that attempts to keep it clearly distinct from *performativity*. The dramatic and the aesthetic – clearly features reflected in voices like that of Pak Daud – may remind his hearers of his operatic background. However, they also help to magically empower his speech/singing. This resonates with recent arguments concerning the development of speech in infants and its relationship to the evolution of human speech and the complex relationship our use of voice has with the vocalizations of nonhuman primates. To be specific, Oller (2014) argues that human infants develop control over the quality of sounds they produce well before they learn to articulate (i.e., to produce sounds we recognize as vowels, consonants, or syllables).

In Chapters 2, 3, and 4, we developed a foundation for thinking clearly and with some sophistication about voice, particularly about the sciences of phonetics and phonology. Knowing the nuts and bolts of something as apparently abstract as acoustic phonetics may give us a sense of how to read a waveform or spectrogram (as in Figure 4.4 and the Appendix) or describe some of the features that make a voice sound like it does. That knowledge can help us understand what makes one healer's voice full like that of a good singer (the so-called "modal" or "operatic" voice) and another sound full of pain, suffering, or weakness ("creaky voice," introduced in Chapter 4).

Both performance and performativity have occupied a very significant place in linguistic anthropology generally. Indeed, performance has been a very fruitful topic of research that is increasingly informed by theory, and that theory sheds light on the relationship between performance and performativity. Consider, for example, the discovery by Michael Silverstein (1976, 2004) and his colleagues that **indexicality** works in two different ways (i.e., there are two kinds of indexes) – *pointing to* a context that is presupposed versus *pointing-beyond-itself*, so to speak, to a context that the index (or indexical sign) brings into being. Some indexes reflect, and others create. Communicative or discursive performances contain or serve as both kinds of index.

Culture and Performance

Across several chapters, you have been reading about the highly poetic **structure** of countless examples of local oratory in contexts that Americans might distinguish as political or religious, though that distinction could not stand in many cultural contexts.

Implicitly, I have emphasized the *universality* of **parallelism**, the cross-cultural similarity of its **functions** – chief among them, perhaps, the marking of speech as ritual oratory. What if a local perspective – such as one of importance in the history of Chinese religion and philosophy, namely the ideal of a balanced relationship between two forces known as *yin* and *yang* (as "both coupled and opposed") – might be reinforced through performance or written artifacts thereof (Chmielewski 1965; Jakobson [1966] 1987:149)? This is a simple example and might raise more questions than it answers. In the following paragraphs, however, I trace the intricate relationships between modes of performance and cultural models of the universe, of persons, in several ethnographic contexts.

Communication and Cosmos: Tewa Stories and the Harvest

As we saw in earlier chapters, rituals are communicative activities. These activities include special kinds of storytelling, including myths describing, for example, the creation of the world – not just describing, but bringing back to the present, that special ritual time of creation. Many indigenous peoples of the American Southwest have a particular understanding of the relationship between rituals they perform and the cosmos. Hopi elders say that if their rituals ceased, it would mean disaster for the cosmos. And those rituals crucially include the telling of special sorts of stories (e.g., sacred winter stories).

For some decades, Paul Kroskrity (1985, 1993) has studied Tewa language and culture in Arizona, often focusing on Tewa verbal art and on one genre of verbal art in particular – stories called *pééyu'u*. But understanding these very special, ritually significant Tewa stories requires a grasp of the language ideologies that surround those stories. Kroskrity had worked with "key **consultant**" Dewey Healing for more than five years on these stories, when Healing shared an unexpected and profound insight. Kroskrity recounts how it suddenly occurred to him that

> despite our deep involvement in analyzing the stories I had not asked him a very basic question about his appreciation of them. I spontaneously remarked "You know after working on these stories with you for so many years, I think I am beginning to understand why they are so well-liked and popular, but I haven't asked you directly, what do you like about the stories?" Without missing a beat, Dewey made eye contact with me, looked off ever so briefly, and returned his gaze to me, saying, "I like the way they make the crops grow." His facial expression was very serious – this was not one of his jokes. I was stunned. (2009b:45)

Kroskrity's shock can be explained, at least in large part, by the stark difference between Tewa (or perhaps Puebloan) and Euro-American **language ideologies** in performance and its relationship to the world. The stories that Kroskrity and Healing were discussing were not even necessarily *about* crops, soil, or rainfall.

Figure 10.3 Corn plays a central role in Tewa life and stories, and traditional stories help the corn to grow. (Fred Kabotie, *Study for Watchtower Mural at Desert View, Grand Canyon*, circa 1932, tempera and watercolor, 13 x 9 in. Collection of the New Mexico Museum of Art. Gift of Steve and Dottie Diamant, 2004 [2004.12.1]. Photo by Blair Clark. © Fred Kabotie Estate)

(See Figure 10.3.) One can only understand Healing's Tewa perspective on verbal art as performance if we take his statement at face value rather than dismiss it or try to interpret it away.

Tewa *pééyu'u* stories have been performed for centuries, and certain rules govern their performance. They must be performed in winter. Healing told Kroskrity that telling *pééyu'u* stories to children is not only analogous with (iconic of) the sprouting of seedlings but indexical of the special time – winter – and place (the kiva) where (and when) seeds are sprouted into seedlings (Kroskrity 2009b:45).

The larger point of the story Kroskrity tells of being "stunned" by Healing's comment is the always fascinating link between performance and culture, which some might define as a set of ideologies.

Two Visions of a Breakthrough into Performance

Steven Caton and Dell Hymes offer useful examples of performance from other parts of the world.

Caton's *Peaks of Yemen I Summon* (1990) is an important contribution to the **ethnography of communication**, a pioneering **ethnography** of poetry and poetic performance. And Caton acknowledges the influence of earlier work, for example, by Dell Hymes (1981) and Dennis Tedlock (1983).

Caton's book includes a marvelous description of a genre of poetic performance that becomes a kind of extended rite of passage for young tribal men in Yemen. Yemeni men perform *bālah* poetry as part of Yemeni tribal wedding rituals, as I mentioned briefly in Chapter 9. During these celebrations, they collectively compose and sing *bālah*, and they include dancing in their performances.

In describing *bālah*, Caton also talks about the interrelated phenomenon of young men attaining manhood as defined in the Yemeni Arabic word *gabīlī* or tribesman. "'How would I [Caton] have to raise my son for him to become a *gabīlī?*' I sometimes asked my tribal friends. One sheikh responded: 'You must teach him four things: the dictates of Islam, how to shoot a gun, how to dance, and how to compose poetry'" (1990:26). Although there are certainly other poetic genres whose mastery contributes to making a tribesman, and despite the fact that young men may compose romantic poetry before participating actively in *bālah* performance, I concentrate on the latter because of its beautiful complexity, its collective composition, the competitiveness that infuses the performance, and the way the *bālah* exemplifies a particular culture of performance, poetics, and manhood.

> The [*bālah*] performance is made up of three concentric circles: the inner one is described by the poet's turn, the middle one comprises the chorus, and the outer one is formed by the seated audience. The penetration of the inner circle by the poet emerging from the outer two and then the exiting back into them is perfectly iconic of the ideal that everyone – whether a member of the audience or the chorus – may be a poet; no one is privileged. In addition, and much more significant, is the fact that the closer someone is to the center, the more intimately he becomes involved in the compositional process: the audience reacts to the poem, the chorus "carries" it (the Arabic word is *shall*, which means lift or carry), and the poet composes it. (Caton 1990:82–83)

The *bālah* deserves our attention also as a kind of enactment of the social order – a culture of society and a social organization of cultural performance. This phrasing shows that the line between "society" and "culture" discussed in Chapter 1 is blurrier than I led you to believe. As Caton puts it, the concentric circles he describes are **iconic** of an ideal (culture) of social organization. Yet the egalitarianism represented by the fact that anyone can contribute to the unfolding poem is only part of what the circles iconically represent. On the one hand, "the performance ought not to depend heavily on the contributions of one person, for then it is no longer felt to be an evenly matched competition" (Caton 1990:82). At the same time, it is clear that the circles represent a hierarchy of skill. The ability to perform is typically unequally distributed in any society.

When reading the following passage, keep in mind that Caton writes from personal experience, linking arms with the young men in the *bālah* chorus:

> When they reach puberty, males are already considered old enough to know how to shoot a gun, dance, and compose poetry, so they are encouraged not only to observe the wedding celebrations but also to participate actively in them. In the poetry performances they usually perform in the chorus, a minimal participation requiring only that they keep the rhythm and the melody distinct while repeating a standard refrain like *lelah wa bālah wa ya lelah hal* (night and *bālah* and O night of the *hal*) or some other combination of words ... Judging by the number of times the more experienced performers reproached us for cutting up the rhythm or failing to enunciate clearly the refrain, these skills did not come especially easily to my young cohorts either. (Caton 1990:52)

Several things mentioned in the preceding paragraph are worth noting. Harkening back to Bauman, performance involves accountability to an audience for how one speaks and not just what one says. Merely by joining the chorus, the inexperienced opened themselves to the apparently stern evaluation of the experienced (presumably their elders).

Note also that the three circles are not stable. That is the point – anyone can contribute. Note too, however, that contributing a solo line involves movement – first in one's face, from an expression of deep concentration to a smile, and next, physically, from the outer to the innermost circle. "Confident that they have composed a well-formed verse, their faces brighten, and one among their number (which varies from two to five or even more) moves decisively toward the circle and *breaks through* the linked arms of the choristers, who close ranks behind him" (Caton 1990:82).

That breakthrough happens to correspond intriguingly to a phrase that Dell Hymes, pioneer of **ethnopoetics**, coined in 1975: *Breakthrough into performance.* His phrase implies that performance is a special mode of communication – and that in situations in which indigenous languages are apparently dying, folklorists and ethnographers of communication are seldom able to "catch" a full-on performance of a traditional tale, for example, since the ritual context and significance of such tales has often been lost. Hymes, in such a situation, had asked his consultant Philip Kahclamat, who at least knew the (Wasco-) Wishram stories, to tell one. Kahclamat chose to tell "The Crier" (Hymes [1975] 1981). Late at night, after drinking many beers while sitting in a booth in the Rainbow Café near the Wasco-Wishram Reservation, sounds like an unpromising setting for breaking through into a performance rich with echoes of the old ways. As Hymes ([1975] 1981:90) writes:

> The special interest of the speech here is that it begins as a report, in the third person, in English ("In the morning he steps out …") and ends as authentic performance, in the first person, in Wishram … The switch into authentic performance, into Wishram, was brief: two sentences, at the end of, or ending, the speech. Code-switching from one language to another is here, I believe, a sign of "breakthrough" into full performance … I take the breaking into Wishram [*Kiksht*] at the end of the speech to imply not only subjective assumption of the role of the speaker, but also momentary forgetting of the immediate audience.

It was a moment in which memories of old ritual oratory temporarily broke through many obstacles – Hymes as audience, the café as setting, the discontinuity between the present and the now distant past – and the oratorical tradition briefly lived again.

There are, of course, a great many differences between the phenomenon that Hymes, speaking figuratively, was to call a "*breakthrough* into performance" and the physical act of brave young Yemeni poets breaking into the inner circle (the only place in the wedding *bālah* performance in which new lines were performed). Both, however, involve at least a momentary shift in the nature of the person stepping into the full performer's role. Both shifted their self-identification. Both shifted their role vis-à-vis the audience (the outer circle in the *bālah*, and Hymes for Kahclamet), the nature of their participation in the communicative event, and the object of their identification. Young Yemeni tribesmen composing perhaps their first poetic lines asserted their identification with experienced poets, and Mr. Kahclamet temporarily stepped into the role of a ritual orator.

Paradoxes of Performance

Performance is a phenomenon defined in relation to six paradoxes, which I explore in this section.

The first paradox is this: Performance can achieve what is apparently impossible. One example that I have already mentioned is the apparent impossibility of stories helping Tewa crops to grow. Another example involves a consummate performer in Catalonia, a comedian called Eugenio, who speaks two languages at once. This is not code-switching – rather it involves "bivalency," or the "simultaneous membership of an element in more than one linguistic system" (Woolard 1998b:6).

Finally, an example that I "perform" for my students can be simultaneously heard as either English or Bangla. When I write it, using a common way of representing Bangla using the roman alphabet, it looks foreign: *b^{h}āb mārle rege ut̪^{h}bo*. But when I say it, my non-Bangla-speaking American students hear "Bob Marley reggae …" followed by something unfamiliar. The /b^h/ sounds to most Americans like a /b/ pronounced strangely. Some might not even notice the aspiration (represented by the raised /h/), since English has no such sound. Thus *b^{h}āb* sounds much like Bob. *Mārle* sounds close enough to Marley, and *rege* to reggae.

But in Bangla, the sentence – including the last word, which sounds most definitely foreign – means 'If you strike a pose (or "show attitude"), I'll get angry (literally, "I will rise up angering")'.

The second paradox regarding performance: Performances of verbal art involve particular performers doing what is expected of them – they perform – and they may be widely known as skilled verbal artists. Still, it is common in local perform-ance traditions for such individuals to not only deny, but to be *obligated* to deny, their qualifications to perform.

Third, in some cultural contexts, the very signs that mark speech as performance may undermine the legitimacy or authenticity of a communicative event *as* per-formative. (By performative, I mean the locally perceived magical quality of some complex of signs to create the goals, conditions, and outcomes of clearly ritual communication.)

Fourth, despite the apparent and real sense in which performance stands out from the ordinary, it is in some way modeled on, if not obviously embedded in, the give and take of everyday interaction. The "standing out from the ordinary" to which I refer can be seen in ritual performance. Features that are sometimes found in everyday talk – which may in itself have a kind of poetry – are intensified in verbal art (i.e., performance) and perhaps nowhere more clearly than in ritual performance. Intensification can be dialed up and down, covered by denial, and hidden in the commonalities of conversation.

The fifth paradox is this: Just as performance is embedded in everyday life – in a spatiotemporally particular context – performances (or their peaks) are also *made to stand out from their surrounding verbal context*. Many words were spoken before and after Lincoln spoke at Gettysburg, but, at least in hindsight, only he delivered a truly great performance. And we know its precise boundaries. It is a "text" – a body of coherent signs, an event of discourse that is fashioned for memorability and quotability, an achievement that requires coherence, a sense that "this is a thing, separate from its context."

Obviously, a political speech – which is surely a performance – is given in a particular time and place and for a particular reason. But it is worth noting that today what we hear from that speech a few minutes or hours later via both old and new media is often just sound bytes. In fact, speechwriters and the **media** conspire to both build into and later lift out of a speech those lines that are designed to be memorable – often passages involving obvious or subtle repetitions, instances of parallelism.

Finally, the sixth paradox: Performances of verbal art typically combine varying degrees of "speaking the past and speaking the present" (Becker 1979). Performances must be creative enough to count as new, yet traditional enough to be recognized but not booed. (You may know that both Igor Stravinsky's *Rite of Spring* and George Gershwin's *Rhapsody in Blue*, two well-known musical compositions, were initially disliked by both audiences and critics for exceeding the limits of propriety because they were too new, too different. Figure 10.4 shows the reaction at the time.)

PARISIANS HISS NEW BALLET

Russian Dancer's Latest Offering, "The Consecration of Spring," a Failure.

HAS TO TURN UP LIGHTS

Manager of Theatre Takes This Means to Stop Hostile Demonstrations as Dance Goes On.

By Marconi Transatlantic Wireless Telegraph to The New York Times.

PARIS, June 7. — "Bluffing the idle rich of Paris through appeals to their

Figure 10.4 Even though audiences today delight in Stravinsky's *Rite of Spring*, the 1913 initial performances were considered disastrous. (*New York Times*, reproduction)

Let's look now at two more detailed examples of the tension between conformity to some tradition or structure and creative play with, or departure from, tradition or structure that characterizes verbal art as performance. Wherever **lament** (sometimes called keening) traditions have been found around the world, they "could generally be defined as poetry of lamentation performed by improvisation, but following traditional verbal expression" (Honko 1974:10). This is certainly true of Karelian lament. (Karelia is a transnational region now lying mostly within Russia, but culturally and linguistically tied to Finland.) The most obvious feature of the special **register** used in Karelian lament is the pervasive use of "circumlocutions" – ways of "beating around the bush" (discussed in the context of "linguistic indirection" in Chapter 9). The lamenter may, for example, avoid direct mention of the deceased over whom a lament might be sung. Alexandra Stepanova has compiled a dictionary of this lament register, with over a thousand circumlocutions (A. Stepanova 2012a). Her daughter Eila Stepanova makes clear, however, that the list of some twelve hundred circumlocutions is not comprehensive, but rather gives a sample – admittedly an exhaustive sample – of all circumlocutions in laments generated according to dozens of formulae (E. Stepanova 2012b). Think of these formulae as a far more complex version of the chord sequence C-F-G-C – and all of the songs that simple sequence has generated.

South Slavic oral song-making traditions provide another interesting example. Something of the ancient narrative art of Homer survived into the twentieth century in these traditions. In the former Yugoslavia, bards known as *guslars* maintained the tradition of oral song-making. As with many other verbal art traditions, folklorists had come to show disdain for oral song-making because of its clichés, its stereotyped repetitiousness. The 1930 publication of Milman Parry's important book *Studies in the Epic Technique of Oral Verse-Making* shook the nascent field of performance studies. As his student Alfred Lord argued, Parry broke out of that inherited tendency toward disdain. Lord ([1960] 2000:30) writes:

> Such terms [as "stock epithets" and "epic clichés"] were either too vague or too restricted. Precision was needed, and the work of Milman Parry was the culmination of that need. The result was a definition of the "formula" as "a group of words which is regularly employed under the same metrical conditions to express a given essential idea" [Parry 1930: 80]. By this definition the ambiguity of "repetitions" was eliminated; we were henceforth to deal with repeated word groups, not with repeated scenes . . .

Verbal Art Experienced: Embodied Responses to Verbal Art

I close this chapter with another paradox, but one very different from the six that strictly concern performance itself. This paradox is about the causes of a performance's effect on its audience.

Many of those who analyze events of verbal art in performance claim that a particular ritual discourse (often encompassing the highest verbal art genres in any community) moves an audience. They further argue that the unfolding patterning or "intratextual movement" that we can trace in an instance of great oratory – the "I Have a Dream" speech or the Gettysburg Address – holds the secret to the audience being moved. The poetic structure, moving from the theme of death to life (Gettysburg Address) or from passive suffering (in the "Litany of Complaint" in the Declaration of Independence) to the highly agentive declaration in its climax, must surely structure or move the feelings of the audience (i.e., it must be performative).

By contrast, another group of scholars tries by various means to elicit from actual audience members (those, for example, who are objects of a Tibetan shaman in Nepal [Desjarlais 1996]) what they experience or have experienced in such sessions, while paying relatively less analytic attention to the unfolding poetic-grammatical-rhetorical structure of the event or the shaman's performance.

Precious little work is being done that balances ethnographic interviews (to elicit the experience, for example, of being healed) with fine-grained ethnopoetic analysis. And, despite the rising interest in "neuroanthropology," I am not aware of any anthropological studies that have attempted to measure physiological or neural responses of audiences to richly contextualized cultural-discursive performances. Many promising articles are coming out of the new field of "cognitive poetics" (Calvo-Merino et al. 2008; De Smedt and De Cruz 2010; Itkonen 2004). Some of these works trace their roots to Dufrenne (1978). Perhaps there will be a role for linguistic anthropologists, cross-trained in neuroanthropology, to contribute to this burgeoning field.

CONCLUSION

Performance is central to culture. Despite variability as to its definition and its modes of enactment and evaluation around the world, performance is the most culturally salient form of communication. As we have seen, its tendency to draw attention to itself and to take on structure that makes it memorable – that makes it appear to be "text," such that a folktale is a text – is part of the very definition of "verbal art as performance" (Bauman 1975).

This chapter brings together from many of the preceding chapters data and arguments pertaining to performativity. In Chapters 11 and 12, we build on what this chapter reveals about performance and its cultural significance (which can, in itself, be a kind of synonym for "magic" or performativity). Much of the global circulation of forms of culture and communication that we examine in Chapter 11 depends on processes of **entextualization**.

SUMMARY

After reading this chapter, you should have a good understanding of the following themes:

- Performativity as a kind of "magic."
- Linguistic elements that characterize performance on the one hand and "a performative utterance" on the other.
- The relationship between key cultural consultants like Dewey Healing and anthropologists like Paul Kroskrity.
- The acceptability of paradoxes in "human sciences" like anthropology.
- The relationship between linguistic anthropology and the study of folklore (folkloristics).

QUESTIONS

1. What is the difference between performance and performativity?
2. How do we best explain their difference as well as their connectedness?
3. Why is performance so important to culture?

EXERCISES

1. To explore your first exposure to folklore, think about what folk genres your parents or teachers shared with you – such as folk songs, nursery rhymes, myths, folk stories, or fairytales. Then respond to the following questions:
   - Describe your first exposure to any of these kinds of folklore.
   - If this folklore was oral, what was the setting or occasion in which you heard or learned it?
   - If it was written, did anyone read it to you, or did you read it on your own?
   - What age were you when you heard or read your first folklore?
   - Did you think it was a product of your own culture and society or the culture of some other society?
   - What attitude did you pick up in your environment toward the folklore you heard or read?
2. Find online (e.g., YouTube, etc.) an example of a classic (explicit) performative from the following types: a wedding, a naming ritual (e.g., a baptism in which a child is given its name), or a trial. Then respond to the following:
   - Describe the individual ceremony and where and how you found it (using what search terms, from what source [e.g., YouTube]).
   - Transcribe the performative utterance.
   - Which of the following features of an explicit performative occur in your example – first-person subject, present tense, metapragmatic verb, and, optionally, a temporal adverb?
3. To explore authenticities/authentic performances, first read Fenigsen and Wilce (2015:181–200). Next search in Google Scholar for articles with "authentic" in the title, and choose one from the first page of hits. Answer the following questions, using the Fenigsen and Wilce article as your framework for responding:
   - On which of the four authenticities does this article focus?
   - What is your evidence? In other words, what features of the particular authenticity you found does the article represent?

   Finally, try a couple more searches, this time using Google instead of Google Scholar:
   - Search for the terms "folk" and "authentic." Choose an interesting-looking hit on the first page of hits, and respond to the same two questions you used in the earlier part of this exercise.
   - Search for the terms "authentic" and "feelings." Choose the first hit on the first page that sheds some light on how our culture connects the concepts of authenticity and feeling or on how our culture defines authenticity. Respond to the same two questions you used before.

ADDITIONAL RESOURCES

Ahearn, Laura M. 2012. *Living Language: An Introduction to Linguistic Anthropology*. Malden, MA: Blackwell Publishers. Chapter 8. Performance, Performativity, and the Constitution of Communities.

Ahearn explores the common ground between performance and performativity, citing a different literature than I have used here.

Bauman, Richard. 1992. *Folklore, Cultural Performances, and Popular Entertainments: A Communications-Centered Handbook*. New York: Oxford University Press.

Bauman draws on his intimate familiarity with the fields of anthropology (including linguistic anthropology), communication, performance, and folklore in assembling this very useful reader.

Samuels, David. 2004. *Putting a Song on Top of It: Expression and Identity on the San Carlos Apache Reservation*. Tucson: University of Arizona Press.

Samuels' book is both ethnography and a fieldwork-oriented work of ethnomusicology. Its attractions include the way he is able to draw on his own participation (performance) with various Apache bands, especially those specializing in an Apache version of country and western music.

11 Globalization, Media, and Emotion Talk

LEARNING OBJECTIVES

After reading this chapter, you should be able to do the following:

- Describe how anthropologists think of globalization.
- Name unique features of anthropological approaches to media.
- Describe how globalization, media, and emotion are linked in our contemporary world.
- Explain the global circulation of emotion as an important new phenomenon.
- Distinguish between old and new media.

Introduction

In this chapter, I address three major themes in contemporary scholarship, particularly in studies of culture and communication. The first two, globalization and mediation, are undoubtedly familiar terms to you. The last one – emotionalization/subjectivization – is likely not. And, as you have certainly come to expect, even familiar terms like globalization and mediation have specialized meanings for our purposes here.

In this chapter, we explore specialized perspectives on how "the global," media influences, and subjective human experience interact to create new ways of thinking and being in our world today. As you might anticipate, we see in this chapter that *language plays a central role* in the globalization of culture. Moreover old, but especially new, media are central to the production and circulation of contemporary forms of language. This chapter distills some of the exciting and recent work in the "anthropology of media," especially by anthropologists concerned with language. Their media-centered ethnographic studies offer insights not only into "**the media**" but also into the nature of emotion and what it means for emotion to be culturally constituted and socially circulated.

The Interconnection of Globalization, Media, and Emotion

As you begin this chapter, you might well wonder how globalization, media, and emotion pertain to one another. Their interconnections have captivated me, at least since I wrote *Crying Shame* (Wilce 2009a). In that book, I traced the damaging impact of globalization on local traditions, especially "crying songs" or laments. The echoes of lament traditions in globally circulating media, albeit distorted and distorting, intrigued me, as did the stark differences in ideologies of emotion in globalizing modernity versus traditions such as ritual wailing. In this chapter, I tell a related but different story about the collaboration of globalization, media, and emotion, one that you may more easily recognize than you would in relation to a perhaps "exotic"-seeming tradition like ritual wailing.

Let us begin by acknowledging that research forms the basis for the information we discuss in this chapter. Anthropologists study processes like globalization, mediation, and subjectivization/emotionalization through ethnographic engagement. That is, we study them "on the ground," in the contexts within which the global meets the local. Participating in ethnographic encounters with more or less unfamiliar groups of people and unfamiliar settings, practices, communication, and ways of thinking is what we do. Such encounters foster a sense of cross-cultural variability and define us as anthropologists (as we discussed in Chapter 7).

The point of ethnographic research is to find what holds true for "this" community, "these" people, at "this" time. Yet we must remember that boundaries between these communities are increasingly porous – as a result of globalization and the mediation of culture that fosters its global circulation.

A few anthropologists have characterized our triad of interacting influences as truly connected (e.g., Graber 2012). A much larger number have addressed the pairing of globalization and media, globalization and emotion, or media and emotion (e.g., Kunreuther 2006; Nakassis and Dean 2007). As we move now into discussions of the individual components of this chapter's triadic theme – globalization, media, and emotion – bear in mind that it is the *interconnections* between them that are most crucial to our understanding.

Globalization, Language, and Communication

As I write this, I am remembering a bumper sticker I once saw. It said, "*Globalization means exporting our jobs & importing their stuff.*" Indeed, globalization is often seen as responsible for closing factories and filling big box stores with goods made in Bangladesh.

Have you heard people express any of the following sentiments? Globalization has taken away our jobs. People feel they have been trampled by globalization. Globalization means inequality and destruction. Globalization has winners and losers; it is not a one-way street (Lechner and Boli 2014:4, 194).

What these statements have in common is an understanding of globalization as a strictly *economic* phenomenon. By contrast, when anthropologists and other social scientists write about globalization, we are referring to the circulation of *culture* – various forms of culture – around the world. While we are very mindful of the economic dimensions of globalization, we insist on the importance of considering other dimensions – communication and the media that carry it and the globally circulating forms of emotion – along with the economic ones.

So what do I mean by globalization? Two features define it. First, it is the rapid, mass movement of people, ideas and ideologies, goods and services, and all that we mean by "culture," including "cultures of emotion." Second, although there have been previous eras or iterations of globalization dating back two millennia or more, the current era is marked by a unique collapsing of time and space and by powerful links to media.

Communication as Work Process and Product

So how do features of language and communication become enmeshed in the processes of globalization, including the economic aspects of these processes? The answer becomes clear when we recognize the particular features in question. As linguistic anthropologist Monica Heller notes, these include the requirement, if economic globalization is to advance, of an intense "management of communication (involving producers, consumers, and national or supranational regulating bodies) across linguistic difference" (2010:104). If you can picture a corporation with offices in Beijing, New Delhi, London, Stockholm, and New York – all trying to work together – then you can understand what Heller means by "management ... across linguistic difference." Just as important, Heller notes, are the following:

> (b) the computerization of the work process, requiring new kinds of language and literacy skills among workers; (c) the growth of the service sector, in largely communication-based form; and (d) responses to the saturation of markets in the form of the development of niche markets (which require localized approaches often including a focus on linguistic specificity) and of the use of symbolic, often linguistic, resources to add value to standardized products. (Heller 2010:104)

As Heller summarizes, communication plays a double role "as the means through which work is accomplished (the work process) and as a product of labor (the work product)" (2010:104). Again I ask you to imagine something – this time a global company whose product is *English itself*, as the commodity purchased by elites. Imagine this real scenario – wealthy families in China sending their children to expensive private English classes to help them get admitted to the most competitive universities in the United States, which can also be seen as centers of what Heller (2010) calls "language work." (Compare Hochschild's [1979:569] concept of "emotion work" – labor in which "feelings are commoditized" – discussed in Chapter 9.)

We misunderstand globalization if we think it is a matter of a one-way, top-down (or vertical) process. As we are beginning to see, it is instead one side of a two-way conversation, the other side being a matter of (g)localization. Before we explore this new word "(g)localization," let's consider the idea that globalization can be "horizontal" – think Bollywood movies from India that were, at least at one time, huge hits even in Muslim areas of Nigeria (Inda and Rosaldo 2002) – as well as "vertical." And what's an example of vertical globalization? You might think of English as a single, globally dominant language displacing other languages, and the Chinese example in the previous paragraph would appear to fit this vertical model. However, in reality, there are many "Englishes" – see the journal *World Englishes* – which problematizes this understanding of the global spread of English.

Global or "Glocal"

The globalization (or **capitalist** expansion) to which Heller refers requires anthropologists to transcend their original vision of fieldwork, which was confined to small face-to-face communities. After all, where shall we find village life (see Figure 11.1) that is pure and unaffected by global flows?

Recent examples of linguistic anthropological fieldwork – indeed, any serious attempt to understand today's world – require recognizing the working of multiple

Figure 11.1 Bangladeshi farmer plowing his field in earlier times. (Photo by author)

pairs, such as the chief couplet that Heller (2010:104) described: language as a central means to late capitalist production on the one hand and, on the other hand, the production of ways of speaking that are themselves forms of **capital**.

Anthropologist Jonathan Friedman describes a similar pairing of simultaneous processes whereby local forms of life in small populations are less and less isolated in how they produce products and ideas; instead they are "reproduced increasingly via the circuits of the larger system" (2003:745). Moreover, global forces that we think of as simply overwhelming all local forms of human life are instead "integrated within the logics of local life worlds" (2003:745).

We encounter the global, in other words, in local form (see Figure 11.2). Think of those McDonald's stores in India with a vegetarian menu (Nandini 2014; Sameer 2012), or the Anglophone tourists who encounter India largely through a local entrepreneur in the film *The Best Exotic Marigold Hotel*, whose values are Western and whose apparently dominant language is English. As Friedman says about the localization of the global and the globalization of the local, "these two processes are dynamically related to one another over time" (2003:745).

It is precisely the paradoxical unity of the two processes Friedman describes – the simultaneous global "flows" and local "knows" of semiotic forms and reflections on them – that others call "glocalization." Citing Levitt (1983) and Herod (2010), linguistic anthropologist Marco Jacquemet writes that "anything global has its

Figure 11.2 The global use of cell phones is made local by this tribal woman in Thailand. (Mula Eshet/robertharding/Getty Images)

locality and any locale is not just global but in particular a node in the spatialized networks of global social relations" (forthcoming).

Concepts such as glocalization serve to remind us of themes I introduced in earlier chapters of this book, particularly the need for a processual perspective on societies, culture, and language – a perspective that calls into question the thing-like nature of these phenomena. These oft-used nouns have, at the very least, become much trickier to define.

Globalization and Superdiversity

The current wave of globalization has involved mass migrations and the diversification of the world's large cities. By contrast, the diversity that has until recently been spoken of most commonly is ethno-national diversity. **Social anthropologist** Steven Vertovec (2007:1024) describes this "old diversity," which has been seen in Britain and many other societies:

> Britain's immigrant and ethnic minority population has conventionally been characterized by large, well-organized African-Caribbean and South Asian communities of citizens originally from Commonwealth countries or formerly colonial territories. (2007:1024)

Of late, however, Vertovec sees in British cities and elsewhere around the world

> a dynamic interplay of variables among an increased number of new, small and scattered, multiple-origin, transnationally connected, socio-economically differentiated and legally stratified immigrants who have arrived over the last decade. (2007:1024)

Vertovec has dubbed this "diversification of diversity" as **superdiversity**.

Perhaps a useful way to think about this is to say that globalization is a process, and superdiversity is a result, a *reflection* of globalization in its present form. And the term superdiversity is useful as a way to designate some features that characterize this era of globalization.

As Blommaert, Rampton, and Spotti (2011:1) see it, superdiversity is the

> tremendous increase in the categories of migrants, not only in terms of nationality, ethnicity, language, and religion, but also in terms of motives, patterns, and itineraries of migration . . . The predictability of the category of "migrant" and of his/her sociocultural features has disappeared. (2011:1)

For instance, Blommaert et al. note that this entails internal diversification of, say, Chinese migrants in "'small' places" scattered across London or Antwerp rather than in the large close-knit "Chinatowns" of the past (2011:1–2).

Where do we see language fitting into this superdiversification? Blommaert et al. (2011) comment at some length on the "Chinese" Antwerp apartment-for-rent notice shown in Figure 11.3.

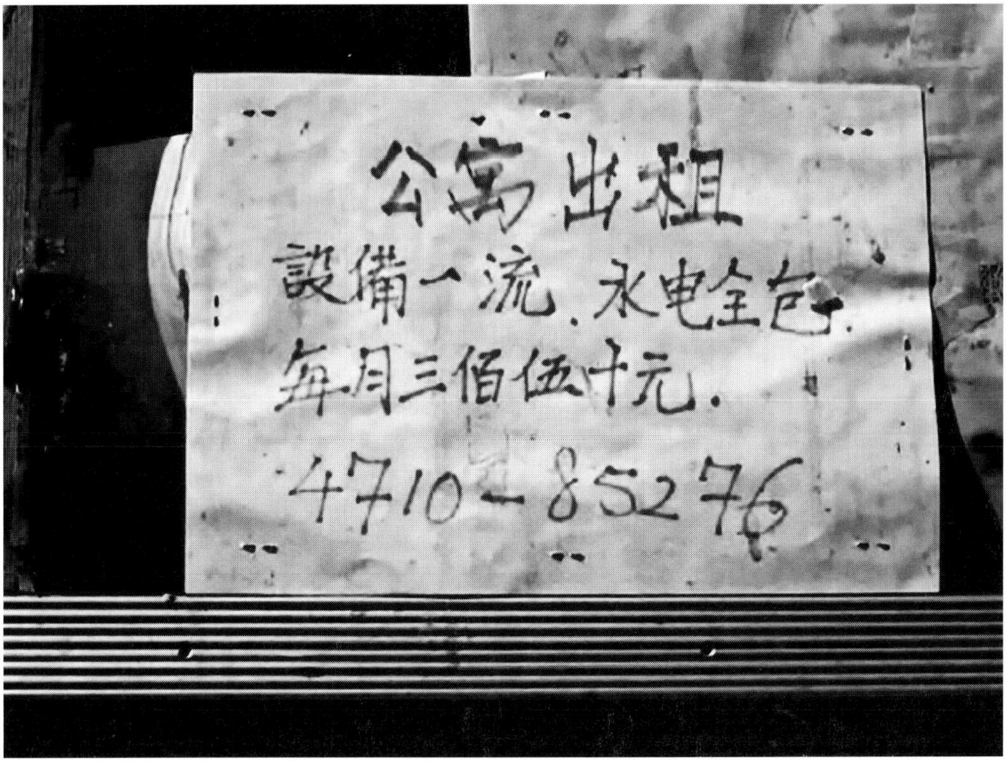

Figure 11.3 A notice in an Antwerp shop window serves as a indirect example of linguistic superdiversity. (© Jan Blommaert 2011. Reprinted with permission)

Note that I placed the adjective "Chinese" in quotation marks in the previous paragraph because it turns out that the sign in Figure 11.3 is handwritten in two scriptal forms: "a mixture of the simplified script which is the norm in the People's Republic of China (PRC) and the traditional script widespread in Hong Kong, Taiwan and earlier generations of the Chinese **diaspora**" (Blommaert et al. 2011:2). Blommaert et al. speculate that the sign's maker is accustomed to the traditional script, but incorporated some of the simplified script – and set the rent in Yuan (the PRC's currency) "rather than the Euro" – to signal a willingness to rent to newer migrants coming from the PRC (2011:2). Note the **indexicality** of this script use as a sign!

Deterritorialization of Discourse

What we have here, then, is a complex play of "home" versus "not-home," the pull of territories (home versus old) and of networks that *transcend* territoriality. **Deterritorialization**, Jacquemet argues, requires "the displacement and dispersion of a subjectivity unrestrained by territorial control" (2005:262). New electronic media – the Web, email, blogs, and instant messaging – exemplify the ways in which the latest wave of globalization has effected a fundamental deterritorialization of discourse.

Scholars interested in sociolinguistic superdiversity are going beyond simplistic core-periphery analysis, which sees clear power cleavages between dominant and subordinate actors. We must not think of the "commodification of language" as something as simple as the worldwide price of a commodity like corn on any given day. Instead, Jacquemet (2016:336) cites Blommaert explaining that, "the ability to speak a globally commodified language, such as English, in a way that is acceptable locally may indicate a 'cosmopolitan' person in that peripheric setting, but that same manner of speaking may, in a global center, point to the inferior status of this speaker." Jacquemet further notes, "Nonstandard deterritorialized speakers often find social and political alliances and smoother lines of communication with other non-standard speakers" (2016:337).

A key implication of what we have been discussing is that, to whatever extent a singular, monolithic "authenticity" emerged with modernity and, as a language ideology, was key to establishing modernity (Bauman and Briggs 2003), *that monolith has broken down* with the rise of glocalization and superdiversity. Wang addresses groups that were once marginalized (under conditions of "high modernity"), along with their forms of language (think here of Québécois French in Heller's analysis, picked up by Wang) (2015). Their linguistic varieties have acquired a new kind of authenticity under conditions Heller describes in terms of the "commodification of language." As Wang (2015:227) explains, such sociolinguistic groups can now "negotiate what it means to be authentic locally in terms of language status and cultural affiliation." This is newly possible as "the roles of language in relation to local identity claims" undergo redefinition, and glocalizing-superdiversifying forces reorganize "the normative systems of producing, distributing and recognizing language resources for identity practices."

Other Perspectives

Compared with other concepts I have introduced in this book, it is important to note that superdiversity is relatively more controversial. Critics point to questions left unanswered by the literature advocating this concept and its relevance to language: Is superdiversity real? Is it "out there," "in the world"? Or is it the product of language ideologies closely linked with nation-states – even in this era of the seeming collapse, or at least the increasing porosity, of the nation-state?

Michael Silverstein is one linguistic anthropologist who questions the newness of superdiversity. Instead he describes a centuries-long history of immigration and invasion that has affected England and its language. He suggests that we transcend a focus on *language communities* that the nation-state might try to impose and instead shift our attention to the diversity we find at the level of the *speech community*, which is small in scale, but large in importance.

As you recall, we explored "speech communities" and "language communities" in Chapter 9, and I at least hinted that, despite appearances, these "communities" are dynamic and constituted by semiotic ideologies. Should we now, following critics of the concept of superdiversity, abandon any pretense that the world out there – the world of speakers moving here and there – is the sole or real locus of change in the nature of diversity? Perhaps instead, we might recognize that we as *hearers* of our new neighbors are the major centers of change.

And how might we be centers of change? As producers and circulators of semiotic ideologies relevant to our new immigrant "neighborhood" and the linguistic varieties we associate with them. As linguistic anthropologist Angela Reyes (2014:367) sees it:

> [T]he change we may be tracing may not be in terms of "speaking subjects" (Foucault 1985:62) as much as in "listening subjects" (Inoue 2006:39): that is, change in ideology, change involving "us" – the perceiver, the overhearer-now-reporter, the [authorized] knowledge producer. As we move about the world, we may not see new things as much as see things anew . . .

Globalization Reviewed

Whether the globalization we are now experiencing is best described as super-diversity or as something we hear/create/define in our neighborhoods, we are living within its interconnections with media influences and emotional themes circulating in our world today. Although we soon explore these interconnections, I want first to summarize the major ideas about globalization that we have considered here – because they form the underpinning for our discussion from here.

- What is commonly called "globalization" is a reality.
- It involves increasingly rapid worldwide flows of not only "goods," but also "culture" and concomitant forms and ideologies of language of the sort this book has been describing.
- Globalization is profoundly linked to the "political economy."
- This means all sorts of capital – green (or hard) capital as well as social/cultural (or soft) capital – are not only on the move but are moving us.
- The movement of all kinds of capital admittedly entails the common idea that globalization is throwing people out of work.
- However, it also entails creating new kinds of work, especially **affective** and communicative labor.
- Such "movement" may better be called **glocalization** than globalization insofar as it always, to some extent, involves *localization*, hybridization, or adaptation.
- Finally, because of the reality of glocalization, the processes we explore here may involve a "diversification of diversity" (i.e., "superdiversity").

Media and Mediation

In this section, we explore two related terms and concepts. When we speak of "the media," we are using a common, shorthand way of referring to the conglomeration of media technologies that are used to reach large, possibly global, audiences.

The more technical term **mediation**, by contrast, refers to the spread of mass media and its increasing cultural and political importance. This use of mediation is not too distant from its use in Chapter 6, where it refers to the coming-between-ness of signs, thus their "mediation" of our experience of the world (i.e., semiotic mediation [Briggs 2011]).

In the course of this discussion, we explore the interconnections of media and mediation with globalization and with the changing roles and views of emotion that are circulating in our world today.

Media Circulating, Culture as Content

As Urban (2001) points out, "cultures" – which for him means *conceptual* systems – are always embodied in objects. Each object serves as a medium for transmitting culture, and only through such media can culture circulate.

However, the word media has taken on a very particular sense in "the age of mechanical reproduction" (Benjamin [1936] 1968). This is the age in which stories or performances circulate not just from mouth to mouth, but in a way that somehow defines the last several centuries vis-à-vis all that came before. The history of "the media" started with print, moved to film and broadcast, and surfaces now as web-mediated communication.

Print communication really took off with the rise of capitalism. "Print capitalism" (Anderson [1983] 1991) was once a powerful hybrid. Now it is only a small part of the larger "culture industry" (Horkheimer and Adorno 1946) – the vast, many-headed commercial enterprise that produces media, arts, entertainment, and infotainment for a consuming public. (See Figure 11.4.)

These media have arisen or proliferated precisely in the age of capitalism in which "all that is solid melts into air" (Berman 1982; Engels et al. 2012:38). As Marx and Engels argued, capitalism "cannot exist without" constantly updating products, production lines, relations, and ideas; thus media under capitalism require a constant stream of new content to generate new sales (see Figure 11.5). There is certainly evidence aplenty to demonstrate the reality of this idea: From an article by freelance writer Imogen O'Rorke about mergers between media outlets and content developers comes the statement, "new *media companies need content to go down their pipes*" (2000, citing Planalp; emphasis added). Or as online media expert Julia McCoy (2015, emphasis in original) points out:

> Right now, 93% of [business to business] marketers use content marketing in their marketing strategy and more than 70% of those marketers are using LinkedIn, Twitter, Facebook, and YouTube to distribute content. Natural search results are among the most-trusted type of web content, and companies are currently spending about 25% of their total marketing budgets on content marketing pursuits. All of these facts can be boiled down to one statement: *companies need content.*

Figure 11.4 An artist's view of "the culture industry." (Adapted from Gordon Haramaki)

Figure 11.5 The commodification of content becomes the new norm in media distribution. (bleakstar/Shutterstock)

Perhaps surprisingly, even "tradition" can be a source of "new" content. The title of O'Rorke's (2000) article is "Old Is the New New." (Interestingly, the *Guardian* webpage on which her article appears includes a button that says "Reuse this content.") I was also able to find online lists of Cinderella movies that have been made, in "attempts at retelling the story, or tailoring it to fit new audiences, or generations" (ComingSoon.net 2015).

Hobsbawm and Ranger (1983) go so far as to argue that the *notion* of tradition was invented to satisfy the dual needs of creating modern nation-states (each needing its own unique body of traditions) and supplying content in the form of books of folktales for early print capitalism. Bauman and Briggs (2003:224) emphasize that the modern state and tradition (e.g., national epics, folklore collections) emerged together, constituting each other.

Media and Transnationalism

Neither isolated nor "un-mediated" societies exist today – if they ever did. Even as long ago as 2000, I saw in Bangladesh, for instance, the circulation of broadcast and electronic media that mark this age as one of greatly intensified globalization. I saw satellite dishes on thatch-roofed village homes whose inhabitants were watching international media content. I heard a Bangladeshi psychiatrist blame a purported upswing in serious mental illness on American cartoons being viewed by too many patients. I visited internet cafes in Dhaka.

New technologies for work and other communication needs have had a substantial effect in speeding the glocalization of culture and have played a major role in creating and sustaining what we may call superdiversity in cities like Antwerp (as we saw in Figure 11.3). New forms of communication are both the increasingly pervasive *process* by which late capitalist production becomes possible and the increasingly common *products* thereof.

A number of factors shape the phenomena that we've been calling by names like globalization, glocalization, mediation, and superdiversity. For Bangladesh, "circular migration" is an important factor – as people move from Bangladesh (especially the northeastern part, called Sylhet) to London *and then back* to Bangladesh again (Gardner 1995). However, media also "migrate" or move – with no respect for national borders. As a result, the borders of nation-states seem increasingly porous; globalization at times threatens to erase borders entirely.

We also hear claims that the multiplicity of communication channels (from television and film to Facebook, Instagram, and smartphone-mediated chat) alienate us from one another – meaning from the sort of embodied co-presence that Duranti (2010) and Husserl (1913) emphasize. Indeed, different scholars think of mediation as humanizing and creative *or* as alienating; they may see it as possible and desirable (Husserl) *or* as impossible as Derrida might have it (Derrida and Bass [1967] 2001; see also Sass 1992).

In the following sections, we consider the perspectives of three scholars of language and communication – Alireza Doostdar, Ilana Gershon, and Marco Jacquemet – on the importance of social media in today's world, in which global flows and even the moving of emotion happen at hyperspeed. Hopefully, these examples can help you decide where you fall in the debate over the humanizing versus dehumanizing potential of mediation, and the possibility (and desirability) versus the impossibility of unmediated human-to-human presence.

Weblogestan

Anthropologist Alireza Doostdar (2004) carried out a fascinating study of the blogo-sphere in Iran, where devotion to the Persian language is part of the discussion. His ethnographic study of Persian-language blogs centers on the "vulgarity debate." When one blogger argued, for instance, that Islam and human rights were incompatible, the heated responses not only rejected that claim and whatever logic was behind it, but also asserted that blogging itself leads to the vulgarization of the Persian language, which is held in high honor by most Iranians.

Such assertions are similar perhaps to those made in the United States about the dumbing-down of English through the "language" of texting (Jones and Schieffelin 2009). The Iranian debate also parallels American debates over the "vulgarity" of gangsta rap, for instance, with lyrics that many consider to be misogynistic (Alim et al. 2008).

Doostdar says that his goal is, in part, to "examine the controversy as a confrontation between bloggers with unequal access to cultural capital" (2004:651). His invocation of capital and the production of value through particular uses of language echoes the words of Heller that we discussed earlier in this chapter. My point here, however, is to emphasize that language is not only the bearer of emotional meanings. Rather, various forms of language – *mediated* forms of language – are also *objects* of emotion and emotional debate. Keep this in mind as we consider Gershon's account of couples breaking up and the argument of her student "informants" over the relative virtues of this or that medium.

Breaking Up in New Media

Having our lives lived in no small part online, with much of our communication involving new media, is obviously quite different from previous times with different dominant modes of communication. Breaking up online is a good example of how new and different many people's lives can be in this age.

Ilana Gershon is an **ethnographer** who studies new media, among other research topics. She writes about a discussion with students:

> On a whim, I asked … "What counts as a bad breakup?" I was expecting answers like, "I found my girlfriend in bed with someone else," or "We yelled at each other until three in the morning," or "He never returned my favorite DVDs." Instead, my students all told me about *mediated breakups* – that is, breakups by texting … or by Facebook. (Gershon 2011:1)

The contingent nature of breaking-up performatives may not be new. It seems likely that "announcing a desire to break up may not result in a breakup" now, but it might not have been "successful" in prior eras either. Gershon and the undergraduate students she interviewed seem to agree that "the media of the message strongly influence whether or not the utterance will be effective" (2010:401–402).

Note that these breakup stories made clear that many media were used in the breakup or the attempt to break up. "Most breakup stories I heard involved a range of media as people gradually realized that what was unfolding was a breakup." In fact, the conversations recounted in these breakup stories "are often scattered interactions that only coalesce into a definitive breakup in hindsight" (2010:402).

The undergraduate students in Gershon's study all had their own "media ideologies," just as we all have language ideologies that filter our understandings of various ways of speaking. Her students experienced different media as possessing different strengths and limitations. They experience different media as "formal or informal, enabling intonation or devoid of intonation, allowing for conversational turn-taking or preventing it, public or private, and so on" (2010:402). As is often the case with language ideologies, however, the students' media ideologies included blind spots. The students "tended to overlook the diversity of other people's beliefs about media. As a consequence, they often claimed that there were widely held beliefs about how a medium affects a message during a breakup, and widely accepted ethical guidelines" (2010:402).

Gershon's book shows that the various sociolects and registers available to communicators in particular communities are far from neutral. They have different effects, despite the way they might seem to be "isosemantic," meaning they use different ways to say the same thing. Likewise, Gershon's undergraduate students do not see the various media that they or their former partners used in breaking up as "functionally interchangeable." They see "face-to-face interaction" as one communicative medium among others, but also as

> a preferable medium during breakups because it contains the widest bandwidth of information, so to speak. My interviewees discussed the pros and cons of co-present communication in much the same ways they discussed the pros and cons of other media. In short, co-presence is no longer widely evaluated by people on the ground as unmarked and unmediated, instead it is taken to be a medium like any other. In this sense, new media ideologies are affecting ideologies of older media, and even transforming what had not been widely defined as a medium into one. (Gershon 2010:402)

I want to mention yet another noteworthy finding of Gershon's study. Other generations, older generations in particular, might presume that those who are growing up in an age of new media take this phenomenon for granted and see it as positive. However, Gershon says, "Those I interviewed were often nostalgic for the times before one had all these technological options … They like to believe that before all these options existed, love and heartbreak were more intelligible" (2010:402–403).

Transidioma: Mobile Media Meeting Mobile People

Transidioma is a complicated concept that rewards our attention insofar as it helps us see how globalization and various forms of mediation work together. Marco Jacquemet coined the term "transidiomatic practices" to describe "the communicative practices of transnational groups that interact using different languages and communicative codes simultaneously present in a range of communicative channels, both local and distant" (Jacquemet 2005:264–265).

More and more, according to Jacquemet, "linguistic communities ... are diffused and overlapping ... groups of people [are] no longer territorially defined [but] think about themselves and communicate using an array of both face-to-face and long-distance media" (2016:330). Jacquemet (2005:262) further explains that

> through the electronic media, people confront new rules and resources for the construction of social identity and cultural belonging (Appadurai 1996) ... [Among other examples,] when Pakistani taxi-drivers in Chicago listen to sermons recorded in mosques in Kabul or Teheran (Appadurai 1996), [what we are witnessing is] the encounter of mobile media practices and transnational people. In this encounter, a new, deterritorialized social identity takes shape, light-years away from the corporate logic of the nation-state. (2005:262)

In other words, what is variously called post- or late-modernity is fostered by rapid globalization and globalizing mass media. And crucially, our contemporary condition leads to a global political economy that sharply contrasts with that of early or "high" modernity. Globalization breaks down the territorial separations that defined the political economy of earlier forms of modernity. As Jacquemet (2005:261) puts it:

> Three of the most significant outcomes of this process are: (1) the sustained development of diasporic social formations, in which people bear multiple linguistic allegiances and cultural belongings; (2) the emergence of media idioms (such as the use of global English in news broadcasting, advertising, or electronic mailing lists) that presuppose translocal modes of production and reception, enabling social groups to access procedural knowledge of the world through the media; and (3) the formation of global power elites and locally based semiotic operators that use knowledge of international languages as commodities and tools to secure, in the former case, a dominant position in the world, and for the latter, to engage in a process of social and geographical (mostly south–north) mobility.

A unique feature of Jacquemet's transidioma is that it points to a multilingualism involving multiple media. For example, in "Adriatic transidiomatic environments" and specifically Albanian households, a handful of languages all clamor for attention on different media – Italian soap operas on TV, Internet content mostly in English, conversation as a live face-to-face medium of communication that in these households takes place not only in standard Albanian or "exotic" varieties such as

Arberesh, "the variety of Albanian brought to southern Italy in the 15th century by Catholic refugees from Northern Albania, fleeing the Ottoman invasion" (Jacquemet 2005:269), but in as many languages as the countries their migratory members have lived in (likely Germany, Greece, the United States).

The vision of this transcendence of any one idiom spoken by a people in a place as part of a polity – which Jacquemet has dubbed "transidioma" – is a fine example of why linguistic anthropologists see special and positive meaning in the myth of Babel, the scattering of people from their monolingual tower in the biblical story.

Media Circulating Subjectivity

We have been talking about a wide variety of media forms and the ways they are inspiring and facilitating changes in communication **styles** and possibilities. Here we focus in particular on how globally circulating media forms are spreading "modern subjectivity" (Abu-Lughod 2000). In fact, even at the turn of the last century, anthropologist Lila Abu-Lughod was already speaking of the "growing cultural hegemony" of media in

> engendering new modes of subjectivity and new discourses on personhood, ones that we could recognize as "modern" in their emphasis on the individual . . . Psychologizing, buttressed by the whole discourse of psychoanalysis with its vivid conjuring of a rich and conflictual inner world, is also instrumental in constructing modern subjects. And the discourse of feelings and emotion – the very stuff of melodrama – is essential to the psychological. (2000:95)

Abu-Lughod speaks of a global "psychologizing," carried by forms from mass media, including television melodramas, to face-to-face media, even including taxi rides (Marsilli-Vargas 2014, 2016). This tendency shines like a sun that never sets on the global reach of psychologizing media (Debord 1994: see especially pp. 12 and 15).

A Brief Nod to Mediatization

Before we shift our gaze more specifically to emotion and subjectivity in a mediated global context, I want to briefly mention a subtype of mediation, called **mediatization**, that is now grabbing the interest of many linguistic anthropologists.

What do scholars mean by this media(tization)? It has been described as a *dark subtype* of mediation, one that is entangled with the spread of commoditization (or commodification), the process by which more and more of our lives are becoming commodities or objects to be bought and sold. As you might suspect, the advertising industry is a leader in both mediation and commodification.

How might this idea of mediatization be useful to anthropologists? Briggs finds it helpful in describing public health media campaigns that turn knowledge about cholera epidemics into a commodity (Briggs 2004, 2005, 2011; Briggs and

Mantini-Briggs 2003). Marsilli-Vargas (2016) finds the term useful in describing commodifying media that tout the quintessentially modern figure of the psychoanalyst in Argentina. It is worth noting that both authors invoke mediatization in close proximity to their mentions of "affective stance" or "tone" (Briggs 2011:224) or the psychologizing or emotionalizing influence of the spreading psychoanalytic discourse (Marsilli-Vargas 2016:144, 147, 149). Once again, we see that there truly is a link between globalization, mediation, and "emotionalization" (Rose 1999:206).

Emotion and Language: New Globally Circulating Forms

Cultural globalization is often portrayed in terms of increasingly easy and rapid "flows," or processes, of "circulation." These flows are not only of the sorts of *products* we usually imagine – American or European fashions, musical recordings, films and television shows – but of *emotions*, or forms of subjectivity that are increasingly conceived of as emotions. As Heller (2010:104) notes, "Sometimes consuming experiences is more valuable than consuming goods." It also seems true, however, that some newly circulating forms of emotion, emotion-talk, and pedagogies of emotion focus more on making the people they teach be more like emotionally "producing selves, rather than consuming ones" (McElhinny 2016:189).

Particular Experiences of the Global Subjective

The kinds of subjective experiences that global citizens are now exposed to or drawn to vary tremendously. As one example, consumers who have the means to make choices about what to buy now often make those choices based on the subjective: "Whether we accept it or not, people buy things, follow brands, or like pages based on emotion and experience. That's just the way the human mind operates" (Brown 2016). (See Figure 11.6.) Linguistic and semiotic anthropologist Paul Manning, an expert on consumer brands, puts this a bit differently:

> As brands move from being prosthetic figures mediating relations between subjects (producers and consumers) to becoming autonomous subjects in their own right, it becomes possible for consumers to form affective relationships with these figures directly. But brands as persons can be imagined in rather different ways, and the kinds of personalistic relationships they mediate also vary. (2010:45)

As Wilce and Fenigsen (2016), following Taylor, have argued, we see a "massive subjective shift" (Taylor 1992:26) in modern culture. Paul Heelas (2008:33), sociologist of religion, calls this the shift toward "subjective-life spirituality." Thus the focus of religious experience has, at least for some, also shifted significantly, not

Figure 11.6 Product marketing today often targets consumers' subjective emotional responses. (Meriel Jane Waissman/Getty Images)

only from an academic perspective, but in the eyes of religious activists: "They no longer hunger for the Gospel, they hunger for 'religious experience'. It's all about emotion. There is little room for reason" (Pascendi 2009).

Let us consider another example of subjectivity that is particularly interesting for the globalization of language, namely "devotion," which we explore in more detail here.

Devotion as Subjective and as Mediated

The **ethnography** of emotion has often focused on a *particular* emotion that is performed and discussed in a particular way in a particular site of ethnographic fieldwork. Devotion is an example. Note, however, that we should expect "devotion" to mean something different depending on whether its object is the Prophet of Islam (Eisenlohr 2010), Krishna (Lynch 1990), or Jesus or his Sacred Heart (Richo 2007). So it is worth noting here that although globalization may tear down walls and may appear to entail the circulation of stable objects across formerly clearer cultural boundaries, homogeneity may be more apparent than real.

Here we focus on one particular devotional experience. Linguistic anthropologist Patrick Eisenlohr has carried out years of fieldwork among Muslims on the island of Mauritius whose ancestors emigrated from South Asia. Eisenlohr describes conflict there over the legitimacy of the recital of poems of devotion to the Prophet and over the power of electronic mediation to stir legitimate devotion. The context – not one locale (the island of Mauritius) but its ongoing relationship with South Asia as the ancestral homeland for Muslim Mauritians – is crucial here.

Much of Eisenlohr's work has focused on a certain genre of devotional singing that is widespread in the Muslim world – a genre called *na't* – "devotional poems sung in praise of the Prophet Muhammad ... *Na't* is a performative technique creating pious dispositions as well as certain affective stances, especially deep affection and love for the Prophet, resulting in a sense of visceral closeness to him" (Eisenlohr 2010:317).

Interestingly, this example of devotion circulates through various media of sound recording – audiocassettes, compact discs, and websites from which *na't* can be downloaded. Not only the practice of *na't* singing, but the tangible and circulable media are theologically ambiguous. For those who cultivate this devotional practice, however, the media ensure the faithful transmission of *na't*. They enable recitational performances by "accomplished reciters of *na't* (*na't khwān*)" (2010:317) to travel. And the local understanding is that they do so without any loss of quality or sacred authority to "South Asia and its diasporas [such as Mauritius]" (2010:317).

Although the form of *na't* used on Mauritius today is clearly modern, electronic mediation and the transmission it exemplifies are accepted in large part because of the centuries-long Islamic understanding of person-to-person (and generation-to-generation) transmission of the theologically sound teaching and practice called *isnad* (Eisenlohr 2006:242; 2010:325). "The potential for a minimization of temporal and spatial distances enabled by the material frame of technologies of **voice** mediation is appropriated and reworked through established logocentric epistemologies of an authority of voice" (Eisenlohr 2006:241).

The cassette- or CD-carried voices of "accomplished reciters of *na't*," in other words, are regarded as authentic, legitimate, and vouchsafed somehow – in a manner specified by local understandings of how both knowledge and certainty work. Again in Eisenlohr's words, "Here Mauritian Muslims reshape technology according to a genealogical form of Islamic authority centered on a 'safeguarding' of textual and performative transmission through long successions of reliable interlocutors" (2006:241).

We students of culture and communication find the apparently flexible fit between "channels" (media) and "content" (affect such as devotion and religious teaching) here especially interesting. However, it is also important to keep in mind that the singing of *na't* and the attribution of religiously faithful authority to the recorded singers and the tangible media are vehemently rejected by some Muslims in Mauritius, South Asia, and elsewhere in the Muslim world.

And, as I mentioned earlier, it is important to remember that Eisenlohr's work here illustrates linguistic anthropologists' interests in the cultural particularity of emotional text-production-and-circulation, even as we locate that particularity at the busy circulatory intersection of the local and the global.

Feelings of Loss in Language Shift and Language Revitalization

As we have seen, this time of increasing global interconnection involves both gains and losses among particular societies and cultures. One kind of global loss is that of the diversity of languages that have been spoken by various groups over the centuries. Language loss includes losses of culture and of identity, and efforts to "revitalize" threatened languages have been made for a few languages.

We explore present-day language revitalization efforts in great detail in Chapter 12. I foreshadow that discussion here for the following reasons:

- "Language shift" is largely a result of the global dominance of colonial languages and concomitant communicative forms.
- Media play a large role in threatening the status of indigenous languages, but also in some programs designed to revitalize those languages.
- Traditional languages, their status, and the media through which they now more commonly circulate are all emotional matters.

This third point, about the emotions people feel about their languages, is one that linguistic anthropologists like Emily McEwan-Fujita (2010) and Anthony Webster (2010) have recently described. McEwan-Fujita has worked primarily on Gaelic as spoken (albeit less and less) in Scotland. (See Figure 11.7.) She acknowledges the potential duality of "negative affect" in the context of the

> shift from a minority language to a state-sponsored European language, whether they take the form of grief over the loss (Dauenhauer and Dauenhauer 1995), regret and anger about not having the language passed on to oneself by one's parents (MacCaluim 2007:267–268; Newton 2005), or shame at being a speaker of a minority language ... However, the language revitalization efforts that are aimed at halting language shift, particularly language-learning efforts, can also generate negative affect among participants. [This includes]... the embarrassment of becoming a childlike linguistic novice again as an adult, and the painful process of breaking down the old social identity and forging a new one. (Trosset 1986:185)

Like McEwan-Fujita, Anthony Webster has done much to foster recognition of emotion surrounding endangered languages. He argues that it is unfortunate that so many language experts manifest a **referentialist** bias – when, for example, they represent the stakes of language loss primarily in terms of losing the capacity (once "stored" in those languages) to make reference to special plants, for instance.

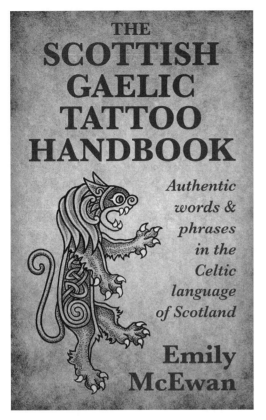

Figure 11.7. One creative way to provide information about Gaelic to different kinds of learners. (*The Scottish Gaelic Tattoo Handbook* front cover © 2016 Bradan Press; lion illustration © 2016 Pat Fish)

This referentialist bias – this representation of language almost exclusively in terms of its referential **function** – is unfortunate because

> such works strip language and grammar of the emotional attachments that speakers have to the uses of their languages and grammars. Such positions replicate a view that sees human emotions and aesthetics as not nearly as important as the science of encoding ecological knowledge. It sees languages as primarily about reference. It forgets the delight that speakers take in language form. As linguistic anthropologists we do a disservice to the speakers of languages if we neglect the feelings they have toward their languages. (Webster 2010:203)

It is worth noting here that the processes of language "contraction" (Hoffman 2006) and of language revitalization result directly, though obviously in different ways, from globalization. We must see, too, that emotions surrounding language (Wilce 2009b) and its revitalization (McEwan-Fujita 2010) play a powerful role, not only reflecting the power of the global but refracting that power.

Bringing Themes Together

It is anthropologist Kathryn Graber (2012) who I find most directly addresses the confluence of emotion surrounding indigenous language, modern media, and globalization. Like McEwan-Fujita, Graber provides evidence of negative affect, including shame, in regards to a felt inability to speak Buryat (the language she studies, which is spoken in Mongolia) in a way perceived as adequate. The media, however, have the potential at least in the case of Buryat to be a source of pride:

> Buryat-language newspaper journalists were respected, it seemed, and generally held in high esteem by readers – not only because they possessed knowledge, but because they shared it through stable, enduring, prestigious literary institutions in which Buryats could take real pride. (Graber 2012:195)

Graber's work makes it abundantly obvious that newspapers and other (e.g., digital) media are related only in complex ways with emotion surrounding the potential loss or maintenance of the Buryat language. This is, in fact, what makes work such as hers significant for a linguistic anthropology that concerns itself with the effects of globalization (e.g., on indigenous peoples and their languages), the nature of media in our contemporary global world, and the anything-but-trivial role that emotion plays in all of these power-drenched phenomena.

A Variety of Forms for the Global Subjective

Exploring globally circulating subjectivities involves looking not only at a range of emotional experience (from consumer decision-making to spiritual devotion and indigenous loss) but also at the variety of media forms that influence and carry these experiences. So next we consider a few of those forms – from the use of television to teach emotions (and emotional expression and control) to children, to the mediation of Shia laments, Egyptian melodramas, and Arab narrative poetry.

Teaching Feelings

In the United States, and rapidly spreading throughout at least the moderately wealthy parts of the world, emotion is being taught explicitly. The channels through which "pedagogies of emotion" (Wilce and Fenigsen 2016) flow include the Public Broadcasting System, which has both television and web components.

As part of a cultural teaching process, as well as for the purposes of entertainment, it is common for very young children to watch television shows. In the United States, the Public Broadcasting System has been a frontrunner in creating television programming for young children that educates as it entertains, since the introduction of the long-running *Sesame Street* series in 1969.

While *Sesame Street* may be better known for introducing preschoolers to counting and reading, the show now also frequently discusses emotions and shows how to cope with different emotions as they arise. For example, in this *Sesame Street* clip (http://bit.ly/24Xqsyk), actress Whoopi Goldberg helps Baby Bear deal with his anger by showing him a vocal and physical exercise that helps him calm down. Notable in this video is the view of anger as a normal, healthy response to the situation.

Another award-winning PBS program, *Daniel Tiger's Neighborhood* (DTN), takes this concept one step further, demonstrating how angry feelings sometimes make it difficult to be calm enough to come up with a solution. "Before children can think clearly enough to deal constructively with their angry feelings, they need self-control in order to slow down and calm down" (PBSKids.org-PBS-Learning-Media 2016). This video clip (http://bit.ly/1UZGIbH) shows DTN's unique take on anger management.

Daniel Tiger's Neighborhood has also, at least on occasion, modeled "I-statements" for its young audience. For those unfamiliar with this concept, teacher Shirley Guerrero contrasts a statement like "You bother me!" by providing an I-statement replacement: "I feel angry when you bother me because I need respect" (Lehrer 2009).

It is worth noting that the Las Vegas public schools produced a *Teachers Guide* for using DTN commentary on the DTN episode "When You Feel Left Out":

> All kids feel hurt when they are ignored or excluded whether at home, at school, on the sports field, or within a group. This engaging video and print curriculum explores true-to-life scenarios in which upper elementary students experience the disappointment and sadness of being left out. It teaches students specific skills to use when they feel left out, how to express their emotions using "I" statements and how to take positive actions to help them feel better. (VegasPBS.org 2015)

In addition to teaching emotional competency via television and in classrooms, emotion pedagogy is actually part of the Head Start Child Development and Early Learning Framework, which states that

> Social & Emotional Development refers to the skills necessary to foster secure attachment with adults, maintain healthy relationships, regulate one's behavior and emotions, and develop a healthy concept of personal identity. Positive social and emotional development provides a critical foundation for lifelong development and learning. (ECLKC-Headstart 2015)

A key question here is whether emotion pedagogies are spreading around the world. Many children's shows – including those from PBS – do seem to circulate internationally. Some are translated, others transculturated (i.e., adapted to fit particular cultural frameworks). One example of programming with a global reach is *Daniel Tiger's Neighborhood*, which is available via the video service Netflix in Norway, Finland, Sweden, France, New Zealand, and Australia. Through other licensing arrangements since its premiere in 2012, DTN is also available in

Germany, Russia, South East Asia, Thailand, the Middle East, Israel, Turkey, Iran, Latin America, and elsewhere. Hence, its messages about emotion and other topics do indeed have global circulation.

In terms of viewer response, an interesting example comes from a website for Indian mothers (Preethi 2016):

> My 3.5 yr old daughter surely is growing up – not just outwardly but in her inner emotional world too. She has a much expanded social life as well with her new school with a lot more kids of all ages. I believe this is the time to help her cope correctly with emotions and social situations. The show Daniel Tiger's Neighborhood offers a lot of help in this regard. My daughter loves watching these episodes!

I don't know where Preethi is (for instance, in India or not) or what being identified as an "Indian Mom" means for her. But, to put it in terms we have emphasized throughout this book, we do know that Preethi *does identify as* an "Indian Mom," specifically one who shepherds her 3.5-year-old daughter through the life passages mediated by Daniel Tiger and his emotion lessons.

Clearly, it is important to look at the impact of globally circulating public and children's television programs. In the future, it would be valuable to intensify academic, particularly *ethnographic*, studies of globalizing media in relation to emotion pedagogies. (Ethnographic media studies typically involve participant observation, as we discussed in Chapter 7 – for instance, watching television with children who are already watching and making note of their responses.) Studies of *Sesame Street* and *Daniel Tiger's Neighborhood* to date have considered these programs as forms of social and emotional learning – a phenomenon that is important in itself (Wilce and Fenigsen 2016).

Feelingful Communication in Our Global Village

Moving beyond mediated emotional learning, I want to share with you a personal example of "feelingful" communication related to digital media. A few years ago, I met an exchange student I'll call Hussein, a man with a laptop and a heart full of songs. These were not just any songs, but Shia Muslim **laments** – songs of mourning (similar in some ways and in others very different from the Karelian laments discussed in earlier chapters). These songs and their compelling lyrics, along with tears and other public signs of grief over a particular set of historic martyrs, help to define Shia Islam vis-à-vis other forms of Islam.

In the process of my interviewing Hussein, it became clear that, for him, many things came together – language, feeling, globally circulating media, and thoughts of memorializing Imam Husayn in Hussein's local Shia shrine in his city and country of origin – in the context of Shia religious practices that pervaded his life. This coming together, this fusion of language and feeling, is the very stuff of culture.

Hussein's laptop contains perhaps hundreds of MP3 files of these Shia laments. Is that where they "live"? Yes and no. Hussein has made them a part of his life. During the course of our interview, when there was a quiet moment as we waited for a file to download, I found him humming. What was he humming? Another lament. Hussein's culture moves around the world with him – in his heart, but often mediated (in this case, via his laptop).

Revisiting Melodrama

And here is another example of media forms helping to develop and circulate cultural information – in this case, Egyptian melodrama. Is "melodrama" capable of producing "the modern subject" in Egypt? Anthropologist Lila Abu-Lughod indicates that such may be the case – at least in 2000, that was the claim she made.

Importantly, however, Abu-Lughod is not asserting that a peculiarly Western "modern subject" was being produced by Egyptian television melodramas. (See Figure 11.8.) By now you won't be surprised that I invoke "glocalization" in regards to Abu-Lughod's subject: Egyptian television producers were drawing on, or at least

Figure 11.8 The two lead actors, Joelle Behlok and Raheed Assaf, from the Arabic melodrama series *The Last Cavalier*, on location. (Courtesy Nasib Bitar, Executive Producer)

working alongside, "folk traditions." These traditions were dramatic in their own way, though "the differences between the emotional styles and imaginaries created by these narrative and poetic traditions and those of television melodramas ... [were] striking" ([Abu-Lughod 2000:96).

Abu-Lughod describes the invention of what we might call an Egyptian-modern subjectivity through a rather old medium (television). This transformation is by no means alone, as we see in traditional poetry that she also comments on.

Oral Narrative Poetry

One such traditional form is Arab oral narrative poetry – especially the Hilali epic, the story of Abu Zayd, studied by anthropologist Susan Slyomovics (1985; 1987). The Abu Zayd story was, and to some extent still is, "recited professionally by socially marginal poets with astonishing verbal talents, not to mention prodigious memories" (Abu-Lughod 2000:97). Thus the tradition is oral.

Yet no tradition remains unchanged. There are now printed versions of the Hilali epic poems. On the one hand, these versions of the old epic now circulating in a new medium are more "complete and sequential, rather than segmented and partial" (2000:97). However, Abu-Lughod (2000:97) notes that

> they also lack the elaborate punning of the performed [version]. This absence of punning indicates two things: a declining attention to the language itself [the poetic or metalingual function a la Jakobson], or poetics, in the printed versions; and a greater reliance on the story, rather than the multiple meanings of the puns, for establishing character.

Note the shift toward a subtle, implicit metadiscourse embracing the centrality of reference over performance and poetics. In place of the crucial features of the older poetic genres, Abu-Lughod writes, "formulaic phrases about tears and their plenitude ... television drama tries to produce the inner beings who feel these emotions through close-ups of facial expressions and melodramatic acting" (2000:99).

CONCLUSION

This chapter explores globalization (primarily defined here as the global circulation of forms of culture and language), media (which we can think of as the concrete bearers of cultural ideas and values, as well as ideologies of language), and the salience of emotion in contemporary cultural globalization/mediation.

Among other themes, the next chapter continues our exploration of the significance of emotion in relation to languages whose vitality has been negatively impacted by cultural globalization and whose best hope for revitalization might or might not lie in media, old or new.

SUMMARY

In this chapter, we explored the complex and powerful relationships between globalization, old and new media, and emotion. After reading it, you should be familiar with the following ideas:

- The meaning of cultural globalization in anthropology.
- The relations between economic globalization, language, and communication.
- What role the media play in cultural globalization.
- The meaning of "mediation" and "mediatization."
- The media by which new (meaning Western? Modern? Postmodern?) concepts, ideologies, and experiences of emotion circulate globally.

QUESTIONS

1. What is it about the use of the term "globalization" in this chapter that sets it apart from common uses (for example, in political rhetoric)?
2. How is it possible to claim that emotions are cultural, that ways of feeling are taught locally and spread globally?
3. Marshall McLuhan (1964) is famous for his dictum, "the medium is the message." What in your view is the relationship between that idea and this book's insistence that systems of communication mediate culture and society?

EXERCISES

1. Watch an episode of a children's television program, such as *Daniel Tiger's Neighborhood* (DTN) – preferably online so you can stop and start the program as needed in order to make detailed notes. If you find references to such issues confronting children such as what to do when they are feeling some specific emotion – and any DTN episode is likely to include some such statements – write down a couple of these statements from the program. What do they tell you about emotion pedagogies?
2. Find two videos of an oral poetry tradition online (e.g., YouTube). You should be able to find examples from West Africa and from Finland, among other places, quite easily. After watching two examples – either two from a similar region, or one each from two separate regions – see what you can learn about them and specifically about how circulation online might have affected the tradition.
3. Do you live within hearing range of a radio station broadcasting in what is, in your country, a minority language? If not, find a broadcast online whose goal is to foster the use of a potentially threatened language. If possible, watch or listen with someone for whom the language being broadcast is their heritage language

(Moore 2012). Afterward, invite that person(s) to talk about what viewing or listening to a show in their own language feels like.

ADDITIONAL RESOURCES

Hoffman, Katherine E. 2008. Mediating the Countryside: Purists and Pundits on Tashelhit Radio. In *We Share Walls: Language, Space, and Gender in Berber Morocco*. K. E. Hoffman, ed. Pp. 195–227. Blackwell Studies in Discourse and Culture. Malden, MA: Wiley-Blackwell.

Like many ethnographies of broadcast media, Hoffman's brings much insight to the controversies surrounding (in this case) radio, particularly how debates over Berber language purism play out over the radio.

Peterson, Mark Allen. 2003. *Anthropology and Mass Communication: Media and Myth in the New Millennium.* Oxford and New York: Berg-Hahn Books.

Probably the best survey of mass communication by an anthropologist, this book is comprehensive and insightful.

2011. Egypt's Media Ecology in a Time of Revolution. *Arab Media and Society* Issue 14. www.arabmediasociety.com/?article=770.

This short article presents a fascinating picture of the role of social media in one of the events that came to be known as "The Arab Spring."

12 Applying Linguistic Anthropology

James Wilce and Martina Volfová

> **LEARNING OBJECTIVES**
>
> After reading this chapter, you should be able to do the following:
>
> - Summarize the history of **applied anthropology**, particularly applied anthropology involving language.
> - Describe the issues uniquely related to culture and communication in the areas where applied/engaged/public anthropologists work.
> - Explain why applied or engaged work has sometimes been controversial.

Introduction

In this chapter, we focus on *applied* linguistic anthropology. We begin with the frequently troubled (and troubling) history of applied anthropological projects involving language. However, the brief history we review here also includes increasingly promising links between theoretical models of **language ideology** – with which you are familiar – and their importance in projects designed to resist **language shift**.

In this chapter, we frequently echo anthropologist Eleanor Nevins (2013), who emphasizes that projects involving communities with traditionally spoken languages that are now in decline consist of more than just documenting that language as it declines. She also emphasizes that language revitalization efforts involve much more than outsiders "suggesting" to Indigenous groups what they should do.

After an extensive look at language revitalization, we then discuss how linguistic anthropology can help improve the quality of practitioner–patient encounters and thus the experience of medicine. This includes engaging with hospitals and other providers that require translation services but often fall back on untrained interpreters, including children, serving as "language brokers." Beyond these brokers, whose task is clearly one of mediation, we also consider two other kinds of mediating technology. The first is the now pervasive use of computers coming between practitioners and patients in literal and figurative ways. The second example is the use of therapy dogs to help children diagnosed with Autism Spectrum Disorder (ASD) to participate in communicative activities that are more challenging without their service dogs.

The final pair of examples we present in this chapter are stories of engagement outside of both medical settings and communities facing "language contraction" that we discuss earlier. The first entails encouraging university students and faculty to break out of the "ivory tower" – to engage with local communities in addressing local linguistic inequality. The second takes place at the national level. It involves linguistic anthropologists joining together to propose policy changes that could affect schools all over the United States. It focuses in particular on schools serving minority populations whose ways of speaking and parenting, especially teaching their children language, have come under fire in the past. In both situations, anthropologists are engaging with local groups to fight stereotypes as well as material inequalities. In doing so, these linguistic anthropologists are drawing on decades of research findings in the area of language socialization.

Chapter 12 is the last chapter in this textbook, and it is appropriate to end on this applied note. After reading examples of linguistic anthropology applied to everyday life issues, you should feel ready to contemplate how you can apply what you have learned *throughout* this book. Indeed, through these examples, you will see how to go from mere thinking about application to actually *applying what you have learned in, about, and from linguistic anthropology*.

The Intertwining of Applied and Theoretical Work

As we begin our discussion, we should recognize that "applied anthropology" is only one of many names for this field. The fact that it goes by several other names reflects the controversies that have surrounded and may continue to surround it. Some anthropologists prefer the adjective "public" (see the Center for A Public Anthropology, at publicanthropology.org). Others prefer the descriptor "engaged" (engagedanthropology.org). Still others avoid compact labels and speak more generally of their ambition to "do" anthropology that is clearly relevant to public policy, or to engage in collaborative efforts of mutual benefit to anthropologists and the communities they work with.

Linguistic anthropological work of this sort – whether labeled applied, public, engaged, or something else – is not necessarily so different from the sort that appears to be purely theoretical. We might see engaged anthropology as *explicit* in its goal of making itself relevant and of benefit to communities, while theoretical work is *implicitly* so. In any case, theoretical studies of culture and communication always have not only a perspective, but also an impact.

Not all linguistic anthropologists strive to find common ground between the so-called applied and the so-called theoretical. Some criticize applied anthropology as ostensibly not theoretical enough. Yet others, including both of this chapter's co-authors, see applied work in our field as making significant theoretical contributions. For us, such contributions begin with the simple yet crucial observation that *anthropological theory is a necessary prerequisite to applied "interventions."*

Areas of Application

Probably the most common challenge to which linguistic anthropologists have applied their models, understandings, and methods is that of Indigenous and minority languages. Language shift often results from situations of language contact – in which one or more smaller, politically and economically weaker languages become gradually replaced by more politically and economically empowered languages, such as English, Spanish, Chinese, and Russian.

In contact situations such as these, Native speakers may first become bilingual, but then gradually cease transmitting their heritage language to their children. There is a strong likelihood that many such languages will continue to "contract" (Hoffman 2008) from their former areas of primacy. Some have referred to this as languages becoming "endangered." However, we should keep in mind that languages differ from plant and animal species in that language speakers *do* have agency. In fact, in some sense, these speakers imbue their *languages* with agency as well. Instead of buying into concepts of endangerment and possible extinction, we hope for and work toward better things. We aim toward "sustainability" in relation to Indigenous languages and "reciprocity" in the interactions between academics and Indigenous activists working to revitalize them (Nevins 2013).

Another domain of sociocultural life to which linguistic anthropology has been and should continue to be applied is health and healing. Although medical anthropology as a field has become more and more *theoretically* savvy, it emerged from *applied* anthropology and continues to produce much work that is applied. That much is literally true. However, the utility of medical anthropology in this context is also metaphorical.

To explain, medical anthropologists have found that in many cases around the world, a declaration of the meaning of an illness (the diagnosis) is the first or perhaps key step toward healing. That can serve as a metaphor for applied anthropology: An anthropological investigation can lead to a practical "diagnostic" insight into a problem. That is, if the study's analysis becomes useful through shedding light on that problem, then this is sufficient for the study to be considered "applied." Thus, it is – or can and should be – a short step from analysis to application, particularly if the "problem-illuminating" function of the analysis is intentional from the outset of the study. As we see in this chapter, this is even more likely if the analysis as well as an intended form of application both arise out of the "reciprocity" that Nevins (2013) mentions – negotiations between affected communities and academics.

Historical Notes on Applied Anthropology and Language

Even as we look at the present and the future of applied linguistic anthropology, it is also important for us to be aware of some of its historical influences. We might say that *linguistic* anthropology and *applied* anthropology share a common three-part origin – in the 1879 birth of the Bureau of American Ethnology; its first director, John Wesley Powell; and the need to understand Native American peoples and their social and cultural organizations (in order to control them). The "genealogical lines" most pertinent to the history of applied linguistic anthropology, though, run through Franz Boas and his students, such as Sapir, Kroeber, and Lowie, who carried out so-called *salvage ethnographies* (Calhoun 2002).

The Notion of Salvaging

The practice of salvage ethnography involved documenting Indigenous languages, which in Boas' times were thought to be on the verge of disappearance. So historically, the focus of Indigenous language research has been on the documentation and language-specific analyses of grammatical elements in the context of language contact. This has sometimes meant failing to address the social and political environments of those Indigenous languages (Kroskrity and Field 2009; Woolard 1998a).

For the Boasians, this meant recording speakers of North American languages on paper or wax cylinders (see Figure 12.1) – practices that produced "texts" whose native authorship was sometimes played down. (See the relationship between Boas and George Hunt, as described by Bauman and Briggs 2003.) These efforts aimed to *preserve* by recording (salvaging) the practices, beliefs, and knowledge of Indigenous people before their seemingly inevitable disappearance.

As anthropologist Barbra Meek argues, this type of documentation provided "a way to count, to geographically locate, and to classify Indigenous populations" (2016:449). These efforts produced countless materials such as word lists, grammatical descriptions, ethnographic notes, and other materials. Anthropologists intended all of these materials to be sources for future generations. However, they presumed that Native peoples would have disappeared. Thus the "future generations" they imagined were Euro-Americans, and the uses they imagined for the materials they prepared involved White people learning about the languages, histories, and social organizations of Indigenous North American groups.

These activities were inherently colonial and extractive in nature, producing materials for audiences that – as conceived by the practitioners of salvage ethnography – rarely, if ever, included the Indigenous groups themselves. However, many contemporary Indigenous communities have defied the predictions and expectations of "inevitable disappearance." Moreover, they have found these sources of information to be vital in the process of reclaiming and revitalizing their languages and restoring and strengthening their cultural practices.

Figure 12.1 Ethnomusicologist Frances Densmore and Blackfoot chief Mountain Chief, *c*. 1916, listening to a recording they made for the Bureau of American Ethnology. (United States Library of Congress)

Admittedly, access to these materials has often been difficult – because, for example, they were transcribed using the International Phonetic Alphabet (see the Appendix). That means that the materials' usability for community members without training in archival research and linguistics has been limited. However, community members themselves are increasingly becoming trained scholars and researchers in the fields of linguistics, anthropology, and archeology, which has meant opening up previously esoteric archives for contemporary Native use.

Applying Linguistic Anthropology and the Analysis of Language Ideologies

In close conjunction with opening Indigenous cultural archives for contemporary Native use, another positive development in the history of applied linguistic anthropology entails applied work focusing on language ideologies.

Since Silverstein first introduced the term to linguistic anthropology (1979), language ideologies have been magnets for important theoretical work. From the outset, this work has challenged the Boasian view of culture as "jailor" (see Chapter 1). In this view, culture's chief manifestation is language (Bauman and Briggs 2003), but instead of empowering speakers, language supposedly limits its users from imagining their experiences differently. Work on language ideologies has specifically challenged Boas' notion that native speakers' understandings of language are almost all unconscious or – if conscious – so distorted as to be worthless to the scientific linguist. As you have seen in many examples by now, language ideologies are, in fact, quite often very conscious indeed. Moreover, they nearly always figure largely in the production or reproduction of the social order. They are thus extremely important.

Although their theoretical significance makes the discovery of language ideologies itself an important contribution (again, tracing to Silverstein 1979), a very important shift has taken place more recently. That shift involves a group of scholars who have been largely responsible for releasing the notion of language ideologies from its isolation in the "ivory tower." Their goal, and often the fortuitous result of their work, is that language ideologies now be subject to clarification. Particularly in the Native American communities where these scholars have worked local attitudes toward language, its speakers, and its functions have been relatively conscious, often competing/conflicting, and hugely consequential. However, now that this new group of linguistic anthropologists is working *alongside* tribal scholars and activists, they hope that this **ideological clarification** (Fishman 1992; Kroskrity 2009a) will assist Native communities in addressing and overcoming the possible inter-ideological conflicts that sometimes stymy applied work.

It follows that recent Indigenous language research in anthropology and linguistics has largely shifted away from the salvage-oriented model to a kind of applied linguistic anthropology that is first and foremost *collaborative*. The goal of this work is to engage in research that is of mutual interest and benefit to all parties involved. Here, both Indigenous communities and researchers (who may or may not be Indigenous themselves) are motivated to preserve, maintain, or revitalize languages that have been in the process of language shift. To accomplish these aims requires gaining a better understanding of local language practices and their impact vis-à-vis language shift (or maintenance). In fact, collaboration in these and other related fields has become the norm for practice. It reflects the growing trend to reexamine the role of both the researcher and "the researched" (Leonard and Haynes 2010). It is now hard to imagine conducting a research project without in-depth consultation and collaboration, where researchers and communities share common goals and motivations in research and practical outcomes (i.e., language preservation.)

With all of that said, let us look specifically at the involvement of linguistic anthropology in the area of language revitalization.

Revitalizing Language: Indigenous Agency and Academic Reciprocity

In Indigenous communities in North America, as in many parts of the world, rapid shift from Indigenous languages to colonial national languages has reduced the frequency with which children acquire ancestral languages as their mother tongues.

Many scholars have framed language shift and loss as a language socialization issue (Bunte 2009; Henne-Ochoa and Bauman 2015; Kroskrity 2012; Kulick 1998; Meek 2007, 2010; Nevins 2004). That is, these scholars portray language shift as typically involving an inability or failure to transmit the minority or threatened language across generations. Consequently, language revitalization efforts have generally been concerned with restoring this disrupted transmission and reversing shift.

Even languages such as Navajo and Inuktitut, which have relatively robust populations of speakers, have been affected by this wider trend (Dorais 2010; Field 2009; Lee 2007). Despite positive examples of reversing language shift from elsewhere in the world (including Maori, Hawaiian, and Hebrew), language preservation in Indigenous communities in Canada and the United States has proven difficult. This is partly because of the high degree of linguistic diversity on the North American continent and the relatively small sizes of most language communities, in contrast to Maori and Hawaiian speech communities, which are the only Indigenous languages in New Zealand and Hawaii respectively (Ahlers 2006:59).

Just to give an example of North American linguistic diversity, let's follow the western edge of the continent. Historically, what is now the State of California was home to between 80 to 90 languages from twenty distinct language families (University of California Regents 2015–2016). Unfortunately, many of these languages are no longer being spoken. British Columbia, the westernmost province of Canada, is currently home to more than 30 Indigenous languages and as many as 60 **dialects**. Further north, eight distinct languages with a multiplicity of dialects are present in the Yukon Territory (Yukon Native Language Centre 2016). Alaska is home to at least 20 different languages from four distinct language families, all with their own many dialects.

Such diversity, together with the relatively small size of most language communities, poses limitations on human and financial resources, as well as on general institutional support in terms of language-specific teacher training and language material development, for example.

By contrast, Hebrew, one of the official languages of Israel, is spoken by the majority of the state's population, enjoying high prestige and political power. Although Hebrew ceased being spoken somewhere around AD 300, it was revived in the nineteenth century. Today, there are millions of Modern Hebrew speakers in many parts of the world (Blau 1981; Shohamy 2008).

The patterns of language shift and language loss in North America have not been uniform (Mithun 1998), requiring diverse, locally specific responses. Further, contemporary Indigenous communities are not linguistically homogeneous but are instead "organizations of diversity" (Wallace 1952; Wallace and Grumet 2004). In addition to varieties of English, a given community might have speakers of several Indigenous languages or a number of different dialects of an Indigenous language present. Let me (MV) give one example of a small community (of around one thousand people) that I am familiar with in northern Canada. In addition to several varieties of English, French, Spanish, and most recently Tagalog, I have observed at least four dialects of the local Dene language, Kaska, as well as at least two other neighboring Indigenous languages – one closely related (Tahltan), and one distantly related (Tlingit).

The significance of language diversity, both historically and contemporarily, is not just relevant to understanding local linguistic landscapes. Rather, as Hill (2006) argues, the organization of diversity has real consequences for language work and should not be overlooked. Especially important is how linguistic resources of the Indigenous or minority language (versus the other, more dominant language) are distributed "across the repertoire of possible speech events and acts, across the kinds of speakers and addressees, across channels, across affective keys" (Hill 2006:217–218). In other words, the questions of what domains of language use are available to people and how this plays out in language socialization and language transmission are crucial.

In places with high language diversity, such as those mentioned previously, we might wonder whether it is feasible to bring smaller languages into everyday use. In fact, in cases such as Miami, an Algonquian language (Leonard 2007), and Nsyilxcn (the language also known as Okanagan; see Johnson 2012), language efforts suggest that significant language revitalization is possible, even for a small language community. Such achievements challenge what Meek (2011) calls the "expectation of failure" that often surrounds both Indigenous language learners and their languages. Additionally, linguist Leanne Hinton's edited volume of essays (2013), detailing a range of individual and family efforts from diverse contexts in many parts of the world, challenges us to think about what it means for language revitalization to be successful and who gets to make that judgment.

The New Turn: In Detail

These positive experiences signal a remarkable change that is taking place in applied linguistic anthropology in the study of the Indigenous languages of the Americas – a change in the direction of "reciprocity," sometimes described as anthropology "giving back" to the communities they have studied/are studying. The change has occurred despite the continued presence of a "salvage-ist" thread in Americanist linguistics, meaning not necessarily in linguistic anthropology but in linguistics (the study of language and its **structure**).

The recent inclusion of Indigenous voices in the interpretation and reinterpretation of the various collections of language data and materials has, in many cases, contributed to correcting the historical record. Additionally, a number of contemporary institutions and holders of extensive language and artifact collections have begun to provide training for community members wishing to use these materials. For example, the Smithsonian Institution's collaborative initiative "Recovering Voices" (see Figure 12.2) provides funding and logistics support to community groups wishing to engage in object and archival research pertaining to their

Figure 12.2 The Smithsonian Institution's "Recovering Voices" program assists tribal members in doing archival research into their heritage. (Recovering Voices, Smithsonian Institution, Photographer Judith Andrews)

languages and cultural heritage through the Community Research Program. (See resources available at recoveringvoices.si.edu.) Community members apply to the "Community Research Program" or the "Breath of Life" program (nationalbreatho-flife.org). Applicants accepted in the "Breath of Life" program visit the Smithsonian Institution and learn, among other things, how to work with archival materials in recovering their tribal voice (i.e., their indigenous language).

Facing "Ordeals of Language"

Despite recent advances, language revitalization efforts continue to be challenging because of the enduring social and political inequalities of speakers and, in turn, of their languages. Acknowledging the external forces stemming from sustained oppression and unequal political economy, Jane Hill (1993) explores how language practices produced within communities might be leading to language change, shift, and attrition. Hill highlights the deep anxieties about "boundaries" and the construction of difference (1993:82–84). Communities can go from at one time unself-conscious language use to a situation of heightened concern and anxiety over matters of language. Hill argues that there is a need to attend to moments when speakers of minority languages "convert the subordination of their community into an unfavorable evaluation of the language" (1993:83).

This manifests in many forms, including a process that linguistic anthropologist Anthony Webster (2012) calls "ordeals of language" arising from a language being treated as an object of scrutiny. Such ordeals may result in reluctance to speak the language to avoid confirming outsiders' negative stereotypes, for example. Webster argues that ordeals of language suggest the ongoing tensions found in the basic inequalities of languages and their speakers.

In her ethnographic work, Meek (2010) highlights the presence of what she calls "disjunctures" – defined as everyday points of discontinuity and contradiction that "interrupt the flow of action, communication, or thought" (2010:x). These disjunctures, Meek argues, result from multiple, conflicting and shifting language ideologies and semiotic practices, ultimately constraining revitalization efforts. Many such disjunctures become visible in socialization practices where "ideologies of respect" are highlighted – for example, in common directives to encourage children to sit quietly and listen to elders in order to learn, as opposed to actively interacting with elders by asking questions. Meek also notes that Indigenous language use is generally associated with elders, who are often seen as living archives. As a result, the focus of language activities where elders are present is on the documentation of this knowledge (both linguistic and cultural), rather than on creating new speakers. The end result, Meek argues, is that there has been no substantial change in language learning routines over time, including routines in local school programs. While language revitalization generally aims to reestablish past linguistic forms and connectivity across events, it must also strive to establish new lexical terms to reflect the everyday lives of contemporary people.

Working for decades with Tlingit and Haida peoples in southeastern Alaska, linguist Richard Dauenhauer and poet Nora Dauenhauer learned that communities displayed strongly held ideas about language, and these ideas were not always evenly or uniformly held by everyone; furthermore, an individual could hold a set of ideas and feelings that were conflicting or even contrary to language preservation. They found "a broad gap between verbally expressed goals, on the one hand (generally advocating language and cultural preservation) and unstated but deeply felt emotions and anxieties on the other (generally advocating for or contributing to abandonment)" (Dauenhauer and Dauenhauer 1998:62–63). The Dauenhauers argue that these tensions stem from Indigenous peoples' experiences of historical oppression, including boarding school experiences that often included harsh suppression of Native language speaking. (See Figure 12.3.) They traced some of these difficulties and failures of local programs to erroneous assumptions that there was a unified, community-wide agreement to support language renewal efforts.

Working with Language Ideologies, Working in Teams

In anthropology, scholars have recognized the importance of the sociolinguistic practices and beliefs about language and have been documenting and investigating how these practices and beliefs might contribute to or affect language changes. As we discussed earlier in this chapter, Michael Silverstein was one of the first to

Figure 12.3 Before and after photos of Tom Torlino at Carlisle Indian Industrial School, whose founder's slogan was "Kill the Indian, save the man." Students at most boarding schools were punished for speaking their own languages, and some died of malnutrition and distress. (Farrell 2015)

acknowledge ideological dimensions of language in his 1979 article, where he coined the term "language ideology" and defined it as the "set of beliefs about language articulated by users as a rationalization or justification of perceived structure and use" (1979:193).

Others have since expanded on this definition. For example, linguistic anthropologist Judith Irvine defines language ideologies as "cultural systems of ideas about social and linguistic relationships, together with their loading of moral and political interests" (Irvine 1989:255). Kathryn Woolard, also a linguistic anthropologist, sees language ideology as "a mediating link between social forms and forms of talk." She argues that language ideologies are never only about language. Rather, they "enact ties of language to identity, to aesthetics, to morality, and to epistemology. Through such linkages, they underpin not only linguistic form and use, but also the very notion of the person and the social group" (Woolard 1998a:3).

These perspectives convincingly assert that any attempt at examining language use must attend to language ideologies and describe how they become salient in practice. They also highlight the fact that communities are never monolithic and even within the same community, speakers are often juggling multiple, at times contradictory, language ideologies. Such complexities cannot be overlooked if we are to fully understand the driving forces behind communities' language change and, ultimately, language shift (e.g., Kroskrity and Field 2009; Kulick 1998; Nevins 2004).

In addition to identifying and clarifying language ideologies, which proves vital to the effectiveness, sustainability, and longevity of language revitalization programs, linguistic anthropologist Christopher Loether (2009) shows that in some cases there is a need for what he calls "ideological manipulation." Loether argues that "addressing and resolving [these] insecurities typically involves raising community awareness about the impact of colonial and hegemonic language ideologies on local thinking about language and communication." Taming these insecurities also involves "recognition of indigenous beliefs and practices regarding heritage language" (2009:238–239). Once these ideologies are recognized, they can be "manipulated" to serve as a *decolonizing* force, recognizing oppressive, imposed concepts and aiding in locating a foundation of indigenous beliefs and feelings that will support language renewal efforts. This ideological manipulation, Loether argues, should take place on individual, family and community levels.

In my (MV) research working in a Shoshone classroom, I observed the teacher's skillful mitigation of various ideological tensions between institutional and community-based pedagogical models. First and foremost, the teacher was a Shoshone community member. Thus he understood the need for deeply contextualized language learning, incorporating the Shoshone worldview and traditional knowledge into his teaching. However, he was also trained in linguistics and often described himself as "a language nerd." This formal training helped him understand the rich morphological structure so prevalent in the Shoshone language. He called this union of non-Native and Native approaches in his classroom "indigenizing the teacher's toolbox" and frequently advocated for this approach in his community. Unfortunately, this approach did not always go over well. As a result, the teacher engaged in an ongoing dialog with others, addressing some of the conflicting ideologies, combining and manipulating certain elements of both approaches in order to respond to the differing orientations toward language, with hope to minimize tensions and conflicts (Volfová 2013).

As we have seen, language scholars have paid considerable attention to a broad range of language ideologies. Yet, in the context of language endangerment or "contraction" (Hoffman 2008), most scholars have focused on elders, who are often also speakers of the Indigenous language. In contrast, less attention has been paid to children and youth, whose knowledge of the Indigenous language may be limited, but whose role in language renewal is pivotal. Similarly insufficient has been the investigation of the intersection of language ideologies between different generations. Richard Henne-Ochoa and Richard Bauman (2015) illustrate how a Lakota high school speech contest became a heightened public occasion for different generations to voice at times differing or even conflicting language ideologies that frame all considerations of language and culture at Pine Ridge Reservation. The contest facilitated what the authors call "culture talk." Such talk was not just metadiscourse about culture or even talk of language as an essential component and a vehicle of culture and cultural expression. Rather, it was simultaneously a public declaration and display of commitment to cultural maintenance (Henne-Ochoa and Bauman 2015:130).

In the same vein, linguistic anthropologist Jacqueline Messing (2014) focuses on Mexicano (Nahuatl) youth and young adults' shifting ideologies of indigeneity and modernity, influenced by globalizing forces and societal discourses that denigrate Indigenous languages and identities. She highlights the importance of studying young people's ambivalence toward their ancestral languages stemming from, as Messing argues, a sociohistorical response to minoritized status.

Similarly, Tiffany Lee (2007), scholar in Native American studies, finds that for young people, learning Navajo is more than just mastering language skills; it also involves overcoming ideological and emotional obstacles such as strong peer pressure to conform to mainstream values. These include, for example, the use of English as a tool for gaining access to better employment opportunities, as well as overcoming teasing and at times ridicule for speaking Navajo. In fact, Lee acknowledges the sensitivity of today's teenagers to criticism and ridicule, and she shows that the more young people were teased, the less they were able to understand elders or be willing to participate in activities using Navajo. Lee also found that, counter to the common perceptions that youth generally don't care about their ancestral languages, Navajo teens do understand the value of Navajo language and culture. In fact, they strongly desire more effective opportunities to learn it.

Educational linguist Leisy Wyman (2014) conducted a longitudinal study, tracing the process of a community-wide language shift from Yup'ik to English in a southwestern Alaskan village. Her study demonstrates the importance of focusing on young people's ideas and feelings about language and how they might be reflected in the young people's linguistic practices. By focusing on these aspects, Wyman argues that it is possible to highlight how societal forces, such as schooling, for example, shape the maintenance or the disruption of local languages and knowledge systems.

Meek argues that young people's views on their ancestral language issues are not simply an incomplete version of an adult's view. She explains that "an exploration of this difference is critical to understanding, and perhaps even predicting, future linguistic practices, including practices seminal to preservation and maintenance of any endangered language variety" (2007:24). Therefore, paying close attention to the experiences of young language learners holds the potential to uncover the subtle ways in which children can affect or transform language ideologies.

Researchers have made positive steps toward understanding how children and young learners are interpreting, conceptualizing, and responding to the sociolinguistic conditions of their ancestral languages and the effects these have on language shift and revitalization (for example, Wyman et al. 2014). Overall, however, this remains a relatively underexplored area in the language revitalization literature – and an opportunity for more applied, collaborative work.

Language Socialization/Ideologies

Socialization *through* the use of language involves the speech children grow up hearing, including important cultural lessons imparted in language, while socialization *to* particular, culturally and situationally appropriate language use involves direct modeling of how to speak, e.g. "Say 'excuse me'!" Through ethnographic observations of the ways caregivers and young children interact with each other, Ochs and Schieffelin (1984) demonstrate that the processes through which an individual becomes a linguistically and culturally competent member of society vary across cultures. The authors specifically look at how caregivers and young children interact through language and how these interactions are shaped by cultural values shared through specific language use. It is therefore unsurprising that this process is closely linked with a variety of language ideologies in general and with ideologies concerning language acquisition in particular.

Understanding culturally specific ideas about the process of language socialization becomes especially important in the context of Indigenous language revitalization and maintenance, where unclarified language ideologies about how one is socialized into language use can have a major effect on whether the efforts succeed or fail (Kroskrity 2009a). For example, Meek (2007:28) identifies an important barrier to Kaska language learning, namely the association of Kaska language use solely with elders (see Figure 12.4). This means that language becomes an index not only of generational differences but also of hierarchical status differences. Meek also observes that discourses linking respect for elders with being quiet and

Figure 12.4 In the Yuchi Language Project, a tribal elder interacts with children to save seeds and cook pumpkin for a traditional dish. (Yuchi Language Project, Sapulpa, Oklahoma)

listening encouraged young people to be passive in their interactions with elders. This in turn "constrained their opportunities to speak Kaska in spaces or during events considered to be ideal places for learning, practicing, and speaking Kaska" (2007:33).

In my (MV) research with Shoshone and Goshute youth, listening and observing as a way to learn was frequently highlighted by elders as well. However, the youth expressed some frustration with this approach. They felt their learning progress was slow, especially since, for many young people, opportunities for regularly interacting with elders were limited. They found that creating peer-learning opportunities was an effective way not only to complement listening and observing elders, but also to support one another in the process of acquiring the language (Volfová 2013).

Eleanor Nevins (2004) describes how in the process of designing culturally relevant language instruction materials for an Apache language project, the development team encountered two conflicting language ideologies coexisting in the community, each informing different pedagogical models of language acquisition. The first pedagogical model is what Nevins calls the institutional pedagogical model or classroom teaching model, which relies on the development and use of materials such as word lists and vocabulary flashcards focused on memorization of vocabulary and development of correct pronunciation. In contrast, the second pedagogical model understands language acquisition as a process that is more broadly dispersed through families and homes, placing Apache elders at the center of the learning process. Nevins' research points to the importance of considering local ways of knowing – of learning and of explicit and implicit ways of teaching – and seeing how they can be better adopted into the existing and any future language programming to increase their effectiveness and sustainability.

Summing Up Collaborative Work in Revitalizing Indigenous Languages

The process of language shift and language loss is complex, multifaceted, and often emotionally difficult for the communities involved, partly because Indigenous languages are typically important markers of Indigenous identity. This process of language shift usually occurs over some period of time, as language transmission from one generation to the next diminishes gradually. Hill (1993) points out that forces of language shift are located not only in the past but also in the practices, feelings, and attitudes of contemporary people.

Linguistic anthropologists have been especially instrumental in illuminating some of the ideological aspects of language shift and how these aspects become salient in practice. Such studies have been important in identifying barriers to language transmission and designing appropriate interventions to stop or reverse ongoing language shift. Some scholars as well as many community activists and international organizations have linked loss of languages to issues of social justice,

Figure 12.5 The National Centre for Truth and Reconciliation, University of Manitoba, has recommendations for specific ways to address past damage to Aboriginal peoples, including ways to directly support Aboriginal languages.

human rights, and Indigenous people's rights. They have advocated for broader national and global efforts to support Indigenous language revitalization efforts.

For example, in Canada, the benefits of maintaining First Nations languages were acknowledged nationally in 2015, when the Truth and Reconciliation Commission of Canada released its final report, with *94 Calls to Action* to redress the legacy of Canadian residential schools. (See Figure 12.5.) These calls for action are wide-ranging, including important issues concerning Indigenous child welfare, the justice system, public health, and education, among others. Notably, five of the calls to action speak directly to issues related to the support and promotion of Aboriginal languages and cultures as a way to advance the national process of healing and reconciliation.

Although this is changing rapidly – especially in projects aimed at revitalizing Indigenous languages – self-designated applied work has been relatively rare in linguistic anthropology in comparison with work that does not involve applied interventions. Work on language ideologies is full of promise in relation to community initiatives – but it has yet to leap the fence surrounding the ivory tower in any consistent way.

Before leaving this discussion of language revitalization and Indigenous language ideologies, it is important to acknowledge the rich literature on self-reflexivity in anthropology – specifically linguistic anthropologists' reflections on our own ideologies, practices, and rhetoric (Collins 1998; Hill 2002; Muehlmann 2012; Speas 2009). Linguistic anthropologists must ask why applied work is relatively rare in the field and need to explore specifically why some studies undertaken explicitly in the hope of making contributions to, say, communities whose languages are "contracting" (Hoffman 2008) do run into difficulty.

Medicine as a Realm for Applying Linguistic Anthropology

Having explored language revitalization as a focus of applied linguistic anthropology, we turn now to a second area where insights from our discipline can be valuable.

Before discussing our perspectives on medicine, health, and healing, though, we must first make clear that medical anthropology is not, as is sometimes thought, exclusively a subfield of **sociocultural anthropology**. Fruitful and critical insights into medicine, broadly defined, are as likely to come from linguistic anthropology as from cultural anthropology. On the other hand, linguistic anthropologists who wish to work on issues related to medicine must also learn about what our sociocultural colleagues are doing in medical anthropology.

As just one example, we can learn from those sociocultural anthropologists who critique the various editions of the *Diagnostic and Statistical Manual of Mental Disorders* – informally called the DSM, the "bible" of psychiatry and psychiatric diagnosis. These include Gaines' critique (1992) of the DSMs as whole categorical systems and Young's critique (1995a) of the discourse on one specific DSM category, Post-Traumatic Stress Disorder. At the same time, the reverse is also true: If we can take cues from sociocultural anthropologists, we can give some as well.

What We Have to Offer

Medical researchers of many stripes recognize that there are problems in biomedicine that linguistic anthropologists may be able to see – and questions we might be able to answer – with special clarity because of our training: What are relationships in medical encounters like, and what *could* they be? Where is medical meaning made? And what is the role of the linguistic anthropologist specializing in medicine, health, and healing?

I (JW) answer these questions in reverse order, starting with *our role in applied medical anthropology*. In analyzing medical discourse, linguistic anthropologists take a critical perspective focused on the *power* that is unavoidably present whenever the world of medicine meets "the lifeworld" (Mishler 1984). To explain, the lifeworld is the world as we inhabit it – "warmly," without much cold, hard analysis. It is a precious gift by contrast with the "technocratic consciousness" of the world of medicine – a potentially oppressive fusion of bureaucracy and technology (Habermas and Seidman 1989:253; see also Mishler 1984:97). Therefore, linguistic anthropologists focus on the power differential in medical encounters in order to find ways to improve the *experience* of medical care and its *outcomes* (Waitzkin 1991).

Where is medical meaning made? Medical meaning and "the meaning of medicine" are not quite the same, but they must both be kept in close relation to "the lifeworld." As a result, when linguistic anthropologists look at the power differential in medical discourse, we see the problems created when health-care providers think about and talk to patients in a parental and paternalistic way. We also see power in attributions, studied under the rubric of "social labeling theory" (Waxler 1974). To elaborate, "patients" are in actuality individuals with full lives of their own and complex *self-identifications* (of the sort discussed in Chapter 1) who, in the medical setting only, become reduced, sometimes exclusively, to a limiting *identity-label* as "patients" (Dallaire 2000; Sherlock and Kielich 1991).

We also see problems in one-to-one interactions when health-care providers focus on whether patients' "beliefs" are true or false – or when they assume that patients have "beliefs," while they (practitioners) have "knowledge" (Good 1994). It follows then that "success" in a medical encounter cannot be measured in terms of patient "compliance," as it was in older "medical communication" literature (e.g., Burgoon 1987). A "judgment" about compliance – meaning whether or not patients follow doctors' orders – cannot be made without at least considering whether patients were offered the opportunity to provide input into those orders or not.

As important as it is to examine these direct doctor–patient interactions, we, as linguistic anthropologists, also need to examine meaning in other medical encounters. Such encounters may include meetings of various practitioners in grand rounds (Good and Delvecchio-Good 2000), medical school lectures (Luhrmann 2000), discussions of chart notes in a clinic (Atkinson 1999; Young 1995b), and even the fusion of direct medical care with public health perspectives. These are all settings in which medical meaning is made (and often reinforced).

What should the relationship in the medical encounter be? As mentioned previously, the doctor–patient interaction during medical encounters is all too often paternalistic, whereas it should be anything but. Looking from a broader perspective, it appears that all too often in the world of medicine today, the dominance of "technocratic consciousness" defines the nature of these encounters.

It is important to note that **ethnographers** have also documented healing encounters that are humane as well as touched with spirit, as understood locally (e.g., Briggs and Mantini-Briggs 2003). Nonetheless, there is clearly work for us to do here. It is my hope and belief that critical ethnographic discourse analyses can help determine how medical encounters can become more about the return of something lost – we may call it "soul" – and the restoration of "vitality" (Desjarlais 1996).

With all of this as context, we look now at a wide sampling of situations in which applied linguistic anthropology can offer unique understandings of medical problems and possible solutions – in cultural competence training, the use of family "language brokers" in patient–practitioner encounters, the role of computers in these direct encounters, and of effective communication in autism.

Cultural Competence in Medicine

The term "cultural competence" has become something of a buzzword in medicine, as well as in areas of social service delivery. It may have first been used in health care by social worker Terry Cross et al. in 1989, and it refers to

> how the system of care can more effectively deal with cultural differences and related treatment issues ... Service adaptations developed in response to cultural diversity may impact on intake and client identification, assessment and treatment, communication and interviewing, case management, out-of-home care, and guiding principles. (Cross et al. 1989:1)

While the focus Cross describes is one linguistic anthropologists, of course, see value in, I (JW) explore here my concerns about cultural competence training programs for health-care workers that are now widely used. My concern is about the need to processualize key concepts that are instead often "essentialized."

As we have discussed elsewhere in this book, essentializing involves erroneous assumptions that somehow all members of some group share some essence (X) related to its "culture," something that makes them all Xs. In the field of medicine, if cultural competence rests on an essentialist view of culture, that has the potential to do harm at many levels.

This, of course, is not just my perspective. Others have pioneered anti-essentialist approaches that are relevant here. Medical anthropologists like Santiago-Irizarry as well as Kleinman and Benson warn against essentializing representations or invocations of culture or cultural competence in medical practice (Kleinman and Benson 2006; Santiago-Irizarry 1996, 2001).

Vilma Santiago-Irizarry offers an insightful ethnography of the well-intentioned but ultimately essentializing nature of "three bilingual, bicultural psychiatric programs for Hispanics" in New York City (1996:3). The programs were "predicated upon a notion codified as 'cultural sensitivity' and the attendant production of 'culturally sensitive' models of psychiatric assessment and treatment" (1996:6). The problem with these programs was a failure to recognize the range of diversity within and between "Hispanic" communities in New York as well as the diverse ways of languaging in Spanish. For example, the three programs instead treated "Latino 'character'" and "the Spanish language" as essentially different from English and specifically as "more 'expressive' than English." Santiago-Irizarry explains that, "Latino staff further bolstered the attribution of a 'naturally' therapeutic quality to Spanish, and to Latino-ness, within local language and cultural ideologies" (2001:89). Clearly such notions exemplify the semiotic ideologies we explore in this book.

In place of what often passes for cultural competency training, Arthur Kleinman and Peter Benson (2006) advocate teaching clinicians to conduct a kind of "mini-ethnography" of their patients, with all that they bring to the clinic – their lives and often family members. Kleinman and Benson call for clinicians to adopt a six-step practice of "culturally informed care," which they sharply distinguish from "cultural competency." The aim of culturally informed care is to uncover

> what really matters, what is really at stake for patients, their families, and, at times, their communities. If we were to reduce the six steps of culturally informed care to one activity that even the busiest clinician should be able to find time to do, it would be to routinely ask patients (and where appropriate family members) what matters most to them in the experience of illness and treatment. The clinicians can then use that crucial information in thinking through treatment decisions and negotiating with patients. (Kleinman and Benson 2006:1676).

Translation in Medical Settings

Part of providing medical treatment involves another issue related to cultural, specifically linguistic, differences: It is not uncommon for health-care providers to need information from patients whose languages they do not know. How they get that information is a topic of study for linguistic anthropologists, among others.

The need for translated and interpreted medical information is a growing area of concern as the exploding global circulation of people, goods, and ideas that defines late modernity necessitates armies of medical interpreters/translators. Yet too many of those armies include unpaid "conscripts" – patients' family members, including non-adult children (Cohen et al. 1999), hospital staff who are not trained as interpreters (Elderkin-Thompson et al. 2001), and even sometimes strangers in waiting rooms (Flores 2006).

When medical professionals get information from unskilled or personally involved translators/interpreters, their ability to make appropriate treatment and other decisions can be affected. This can happen, for instance, when interpreters do not convey everything that patients say, resulting in distortion (Aranguri et al. 2006). Patients' children (see Figure 12.6) are especially likely to avoid sensitive issues (Flores 2006) that may need to be addressed. And unskilled translators may not understand medical concepts well enough to explain them adequately

Figure 12.6 Should this teenager serve as his mother's interpreter or "language broker" in this meeting with a doctor? (Rick Gomez/Getty Images)

to patients. Clearly, interpreters and their particular communicative **styles** can affect clinical outcomes (Preloran et al. 2005).

In reality, this ad hoc approach to medical interpretation in the United States reflects a devaluation of subordinate languages and their speakers, who may be seen as racialized classes of people associated with "ignorance" (Briggs 2005).

However, translation in and beyond the clinic involves more than an exact transfer of information across difference: It also involves power (Giordano 2008). As an example of this crucial problem, a Xhosa translation of the Beck Depression Inventory (Beck 1976) was produced in South Africa during the time of apartheid. Although a translation team took steps to ensure the translation's "accuracy," including back translation and having "bilinguals take the same test in two languages" (Drennan et al. 1991:367), they failed to address the inevitable "power differential" (1991:361). That is to say the team's own discourse reflected the kind of essentializing relativism that buttressed apartheid, including the "folk-Whorfian" notion (Silverstein 2000) that populations either have or lack a word for X (e.g., sadness) and that lacking a word for X reflects primitiveness. Such discourse structured the team's attempts to grapple with difference and sameness (Drennan et al. 1991:371–373), resulting in the reproduction of social inequality.

What interventions could potentially be inspired by linguistic anthropologists' approach to culture and communication? Aranguri et al. (2006) – rightly, in my opinion – start by emphasizing the need for "increasing awareness of the magnitude of the problems posed by speaking through an interpreter."

Beyond that, it becomes more complex. For example, linguistic anthropologists who study "child language brokering" (García-Sánchez 2014; Reynolds and Faulstich Orellana 2014:315) encourage a view of the situation that goes far beyond the child. (The term "language brokering" refers to the practice of making use of multilingual children to enable communication between families and health-care practitioners, and also in schools.) These linguistic anthropologists are looking for ways to better understand, and perhaps eventually improve, communication between two parties who do not share a common language – such as practitioners and patients. Improvement would require a recognition of "the ways in which ideologies of language shape cross-generational linguistic exchanges in zones of cultural contact," with "broader attention to bilingual communicative repertoires" (Reynolds and Faulstich Orellana 2014:315).

Jennifer Reynolds and Marjorie Faultstich Orellana's research team regards its analysis of child language brokering as a critical intervention. But theirs is no simplistic criticism. Indeed, they also cite evidence of the benefits to children engaged in language brokering. Some of those benefits are tangible (e.g., improved school standardized test results). Others are intangible. For example, research carried out by Valdés indicates that intense involvement in language brokering may reveal linguistic giftedness (Reynolds and Faulstich Orellana 2014:318, citing Valdés et al. [2003] 2014). Might it also encourage such giftedness?

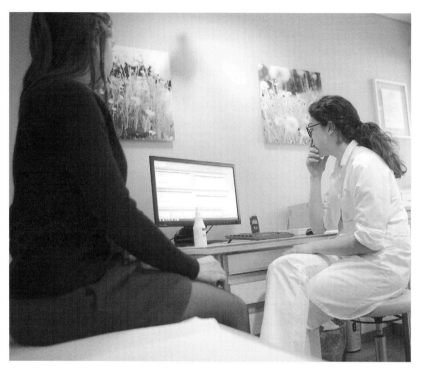

Figure 12.7 Computers are changing the nature of the doctor–patient interaction. (Universal Images Group/Getty Images)

Electronic Medical Records

In addition to the one-on-one medical encounters between practitioners and patients that we've discussed, linguistic anthropologists need to consider encounters in which a computer becomes part of the conversation, with the practitioner recording medical information *while meeting with the patient.* (See Figure 12.7.)

Of the research that has been done in this area, the ethnographic work by Peden (2012) and by Swinglehurst (2014) (see also Vinkhuyzen et al. 2012) is particularly promising. Swinglehurst argues, for example, that viewing a computer as simply mediating between practitioners and patients may be naïve. It is probably more accurate to see in this technology not a third member of a triad, but a tool that is more securely in the hands of the practitioner than the patient. Rather than mediating, it may reinforce what we have already stressed about medical encounters – a fundamental asymmetry of power. The solution, then, must involve some sort of renegotiation of that power balance.

Going one step further, we need to consider the resulting electronic medical records (EMR) themselves. Because they contain information about the patient from only the practitioner's perspective, biomedicine's power asserts itself in these records as well (Martin and Wall 2008; Reich 2012). It is a positive thing that some health-care practitioners, as well as corporations and universities involved in EMR, have invited researchers, including anthropologists, to investigate EMR's effects. However, this is an area where linguistic anthropologists can do more.

Autism Spectrum Disorders

In our discussion of linguistic anthropological engagement with medical issues, our focus thus far has primarily been on language in institutional contexts. Like its cousin, conversation analysis (Antaki 2011), linguistic anthropology can also contribute to our understanding of conditions whose very *diagnosis* involves particular ways of using language or the difficulty therein. Autism is one such condition.

A group of linguistic anthropologists led by Elinor Ochs and Olga Solomon (Ochs et al. 2005) has been studying Autism Spectrum Disorders (which includes the range of developmental challenges in autism from mild to severe). Their work focuses on how children are affected by these disorders, how they and their families cope, and most recently, how insights from linguistic anthropological studies of autism can be applied, making a difference for affected families.

Consider this example. Let's say a speech therapist interacts with a child with autism. The therapist looks directly at the child – as many of us are culturally prone to do. However, the direct eye contact disturbs the child, rather than feeling to him like a positive connection. (It is worth noting that my use of masculine pronouns here is intentional, because epidemiological studies of autism have for decades found a stable ratio of three or four boys to every one girl diagnosed (Bryson 1996).) If the speech therapist in this example could find an alternative to the engrained disposition for eye-to-eye contact, this might improve the chances of establishing a positive connection with the child.

In fact, one of Ochs and Solomon's studies (2010) compared the two physical arrangements of boy and therapist and found just such a striking difference in the outcome of the two modes of alignment. In the first, a therapist and an aide struggled to keep the boy with autism facing them directly (2010:81). The second arrangement involved the speech pathologist sitting *next to* the young male patient. In that scenario, the two established a mutual gaze on an item in front of them, an object of importance to the boy's school lesson – a flashcard containing a word to be learned and pronounced (2010:82). This arrangement succeeded not only in securing mutuality of gaze on an important object, but in doing so without physical restraint (2010:82). This research is an excellent example of an engaged study of culture – in this case, a study of the therapist's engrained **habitus** – including her mode of communication (Bourdieu [1972] 1977, discussed in Chapter 2).

The **interlocutor's** physical alignment is not all that matters for individuals with ASD. Her speech style matters too. In the unsuccessful arrangement just described, the therapist attempted to get the boy with ASD to face her. Equally problematic, however, was the fact that she spoke to him dramatically. The more successful encounter involved not only the pair mutually focusing on the card in front of them, but the therapist speaking in a less emotional way – speaking in a

Figure 12.8 Therapy dogs can provide both obvious and subtle assistance to children with autism. (Alyn Stafford/Getty Images)

manner that was clear, clipped, and predictable, addressing a narrow range of topics (Ochs and Solomon 2010:79, 81).

Solomon has also been involved in other studies of children with ASD – using interventions involving a therapy dog. (See Figure 12.8.) Such dogs can serve a mediating role in the life of a child with ASD, facilitating interaction with family members and others. Therapy/service dogs provide a series of proximal, predictable, and predominantly nonverbal interactions, which make for an ideal interactional setup for children with ASD (Solomon 2010:156).

Studies like Solomon's have challenged dominant understandings that children with ASD lack Theory of Mind (discussed in Chapter 6). Such understandings would indicate that children with ASD have a diminished capacity for empathy with others, both human and animal (Solomon 2015:332, 337). But Solomon demonstrates the capacity of "Kid," a 9-year-old girl with ASD, to experience situations from the perspective of her therapy dog (2015:335). Kid further demonstrates her empathetic capacity when she tells her parents she is worried that their family dog might be jealous of her therapy dog (named Crystal), since Kid rarely plays with the family dog (2015:337). Solomon also notes that Kid demonstrates an ability to join in *mutual play* in which she brushes Crystal along with her two younger sisters. In fact, Kid points out to the dog's trainer that she is holding Crystal while her sisters brush her (Solomon 2010:154), which we might describe as being engaged in collaborative play.

Spreading success stories like these can help families of children with ASD to more frequently produce situations in which their children experience greater social ease. In such situations, children with ASD can, to some degree, defy expectations. For example, they can demonstrate "a use of language [that] is generative" rather than merely repeating or echoing what an interlocutor has just said. This can achieve what family members probably do on a regular basis by building communication together – for example, building one's own utterances onto those of interlocutors while at the same time doing so "to express [their] own meaning and [their] own intentions" (Solomon 2010:154).

Through this kind of research, linguistic anthropologists have brought a new depth of understanding to the ways in which children with ASD process social interactions and emotions. This understanding has helped these children be more completely understood by and integrated into the communities in which they live.

Two Final Examples: Linguistic Anthropology in Action

So far, we have explored applied linguistic anthropology in two major areas – language revitalization and settings related to illness and health. Before we end this chapter, let's look at applied work in two other areas, just to emphasize that, truly, wherever people are talking and interacting, there is room for linguistic anthropology to be of use.

Partnership in SKILLS

Mary Bucholtz, Dolores Inés Casillas, and Jin Sook Lee (2015) have broken down walls between academe and community by developing a research and applied program in the public school system. (Note that Bucholtz and colleagues use the term "sociocultural linguistics" as an umbrella term including linguistic anthropology and related fields.) What Bucholtz and colleagues describe is a unique example of an educational partnership in sociocultural linguistics. This vision of partnership reflects precisely the kind of contemporary applied linguistic anthropology that we have been encountering from the start of this chapter. It goes a long way toward fixing what has been troublesome in regards to applied linguistic anthropology:

> an educational partnership in sociocultural linguistics that conceptualizes effective collaboration as both multidimensional and multidirectional in its impact and benefits. The program we discuss here, School Kids Investigating Language in Life and Society (SKILLS), is multidimensional in that it involves not only academic outreach, but also graduate, undergraduate, and teacher training as well as original research conducted by students in their local communities as well as

> university-based members of the SKILLS team; it is multidirectional in that these research, training, and learning activities are carried out by all SKILLS team members, ranging from the university faculty who direct the program, to the public school teachers and graduate students who implement it, to the undergraduates who provide assistance for it, to the public school students who learn and conduct research within the program. In this way, the SKILLS program positions all participants as both experts and learners (see also Lee and Bucholtz 2015). (Bucholtz et al. 2015:230)

It is appropriate to mention here that Mary Bucholtz received the first Society for Linguistic Anthropology Award for Public Outreach and Community Service as the creator and director of this SKILLS Program. Hopefully, the award will encourage similar programs in the future.

Debunking "The Gap," Listening Differently

Finally, let's look at a 2015 forum that appeared in the *Journal of Linguistic Anthropology*, titled "Bridging the 'Language Gap.'" (The JLA is the main publication of the Society for Linguistic Anthropology [see linguisticanthropology.org], a member-organization of the American Anthropological Association [see aaanet.org].)

This forum provides a very different kind of example of applied linguistic anthropology from the others we've explored in this chapter, yet it is an important example to illustrate the wide range of ways our field can have influence in the world.

The twelve contributors to this invited forum call into question ideas about language and mind that underlie a powerful concept called "the language gap." This phrase began to filter into thinking about educational policy in the 1990s (Hart and Risley 1995). Put simply, the claim was that children's language-learning environments in "low-income racialized communities" (Avineri et al. 2015) are impoverished, and that poverty is measurable in the numbers of words these children hear at home on an everyday basis, in sharp contrast with the number of words heard by children raised in middle-class homes.

The 2015 forum's contributors take issue with the idea that economically challenged families produce linguistically impoverished environments and that word counts accurately represent linguistic poverty or wealth. They assert that since the 1970s the programs that have been most effective have *not* been based on isolated measures, let alone word counts. Successful interventions instead "took into consideration health, high levels of parental involvement, sustained involvement in reading, engaging in sociodramatic play, and experiencing events and locales beyond communities of parents" (Avineri et al. 2015:69).

Yet how is this "applied" anthropology? First, the forum contributors expose the dominant policy talk – about families, race, poverty, and wealth – as being loaded with *implicit* and *essentializing* concepts:

> Notions that motivate the Language Gap, like words are knowledge ... parents should be teachers ... and books are the magic bullet ... are in many cases unquestioned within these circulating discourses. Examining structural inequalities around power and poverty allows us to ask ourselves not only who is doing the talking but also who the listeners are, and what their range of subjectivities are ... This can reframe the conversation as a whole by not allowing diverse communities to be cast as static, deficient entities in need of help.

Part of the forum's goal, then, is to "*disrupt* the communicative common sense surrounding the so-called language gap" (Avineri 2015:78; emphasis added).

However, they go far beyond creating initial awareness of these unexamined biases. In their joint conclusion, the forum contributors envision a future based on "social justice," in which schools, for example, focus on *listening differently to children* rather than on the supposed weakness of how children speak or are (not) spoken to at home. This new form of listening focuses on the *strengths* of children's families and communities:

> We can then focus instead on what students have (and not what they don't), recognizing that they are ideally positioned to serve as resources that contribute to the conversation in unique ways ... This forward-thinking, progressive disposition allows us to broaden the discussion with a social justice orientation. Instead of intently focusing on modifying the language patterns of children who struggle academically, we propose rethinking the way schools and other educational programs engage students and families from linguistically diverse backgrounds such that what is highlighted is not deficits but strengths. (Avineri et al. 2015:81)

CONCLUSION

A number of institutions, from schools to doctor's offices and hospitals, have been sites of anthropological research. In this chapter, we explored past, present, and possible future applied linguistic anthropological research in such settings (and beyond – in homes, for example).

We have focused much of this chapter on one of the most fruitful areas for such "engaged" research – collaborative programs aimed at assisting Indigenous communities in revitalizing their ancestral languages. We have also looked at applied linguistic anthropology in other settings, showing the range of projects that are possible. I hope that by mentioning this variety of worthwhile applied efforts, you will be encouraged to consider an engaged approach to your own academic study.

It is appropriate for us to conclude this book with this particular chapter. The book as a whole answers the "so-what question" about linguistic anthropology. This chapter addresses a variety of answers to the more specific question, "What can you *do* with all this?" In this chapter, we have responded to this question by showing the power and utility of linguistic anthropology in relation to urgent practical matters: training in cultural awareness for health-care providers, the pros and cons of new medical technology, the complexities of disorders like autism, children's roles as language brokers and as subjects of controversies like the so-called "language gap," as well as models of Indigenous language revitalization.

Throughout this book, we have argued that understanding language is not only about understanding its structure, but also its wide-ranging *functions* – from social-indexical and participation-managing to poetic and emotional functions. We end this discussion with a threefold functional definition of language, loosely borrowed from Hanks (1996):

- Language is a **representational system** governed by rules that are more or less conscious.
- Language is a tool for action, interaction, thought, social cognition, and carrying out social tasks.
- Language is a crucial generator and object of value, as we express our attachments to and our valuing of things through language.

Perhaps as you go forward from here, you will carry with you a new appreciation for all that language can do for you and all that you can do with it.

SUMMARY

In this chapter, we explored various applications of linguistic anthropology. You should now be familiar with the following ideas:

- Project collaboration between academics and communities.
- Connections between theoretic and applied dimensions of linguistic anthropology.
- The importance of language shift in Indigenous languages and efforts to resist shift and revitalize those languages.

QUESTIONS

1. What factors mentioned in this chapter contribute to the complexities and sensitivities of applied anthropology?
2. Why might non-Indigenous people assume that the initiative and shape of a project to revitalize an Indigenous language would come from outside of the Indigenous population?
3. You may have found "language ideologies" a difficult concept to grasp when you first encountered it in this book, and it may still be. Can you think of other challenging concepts from other sciences – biological, physical, or social – that have turned out to have proven applied potential?

EXERCISES

1. Where is the nearest community of Indigenous language speakers in relation to your university? What can you find out about this community and the current status of its primary language?

2. Does your university offer service learning opportunities or perhaps something more like the SKILLS project organized by Mary Bucholtz and described in this chapter? Investigate the range of opportunities. Decide for yourself whether you might join a project that's available in your area, both to gain from it and possibly to share with it some insights related to what you have read in this book.

3. Watch a fictional medical television show or find a video of doctor–patient interactions online. How are the interactions like and unlike your own experiences? Do your health-care practitioners and their office staff give evidence of wanting to improve their services? Decide whether sharing your own experiences with providers might be welcome and possibly useful for you.

ADDITIONAL RESOURCES

Briggs, Charles L. 2005. Communicability, Racial Discourse, and Disease. *Annual Review of Anthropology* 34:269–291.

Briggs epitomizes critical linguistic and medical anthropology, pointing to problems that particularly affect racialized minorities in their struggles to obtain good health and health care.

Clemente, Ignasi. 2015. *Uncertain Futures: Communication and Culture in Childhood Cancer Treatment.* Chichester and Hoboken, NJ: John Wiley & Sons.

Clemente's book promises to stimulate a range of reactions, from frustration with the way children with cancer are treated to understanding reasons behind cultural patterns of nondisclosure of cancer news, to hope that cancer care can be improved and language patterns can play an important role therein.

Hill, Jane H. 2002. "Expert Rhetorics" in Advocacy for Endangered Languages: Who Is Listening, and What Do They Hear? *Journal of Linguistic Anthropology* 12(2):119–133.

Hill's essay has done as much as any other to challenge the way Indigenous languages, their current status, and their possible futures are discussed. In doing so, Hill has stimulated a generation of critical thought and new visions for collaboration of all sorts. We owe her our enormous gratitude.

Murray, Stephen O. 1983. *Group Formation in Social Science.* Carbondale, IL: Linguistic Research.

Murray's work on the history of linguistic anthropology is a tour de force, well worth reading for anyone interested in how historians look at any science.

APPENDIX
IPA and Other Specialized Marks

Especially in Chapter 4 of this book, you will find some marks – quotation marks, slash marks, and square brackets – setting off individual letters and sometimes groups of letters in the text. You will also find some unfamiliar symbols enclosed in these marks. In this appendix, we explore a bit of the story behind those marks and symbols.

I put these bits of the story in an appendix instead of in Chapter 4 because they are parts of a more specialized understanding than you need at this level of linguistic anthropology. Nonetheless, they provide an interesting glimpse of some of the technical aspects of our discipline that are worth being aware of.

First, we'll talk about these specialized marks, then about what are called IPA symbols, and then a few last details about phonetic transcription options more generally.

Specialized Uses of Punctuation Marks

Let's begin by explaining how three basic marks are used in discussions about languages and their sound components.

- **Quotation marks** around an individual letter indicate I have something to say about that specific letter. I am not saying anything about the *sound* of that letter, only about the letter itself.
  (Example: *The letter "p" can be pronounced differently in different words.*)
- **Slash marks** around a letter indicate I'm talking about a phoneme. (Think of phonemes in pairs – two objectively similar sounds that are distinct enough to native speakers as to change a word's semantic meaning.)
  (Example: *Because /p/ and /b/ are different phonemes in English, replacing one with the other changes the meaning in words like "pat" and "bat."*)
- **Square brackets** around one or more letters (or symbols) indicate I'm talking about an allophone. (Allophones are such subtle variations on a phoneme that a native speaker is not even aware of them, even though waveforms and spectrograms do show the difference.)
  (Example: *English has one /p/ phoneme. Its speakers pronounce the two consonants in "pat" [pʰ] and "spat" [p] differently, yet perceive no difference.*)

So these specialized marks in a text tell us whether we're talking about a letter, a phoneme, or an allophone. Talking about a specific letter – "p" – is easy to understand. Phonemes – /p/ and /b/ – can be harder, and perhaps allophones – [pʰ] and [p] – are harder still. Yet it is these phonemes and allophones that are often represented by the unfamiliar symbols that we talk about next.

IPA Symbols

IPA stands for the International Phonetic Alphabet. The symbols that make up the IPA have nothing to do with a specific language. Instead, they represent all of the sounds used in all human languages – objectively, not as perceived by native speakers of any given language. Each IPA symbol represents precisely one sound – always and only that sound.

The idea of creating an alphabet of unique symbols representing the individual sounds of human speech came from French and British language teachers in the late 1880s. Yet the IPA system is still used today for phonetic and phonemic transcription of any language. That makes it useful for singers and actors as well as foreign language learners and speech-language pathologists, to name a few. Of course, it is useful as well to linguistic anthropologists, as we have seen in Chapter 4.

IPA symbols are primarily based on Latin and Greek letters, but they are used in different ways. Although there are nearly 160 unique symbols, they are made up of two basic building blocks: letters and diacritical marks. Some symbols use only letters – like "p." Some combine a letter and a diacritical mark, which indicates a different pronunciation than the letter alone would have – like [pʰ]. It is the precise combination of IPA symbols that tells us exactly how to pronounce any word, even when we don't know the language it comes from.

For example, one of the IPA symbols is the phoneme /ŋ/, as you saw in Figure 4.1. In that figure, it is one of four phonemes making up the word "going." It would be easy to think of /ŋ/ as being the same as "ng" in English, but that would be "scientifically" imprecise: Especially in a language like English, letters aren't always pronounced as you would expect them to be. The words "take" and "steak" don't look like they would rhyme, but their IPA designations show that they do – [tʰ]ek and s[t]ek.

I won't attempt an in-depth explanation of IPA symbols here, but let me give you a few more examples. If you saw a word written as [pʰæt], you might assume it referred to someone who was overweight. In reality, though, the [pʰ] is not the same as the English letter combination "ph"; instead, the allophone [pʰ] is always a /p/ with a puff of air (i.e., an aspiration) after it. Try saying "pat" [pʰæt] and "spat" [spæt] in front of a candle flame, and you will find it is the aspirated sound – [pʰ] – that leaves you in darkness. Moreover, if you have no candles on hand, you can also see this aspiration by using software like Praat to create waveforms and spectrograms of subtle sound distinctions, as shown in Figure A.1. (Waveforms are pictures of frequency or pitch, and spectrograms depict differences in voice

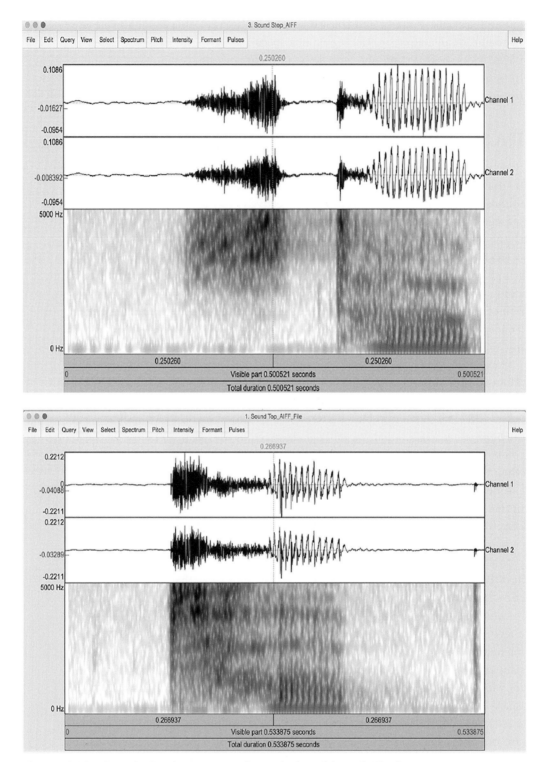

Figure A.1 Waveforms (top) and spectrograms (bottom) of two /t/ sounds. The figure represents one stereo recording each of two distinct words as pronounced by the author. The pair of waveforms for each word, labeled "Channel 1" and "Channel 2," reflects this stereo recording. Notice the low energy at the beginning of the word "stop" on the top – the *unaspirated* [t], and the high energy at the beginning of the word "top" on the bottom – the *aspirated* [tʰ]. (Illustration by author)

quality, including differences not only between vowels, but also between your voice and your friend's.)

The letter combination "sh" provides another example of how the spelling of an English word doesn't tell us how to pronounce it. The "sh" can represent two separate sounds (as in "grasshopper") or a single sound (as in "ship"). By contrast, IPA provides us with the symbol [ʃ], which can only represent one possible sound (that of the "sh" in "ship").

Finally, I want to share one longer IPA example, using the musical *My Fair Lady*, which I discussed briefly in Chapter 8. There, I mentioned the silly sentence Professor Henry Higgins used to model "proper English" for Eliza Doolittle: "The rain in Spain falls mainly in the plain." Higgins' lesson for Eliza was about "pure vowels" versus diphthongs. (Diphthongs are two vowels back to back – so close that most English speakers experience them as a single vowel.) Let me show you how Higgins pronounced this sentence in his "proper British" accent:

IPA system: ðə ren in spen falz menli in ðə plen
English approximation: The reyn in Speyn falls meynly in the pleyn

And here's how Eliza's original "Cockney" accent would look:

IPA system: ðə rain in spain falz mainli in ðə plain
English approximation: The rhine in Spine falls minely in the pline

My point is that IPA is a scientific tool, whereas English spelling is anything but. IPA can therefore represent any pronunciation much more efficiently, predictably, and – once you learn it – sensibly.

I am obviously giving you a very brief glimpse into the IPA system – along with a dash of acoustic phonetics (the acoustic physics-based study of human sounds). Perhaps what is most important is just to know that IPA exists, and it can be extremely useful in the situations it was designed for. As you need it in the future, you will be able to learn it when it's applicable. Like any alphabet, you don't need to know every bit of it to be able to begin using it, and you can build on what you learn over time.

A Few Last Glimpses

As promised, I want to provide a bit more context for the IPA. First of all, it's worth knowing that it has been modified somewhat since its creation in 1888. Many of the revisions happened fairly early in its history (between 1900 and 1932), and then again in 1989. However, the essential idea of using symbols to represent the myriad sounds that make up human speech has been there from the beginning.

Originally, the sounds that were represented in the IPA system were those we would identify directly with speech itself, including phones, phonemes, allophones, and intonation. Then an addition, called the Extensions to the International Phonetic Alphabet, was adopted in 1994; it provides symbols to represent other speech-related sounds, sometimes called disordered speech, including those made because of a cleft palate or a lisp.

Although the IPA system is capable of representing the sounds of all known languages, including, for instance, the so-called click languages, IPA is not the only system around. There is also the North American Phonetic Alphabet, which was developed by American and European anthropologists and language scientists; it has been used with some Indigenous languages as well as Arabic and numerous European languages. I use another system – "standard orientalist" transcription – in representing Bangla (Bengali), partly because of its "orientalist" use of macrons on some vowels. (A macron is a diacritical mark, a straight bar above a vowel.) Additionally, some researchers use some IPA symbols along with other symbols and notations of their own devising, so it is possible to encounter unusual variants from time to time. Nonetheless, IPA is the best-known and most widely used system, so it is worth having at least a general understanding of. It is just one of many tools in the linguistic anthropologist's toolkit.

GLOSSARY

Accusative case: marks a noun phrase as serving the grammatical role of direct object of a sentence.

Affect, affective: distinguished by some scholars from emotion (usually treated as less tightly connected to language), but here used as synonym for emotion/emotional.

Affix, affixes: a term that includes prefixes, suffixes, and infixes.

Agency: the ability to act, as conferred by a society that creates the necessary context and provides the necessary skills, moral boundaries, and so on; and, in acting, exerting influence over others, and becoming subject to moral judgment.

Alliteration: sonic, acoustic, or phonetic parallelism involving the repetition of sound segments at the beginnings of words, phrases, or larger poetic units.

Allomorph: a particular phonetic realization of a morpheme, one suited to its phonetic environment.

Allophone: a phone or sound in a particular language that is produced in response to a certain sound environment. Substituting one allophone of the same phoneme for another never changes the meaning of the word it is part of. Only substituting one phoneme for another (such as in English substituting /b/ for /p/ to make /bat/ instead of /pat/) – sometimes called substituting two allophones of two phonemes – can change word meaning.

Anthropological perspective: typically a holistic and relativistic perspective, situating a phenomenon like language or communication in its context – evolutionary/ biological, historical or prehistorical, or cultural – a setting with its own logic.

Anthropology: an approach to the study of humankind that, in the United States especially, integrates biological, archaeological, cultural, and linguistic perspectives.

Applied anthropology: sometimes known as public anthropology, an approach to the issues that commonly concern anthropologists, with an emphasis on bringing anthropological insights to bear on those issues as they affect actual communities; sometimes considered a separate subfield.

Arbitrary, arbitrariness: in Saussurean **semiology** or **structuralism**, the nature of the sign, in which the **signifier** can always be replaced (as it is in translating between languages), in other words, the unmotivated quality of the signifier.

Articulation: (in phonetics) the coming together of parts of human vocal anatomy (throat, mouth, teeth, lips) at certain **places of articulation** (e.g., the two lips, bilabial place) in certain **manners of articulation** (e.g., stopping the flow of air [e.g., stops], channeling it through the nose [nasals]).

Aspect: as a linguistic term, denotes dimensions of a verb's meaning that pertain to qualities of events, such as duration, whether the event is depicted as completed or in progress, whether it is repeated or occurs but once, and so on; may be entangled with tense, but is a very different analytic concept.

Attunement: a metaphor for **behavioral synchrony (mutual attunement)**.

Augmentative: linguistic forms used to express negative social-indexical stance toward a referent or object of discussion, with a superficial semantic connection to largeness of size.

Authenticities: represented in this book as ways of claiming legitimacy for one communicative act based on several distinct relationships with a prior act or state.

Behavioral synchrony/mutual attunement: as used in relation to its manifestation in human interaction, two or more **interlocutors** falling into a pattern in which they perform the same action, such as crossing their legs, at the same time, which is said to reflect mutual attunement, a state of mutual orientation one to the other.

Body: seen in linguistic anthropology as an important object of communication, but particularly as the most important ground of communication (see **embodiment**).

Bound morphemes: morphemes that occur only as parts of words, never on their own (see **free morphemes**).

Capital: from the perspective of many social scientists, includes values or valuables that are "cultural" or "symbolic" (as in "cultural capital") as well as what Marx had in mind in writing his famous book, *Capital* – namely, control over land, factories, or corporations ("hard," "green," or "material" capital).

Capitalism: a mode of socio-political-economic organization in which a minority controls the "means of production" – land, factories, corporations – and others are left to sell their labor to those in control at a deep discount.

Case: affixal system (i.e., a system involving prefixes or suffixes that mark the relationship of the noun phrase to the sentence as a whole, or the verb phrase) (see **ergative**).

Clause: a basic sentence (an independent clause) or incomplete sentence (dependent clause); building block of complex sentences.

Code-switching: changing one's linguistic variety in the middle of a speech event (for instance, in a Tewa conversation in which Hopi, Tewa, and English might be used).

Commodification: turning relationships, skills, practices, and human products into saleable items whose value is increasingly economic; in some conventions, a synonym of commoditization or commercialization.

Communication: semiosis, the process of making, sending, and receiving signs; usually implies intentionality but not humanness.

Complement clause: a clause (or minimal sentence) involving a word that serves as a complementizer – a word required in order to introduce the clause – and typically hinging on verbs of speaking or knowing; examples include "She knew that_____," or "He said that _____."

Compositionality: the trait of language whereby messages are composed of smaller linguistic elements, which are in turn composed of yet smaller elements.

Conduit metaphor: a widely critiqued model of communication depicting speech-in-interaction as a matter of exchanging information, which is viewed as trans-contextual and trans-linguistic, as a liquid might flow through a conduit or pipe.

Conduit model: a concept of communication as a relationship between sender and receiver, mediated by a conduit through which the message flows as though the conduit – language – has no influence on the message.

Consultants: a term used in contemporary anthropology to denote cultural insiders with enough local knowledge to make them important sources of insight in, for example, ethnographic **interviews**. (Replaces the now dispreferred term "informants".)

Context: a notoriously difficult thing to define and to discuss without **reifying** the phenomenon (see the more processual concept **contextualization**).

Contextualizing, contextualization: process whereby talk is fitted to context or made to index context, particularly in the sense of making speech appropriate to context (see **indexicality**).

Contextualization cues: signals built into language-in-interaction that signal context to mutual interlocutors (see **framing devices**).

Conversation: in conversation analysis and linguistic anthropology, a type or genre of interaction involving a very limited number of people and a system of allocating turns-at-talk that is internal, as opposed to genres like presidential debates in which turns are allotted by a moderator rather than the debating candidates.

Conversation analysis: a descendant of **ethnomethodology**, an empiricist approach to the study of particular conversations as contexts capable in and of themselves of revealing local cultural meaning; analysis guided by the axiom that each **interlocutor** reveals an understanding of the previous turn in his or her turn, and the latter constrains to some extent the following turn.

Creaky voice: voice quality resulting from very low-energy vocal output; also called "vocal fry."

Culcha: often found in quote marks; a way of spelling and pronouncing "culture" that is tongue-in-cheek, a means of referring not to what anthropologists call culture but to some level of "civilized" sense, experience, and intelligence that one has or lacks.

Cultural anthropologists: anthropologists whose focus is on contemporary (though historically shaped) manifestations of human culture.

Cultural reasoning: a way of reasoning and producing discourse about Others that enables elites, such as national and international public health officers, to use **essentializing** representations of people by invoking the concept of culture instead of race, in an era when it has become untenable to attribute stupidity, for instance, to a "race."

Culture: a complex interlocking set of processes producing often contradictory local principles guiding human thought and action together with the products of thought and action in a society.

"The cultural": the level of human reality defined by culture.

Decontextualization: removing discourse from its original context and thereby treating it as **text**.

Deictic: a term used for indexical linguistic elements such as first- and second-person pronouns and demonstratives.

Denotative meaning: the purportedly transcontextual meaning of linguistic forms like words; the type of meaning found in dictionaries; roughly the equivalent of **referential** meaning.

Deterritorialization: processes contributing to weakening of the nation-state, with its geographical boundaries, as the defining polity of the modern era.

Diagrammatic icon: a complex sign that represents something (see **object**) insofar as the relationship between the parts of the sign is held to be similar to the relationship between parts of its object, such as the diagram of an American football play, but also many examples of ritual discourse insofar as it represents the cosmic or transformative outcome toward which the ritual is aimed.

Dialect: technically, a regional variant, one among many such variants treated scientifically equal to each other; in dominant language ideology, an inferior, often unwritten, variety.

Diaspora/diasporic: the uprooting of societies from their traditional territories, their scattering around the world (see **deterritorialization**).

Diminutive: linguistic forms typically used to express endearment, a social-indexical meaning, with a surficial semantic connection to small size (see **augmentative**).

Discourse: language in use, be it spoken or written; an instance of discourse is typically bounded, recordable, and empirically analyzable; that is, linguistic anthropologists use discourse quite literally, almost always in the singular, in contrast with Foucault's reference to discourses.

Divination: as viewed from outside the circle of belief and practice, an esoteric and randomizing means of discovering information and constituting social realities.

Embodiment, embodied signs: achieved via bodily activity, material in its manifestation, as in all forms of human linguistic activity.

Emergence: the phenomenon in which qualities of complexity emerge from multiplexity (i.e., in which wholes take on features that are greater in complexity than any features that might exist simply as the sum of the parts of some complex whole); examples include the mounds that African termites build.

Enregisterment: the process by which semiotic forms, and particularly linguistic varieties, come to be associated ("culture-internally" [Agha 2007]) with particular situations and skills, and recognized as coherent members of a set of features – i.e., a register.

Entextualization: the process of making discourse (especially talk) memorable and thus removable from one context and re-insertable in another; at the heart of performance.

Ergative: a noun case, and hence a nominal construction that marks nouns as serving the semantic role of true agents (doers of actions); subjects of transitive verbs that can be associated with the structures of sociopolitical power; ergative is used in roughly half of the world's languages.

Essentialist/essentializing: in relation to a society, the view that its members all share some essence (X) related to its culture, something that makes them all X's.

Ethnographer: one who practices ethnography, an ethnographic form of research involving the qualitative method centered on sharing everyday life with a group of people.

Ethnographic discourse analysis: combining qualitative analysis of **discourse** with ethnography; a set of methods that linguistic anthropologists often identify as their own, methods that define their field.

Ethnography: in social science, a set of mostly qualitative methods for the study of peoples (i.e., societies, from the community to nation-state and beyond) and their ways of being (i.e., cultures), involving the sharing of everyday life with them.

Ethnography of communication: following a model developed in the 1960s, a holistic-comparative study of forms of communication in a particular community (see **ethnographic discourse analysis**).

Ethnomethodology: the social theory that asserts that everyday actors in everyday interaction demonstrate their understandings of the events they participate in, while engaging in sequentially organized activity, especially conversation; interpretive actions by everyday actors that can be read by social scientists.

Ethnopoetics (see also **poetics**): cross-culturally and cross-linguistically diverse forms of poetics – especially forms of parallelism – that are typically manifest in, and regarded as a marker of, performance, and the study thereof (see **parallelism, performance**).

Evolutionary processes: processes by which **hominids**, for example, and their forms of communication – particularly language – have changed at the level of the species; any species-level change driven by natural selection.

False belief test: the name of a test used in an experiment, often involving children of two different ages, especially around the ages of 3 and 5 years, designed to tell whether the child can imagine others' minds (i.e., whether the child has acquired **Theory of Mind**).

Figure-ground: a notion developed in Gestalt psychology and made famous by illustrations in psychology textbooks (under the topic of perception).

Folklore: genres of performance originating at the local level, long thought to be the exclusive domain of face-to-face traditional societies, now recognized as pervading all societies, but characterized by processes that cause productions and performances to appear traditional and thus characterized by semiotic ideologies pertaining to tradition.

Frame: metacommunicative information provided in interaction that enables addressees to understand what sort of message is being sent.

Framing devices: metasignals or metasigns that indicate to sign receivers how to interpret the object signs to which they point.

Free morphemes: morphemes that occur as independent forms, especially whole words.

Function(s): a term conceived differently, but usefully, by various figures in the history of anthropology and applied variously to language, **social structure**, and the fit between human biological needs and sociocultural forms and practices.

Genre, speech genre: a type of written or spoken communication; in linguistic anthropology and related fields, most often a type of speech defined by its context and norms governing its production and reception.

Gestures: visible signs separate from but complementary to speech; may include iconic, indexical, and symbolic dimensions of meaning.

Globalization: mass migrations, the diversification of the world's large cities, the rapid flow of goods and ideas around the world.

Glocalization: process by which global flows of culture rely in large part on local uptake, hybridization, or adaptation.

Grammaticalization: process whereby words phrases are reduced to bound morphemes (prefixes and suffixes).

Habitus: the engrained bodily dispositions we have as a result of our cultural and socioeconomic background (see **practice theory**).

Hominids (Family Hominidae): the family of primates that encompasses all great apes alive today, including our genus (Homo) and the extinct australopithecines.

Honorifics: linguistic and especially grammaticalized means for showing deference or honor – for example, to an addressee or a referent; sometimes, with particularly complex honorific systems such as the Javanese, honorifics are called speech levels.

Icon: in C. S. Peirce's **semiotic**, a sign that represents its object by resembling it.

Iconic, iconicity: pertaining to some kind of resemblance between sign(-vehicle) and object, sharing a quality with a semiotic object, the quality possessed by icons in Peirce's sense.

Iconization: a process that transforms a contingent indexical relationship or association between speech and speakers and turns it into an icon, representing a group's communicative patterns as a direct representation of its essence.

Identification: actions involving emotion, and often language, linking oneself to another individual, a group, or a practice (identifying with____, identifying as ____), which is the object of identification.

Ideological clarification: in applied linguistic anthropology, a community-level process addressing conflict over visions of language and its revitalization.

Ideologies: ideas, less fully formed notions, and evaluative stances that are shared by some social group, tied in significant ways to structures of power, and partial in their representations, and thus to some extent distorting (see **language ideologies**).

Image (imagistic icon): an icon involving a simple resemblance between one whole sign and one whole object, in contrast with a **diagrammatic icon**.

Index: in Peirce's **semiotic**, a sign that in some sense points to what it stands for or in some ways represents, such as smoke "pointing" to its source (fire); a sign whose meaning is radically dependent on, or helps create, context.

Indexical: having the character of an index; the function of that class of signs whose meaning is contextual, that point to or help create context.

Indexicality: indexical function, involving the pointing or contextual function of signs; includes presupposing as well as creative subtypes.

Indexicalities: multiple ways in which signs can point to their objects.

Intention: as used in phenomenology, an orientation toward something.

Interlocutor: a partner in an interaction or conversational exchange.

Interpretant: in Peirce's **semiotic**, one member of the triad (the other two being sign-vehicle and object) constituting the sign; in the case of a dynamical interpretant, the sign's effect.

Intersubjectivity: shared experience, feelings, and thoughts, which all add up to sharing a sense of the event, a sense of "what's going on here."

Interview: a type of interaction in which topical focus of the talk, and turn-taking, are driven by the person asking the questions; a genre that is often foreign to any given sociocultural setting, particularly where mass media penetration is minimal; a form of ethnographic fieldwork that linguistic anthropologists often prefer to engage in after some time of observation and participant observation (see **playback interview**).

Intonation: the melodic pattern of a spoken phrase or utterance; in contrast with the tone on which the shorter segments known as syllables are pronounced, intonation is **suprasegmental**, straddling a group of words.

Intratextual movement: movement within a text (e.g., a shift over textual time from passive to active **voice**, or from one grammatical **mood** to another).

Lament: a type or genre of performance that was once culturally obligatory in perhaps most societies around the world; tuneful, texted weeping; crying songs; vocal productions combining melody, icons of crying, and words; also called dirge, especially in funerary ritual.

Language game: philosopher Ludwig Wittgenstein's term for a context-particular linguistic practice or act of speaking; closely related to **speech act**.

Language ideologies: ideas about language and its relations to groups of speakers or to the world more broadly; ideas that share the defining features of ideologies (see **ideologies**).

Language shift: process whereby indigenous languages give way to dominant languages – typically globally circulating languages with a colonial history in the geographical area where shift takes place.

Language socialization: the sometimes unconscious process of training novices to a society or group – such as children or new members of a religious sect – to act appropriately; a process taking place through the use of language and including targeted lessons to the particular use of language appropriate to the social group in question.

Languaging: as a descriptor for our species, it characterizes us as using language, and doing so as a unique mode of action aimed at goals.

Latching: term used in conversation analysis for a particular relationship between two turns-at-talk or two utterances called "zero gap, zero overlap."

Lexical: pertaining to words, the lexicon or complete set of words of a language.

Linguistic anthropology: part of the larger discipline of anthropology, which is the study of humankind from many angles; the anthropological subfield that mines practices of communication, and language in particular, for their sociocultural significance;

the study of human life, human culture, human societies through the social production, exchange, circulation, and reception of signs in society.

Linguistic relativity: the axiom or foundational principle in linguistic anthropology that language stands between us and our world, serving as a lens or a filter to influence our experience of the world, inspiring most of the interesting questions about the power of language that linguistic anthropologists pursue; less frequently referred to as linguistic relativism.

Linguistic structure: from a formalist perspective, the structure(s) unique to language, structures not directly dependent on or reflective of other systems (e.g., social structure).

Litany: series of elements, often characterized by some form of parallelism (e.g., "Litany of Complaint" section of the Declaration of Independence); a series of religious lines spoken, chanted, or sung in a ritual or liturgical context, often in antiphonal form.

Manner of articulation: see **articulation**.

Materialism: one of several theories deriving from the work of Karl Marx that assert the causal significance of the distribution of wealth; can also refer to practice theory and anthropological theories of embodiment, or of the materiality of signs, among other things.

Media: the plural noun that encompasses modes of communication, means of transmitting communicative forms.

Mediation: coming between two phenomena, building bridges between them, providing a channel that directs the flow between them (see **semiotic mediation**); in the context of the media, mediation is a very particular kind of coming between – the spread of mass media and its increasing cultural and political importance.

Mediatization: the state of affairs in which commoditized media shapes and frames communication processes and societies (i.e., in which mediation fuses with commoditization).

Metacommunication: communication about communication; signals, sometimes in one communicative medium such as the face, that help recipients interpret signals in another medium, sent simultaneously, such as a grammatical sentence uttered in a particular tone of voice.

Metaculture: culture about culture, such as a review (metaculture) of a film (culture) or an advertisement (metaculture) for a film, an article of clothing, or an adventure (culture).

Metalanguage/metalinguistic capacity: language about language, or its self-reflexive capacity (e.g., this textbook, or the statement "I'm sorry I swore").

Metasemiotic: the quality by which a sign exists as a reflection on another sign that is regarded as more basic or primary.

Metasign/metasignal: a sign about a sign; one sign that frames another (see **metacommunication**).

Micro-interaction: the tiny communicative acts or signals, often aligned so closely with each other in time that we call them synchronous; acts and signals that enable two people (e.g., a caregiver and baby) to sense they are "on the same page."

Minimal pair: two words that differ only in one pair of closely related sounds, a concept central to phonology, applying not cross-linguistically but in a single language.

Mirror neurons: brain cells (neurons) that are stimulated (i.e., that "fire") both when perceiving another being performing a particular action and when carrying out the same action oneself; discovered in monkey and human brains in the 1980s; considered by some scientists to be the anatomical basis of **intersubjectivity**.

Mock Spanish: Jane Hill's term for a variety of covert racist discourse whose function, whether conscious or more likely not, is to associate Spanish speakers with negative stereotypes.

Modalities: types of signs; means or channels of communication, including visual (e.g., gestures, writing systems) and audible (e.g., speech or spoken language, prosody, as well as nonlinguistic but meaningful sounds such as sighs).

Mood/grammatical modality: linguists' terms for verb forms or the stances they denote, or morphemes marking verbs for their speech-act function.

Morpheme: the smallest meaningful or meaning-bearing unit of human language; words (**free morphemes**) or affixes (**bound morphemes**, such as prefixes and suffixes).

Morphology: rules for word-building, such as languages that are analytic (having few words built from smaller morphemes) or inflectional (having many words built from other morphemes); the study of this phenomenon, also called morphology.

Motivated: in Saussurean **semiology** or structuralism, the existence of a reason that a phonetic structure, signifier, or sound shape is linked to a particular "**signified**," as in onomatopoeia, and considered unimportant by Saussure, whereas in **Peircean semiotic**, **indexicality** and **iconicity** are two forms of motivation, and only **symbols** are arbitrarily related to what Peirce called their **objects**.

Moves (conversational moves, interactional moves): a term borrowed from game theory and used to describe an utterance (a groan, a shout, a sentence) as part of a **language game**.

Multimodal communication (or semiotic multimodality): communication, such as the kind characteristic of face-to-face human interaction, that naturally involves multiple sign-types (e.g., speech, gesture, drawing in the dirt, writing, and so on).

Nasalization: either the phonemic process of producing sounds using an airflow that avoids the oral path in preference for the nasal path (as in the English phonemes /m/and /n/), or making sounds twangy (and thus colored by local cultural values, but not such as to change the denotative meaning) by producing them with a substantial amount of the air moving through the nose.

Naturally occurring: events of social and typically linguistic interaction that are occurring, or would have occurred, regardless of the presence of the anthropologist; the preferred object or focus of study in linguistic anthropology; for some in the field, naturally occurring interaction contrasts with interviews, while others define "natural" in relative terms, so that discursive behavior in an interview is natural to that context.

New media: computer-based and social media; sometimes called Web 2.0.

Nominalization: the process, in acts of discourse, of turning verbs or verb phrases into nouns or noun phrases.

Nominative: a **case** that marks noun phrases in, for example, Indo-European languages, as serving the grammatical role of subject in a sentence, regardless of the true (semantic) role of the subject; a case used to mark both transitive and intransitive subjects.

Object: in Peirce's **semiotic**, that which a sign represents.

Operationalize, operationalizing: defining an object of study through some "operation" so that it is possible to determine whether or not some thing or process is an example.

Oratory: speech publicly performed and thus audience-centered, as in a political ritual or some other ritual context; speech as **verbal art**.

Overlap: the relatively value-neutral way to refer to a kind of interruption that is minimal and does not result in a topic change.

Parallelism: the key principle of **poetics** and **performance**; the repetition of linguistic features in close proximity, typically paired segments, within a text; may be phonological, semantic, morphological, or syntactic.

Participant observation: an important ethnographic method used by linguistic and sociocultural anthropologists in which the ethnographer joins in the activities of the people being studied while remaining a conscious observer, noticing what is happening – including what she or he is feeling.

Peircean: pertaining to the American philosopher Charles Sanders Peirce and particularly his theory of **semiotic**.

Performance: a mode of discourse production in which the producer is held accountable not only for what is said but how it is said; defined by intensive parallelism in many genres of discourse performance; distinct from **performativity**.

Performative: an utterance that functions not to refer to some fact about the world but to create such a fact, as in rituals such as naming someone or something (e.g., a ship).

Performativity: of or pertaining to a performative utterance; magical power, as in the power of ritual to perform what it might appear only to refer to, or to speak about.

Person: in the language sciences, the threefold possibilities of the subject of a verb; three speech-interactional roles: speaker (first-person), addressee (second-person), and referent (third-person, which can include a noun phrase that is referred to but is neither speaker nor addressee).

Phenomenology: the philosophical school of thought, originating with such figures as Edmund Husserl, that attempts to analyze experience in itself, or the study of things (phenomena) as they appear; the study of lived experience; the basis for **embodiment** theory, operating under the assumption that perceiving and understanding are active processes, that intention is best understood as an orientation (often embodied).

Phonation: the production of voiced (as opposed to whispered) sound by the human vocal anatomy (see **voice quality**).

Phones: the sounds used in a particular language, including allophones of the same phonemes and allophones of different phonemes.

Phonemes: sounds whose reality or significance in word-building is recognized at least semi-consciously by speakers of a particular language, who can thus use them to create semantically contrasting words (as when English speakers use /b/ or /p/ in making the contrasting pair, "bat" versus "pat") (see **minimal pair**).

Phonemic difference: the difference between two sounds, for which it is true that substituting one (such as /b/) for another (/p/) changes the **semantic meaning** of a word that is constituted by otherwise identical sounds ("pat" instead of "bat," both ending with the sounds -æt, where æ is the International Phonetic Alphabet symbol representing the vowel sound English speakers produce in those two words).

Phonetics: the study of linguistic sounds, often from a global and comparative perspective, focusing on the objective characteristics of sounds; also denotes phonetic phenomena themselves, especially phonetic differences (i.e., objective differences that are often outside the awareness of speakers) (see **articulation**).

Phonology: particular human linguistic **sound systems** or the study thereof, focusing on those sounds that are locally, culturally meaningful to a community of speakers (phonemes).

Phonotactic rules: rules determining, in a particular language, what sounds can co-occur in immediate proximity, including rules governing consonant clusters – which can consist of many consonants (in Slavic languages, for example) – or lack thereof (so that syllables may consist, in other languages, only of a vowel, or one consonant and one vowel).

Place of articulation: see **articulation**.

Playback interview: an interview, typically with someone who has been a participant in an event of naturalistic interaction that has already been recorded, in which portions of the recording are played back while a new recording is made of the participant commenting on the original recording.

Poetics: ways and means by which discourse becomes poetic text – through parallelism in particular – or the study thereof (see **ethnopoetics**).

Polysemous: carrying multiple meanings, as typified by signs referred to in the technical **Peircean** sense as **symbols**.

Practice: human social action, organized as the outworking of the **habitus**; the object of **practice theory**, in which practice mediates between agency and structure.

Practice theory: sometimes described in relation to poststructuralism, for example in anthropology, a theory that tries to account for both agency and **structure**, and to explore how they interact; builds on late twentieth-century forms of **materialism**.

Pragmatic meaning: meaning as action; the acts (meaning-acts or **speech acts**) performed by words (phrases, sentences, and so on).

Pragmatic(s): an approach to language, or school of linguistic thought, concerning itself with meaning as action.

Presupposing: for our purposes, the quality of an index whose indexicality relies on shared understanding or context, such as the word "that" in a sentence like "Look at that!"

Primates: an order of the class Mammalia (mammals) that includes prosimians, monkeys, and apes (among which humans are classified).

Processualization: in social theory/social sciences, the increasing tendency to reject "thing"-like models (i.e., reification) – of culture or language, for example – in favor of process-oriented models and the adoption of terms that fit those models, such as "languaging."

Prosody: sound features not involved in production of semantic meaning, but often used to produce pragmatic or indexical meaning (e.g., speech tempo, pitch or intonation patterns, **voice quality**).

Protoculture: the middle ground between behavior determined genetically or learned through trial-and-error and full-blown culture as a symbolically transmitted behavioral complex.

Race: a cultural construct separating populations on the basis of differences that scientists find it useful to conceive of as falling somewhere on a continuum, since human biologists have found greater genetic diversity within so-called racial populations than between them; a concept undergirding racism, labeled by some as a "cultural project."

Recontextualization: the process of placing **decontextualized** discourse (treated as **text**) into a new context.

Recursivity: the phenomenon, shared by all natural human languages, wherein a **structure** (e.g., a sentence) can be built out of two iterations of that structure (here, two sentences).

Reference: in the language sciences, the act of referring or denoting, picking something out of the world and saying something about it.

Referent: the object of, or the thing denoted by, a linguistic sign.

Referential: an adjective that describes the function of reference, a function also called denotative-referential or semantico-referential.

Referentialist: a language ideology that reduces the function of language to referring/denoting.

Reflective/reflexive: capable of reflecting on itself, as is uniquely true of language as perhaps the only sign system with that ability (see **metasign**, **metacommunication**).

Register: set of signs – linguistic or more broadly semiotic – used to perform a very particular social role with special expertise (e.g., "medicalese" or "legalese") or to perform a more general social value, such as politeness.

Reifying/reification: process by which dynamic complexity is reduced – at least in thought, perception, and discourse – to a less dynamic and more object- or thing-like phenomenon.

Relative pronoun: words such as "which," "that," "who," and "whom" that introduce relative clauses.

Representamen: in Peircean semiotic, a term that encompasses signs which, in some of Peirce's writings, were restricted to meaning linked to mental phenomena.

Representational system: language as a system whose functions include the semantico-referential function

Ritual: activity, typically social, aiming to uphold or change the order of things, often the cosmic order.

Ritual specialist: those with the special, locally recognized, knowledge needed to effectively carry out or lead ritual activity, to whom mystical powers are often attributed.

Rock art: pictographs (rock paintings) and petroglyphs (rock carvings).

Sacralize/sacralization: making something sacred by treating it as such (e.g., in a ritual event).

Semantic meaning: in language (and only existing in language), refers to denotative or referential meaning; in contrast with indexical or pragmatic meaning, which is radically context-bound, the supposedly transcontextual meaning of, for example, a word or phrase.

Semantics: the study of semantic meaning (denotative-referential meaning in language), as distinct from **pragmatics**, which is the study of pragmatic meaning.

Semiology: the sign theory of Ferdinand de Saussure; contrasts with Peircean **semiotic**.

Semiosis: Peirce's term for the production, circulation, interpretation, and effects of signs; treated in this book as a synonym of **communication**.

Semiotic: by itself, Peirce's term for the study of **signs**, a study that other scholars usually call semiotics.

Semiotic mediation: the coming-between-ness of signs in relation to the world and our experience of it, and thus the power of signs to channel that experience.

Semiotic multimodality: see **multimodal communication**.

Semiotics: the scientific study of signs, referred to as **semiotic** by Peirce.

Shaman: usually male, one who specializes in healing rituals, calling and retrieving lost souls, engaging in soul travel; often uses a multimodal shamanic register, in which a typically esoteric speech register plays an important role.

Sign: in Peircean **semiotic**, the whole constituted by the triadic relationship between sign-vehicle, object, and interpretant; sometimes used to designate the sign-vehicle only; for Saussure, refers to the whole constituted by the dyad signifier and the signified.

Sign-vehicle: in Peircean **semiotic**, the sign or carrier thereof; the linguistic sign being a word or larger unit; a biological sign being, for example, a string of DNA.

Signified: in Saussurean **semiology**, the concept for which a sound-image (word) stands.

Signifier: in Saussurean **semiology**, the material or sensate product impressing itself on our senses, in contrast with that impression – the semiological concept.

The social: the realm of reality that encompasses the phenomena pertaining to society or societies, especially the complexity of interaction that brings about enduring relations (as well as challenging or fracturing them).

Social address: variables that locate someone in social space, like gender, class, and ethnicity.

Social anthropology: the version of anthropology associated with Great Britain and Commonwealth countries that focuses on human societies and their structure (today, often spoken of in conjunction with cultural anthropology or sociocultural anthropology).

Social fractions: locally/culturally defined divisions within a society or community such as gender, class, race, and ethnicity (see **social address**).

Social structure: "all social relations of person to person" yet viewed not as individuals but representatives of categories and groups differentiated "by their social role" (Radcliffe-Brown 1940:2).

Socialization: processes through which insiders enable novices to become competent actors or insiders vis-à-vis a particular society.

Social activity, social action: a joint activity such as eating together or playing chess; inclusive of activities defined or dominated by speaking, signing, writing, and others.

Society: a population, an organization of groups and individuals interacting and often collaborating, their relationships and activities reflecting a shared culture.

Sociocultural anthropology: the subfield of anthropology that studies contemporary societies (populations) and their cultures (practices, products, norms, values).

Sociolect: a **speech variety** associated with a particular group of people defined by socio-demographic features like sex or gender, or socioeconomic class.

Sound iconism: the quality of speech sounds that, from a culture-internal perspective, are felt to resemble their referential object or sound like what they mean, including onomatopoeia.

Sound system: a system of phones (sounds) belonging to one particular language, some of which are consciously manipulated to make unique words, others unconsciously produced in response to other sounds in the immediate linguistic environment (e.g., within a word, such as the [t] "stick" in contrast with the [t^h] in "tick," "scat" with [k] sound in contrast with "cat," with [k^h]) (see **phone**, **allophone**, **phoneme**, **phonetics**, **structuralism**).

Speech act: action performed exclusively or saliently through speaking; the social actions conventionally performed by certain utterances or types of utterance such as praising, thanking, asking, begging/appealing, or issuing a directive; a particular pragmatic genre or type; a grammatical **mood** or modality (see **agency**, **language game**, **performative/performativity**).

Speech variety: umbrella term used by sociolinguists and linguistic anthropologists to refer, for example, to a **dialect**, **sociolect**, or **register**.

Stance: the lexical and grammatical encoding of speaker's evaluation of, especially affective attitude toward, speaker's utterance (affective stance); marking to encode the speaker's degree of certainty regarding the utterance (evidential stance).

Standard languages: technically standard linguistic varieties, products of language ideologies that arose along with modern nation-states (see **dialect**, **sociolect**, **vernacular**).

Structure: in the social and semiotic sciences, a set treated as such, following its own rules; can denote a set of linguistic features – phonetic, lexical, poetic, or termino-logical (as in kin terms); a relationship in which contrastive features are embedded (/b/ versus /p/, sister versus wife, father versus uncle); treated, in **structuralism**, as abstractable from its immediate and longer-term temporal context.

Structuralism: the movement in intellectual history often said to have originated with Saussure; theory asserting that no element in a system of **signs** has a meaning by itself but, rather, has meaning only in relationship to some opposing sign (see **signifier** and **signified**, **structure**).

Style, stylistic function: emphasis or any other phonetic difference, as long as it is not used to create phonemic difference; may refer to features indicative of speech-**performance**.

Subjectivity: our inner life; in this book, the term denoting a simple fact or real realm, never used as a derogatory term (e.g., to denote something unscientific).

Superdiversity: newly intensified forms of human social diversity resulting from new kinds of migration, new patterns of **diasporic** residence.

Suprasegmental: straddling segments such as individual sounds, morphemes, words, or sentences; a linguistic feature accomplished in, and only by, straddling such segments as, for example, intonation stretches across a whole sentence or utterance.

Symbol, symbolic, symbolicity: a sign whose relationship to an **object** is **arbitrary** or unmotivated (i.e., it is symbolic or characterized by symbolicity); in Peircean **semiotic**, a symbol has meaning only by virtue of a law-like relationship, especially a cultural convention.

Syntax, syntactic structure: rules governing the order of words within phrases, and phrases within clauses and sentences, or the study thereof.

Tense-aspect: two conceptually distinct categories often found together, tense indexing time relative to the moment of communication and aspect denoting (as Peircean symbol carrying denotative-referential meaning) the fine-grained nature of time in the event.

Text: a body of signs whose coherence makes it meaningful, culture-internally; a strip of discourse shaped for broad reception (i.e., structured in such a way as to be memorable, prepared for removal from one context and reinvoked in another).

Textuality: coherence, particularly at the level of the text, the work, the speech act (defining those acts broadly to include examples such as a sermon, political speech, or ritual), or discourse **structure**, often created by parallelism, patterns of repetition.

Theory of Mind: natural theories, concepts, or notions of other beings' inner states; at its highest level entailing profound empathy; at an intermediate level, the understanding that others can have false beliefs – an understanding only achieved after four or five years of normal human (childhood) development; at a primitive level, it underlies the capacity for deception among higher primates (see **false belief test**, **intersubjectivity**, **mirror neurons**).

Transcribing: in linguistic anthropology, the first step in analyzing recordings of spoken discourse, each act of transcribing reflecting the type of discourse recorded and the theoretical viewpoint on language the transcriber adopts as appropriate to an event of discourse.

Transidioma/transidiomatic: the communicative practices of transnational groups that interact using different languages and communicative codes simultaneously present in a range of communicative channels, both local and distant.

Tropes: figures of speech such as metaphor, metonym, synecdoche, and irony.

Verbal art: language refined for **performance** and governed by local **ethnopoetic** norms.

Vernacular: a term reflecting a standardist language ideology (i.e., connoting a nonstandard or informal, colloquial **speech variety**).

Voice: refers to "passive voice" ("patients" as grammatical subjects) or "active voice" ("agents" and other semantic "cases" as grammatical subjects).

Voice quality: manner of **phonation** or voicing, such as whispery and **creaky voice** and singing voice; sometimes synonymous with timbre.

Voiced sounds: sounds produced with vibration of the larynx (such as /b/, /d/, /g/, /z/, and /m/).

Voiceless sounds: whispered sounds (i.e., those made without the vibration of the larynx such as /p/, /t/, /k/, and /s/).

Whorfian effects: the sorts of cognitive effects, the effects on what Whorf referred to as worldview that language potentially has (see **linguistic relativity**).

REFERENCES CITED

Abu-Lughod, Lila. 1991. Writing against Culture. In *Recapturing Anthropology: Working in the Present*. R .G. Fox, ed. Pp. 137–162. Santa Fe, NM: School of American Research Press.

2000. Modern Subjects: Egyptian Melodrama and Postcolonial Difference. In *Questions of Modernity*. T. Mitchell, ed. Pp. 87–114. Minneapolis: University of Minnesota Press.

Agar, Michael. 1996. *Language Shock*. New York: Harper Paperbacks.

Agha, Asif. 2005. Voice, Footing, Enregisterment. *Journal of Linguistic Anthropology* 15(1):38–59.

2007. *Language and Social Relations*. Cambridge University Press.

2011. Commodity Registers. *Journal of Linguistic Anthropology* 21(1):22–53.

Ahearn, Laura M. 2001. Language and Agency. *Annual Review of Anthropology* 30:109–137.

2012 *Living Language: An Introduction to Linguistic Anthropology*. Malden, MA: Blackwell Publishers.

Ahlers, Jocelyn, C. 2006. Framing Discourse: Creating Community through Native Language Use. *Journal of Linguistic Anthropology* 16(1):58–75.

Alibali, Martha W. 2005. Gesture in Spatial Cognition: Expressing, Communicating, and Thinking about Spatial Information. *Spatial Cognition & Computation: An Interdisciplinary Journal* 5(4):307–331.

Alibali, Martha W., R. C. Spencer, and S. Kita. 2004. Spontaneous Gestures Influence Strategy Choice in Problem Solving. Paper presented at the Biennial Meeting of the Society for Research in Child Development, Atlanta, Georgia.

Alim, H. Samy. 2006. *Roc the Mic Right: The Language of Hip Hop Culture*. New York: Routledge.

Alim, H. Samy, A. Ibrahim, and Alastair Pennycook. 2008. *Global Linguistic Flows: Hip Hop Cultures, Youth Identities, and the Politics of Language*. New York and London: Taylor & Francis.

Amantea, Carlos. 1989. *The Lourdes of Arizona*. San Diego, CA: Mho & Mho Works.

American Anthropological Association. 2016. Race: Are We So Different? www.understandingrace.org.

Anderson, Benedict R. O'G. [1983] 1991. *Imagined Communities: Reflections on the Origin and Spread of Nationalism*. London and New York: Verso.

Antaki, Charles. 2011. Six Kinds of Applied Conversation Analysis. In *Applied Conversation Analysis: Intervention and Change in Institutional Talk*. C. Antaki, ed. Pp. 1–14. London: Palgrave/Macmillan.

Antaki, Charles, Rebecca Barnes, and Ivan Leudar. 2005. Self-Disclosure as a Situated Interactional Practice. *British Journal of Social Psychology* 44(2):181–199.

Appadurai, Arjun. 1996. *Modernity at Large: Cultural Dimensions of Globalization*. Minneapolis: University of Minnesota Press.

Aranguri, Cesar, Brad Davidson, and Robert Ramirez. 2006. Patterns of Communication through Interpreters: A Detailed Sociolinguistic Analysis. *Journal of General Internal Medicine* 21(6):623–629.

Arbib, Michael A. 2011. From Mirror Neurons to Complex Imitation in the Evolution of Language and Tool Use. *Annual Review of Anthropology* 40(1):257–273.

Atkinson, Dwight. 1992. The Evolution of Medical Research Writing from 1735–1985. The Case of the *Edinburgh Medical Journal*. *Applied Linguistics* 13(4):337–374.

Atkinson, Paul. 1999. Medical Discourse, Evidentiality and the Construction of Professional Responsibility. In *Talk, Work and Institutional Order: Discourse in Medical, Mediation and Management Settings*. S. Sarangi and C. Roberts, eds. Pp. 75–107. Berlin: Mouton de Gruyter.

Austin, John L. 1962. *How to Do Things with Words*. Cambridge, MA: Harvard University Press.

Avineri, Netta, Eric Johnson, Shirley Brice-Heath, Teresa McCarty, Elinor Ochs, Tamar Kremer-Sadlik, Susan Blum, Ana Celia Zentella, Jonathan Rosa, and Nelson Flores. 2015. Invited Forum: Bridging the "Language Gap." *Journal of Linguistic Anthropology* 25(1):66–86.

Bailey, Garrick, and James Peoples. 2013. *Essentials of Cultural Anthropology*. Belmont, CA: Cengage Learning.

Bakhtin, Mikhail M. 1981. Discourse in the Novel. In *The Dialogic Imagination*. M. Bakhtin, ed. Pp. 259–422. Austin: University of Texas Press.

[1975] 1981. *The Dialogic Imagination*. Austin: University of Texas Press.

1984a. *The Problems of Dostoevsky's Poetics*. C. Emerson, trans. Theory and History of Literature, Volume 8. Minneapolis: University of Minnesota Press.

1984b. *Rabelais and His World*. Bloomington: Indiana University Press.

1986. *Speech Genres and Other Late Essays*. Austin: University of Texas Press.

Barth, Fredrik. 1969. Introduction. In *Ethnic Groups and Boundaries: The Social Organization of Cultural Difference*. F. Barth, ed. Boston: Little, Brown and Company.

Basso, Keith. 1979. Joking Imitations of Anglo-Americans: Interpretive Functions. In *Portraits of the Whiteman: Linguistic Play and Cultural Symbols among the Western Apache*. Pp. 35–64. New York: Cambridge University Press.

Bataille, Georges, and Carl R. Lovitt. 1979. The Psychological Structure of Fascism. *New German Critique*, no. 16:64–87.

Bateson, Gregory. [1936] 1958. *Naven*. Stanford University Press.

1972. *Steps to an Ecology of Mind*. Scranton, PA: Chandler.

Bauman, Richard. 1975. Verbal Art as Performance. *American Anthropologist* 77:290–311.

1999. Genre. *Journal of Linguistic Anthropology* (Special Issue: *Language Matters in Anthropology: A Lexicon for the Millennium*) 9:84–87.

Bauman, Richard, and Charles Briggs. 1990. Poetics and Performance as Critical Perspectives on Language and Social Life. *Annual Review of Anthropology* 19(1):59–88.

2003 *Voices of Modernity: Language Ideologies and the Politics of Inequality*. Cambridge University Press.

Beck, Aaron T. 1976. *Cognitive Therapy and Emotional Disorders*. New York: International Universities Press.

Beck, Guy L. 1993. *Sonic Theology: Hinduism and Sacred Sound*. Columbia: University of South Carolina Press.

Becker, Alton L. 1979. Text-Building, Epistemology, and Aesthetics in Javanese Shadow Theatre. In *The Imagination of Reality*. A. L. Becker and A. Yengoyan, eds. Pp. 211–243. Norwood, NJ: Ablex.

    1991. A Short Essay on Languaging. In *Research and Reflexivity*. F. Steier, ed. Pp. 226–234. Newbury Park, CA: Sage.

Beckett, Samuel. 1956. *Waiting for Godot: Tragicomedy in Two Acts*. New York: Faber & Faber.

Ben-Amos, Dan. 1971. Toward a Definition of Folklore in Context. *The Journal of American Folklore* 84(331):3–15.

Bender, Margaret. 2008. Up to Center: Indexicality and Voice in Cherokee Medicinal Texts. Unpublished ms.

Benjamin, Walter. [1936] 1968. The Work of Art in the Age of Mechanical Reproduction. In *Illuminations: Essays and Reflections*. H. Arendt, ed. Pp. 217–251. New York: Schocken Books.

Berkenkotter, Carol. 2008. *Patient Tales: Case Histories and the Uses of Narrative in Psychiatry*. Charleston: University of South Carolina Press.

Berlin, Adele. 1979. Grammatical Aspects of Biblical Parallelism. *Hebrew Union College Annual* 50:17–43.

Berman, Marshall. 1982. *All That Is Solid Melts into Air: The Experience of Modernity*. New York: Simon and Schuster.

Besnier, Niko. 1990. Language and Affect. *Annual Review of Anthropology* 19:419–451.

    1995 *Literacy, Emotion, and Authority: Reading and Writing on a Polynesian Atoll*. Cambridge University Press.

Bialecki, Jon, Naomi Haynes, and Joel Robbins. 2008. The Anthropology of Christianity. *Religion Compass* 2(6):1139–1158.

Biber, Douglas, and Randi Reppen. 1998. Comparing Native and Learner Perspectives on English Grammar: A Study of Complement Clauses. In *Learner English on Computer*. Sylviane Granger, ed. Pp. 145–158. New York: Longman.

Bilaniuk, Laada. 2003. Gender, Language Attittudes, and Language Status in Ukraine. *Language in Society* 32(1):47–78.

Blau, Joshua. 1981. *The Renaissance of Modern Hebrew and Modern Standard Arabic: Parallels and Differences in the Revival of Two Semitic Languages*. Berkeley and London: University of California Press.

Blom, Jan-Petter, and John J. Gumperz. 1972. Social Meaning in Linguistic Structures: Code-Switching in Norway. In *Directions in Sociolinguistics: The Ethnography of Communication*. J. Gumperz and D. Hymes, eds. Pp. 407–434. New York: Holt. Reprinted Basil Blackwell.

Blommaert, Jan, and Ben Rampton. 2011. Language and Superdiversity. *Diversities* (Special Issue: *Language and Superdiversities*, ed. J. Blommaert, B. Rampton, and M. Spotti) 13(2):1–22.

Blommaert, Jan, and Piia Varis. 2015. Culture as Accent: The Cultural Logic of Hijabistas. *Semiotica* (Special Issue: *De-Essentializing Authenticity: A Semiotic Approach*, ed. Janina Fenigsen and James M. Wilce) 203(1–4):153–177.

Boas, Franz. [1911] 1966. Introduction to Handbook of American Indian Languages. In *Introduction to Handbook of American Indian Languages* and *Indian Linguistic Families of America North of Mexico*, Franz Boas; J. W. Powell, eds. Lincoln, NE and London: University of Nebraska Press.

Bochnak, Ryan, and Eva Csipak. 2014. A New Metalinguistic Degree Morpheme. *Semantics and Linguistic Theory* 24:432–452.

Bonner, Donna M. 2001. Garifuna Children's Language Shame: Ethnic Stereotypes, National Affiliation, and Transnational Immigration as Factors in Language Choice in Southern Belize. *Language in Society* 30(1):81–96.

Bonvillain, Nancy. 2003. *Language, Culture, and Communication: The Meaning of Messages.* Upper Saddle River, NJ: Prentice-Hall.

Botha, Rudolf. 2009. On Musilanguage/"Hmmmmm" as an Evolutionary Precursor to Language. *Language & Communication* 29(1):61–76.

Bourdieu, Pierre. 1977. The Economics of Linguistic Exchanges. *Social Science Information* 16(6):645–668.

    [1972] 1977. *Outline of a Theory of Practice.* R. Nice, trans. Cambridge Studies in Social and Cultural Anthropology, 6. Cambridge University Press.

    1991. *Language and Symbolic Power.* J. B. Thompson, trans. Cambridge, MA: Harvard University Press.

Boyers, Robert. 1971. *R. D. Laing and Anti-Psychiatry.* New York: Octagon Books.

Brenneis, Donald. 1987. Talk and Transformation. *Man* (n.s.) 22(3):499–510.

Briggs, Charles L. 1984. Learning How to Ask: Native Metacommunicative Competence and the Incompetence of Field Workers. *Language in Society* 13:1–28.

    1993. Personal Sentiments and Polyphonic Voices in Warao Women's Ritual Wailing: Music and Poetics in a Critical and Collective Discourse. *American Anthropologist* 95(4):929–957.

    1996. The Meaning of Nonsense, the Poetics of Embodiment, and the Production of Power in Warao Healing. In *The Performance of Healing.* C. Laderman and M. Roseman, eds. Pp. 185–232. New York: Routledge.

    2004. Theorizing Modernity Conspiratorially: Science, Scale, and the Political Economy of Public Discourse in Explanations of a Cholera Epidemic. *American Ethnologist* 31(2):164–187.

    2005. Communicability, Racial Discourse, and Disease. *Annual Review of Anthropology* 34:269–291.

    2011. On Virtual Epidemics and the Mediatization of Public Health. *Language and Communication* 31(3):217–228.

Briggs, Charles L., and Daniel C. Hallin. 2007. Biocommunicability: The Neoliberal Subject and Its Contradictions in News Coverage of Health Issues. *Social Text* 25(4):43–66.

Briggs, Charles L., and Clara Mantini-Briggs. 2003. *Stories in the Time of Cholera: Racial Profiling during a Medical Nightmare.* Berkeley: University of California Press.

Brown, Christina. 2016. Personality in Web Design: It's All about Emotion. https://savyagency.com/personality-in-web-design-its-all-about-emotion/.

Brown, Penelope, and Stephen Levinson. 1987. *Politeness: Some Universals in Language Usage.* Studies in Interactional Sociolinguistics, 4. Cambridge University Press.

Brown, Steven. 2001. Are Music and Language Homologues? *Annals of the New York Academy of Sciences* 930:372–374.

Brown, Stuart L. 1994. Animals at Play. *National Geographic* 186(6):2–35.

Bruner, Jerome. 1990. *Acts of Meaning.* Cambridge, MA: Harvard University Press.

Bryson, Susan E. 1996. Brief Report: Epidemiology of Autism. *Journal of Autism and Developmental Disorders* 26(2):165–167.

Buber, Martin. [1923] 2004. *I and Thou*. London: Continuum.

Bucholtz, Mary. 2011. Race and the Re-Embodied Voice in Hollywood Film. *Language & Communication* 31(3):255–265.

Bucholtz, Mary, Dolores Inés Casillas, and Jin Sook Lee. 2015. Team Collaboration and Educational Partnership in Sociocultural Linguistics. *American Speech* 90(2):230–245.

Bunte, Pamela, A. 2009. "You Keep Not Listening with Your Ears!": Language Ideologies, Language Socialization, and Paiute Identity. In *Native American Language Ideologies: Beliefs, Practices, and Struggles in Indian Country*. P. V. Kroskrity and M. C. Field, eds. Pp. 172–189. Tucson: University of Arizona Press.

Burgoon, Judee K. 1987. Relational Communication, Satisfaction, Compliance-Gaining Strategies and Compliance in Communication between Physicians and Patients. *Communication Monographs* 54(3):307–324.

Butler, Judith. 2013. *Excitable Speech: A Politics of the Performative*. London and New York: Taylor & Francis.

Byrne, Richard W., and Andrew Whiten. 1990. Tactical Deception in Primates: The 1990 Database. Primate Report 27:1–101.

Calhoun, Craig J. 2002. Salvage Ethnography. In *Dictionary of the Social Sciences*. C. J. Calhoun, ed. P. 424. Oxford University Press.

Calvo-Merino, B., C. Jola, D. E. Glaser, and P. Haggard. 2008. Towards a Sensorimotor Aesthetics of Performing Art. *Consciousness & Cognition* 17(3):911–922.

Cann, Ronnie. 1993. *Formal Semantics: An Introduction*. Cambridge University Press.

Capps, Lisa, and Elinor Ochs. 1995. *Constructing Panic: The Discourse of Agoraphobia*. Cambridge, MA: Harvard University Press.

Caraveli, Ana. 1986. The Bitter Wounding: The Lament as Social Protest in Rural Greece. In *Gender and Power in Rural Greece*. J. Dubisch, ed. Pp. 169–192. Princeton University Press.

Carroll, Lewis. 1872. *Through the Looking-Glass and What Alice Found There (Illustrated by John Tenniel)*. London: A. A. Knopf.

Cäsar, Cristiane, Richard W. Byrne, William Hoppitt, Robert J. Young, and Klaus Zuberbühler. 2012. Evidence for Semantic Communication in Titi Monkey Alarm Calls. *Animal Behaviour* 84(4):405–411.

Caton, Steven C. 1990. *"Peaks of Yemen I Summon": Poetry as Cultural Practice in a North Yemeni Tribe*. Berkeley and Los Angeles: University of California Press.

    2006. *Yemen Chronicle: An Anthropology of War and Mediation*. New York: Farrar, Straus and Giroux.

Cavanaugh, Jillian R., Kathleen C. Riley, Alexandra Jaffe, Christine Jourdan, Martha Karrebæk, and Amy Paugh. 2014. What Words Bring to the Table: The Linguistic Anthropological Toolkit as Applied to the Study of Food. *Journal of Linguistic Anthropology* 24(1):84–97.

Ch'en, Kuo-tung, and James Greenbaum (trans.). 1998. Temple Lamentation and Robe-Burning – Gestures of Social Protest in Seventeenth-Century China. *East Asian History* (Canberra) 15–16:33–52.

Chafe, Wallace. 1993. Prosodic and Functional Units of Language. In *Talking Data: Transcription and Coding in Discourse Research*. J. A. Edwards and M. D. Lampert, eds. Pp. 33–44. Hillsdale, NJ, Hove, and London: Lawrence Erlbaum.

1997. *The Importance of Native American Languages*. The David Skomp Distinguished Lectures in Anthropology. Bloomington: Department of Anthropology, Indiana University.

Chmielewski, Janusz. 1965. Notes on Early Chinese Logic. *Rocznik Orientalistyczny* 28(2):87–111.

Chun, Elaine W. 2001. The Construction of White, Black, and Korean American Identities through African American Vernacular English. *Journal of Linguistic Anthropology* 11(1):52–64.

Clancy, Patricia M. 1986. The Acquisition of Communicative Style in Japanese. In *Language Socialization across Cultures*. B. B. Schieffelin and E. Ochs, eds. Pp. 213–247. Cambridge University Press.

Clemente, Ignasi. 2015. *Uncertain Futures: Communication and Culture in Childhood Cancer Treatment*. Chichester and Hoboken, NJ: John Wiley & Sons.

Coburn, William J. 2001. Subjectivity, Emotional Resonance, and the Sense of the Real. *Psychoanalytic Psychology* 18(2):303–319.

Cohen, Suzanne, Jo Moran-Ellis, and Chris Smaje. 1999. Children as Informal Interpreters in GP Consultations: Pragmatics and Ideology. *Sociology of Health & Illness* 21(2):163–186.

Cohn, Bernard. 1985. The Command of Language and the Language of Command. *Subaltern Studies* 4:276–329.

Collins, James. 1998. Our Ideologies and Theirs. In *Language Ideologies: Practice and Theory*. B. B. Schieffelin, K. A. Woolard, and P. V. Kroskrity, eds. Pp. 256–270. New York: Oxford University Press.

ComingSoon.net. 2015. List of All Cinderella Movies: A History 1899 to 2015. www.comingsoon.net/movies/news/402597-list-of-cinderella-movies - /slide/1 (retrieved 6/12/16).

Cooren, François. 2012. Communication Theory at the Center: Ventriloquism and the Communicative Constitution of Reality. *Journal of Communication* 62(1):1–20.

Corwin, Anna Insolio. 2007. Beyond He and She: The Linguistic Construction of Gender among Genderqueer Individuals. Master's thesis, Northern Arizona University.

Coward, Harold. 1993. Foreword. In *Sonic Theology: Hinduism and Sacred Sound*. G. L. Beck, ed. Pp. xi–xii. Columbia: University of South Carolina Press.

Craine, Ian. 2013. How the Slapstick Came to Be Applied to Marjorie Beebe's Bottom: Mack Sennett's Talkie Star and Slapstick's Roots in Commedia Dell' Arte and Pantomime. *The Journal of Popular Culture* 46(3):501–523.

Crapanzano, Vincent. 2000. *Serving the Word: Literalism in America from the Pulpit to the Bench*. New York: New Press (distributed by W. W. Norton).

Crissman, Lawrence W. 1967. The Segmentary Structure of Urban Overseas Chinese Communities. *Man* 2(2):185–204.

Cross, Terry L., Barbara J. Bazron, Karl W. Dennis, and Mareasa R. Isaacs. 1989. *Towards a Culturally Competent System of Care: A Monograph on Effective Services for Minority Children Who Are Severely Emotionally Disturbed*. Washington, DC: Georgetown University Child Development Center, National Institute of Mental Health's Child and Adolescent Service System Program (CASSP). Technical Assistance Center.

Crow, Timothy J. 2000. Schizophrenia as the Price That Homo Sapiens Pays for Language: A Resolution of the Central Paradox in the Origin of the Species. *Brain Research Reviews* 31:118–129.

Csordas, Thomas. [1988] 1990. Embodiment as a Paradigm for Anthropology (Stirling Award Essay). *Ethos* 18:5–47.

Dallaire, Bernadette. 2000. Book Review: *Being Mentally Ill: A Sociological Theory*, Third Edition (by Thomas Scheff). *Ethical Human Sciences and Services* 2(2):129–131.

Danziger, Eve. 2005. The Eye of the Beholder: How Linguistic Categorization Affects "Natural" Experience. In *Complexities: Anthropological Challenges to Reductive Accounts of Social Life*. S. McKinnon and S. Silverman, eds. Pp. 64–80. Chicago University Press.

2010. Deixis, Gesture, and Cognition in Spatial Frame of Reference Typology. *Studies in Language* 34(1):167–185.

2011 Distinguishing Three-Dimensional Forms from Their Mirror-Images: Whorfian Results from Users of Intrinsic Frames of Linguistic Reference. *Language Sciences* 33(6):853–867.

Das, Veena. 1996. Language and the Body: Transactions in the Construction of Pain. *Daedalus* 125(1):67–91.

Dauenhauer, Nora Marks, and Richard Dauenhauer. 1998. Technical, Emotional, and Ideological Issues in Reversing Language Shift: Examples from Southeast Alaska. In *Endangered Languages: Current Issues and Future Prospects*. L. A. Grenoble and L. J. Whaley, eds. Pp. 57–98. Cambridge University Press.

Dauenhauer, Richard, and Nora Marks Dauenhauer. 1995. Oral Literature Embodied and Disembodied. In *Aspects of Oral Communication*. U. Quasthoff, ed. Pp. 91–111. Berlin: Walter de Gruyter.

De Fina, Anna, and Sabina Perrino, eds. 2011. Interviews Vs. "Natural" Contexts: A False Dilemma. *Language in Society* (Special Issue). 40(1).

De Smedt, J., and H. De Cruz. 2010. Toward an Integrative Approach of Cognitive Neuroscientific and Evolutionary Psychological Studies of Art. *Evolutionary Psychology* 8(4):695–719.

de Villiers, Peter A., and Jill G. de Villiers. 2012. Deception Dissociates from False Belief Reasoning in Deaf Children: Implications for the Implicit Versus Explicit Theory of Mind Distinction. *British Journal of Developmental Psychology* 30(1): 188–209 (Special Issue: Implicit and Explicit Theory of Mind).

Debord, Guy. 1994. *The Society of the Spectacle*. D. Nicholson-Smith, trans. New York: Zone Books.

Derrida, Jacques. 1977. Signature Event Context. In *Limited Inc*. G. Graff, ed. Pp. 1–24. Chicago: Northwestern University Press.

Derrida, Jacques, and Alan Bass. [1967] 2001. Structure, Sign, and Play in the Discourse of the Human Sciences [La structure, le signe et le jeu dans le discours des sciences humaines]. In *Writing and Difference* [*L'écriture et la différence*]. A. Bass, ed. Pp. 278–294. London: Routledge.

Desjarlais, Robert. 1996. Presence. In *The Performance of Healing*. C. Laderman and M. Roseman, eds. Pp. 143–164. New York: Routledge.

2000. Echoes of a Yolmo Buddhist's Life, in Death. *Cultural Anthropology* 15(2):260–293.

2003. *Sensory Biographies: Lives and Deaths among Nepal's Yolmo Buddhists*. Berkeley: University of California Press.

2011. *Counterplay: An Anthropologist at the Chessboard*. Berkeley: University of California Press.

Desjarlais, Robert, and C. Jason Throop. 2011. Phenomenological Approaches in Anthropology. *Annual Review of Anthropology* 40:87–102.

Dimock, Edward C. 1989. Symbolic Forms in Bengali. In *The Sound of Silent Guns and Other Essays*. E. C. Dimock, ed. Pp. 52–61. Delhi: Oxford University Press.

Dixon, Robert M. W. 1972. *The Dyirbal Language of North Queensland*. Cambridge University Press.

Doostdar, Alireza. 2004. "The Vulgar Spirit of Blogging": On Language, Culture, and Power in Persian Weblogestan. *American Anthropologist* 106(4):651–662.

Dorais, Louise-Jacques. 2010. *The Language of the Inuit: Syntax, Semantics, and Society in the Arctic*. Montreal and Kingston: McGill-Queen's University Press.

Drennan, Gerard, Ann Levett, and Leslie Swartz. 1991. Hidden Dimensions of Power and Resistance in the Translation Process: A South African Study. *Culture, Medicine, and Psychiatry* 15(3):361–381.

Dufrenne, Mikel. 1978. The Phenomenological Approach to Poetry. In *Crosscurrents in Phenomenology*. R. Bruzina and B. Wilshire, eds. Pp. 109–119. Dordrecht: Springer.

Duranti, Alessandro. 1994. *From Grammar to Politics: Linguistic Anthropology in a Western Samoan Village*. Berkeley and Los Angeles: University of California Press.

1997. *Linguistic Anthropology*. Cambridge University Press.

2003. Language as Culture in US Anthropology: Three Paradigms. *Current Anthropology* 44(3):323–348.

2009. The Relevance of Husserl's Theory to Language Socialization. *Journal of Linguistic Anthropology* 19(2):205–226.

2010. Husserl, Intersubjectivity and Anthropology. *Anthropological Theory* 10(1–2):16–35.

Duranti, Alessandro, and Donald Brenneis. 1986. The Audience as Co-Author: An Introduction. *Text* (Special Issue: *The Audience as Co-Author*, ed. A. Duranti and D. Brenneis) 6(3):239–347.

Duranti, Alessandro, Elinor Ochs, and Bambi B. Schieffelin. 2011. *The Handbook of Language Socialization*. Numa Markee, ed. Malden, MA and Chichester: John Wiley & Sons.

Eckert, Penelope. 2000. *Linguistic Variation as Social Practice: The Linguistic Construction of Identity in Belten High*. Malden, MA: Blackwell Publishers.

Eckert, Penelope, and Sally McConnell-Ginet. 1992. Think Practically and Look Locally: Language and Gender as Community-Based Practice. *Annual Review of Anthropology* 21:461–490.

2003 *Language and Gender*. Cambridge University Press.

ECLKC-Headstart, 2015. Early Childhood Learning and Knowledge Center. Social and Emotional Development. US Department of Health and Social and Human Services, Washington, DC. https://eclkc.ohs.acf.hhs.gov/hslc.

Eira, Christina, and Tonya N. Stebbins. 2008. Authenticities and Lineages: Revisiting Concepts of Continuity and Change in Language. *International Journal of the Sociology of Language* 189(1):1–30.

Eisenlohr, Patrick. 2006. As Makkah Is Sweet and Beloved, So Is Madina. *American Ethnologist* 33(2):230–245.

2010 Materialities of Entextualization: The Domestication of Sound Reproduction in Mauritian Muslim Devotional Practices. *Journal of Linguistic Anthropology* 20(2):314–333.

Elderkin-Thompson, Virginia, Roxane Cohen Silver, and Howard Waitzkin. 2001. When Nurses Double as Interpreters: A Study of Spanish-Speaking Patients in a US Primary Care Setting. *Social Science & Medicine* 52(9):1343–1358.

Emery, Nathan J, and Nicola S. Clayton. 2004. The Mentality of Crows: Convergent Evolution of Intelligence in Corvids and Apes. *Science* 306(5703):1903–1907.

Enfield, N. J. 2015. Linguistic Relativity from Reference to Agency. *Annual Review of Anthropology* 44(1):207–224.

Engels, Friedrich, Karl Marx, and Eric Hobsbawm. 2012. *The Communist Manifesto: A Modern Edition*. London: Verso Books.

Erickson, Frederick, and Jeffrey Shultz. 1982. *The Counselor as Gatekeeper: Social Interaction in Interviews*. New York: Academic Press.

Errington, J. Joseph. 1988. *Structure and Style in Javanese: A Semiotic View of Linguistic Etiquette*. Philadelphia: University of Pennsylvania.

Evans, Cristopher S., and Peter Marler. 1995. Language and Animal Communication: Parallels and Contrasts. In *Comparative Approaches to Cognitive Science*. H. L. Roitblat and J.-A. Meyer, eds. Pp. 341–382. Cambridge, MA: MIT Press.

Fajans, Jane. 2014. Exoticizing the Familiar, Familiarizing the Exotic. In *Local Knowledges, Local Practices: Writing in the Disciplines at Cornell*. J. Monroe, ed. Pp. 83–89: University of Pittsburgh Press.

Falk, Dean. 2009. *Finding Our Tongues: Mothers, Infants and the Origins of Language*. New York: Basic Books.

Farber, Seth. 2006. *Lunching with Lunatics: Adventures of a Maverick Psychologist*. Manchester: Critical Vision. www.sethhfarber.com/lunching_with_lunatics_ adventures_of_a_renegade_psychologist_69224.htm.

Farnell, Brenda M. 1995. *Do You See What I Mean? Plains Indian Sign Talk and the Embodiment of Action*. Austin: University of Texas Press.

Farrell, Brenna. 2015. Photos: Before and After Carlisle. Radiolab.org. Radiolab.org/ Story/Photos-before-and-after-Carlisle/ (Retrieved 6/16/16). Photo blog, Vol. 2016.

Feld, Steve, and Aaron Fox. 1994. Music and Language. *Annual Review of Anthropology* 23:25–53.

Feld, Steve, Aaron A. Fox, Thomas Porcello, and David Samuels. 2004. Vocal Anthropology: From the Music of Language to the Language of Song. In *A Companion to Linguistic Anthropology*. A. Duranti, ed. Pp. 321–345. Malden, MA: Blackwell Publishers.

Feld, Steven. 1990. *Sound and Sentiment: Birds, Weeping, Poetics, and Song in Kaluli Expression*. Philadelphia: University of Pennsylvania Press.

Feldman, Ruth. 2007. Mother-Infant Synchrony and the Development of Moral Orientation in Childhood and Adolescence: Direct and Indirect Mechanisms of Developmental Continuity. *American Journal of Orthopsychiatry* 77(4):582–597.

Fenigsen, Janina. 1999. "A Broke-up Mirror": Representing Bajan in Print. *Cultural Anthropology* 14(1):61–87.

— 2005. Meaningful Routines: Meaning-Making and the Face-Value of Barbadian Greetings. In *Politeness and Face in Caribbean Creoles*. S. Mühleisen and B. Migge, eds. Pp. 169–194. Amsterdam: John Benjamins.

— 2007. From Apartheid to Incorporation: The Emergence and Transformations of Modern Language Community in Barbados, West Indies. *Pragmatics (IPrA)* 17(2):231–262.

Fenigsen, Janina, and James M. Wilce. 2015. Authenticities: A Semiotic Exploration. *Recherches sémiotiques/Semiotic Inquiry* (Special Issue: *Semiotics in Anthropology Today*, ed. Sally Ann Ness) 32(1–2-3):181–200.

Fichtel, Claudia, Susan Perry, and Julie Gros-Louis. 2005. Alarm Calls of White-Faced Capuchin Monkeys: An Acoustic Analysis. *Animal Behaviour* 70(1):165–176.

Field, Margaret C. 2009. Changing Navajo Language Ideologies and Changing Language Use. In *Native American Language Ideologies: Beliefs, Practices, and Struggles in Indian Country*. P. Kroskrity and M. C. FIeld, eds. Pp. 31–47. Tucson: University of Arizona Press.

Finegan, Edward. 2007. *Language: Its Structure and Use*. Boston, MA: Thomson Wadsworth.

Fischer, John L. 1961. The Retention Rate of Chamorro Basic Vocabulary. *Lingua* 10:255–266.

Fishman, Joshua A. 1992. Three Dilemmas of Organized Efforts to Reverse Language Shift. In *Status Change of Languages*. U. Ammon and M. Hellinger, eds. Pp. 285–293. Berlin and New York: Walter de Gruyter.

Flores, Glenn. 2006. Language Barriers to Health Care in the United States. *New England Journal of Medicine* 355(3):229–231.

Foucault, Michel. [1969] 1972. *The Archaeology of Knowledge and the Discourse on Language*. New York: Pantheon Books.

1985. The Order of Discourse. In *Untying the Text: A Post-Structuralist Reader*. R. Young, ed. Pp. 48–78. Boston and London: Routledge & Kegan Paul.

1990. The Incitement to Discourse. In *The History of Sexuality: An Introduction*. M. Foucault, ed. Pp. 17–35. New York: Vintage.

Fox, James J., ed. 1988. *To Speak in Pairs: Essays on the Ritual Languages of Eastern Indonesia*. Cambridge Studies in Oral and Literate Culture, 15. Cambridge and New York: Cambridge University Press.

1989. "Our Ancestors Spoke in Pairs": Rotinese Views of Language, Dialect, and Code. In *Explorations in the Ethnography of Speaking*. R. Bauman and J. Sherzer, eds. Pp. 65–85. Cambridge University Press.

2014. *Explorations in Semantic Parallelism*. Canberra: Australian National University E-Press.

Francis, Norbert. 2012. Poetry and Narrative: An Evolutionary Perspective on the Cognition of Verbal Art. *Neohelicon* 39(2):267–294.

Freud, Sigmund. 2003. *The Wolfman and Other Cases by Sigmund Freud*. L. A. Huish, trans. London and New York: Penguin Classics.

Friedman, Jonathan. 1994. *Cultural Identity and Global Process*. London and Thousand Oaks, CA: Sage Publications.

2003. Globalizing Languages: Ideologies and Realities of the Contemporary Global System. *American Anthropologist* 105(4):744–752.

Friedrich, Paul. 1986. *The Language Parallax: Linguistic Relativism and Poetic Indeterminacy*. Austin: University of Texas.

Frog, and Eila Stepanova. 2011. Alliteration in (Balto-) Finnic Languages. In *Alliteration in Culture*. J. Roper, ed. Pp. 195–218. Houndmills: Palgrave Macmillan.

Fuss, Diana. 1995. *Identification Papers*. London and New York: Routledge.

Gaines, Atwood. 1992. From DSM-I to DSM-IIIR; Voices of Self, Mastery and the Other: A Cultural Constructivist Reading of US Psychiatric Classification. *Social Science and Medicine* 35(1):3–24.

Gal, Susan. 2006. Contradictions of Standard Language in Europe: Implications for the Study of Practices and Publics. *Social Anthropology* 14(2):163–181.

García-Sánchez, Inmaculada. 2014 *Language and Muslim Childhoods: The Politics of Belonging*. Chichester and Malden, MA: John Wiley & Sons.

Gardner, Katy. 1995. *Global Migrants, Local Lives: Travel and Transformation in Rural Bangladesh*. Oxford and New York: Clarendon Press/Oxford University Press.

Garfinkel, Harold. 1967. *Studies in Ethnomethodology*. Englewood Cliffs, NJ: Prentice-Hall.

Geertz, Clifford. 1973. Thick Description: Toward an Interpretive Theory of Culture. In *The Interpretation of Cultures: Selected Essays by Clifford Geertz*. C. Geertz, ed. Pp. 3–32. New York: Basic Books.

2000. *Local Knowledge: Further Essays in Interpretive Anthropology* (3rd edn.). New York: Basic Books.

Gendron, Maria, Kristen A. Lindquist, Lawrence Barsalou, and Lisa Feldman Barrett. 2012. Emotion Words Shape Emotion Percepts. *Emotion* 12(2):314–325.

Gerard, Ralph W. 1943. Synchrony in Flock Wheeling. *Science (New York, NY)* 97(2511):160–161.

Gershon, Ilana. 2010. Breaking Up Is Hard to Do: Media Switching and Media Ideologies. *Journal of Linguistic Anthropology* 20(2):389–405.

2011. *The Breakup 2.0: Disconnecting over New Media*. Ithaca, NY: Cornell University Press.

Giddens, Anthony. 1979. *Central Problems in Social Theory: Action, Structure and Contradiction in Social Analysis*. Berkeley and Los Angeles: University of California Press.

Giordano, Cristiana. 2008. Practices of Translation and the Making of Migrant Subjectivities in Contemporary Italy. *American Ethnologist* 35(4):588–606.

Goffman, Erving. 1964. The Neglected Situation. *American Anthropologist* n.s. 66(6), Part 2: The Ethnography of Communication: 133–136.

[1959] 1973. *The Presentation of Self in Everyday Life*. Woodstock, NY: Overlook Press.

1974. *Frame Analysis: An Essay on the Organization of Experience*. Cambridge, MA: Harvard University Press.

1981 *Forms of Talk*. Philadelphia: University of Pennsylvania Press.

Good, Byron J. 1994. *Medicine, Rationality, and Experience: An Anthropological Perspective*. Cambridge University Press.

Good, Byron, and Mary Jo Delvecchio-Good. 2000. "Fiction" and "Historicity" in Doctors' Stories: Social and Narrative Dimensions of Learning Medicine. In *Narrative and the Cultural Construction of Illness and Healing*. C. Mattingly and L. C. Garro, eds. Pp. 50–69. Berkeley: University of California Press.

Goodall, Jane. 1986. *The Chimpanzees of Gombe*. Cambridge, MA: Belknap Press of Harvard University Press.

Goodwin, Charles. 1979. The Interactive Construction of a Sentence in Natural Conversation. In *Everyday Language*. G. Psathas, ed. Pp. 97–121. New York: Irvington.

1994. Professional Vision. *American Anthropologist* 96(3):606–633.

Goodwin, Charles, and Marjorie H. Goodwin. 1987. Children's Arguing. In *Language, Gender, and Sex in Comparative Perspective*. S. U. Philips, S. Steele, and C. Tanz, eds. Pp. 200–248. Cambridge University Press.

1992. Context, Activity, and Participation. In *The Contextualization of Language*. P. Auer and A. Di Luzio, eds. Pp. 77–100. Amsterdam: John Benajamins.

Goodwin, Marjorie H. 1990. *He-Said-She-Said: Talk as Social Organization among Children*. Bloomington: Indiana University Press.

2006. *The Hidden Life of Girls: Games of Stance, Status, and Exclusion*. Malden, MA: Blackwell Publishers.

Goody, Jack, and Ian Watt. 1963. The Consequences of Literacy. *Comparative Studies in Society and History* 5(3):306–326, 332–345.

Graber, Kathryn Elizabeth. 2012. *Knowledge and Authority in Shift: A Linguistic Ethnography of Multilingual News Media in the Buryat Territories of Russia*. Ann Arbor: The University of Michigan Press.

Gratier, Maya, and Colwyn Trevarthen. 2008. Musical Narrative and Motives for Culture in Mother-Infant Vocal Interaction. *Journal of Consciousness Studies* 15:122–158.

Gumperz, John J. 1982. Interethnic Communication. In *Discourse Strategies*. Pp. 172–186. Cambridge University Press.

1996. The Linguistic and Cultural Relativity of Conversational Inference. In *Rethinking Linguistic Relativity*. J. Gumperz and S. Levinson, eds. Pp. 375–406. Cambridge University Press.

Habermas, J., and S. Seidman. 1989. *Jürgen Habermas on Society and Politics: A Reader*. Boston, MA: Beacon Press.

Haeckel, E. H. P. A., and E. R. Lankester. 1883. *The History of Creation: Or, the Development of the Earth and Its Inhabitants by the Action of Natural Causes. A Popular Exposition of the Doctrine of Evolution in General, and of That of Darwin, Goethe, and Lamarck in Particular*. New York: D. Appleton.

Haesler, S., C. Rochefort, B. Georgi, P. Licznerski, P. Osten, and C. Scharff. 2007. Incomplete and Inaccurate Vocal Imitation after Knockdown of FOXP2 in Songbird Basal Ganglia Nucleus Area X. *PLoS Biol* 5(12):e321.

Hall, Stuart. 1988. New Ethnicities. In *Black Film, British Cinema* (Ica Document 7). K. Mercer, ed. Pp. 27–31. London: Institute of Contemporary Art/BIFF.

Halliburton, Murphy. 2005. "Just Some Spirits": The Erosion of Spirit Possession and the Rise of "Tension" in South India. *Medical Anthropology* 24(2):111–144.

Hallowell, A. Irving. 1968. Self, Society and Culture in Phylogenetic Perspective. In *Culture: Man's Adaptive Dimension*. A. Montagu, ed. Pp. 197–261. Oxford University Press.

Halmari, Helena. 2011. Alliteration in Inaugural Addresses: From George Washington to Barack Obama. In *Alliteration in Culture*. J. Roper, ed. Pp. 45–61. London: Palgrave Macmillan.

Hammer, Max. 1974. The Essence of Personal and Transpersonal Psychotherapy. *Psychotherapy: Theory, Research & Practice* 11(3):202–210.

Hanks, William F. 1989. Text and Textuality. *Annual Review of Anthropology* 18:95–127.

1996. *Language and Communicative Practices*. Boulder, CO: Westview.

Hannerz, Ulf. 1992. *Cultural Complexity: Studies in the Social Organization of Meaning*. New York: Columbia University Press.

Harkness, Nicholas. 2011. Culture and Interdiscursivity in Korean Fricative Voice Gestures. *Journal of Linguistic Anthropology* 21(1):99–123.

2013. *Songs of Seoul: An Ethnography of Voice and Voicing in Christian South Korea*. Berkeley: University of California Press.

Hart, Betty, and Todd Risley. 1995. *Meaningful Differences in the Everyday Experience of Young American Children*. Baltimore: Paul H. Brookes.

Hart, Jerome Alfred. 1910. *A Vigilante Girl*. New York: A. L. Burt.

Haviland, John B. 2004. Gesture. In *Companion to Linguistic Anthropology*. A. Duranti, ed. Pp. 197–221. Malden, MA: Blackwell Publishers.

Hay, Jennifer, and Katie Drager. 2007. Sociophonetics. *Annual Review of Anthropology* 36(1):89–103.

Heath, Shirley Brice. 1978. *Teacher Talk: Language in the Classroom*. Language in Education: Theory and Practice 9. Pp. 1–33. Document #158 575FL. 009 676 (ERIC Clearinghouse on Languages and linguistics, Arlington, VA, Sponsored by the National Institute of Education, Washington, DC).

Heelas, Paul. 2008. *Spiritualities of Life: New Age Romanticism and Consumptive Capitalism*. Malden, MA: Wiley-Blackwell.

Heller, Monica. 2010. The Commodification of Language. *Annual Review of Anthropology* 39(1):101–114.

Henne-Ochoa, Richard, and Richard Bauman. 2015. Who Is Responsible for Saving the Language? Performing Generation in the Face of Language Shift. *Journal of Linguistic Anthropology* 25(2):128–149.

Herder, Johann Gottfried. 1772. *Abhandlung Über Den Ursprung Der Sprache* [Essay on the origin of language]. Berlin: Christian Friedrich Voss.

Herman, Louis M. 2012. Body and Self in Dolphins [Review]. *Consciousness and Cognition* 21:526–545.

Herod, Andrew. 2010. *Scale: Key Ideas in Geography*. New York: Routledge.

Herrick, Francis H. 1911. Nests and Nest-Building in Birds: Part I. *Journal of Animal Behavior* 1(3):159–192.

Herzog, Werner. 2011. *Cave of Forgotten Dreams: Sundance Selects*. Washington, DC: IFC Film.

Hill, Jane H. 1993. Structure and Practice in Language Shift. In *Progression and Regression in Language: Sociocultural, Neuropsychological, and Linguistic Perspectives*. K. Hyltenstam and Åke Viberg, eds. Pp. 68–93. Cambridge University Press.

1995a. Mock Spanish: A Site for the Indexical Reproduction of Racism in American English. In *Language & Culture: Symposium*. D. J. Glick, ed. www.cs.uChicago.edu/l-c/archives/subs/.

1995b. The Voices of Don Gabriel: Responsibility and Self in a Modern Mexicano Narrative. In *The Dialogic Emergence of Culture*. D. Tedlock and B. Mannheim, eds. Pp. 97–147. Urbana and Chicago: University of Illinois Press.

2002. "Expert Rhetorics" in Advocacy for Endangered Languages: Who Is Listening, and What Do They Hear? *Journal of Linguistic Anthropology* 12(2):119–133.

2006. The Ethnography of Language and Language Documentation. *In Essentials of Language Documentation*. J. Gippert, N. P. Himmelmann, and U. Mosel, eds. Pp. 113–128. Berlin and New York: Walter de Gruyter.

2009. *The Everyday Language of White Racism*. Malden, MA: Wiley-Blackwell.

Hill, Jane H., and Bruce Mannheim. 1992. Language and Worldview. *Annual Reviews in Anthropology* 21:381–406.

Hinton, Leanne. 2013. *Bringing Our Languages Home: Language Revitalization for Families*. Berkeley: Heyday.

Hobsbawm, Eric, and Terence Ranger, eds. 1983. *The Invention of Tradition*. Cambridge and New York: Cambridge University Press.

Hochschild, Arlie. 1979. Emotion Work, Feeling Rules, and Social Structure. *American Journal of Sociology* 85(3):551–575.

Hoffman, Katherine. 2006. Berber Language Ideologies, Maintenance, and Contraction: Gendered Variation in the Indigenous Margins of Morocco. *Language and Communication* 26(1):144–167.

2008. *We Share Walls: Language, Space, and Gender in Berber Morocco*, Vol. II. Malden, MA: Wiley-Blackwell.

Holmes, N. P., and C. Spence. 2005. Visual Bias of Unseen Hand Position with a Mirror: Spatial and Temporal Factors. *Experimental Brain Research* 166(3):489–497.

Honko, Lauri. 1974. Balto-Finnic Lament Poetry. *Studia Fennica* 17:9–61.

Hoopes, James, ed. 1991. *Peirce on Signs: Writings on Semiotic by Charles Sanders Peirce*. Chapel Hill: University of North Carolina Press.

Hopper, Paul J., and Elizabeth C. Traugott. 2003. *Grammaticalization*: Cambridge University Press.

Horkheimer, Max, and Theodore W. Adorno. 1946. The Culture Industry: Enlightenment as Mass Deception. In *Dialectic of Enlightenment: Philosophical Fragments*. M. Horkheimer, T. W. Adorno, G. S. Noerr, and E. Jephcot, eds. Pp. 94–136. Stanford University Press.

Hurford, James R. 2008. The Evolution of Human Communication and Language. In *Sociobiology of Communication: An Interdisciplinary Perspective*. P. d'Ettorre and D. P. Hughes, eds. Pp. 249–264. Oxford University Press.

Husserl, Edmund. 1913. Ideen Zu Einer Reinen Phänomenologie Und Phänomenologischen Philosophie. *Jahrbuch für Philosophie und Phänomenogische Forschung* 1(1):1–323.

1931. *Ideas: General Introduction to Pure Phenomenology*. New York: Macmillan Company.

[1913] 1970. *Logical Investigations*. J. N. Findlay, trans. New York: Humanities Press.

Hymes, Dell. 1972. Models of the Interaction of Language and Social Life. In *Directions in Sociolinguistics: The Ethnography of Communication*. J. Gumperz and D. Hymes, eds. Pp. 35–71. New York: Basil Blackwell.

1981. *In Vain I Tried to Tell You: Essays in Native American Ethnopoetics*. Philadelphia: University of Pennsylvania Press.

Inda, Jonathan Xavier, and Renato Rosaldo. 2002. Introduction: A World in Motion. In *The Anthropology of Globalization: A Reader*. J. X. Inda and R. Rosaldo, eds. Pp. 1–36. Oxford and Malden, MA: Blackwell Publishers.

Ingold, Tim. 1991. Becoming Persons: Consciousness and Sociality in Human Evolution. *Cultural Dynamics* 4(3):355–378.

2001. From Complementarity to Obviation: On Dissolving the Boundaries between Social and Biological Anthropology, Archaeology and Psychology. In *Cycles of Contingency: Developmental Systems and Evolution*. S. Oyama, P. E. Griffiths, and R. D. Gray, eds. Pp. 255–279. Cambridge, MA: MIT Press.

Inoue, Miyako. 2006. *Vicarious Language: Gender and Linguistic Modernity in Japan*. Berkeley: University of California Press.

Irvine, Judith. 1989. When Talk Isn't Cheap: Language and Political Economy. *American Ethnologist* 16:248–267.

1990. Registering Affect: Heteroglossia in the Linguistic Expression of Emotion. In *Language and the Politics of Emotion*. C. Lutz and L. Abu-Lughod, eds. Pp. 126–161. Cambridge University Press.

1998. Ideologies of Honorific Language. In *Language Ideologies: Practice and Theory*. B. Schieffelin, K. Woolard, and P. Kroskrity, eds. Pp. 51–67. New York: Oxford University Press.

Irvine, Judith, and Susan Gal. 2000. Language Ideology and Linguistic Differentiation. In *Regimes of Language: Ideologies, Polities, and Identities*. P. Kroskrity, ed. Pp. 35–83. Santa Fe, NM: School of American Research.

Ishaque, Abu. 1955. *Surya-Dighal Bāṛi* [Sun-Crossed (Inauspiciously Aligned) Homestead]. Dhaka: Nowroj Kitabistan.

Ishii, Keiko, Yuri Miyamoto, Kotomi Mayama, and Paula M. Niedenthal. 2011. When Your Smile Fades Away: Cultural Differences in Sensitivity to the Disappearance of Smiles. *Social Psychological and Personality Science* 2(5):516–522.

Itkonen, Matti. 2004. Lived Words: The Phenomenology of Poetry Experienced. In *Analecta Husserliana: Phenomenology of Life: Meeting the Challenges of the Present-Day World*. A.-T. Tymieniecka, ed. Pp. 145–163. Dordrecht: Kluwer Academic Press.

Jacquemet, Marco. 2005. Transidiomatic Practices: Language and Power in the Age of Globalization. *Language and Communication* 25(3):257–277.

— 2016. Language in the Age of Globalization. In *The Routledge Handbook of Linguistic Anthropology*. N. Bonvillain, ed. Pp. 329–347. New York and London: Routledge.

— Forthcoming. Sociolinguistic Superdiversity and Asylum. In *The Routledge Handbook on Language and Superdiversity*. A. Creese and A. Blackledge, eds. London: Taylor & Francis.

Jakobson, Roman. 1929. Romantické Všeslovanství – Nová Slavistika. [Romantic Pan-Slavism – A New Slavistics.] *Čin* 1(1):10–12.

— 1965. Quest for the Essence of Language. *Diogenes* 13(51):21–37.

— [1965] 1987. Quest for the Essence of Language. In *Language in Literature*. K. Pomorska and S. Rudy, eds. Pp. 413–427. Cambridge, MA and London: Harvard University Press.

— [1966] 1987. Grammatical Parallelism and Its Russian Facet. In *Language in Literature*. K. Pomorska and S. Rudy, eds. Pp. 145–179. Cambridge, MA and London: Harvard University Press.

— 1990. The Speech Event and the Functions of Language. In *On Language: Roman Jakobson*. L. R. Waugh and M. Monville-Burston, eds. Pp. 69–79. Cambridge, MA: Harvard University Press.

— [1987] 2002. The Spell of Speech Sounds. In *The Sound Shape of Language*. R. Jakobson and L. R. Waugh, eds. Pp. 181–234. The Hague: Mouton de Gruyter.

Jakobson, Roman, and Krystyna Pomorska. 1990. The Concept of Mark. In *On Language*. L. R. Waugh and M. Monville-Burston, eds. Pp. 134–142. Cambridge, MA: Harvard University Press.

Jerison, Harry J. 1976. Paleoneurology and the Evolution of Mind. *Scientific American* 234 (January):90–101.

Ji, Sungchul. 2002. The Microsemiotics of DNA. *Semiotica* 138(1–4):15–42.

Johnson, Michele K. 2012. k^sup w^u_sq^sup w^a?q^sup w^a?álx (We Begin to Speak): Our Journey within Nsyilxcn (Okanagan) Language Revitalization. *Canadian Journal of Native Education* 35(1):79.

Johnstone, Barbara. 2016. Characterological Figures and Expressive Style in the Enregisterment of Linguistic Variety. In *A Sense of Place: Studies in Language and Region*. B. Johnstone, ed. Cambridge University Press.

Jones, Graham M., and Bambi B. Schieffelin. 2009. Talking Text and Talking Back: "My Bff Jill" from Boob Tube to Youtube. *Journal of Computer-Mediated Communication* 14(4):1050–1079.

Jørgensen, J. N., M. S. Karrebæk, L. M. Madsen, and J. S. Møller. 2011. Polylanguaging in Superdiversity. *Diversities* 13(2):23–38.

Keane, Webb. 2003. Public Speaking: On Indonesian as the Language of the Nation. *Public Culture* 15(3):503–530.

2007. *Christian Moderns: Freedom and Fetish in the Mission Encounter*. Berkeley and Los Angeles: University of California Press.

Keenan, Elinor Ochs. 1974. Norm-Makers, Norm-Breakers: Uses of Speech by Men and Women in a Malagasy Community. In *Explorations in the Ethnography of Speaking*. R. Bauman and J. Sherzer, eds. Pp. 125–143. Cambridge University Press.

Keller, Charles M., and Janet Dixon Keller. 1996. Imaging in Iron, or Thought Is Not Inner Speech. In *Rethinking Linguistic Relativity*. J. Gumperz and S. Levinson, eds. Pp. 115–131. Cambridge University Press.

Keller, Evelyn Fox. 2016. Thinking about Biology and Culture: Can the Natural and Human Sciences Be Integrated? *The Sociological Review Monographs* 64(1):26–41.

Kendon, Adam. 1990. *Conducting Interaction: Patterns of Behavior in Focused Encounters*. Cambridge University Press.

1997. Gesture. *Annual Review of Anthropology* 26(1):109–128.

Kincaid, Harold. 1998. Positivism in the Social Sciences. In *Routledge Encyclopedia of Philosophy: Genealogy to Iqbal*, Vol. IV. E. Craig, ed. Taylor & Francis Group.

Kirby, Christine. 2012. Are "We" Pregnant? A Phenomenological Approach to Investigating the Lived Pregnancy Experience through Discourse and Practice. MA thesis, Northern Arizona University.

Kleinman, Arthur, and Peter Benson. 2006. Anthropology in the Clinic: The Problem of Cultural Competency and How to Fix It. *PLoS Medicine* 3(10/e294):1673–1676.

Kloss, Heinz. 1966. Types of Multilingual Communities: A Discussion of Ten Variables. *Sociological Inquiry* 36(2):135–145.

Kockelman, Paul. 2004. Stance and Subjectivity. *Journal of Linguistic Anthropology* 14(2):127–150.

Kockelmans, Joseph J. 1999. Phenomenology. In *Cambridge Dictionary of Philosophy* (2nd edn.). R. Audi, ed. Pp. 664–666. Cambridge University Press.

Kohut, Heinz. [1977] 2011. *The Restoration of the Self*. University of Chicago Press.

Kolben, Peter. 1731. *The Present State of the Cape of Good Hope: Or, a Particular Account of the Several Nations of the Hottentots: Their Religion, Government, Laws, Customs, Ceremonies, and Opinions; Their Art of War, Professions, Language, Genius, & C. Together with a Short Account of the Dutch Settlement at the Cape. Written Originally in High German, by Peter Kolben. Done into English from the Original by Mr. Medley*. London: Innys, W. (Hathi Trust).

Kolker, Andrew, and Louis Alvarez. 1988. *American Tongues*. USA: PBS. New York: The Center for New American Media. Kolker, Andrew, Louis Alvarez, and Center for New American Media.

Kornblut, Anne E. 2006. The Peculiar Power of the Chattering Class. *New York Times*. Pp. 1, 14.

Kroeber, Alfred Louis. 1917. The Superorganic. *American Anthropologist* 19(2):163–213.

1949. The Concept of Culture in Science. *The Journal of General Education* 3(3):182–196.

Kroskrity, Paul V. 1985. Growing with Stories: Line, Verse, and Genre in an Arizona Tewa Text. *Journal of Anthropological Research* 41:183–199.

1993. *Language, History, and Identity: Ethnolinguistic Studies of the Arizona Tewa*. Tucson: University of Arizona Press.

2009a. Language Renewal as Sites of Language Ideological Struggle: The Need for "Ideological Clarification." In *Indigenous Language Revitalization: Encouragement, Guidance & Lessons Learned*. J. Reyhner and L. Lockard, eds. Pp. 71–83. Flagstaff: Northern Arizona University.

2009b. Narrative Reproductions: Ideologies of Storytelling, Authoritative Words, and Generic Regimentation in the Village of Tewa. *Journal of Linguistic Anthropology* 19(1):40–56.

2012. *Telling Stories in the Face of Danger: Narratives and Language Renewal in Native American Communities*. Norman: University of Oklahoma Press.

Kroskrity, Paul V., and Margaret Field, eds. 2009. *Native American Language Ideologies: Beliefs, Practices, and Struggles in Indian Country*. Tucson: University of Arizona Press.

Kuipers, Joel C. 1989. "Medical Discourse" in Anthropological Context: Views of Language and Power. *Medical Anthropology Quarterly* 3(2):99–123.

Kulick, Don. 1998. Anger, Gender, Language Shift, and the Politics of Revelation in a Papua New Guinean Village. In *Language Ideologies: Practice and Theory*. B. B. Schieffelin, K. A. Woolard, and P. Kroskrity, eds. Oxford Studies in Anthropological Linguistics. New York: Oxford University Press.

2006. Theory in Furs: Masochist Anthropology. *Current Anthropology* 47(6):933–952.

2009. Soccer, Sex and Scandal in Brazil. *Anthropology Now* 1(3):32–42.

Kunreuther, Laura. 2006. Technologies of the Voice: FM Radio, Telephone, and the Nepali Diaspora in Kathmandu. *Cultural Anthropology* 21(3):323–353.

Labov, William. 1968. The Reflections of Social Processes in Linguistic Structure. In *Readings in the Sociology of Language*. J. Fishman, ed. Pp. 240–251. The Hague: Mouton.

1972. *Sociolinguistic Patterns*. Philadelphia: University of Pennsylvania Press.

Laderman, Carol. 1987. The Ambiguity of Symbols in the Structure of Healing. *Social Science and Medicine* 24(4):293–301.

Laing, R. D. 1989. Comments on the Interview with Christy. In *The Lourdes of Arizona*. C. Amantea, ed. Pp. 141–142. San Diego, CA: Mho & Mho Works.

Lambert, Wallace E. 1975. Language Attitudes in a French-American Community. *Linguistics* 158:127–152.

Lambert, Wallace E., R. C. Hodgson, R. C. Gardner, and S. Fillenbaum. 1960. Evaluational Reactions to Spoken Languages. *Journal of Abnormal and Social Psychology* 60(1):44–51.

Lane, Harlan. 1967. The Perception of General American English by Speakers of Southern Dialects. Supported by ERIC (Ed.Gov) Institute of Education Sciences. Ann Arbor: University of Michigan, Center for Research on Language and Language Behavior. http://eric.ed.gov/?id=ED016974.

Latour, Bruno. 1993. *We Have Never Been Modern*. Cambridge, MA: Harvard University Press.

Laver, John. 1980. *The Phonetic Description of Voice Quality*. Cambridge and New York: Cambridge University Press.

Lechner, Frank J., and John Boli. 2014. *The Globalization Reader*. Malden, MA and London: Wiley.

Lee, Benjamin. 1997. *Talking Heads: Language, Metalanguage, and the Semiotics of Subjectivity*. Durham, NC: Duke University Press.

Lee, Jin Sook, and Mary Bucholtz. 2015. Language Socialization across Learning Spaces. In *The Handbook of Classroom Discourse and Interaction*. N. Markee, ed. Pp. 319–336. Malden, MA: Wiley-Blackwell.

Lee, Tiffany S. 2007. "If They Want Navajo to Be Learned, Then They Should Require It in All Schools": Navajo Teenagers' Experiences, Choices, and Demands Regarding Navajo Language. *Wicazo Sa Review* 22(1):7–33.

Lehrer, Jim. 2009. Focus on Social and Emotional Health Raises Test Scores. *PBS News Hour*. American Public Broadcasting System (PBS, Arlington, VA), July 21, 2009.

LeMaster, Barbara. 2006. Language Contraction, Revitalization, and Irish Women. *Journal of Linguistic Anthropology* 16(2):211–228.

Leonard, Wesley Y. 2007. Miami Language Reclamation in the Home: A Case Study. PhD, University of California, Berkeley.

Leonard, Wesley Y., and Erin Haynes. 2010. Making "Collaboration" Collaborative: An Examination of Perspectives that Frame Linguistic Field Research. *Language Documentation & Conservation* 4:268–293.

Leppänen, Sirpa. 2015. Dog Blogs as Ventriloquism: Authentication of the Human Voice. Discourse, *Context & Media* (Special Issue: *Authenticity, Normativity and Social Media*, eds. Sirpa Leppänen, Janus Møller & Thomas Nørreby) 8:63–73.

Lévi-Strauss, Claude. 1963. The Effectiveness of Symbols. In *Structural Anthropology*. Pp. 186–205. New York: Basic Books.

Levin, Norman Balfour. 1965. Contrived Speech in Washington: The Hu Sociolect. *Georgetown University Monograph Series on Languages and Linguistics* 18:115–128.

Levinson, Stephen C., and Judith Holler. 2014. The Origin of Human Multi-Modal Communication. *Philosophical Transactions of the Royal Society B: Biological Sciences* 369(1651):20130302.

Levitt, Theodore. 1983. The Globalization of Markets. *Harvard Business Review*, May–June, 92–102.

Levrez, Clovis, Béatrice Bourdin, Barbara Le Driant, Baudouin Forgeot D'Arc, and Luc Vandromme. 2012. The Impact of Verbal Capacity on Theory of Mind in Deaf and Hard of Hearing Children. *American Annals of the Deaf* 157(1):66–77.

Lewis, Charlton T., and Charles Short. 1891. *A New Latin Dictionary/Harper's Latin Dictionary*. E. A. Andrews, ed. New York and Oxford: Harper and Clarendon.

Lewis, M. Paul, ed. 2009. *Ethnologue: Languages of the World*. Dallas, TX: SIL International.

Lewis, Norman P. 2010. The Myth of Spiro Agnew's "Nattering Nabobs of Negativism." *American Journalism* 27(1):89–115.

Lieberman, Philip. 2007. The Evolution of Human Speech: Its Anatomical and Neural Bases. *Current Anthropology* 48(1):39–66.

Lieberman, Philip, and Robert McCarthy. 2007. Tracking the Evolution of Language and Speech: Comparing Vocal Tracts to Identify Speech Capabilities. *Expedition* 49(1):15–20.

Lindholm, Charles. 2008. *Culture and Authenticity*. Malden, MA: Blackwell Publishers. 2009. How We Became Authentic. *Ethos* 37(148–153).

Lindstrom, Lamont. 1992. Context Contests: Debatable Truth Statements on Tanna (Vanuatu). In *Rethinking Context: Language as an Interactive Phenomenon*. A. Duranti and C. Goodwin, eds. Pp. 101–124. Studies in the Social and Cultural Foundations of Language, 11. Cambridge University Press.

Lippi-Green, Rosina. 1997. *English with an Accent: Language, Ideology, and Discrimination in the United States*. London: Routledge.

Lo, Adrienne, and Heidi Fung. 2012. Language Socialization and Shaming. In *The Handbook of Language Socialization*. A. Duranti, E. Ochs, and B. B. Schieffelin, eds. Pp. 169–189. Malden, MA: Blackwell Publishers.

Lo, Adrienne, and Jenna Kim. 2011. Manufacturing Citizenship: Metapragmatic Framings of Language Competencies in Media Images of Mixed Race Men in South Korea. *Discourse Society* 22(4):440–457.

Loether, Christopher. 2009. Language Revitalization and the Manipulation of Language Ideologies: A Shoshoni Case Study. In *Native American Language Ideologies: Beliefs, Practices, and Struggles in Indian Country*. P. Kroskrity and M. Field, eds. Pp. 238–254. Tucson: University of Arizona Press.

Lönnrot, Elias. 1835. *Kalevala Taikka Vanhoja Karjalan Runoja Suomen Kansan Muinosista Ajoista*. Pori: Laakapainojäljennös.

Lord, Alfred B. [1960] 2000. *The Singer of Tales*. Cambridge, MA: Harvard University Press.

Lowth, Robert, and G. Gregory. [1787] 1829. *Lectures on the Sacred Poetry of the Hebrews*. Andover and New York: Crocker and Brewster.

Lucy, John. 1996. The Scope of Linguistic Relativity: An Analysis and Review of Empirical Research. In *Rethinking Linguistic Relativity*. J. Gumperz and S. Levinson, eds. Pp. 37–69. Studies in the Social and Cultural Foundations of Language, 17. Cambridge University Press.

   1997. Linguistic Relativity. *Annual Review of Anthropology* 26:291–312.

Luhrmann, Tanya. 2000. *Of Two Minds: An Anthropologist Looks at American Psychiatry*. New York: Vintage.

Luuk, Erkki. 2013. The Structure and Evolution of Symbol. *New Ideas in Psychology* 31(2):87–97.

Lynch, Owen, ed. 1990. *Divine Passions: The Social Construction of Emotion in India*. Berkeley: University of California Press.

Lynch, Rene. 2012. Black and Tan: Nike Apologizes for Shoe-Naming Gaffe. *Los Angeles Times*.

Lyon, Margot L. 1994. Emotion as Mediator of Somatic and Social Processes: The Example of Respiration. In *Social Perspectives on Emotion*, Vol. II. W. Wentworth and J. Ryan, eds. Pp. 83–108. Greenwich, CT: JAI Press.

MacCaluim, Alasdair. 2007. *Reversing Language Shift: The Social Identity and Role of Scottish Gaelic Learners*. Belfast: Cló Ollscoil na Banríona.

Macedonia, J. M., and Christopher Evans. 1993. Variation in Mammalian Alarm Call Systems and the Problem of Meaning in Animal Signals. *Ethology* 93(1):177–197.

MacWhinney, Brian. 2005. The Emergence of Grammar from Perspective. In *Language Acquisition, Change and Emergence: Essays in Evolutionary Linguistics*. J. W. Minett and W.S.-Y. Wang, eds. Pp. 95–152. University of Hong Kong Press.

Malinowski, Bronislaw. 1923. The Problem of Meaning in Primitive Languages. In *The Meaning of Meaning: Supplement I*. C. K. Ogden and I. A. Richards, eds. Pp. 296–336. New York: Harcourt, Brace & World.

   1935. *Coral Gardens and Their Magic*, Vol. II: *The Language of Magic and Gardening*. London: George Allen & Unwin.

Malloch, Stephen N., and Colwyn Trevarthen, eds. 2009. *Communicative Musicality: Exploring the Basis of Human Companionship*. Oxford and New York: Oxford University Press.

Manetti, Giovanni. 2010. Ancient Semiotics. In *The Routledge Companion to Semiotics*. P. Cobley, ed. Pp. 13–28. London and New York: Routledge.

Manning, Paul. 2010. The Semiotics of Brand. *Annual Review of Anthropology* 39:33–49.

Manser, M. B., M. B. Bell, and L. B. Fletcher. 2001. The Information that Receivers Extract from Alarm Calls in Suricates. *Proc Biol Sci* 268(1484):2485–2491.

Marsilli-Vargas, Xochitl. 2014. Listening Genres: The Emergence of Relevance Structures through the Reception of Sound. *Journal of Pragmatics* 69:42–51.

2016. The Offline and Online Mediatization of Psychoanalysis in Buenos Aires. *Signs and Society* 4(1):135–153.

Martelle Hayter, Holly. [1994] 2011. Hunter-Gatherers and the Ethnographic Analogy: Theoretical Perspectives. *Totem: The University of Western Ontario Journal of Anthropology* 1(1):39–49.

Martin, Nathaniel, and Patricia Wall. 2008. The Secret Life of Medical Records: A Study of Medical Records and the People Who Manage Them. *Ethnographic Praxis in Industry Conference (EPIC) Proceedings*. Pp. 51–63. Wiley Online Library.

Marx, Karl. [1852] 1978. The Eighteenth Brumaire of Louis Bonaparte. In *The Marx-Engels Reader* (2nd edn.). R. C. Tucker, ed. Pp. 594–617. New York: Norton.

Mathews, Holly. 1992. The Directive Force of Morality Tales in a Mexican Community. In *Human Motives and Cultural Models*. R. D'Andrade and C. Strauss, eds. Pp. 127–161. Cambridge and New York: Cambridge University Press.

Matoesian, Greg. 2005. Struck by Speech Revisited: Embodied Stance in Jurisdictional Discourse. *Journal of Sociolinguistics* 9(2):167–193.

Maturana, Humberto R., and Francisco J. Varela. 1980. *Autopoiesis and Cognition: The Realization of the Living*: Dordrecht: D. Reidel.

Mauss, Marcel. 1973. Techniques of the Body. *Economy and Society* 2(1):70–87.

Mayer, Mercer. 1969. *Frog, Where Are You?* New York: Dial Press.

Maynard, Douglas W., and John Heritage. 2005. Conversation Analysis, Doctor-Patient Interaction and Medical Communication (Series Title: Making Sense of Qualitative Research). *Medical Education* 39:428–435.

McCoy, Julia. 2015. How to Get Ahead with Your Content in 2016. *SEJ: Search Engine Journal*. December 10, 2015. www.searchenginejournal.com/get-ahead-content-2016/146010/, accessed December 3, 2016.

McElhinny, Bonnie. 2016. A Heartfelt Approach: On and Beyond Neoliberalism. *Ethos* 44(2):186–191. (Special Issue: Emotion Pedagogies, ed. J. Fenigsen, J. Wilce, and E. Lowe) 44(2):186–191.

McEwan-Fujita, Emily. 2010. Ideology, Affect, and Socialization in Language Shift and Revitalization: The Experiences of Adults Learning Gaelic in the Western Isles of Scotland. *Language in Society* 39(1):27–64.

McGrew, William C. 1998. Culture in Nonhuman Primates? *Annual Review of Anthropology* 27:301–328.

McKee, Jeffrey K., Frank E. Poirier, and W. Scott Mcgraw. 2015. *Understanding Human Evolution*. Oxford: Taylor & Francis.

McLuhan, Marshall. 1964. *Understanding Media: The Extensions of Man*. New York: McGraw-Hill.

McQuown, Norman A., ed. [1956] 1971. *The Natural History of an Interview*. University of Chicago Microfilm Collection of Manuscripts in Cultural Anthropology, Series 15, numbers 95–98. University of Chicago Library.

Meek, Barbra A. 2007. Respecting the Language of Elders: Ideological Shift and Linguistic Discontinuity in a Northern Athapascan Community. *Journal of Linguistic Anthropology* 17(1):23–43.

2010. *We Are Our Language: An Ethnography of Language Revitalization in a Northern Athabascan Community*. Tucson: University of Arizona Press.

2011. Failing American Indian Languages. *American Indian Culture and Research Journal* 35(2):43–60.

2016. The Politics of Language Endangerment. In *The Routledge Handbook of Linguistic Anthropology*. N. Bonvillain, ed. Pp. 447–462. New York: Taylor & Francis.

Meier, Brian P., and Michael D. Robinson. 2005. The Metaphorical Representation of Affect. *Metaphor and Symbol* 20(4):239–257.

2006. Does "Feeling Down" Mean Seeing Down? Depressive Symptoms and Vertical Selective Attention. *Journal of Research in Personality* 40(4):451–461.

Mendoza-Denton, Norma. 2011. The Semiotic Hitchhiker's Guide to Creaky Voice: Circulation and Gendered Hardcore in a Chicana/o Gang Persona. *Journal of Linguistic Anthropology* 21(2):261–280.

Merriam Webster Dictionary. 2016. "Society": Merriam-Webster, www.merriam-webster.com/dictionary/society?show=0&t=1312580098.

Mertz, Elizabeth, and Richard Parmentier, eds. 1985. *Semiotic Mediation: Sociocultural and Psychological Perspectives*. Orlando: Academic Press.

Mertz, Elizabeth, and Jonathan Yovel. 2000. Metalinguistic Awareness. In *Handbook of Pragmatics*. J. Verschueren, ed. Philadelphia: John Benjamins.

Messing, Jacqueline. 2014. "I Didn't Know You Knew Mexicano!": Shifting Ideologies, Identities, and Ambivalence among Former Youth in Tlaxcala, Mexico. In *Indigenous Youth and Multilingualism: Language Identity, Ideology, and Practice in Dynamic Cultural Worlds*. L. T. Wyman, T. McCarty, and S. E. Nicholas, eds. Pp. 111–148. New York: Routledge.

Mishler, Elliot G. 1984. *The Discourse of Medicine: Dialectics of Medical Interviews*. Norwood, NJ: Ablex.

Mithen, Steven J. 2005. *The Singing Neanderthals: The Origins of Music, Language, Mind, and Body*. Cambridge, MA: Harvard University Press.

Mithun, Marianne. 1998. The Significance of Diversity in Language Endangerment and Preservation. In *Endangered Languages: Current Issues and Future Prospects*. L. A. Grenoble and L. J. Whaley, eds. Pp. 163–191. New York: Cambridge University Press.

Moerman, Michael. 1988. *Talking Culture: Ethnography and Conversation Analysis*. Philadelphia: University of Pennsylvania Press.

Moore, Robert. 2012. Taking up Speech in an Endangered Language: Bilingual Discourse in a Heritage Language Classroom. *Working Papers in Educational Linguistics* 27(2):57–78.

Morris, C. 1938. Foundations of the Theory of Signs. In *International Encyclopedia of Unified Science,* Vol. I, Number 2. O. Neurath, ed. Pp. 77–138. University of Chicago Press.

Morris, Lori. 1998. *A Toughish Problem: The Meaning of -Ish*. The LACUS Forum, 1998, Pp. 207–215. Chapel Hill, NC: Hornbeam Press/Linguistic Association of Canada and the United States.

Muehlmann, Shaylih. 2012. Von Humboldt's Parrot and the Countdown of Last Speakers in the Colorado Delta. *Language and Communication* 32(1):160–168.

Nagy, Naomi, and Patricia Irwin. 2010. Boston (r): Neighbo(r)s Nea(r) and Fa(r). *Language Variation and Change* 22(2):241–278.

Nakano, Tamami, and Shigeru Kitazawa. 2010. Eyeblink Entrainment at Breakpoints of Speech. *Experimental Brain Research* 205:577–581.

Nakano, Tamami, Nobumasa Kato, and Shigeru Kitazawa. 2011. Lack of Eyeblink Entrainments in Autism Spectrum Disorders. *Neuropsychologia* 49(9):2784–2790.

Nakassis, Constantine V., and Melanie A. Dean. 2007. Desire, Youth, and Realism in Tamil Cinema. *Journal of Linguistic Anthropology* 17(1):77–104.

Nandini, A. Satya. 2014. McDonald's Success Story in India. *Journal of Contemporary Research in Management* 9(3):21–31.

Nelson, Kristin L. 2001. *The Art of Reciting the Qur'an.* American University in Cairo Press.

Nevins, M. Eleanor. 2004. Learning to Listen: Confronting Two Meanings of Language Loss in the Contemporary White Mountain Apache Speech Community. *Journal of Linguistic Anthropology* 14(2):269–288.

     2013. *Lessons from Fort Apache: Beyond Language Endangerment and Maintenance* Malden, MA: Wiley-Blackwell.

Newton, Michael. 2005. "This Could Have Been Mine": Scottish Gaelic Learners in North America. *E-Keltoi: Journal of Interdisciplinary Celtic Studies* 1:1–37.

NOAA Magazine. 2005. NOAA and VT Halter Marine Launch Second Fisheries Survey Vessel. www.noaanews.noaa.gov/stories2005/s2471.htm.

NPR. 2012. Coffee Is the New Wine: Here's How You Taste It. www.npr.org/sections/thesalt/2012/08/16/158932704/coffee-is-the-new-wine-heres-how-you-taste-it.

O'Rorke, Imogen. 2000. Old Is the New New.*The Guardian* (Online US edition).

Ochs, Elinor. 1979. Transcription as Theory. In *Developmental Pragmatics*. E. Ochs and B. B. Schieffelin, eds. Pp. 43–72. New York: Academic Press.

     1988. *Culture and Language Development: Language Acquisition and Language Socialization in a Samoan Village.* Cambridge University Press.

Ochs, Elinor, and Lisa Capps. 2001. *Living Narrative: Creating Lives in Everyday Storytelling.* Cambridge, MA: Harvard University Press.

Ochs, Elinor, and Bambi Schieffelin. 1984. Language Acquisition and Socialization: Three Developmental Stories and Their Implications. In *Culture Theory: Essays on Mind, Self, and Emotion*. R. Shweder and R. A. LeVine, eds. Pp. 276–320. New York: Cambridge University Press.

Ochs, Elinor, and Olga Solomon. 2010. Autistic Sociality. *Ethos* 38(1):69–92.

Ochs, Elinor, Olga Solomon, and Laura Sterponi. 2005. Limitations and Transformations of Habitus in Child-Directed Communication. *Discourse Studies* 7(4–5):547–583.

OED Online. 2016a. *"Culcha, N."* Oxford University Press.

     2016b. *"Culture, N."* Oxford University Press, www.oed.com/view/Entry/45746?result=1&rskey=IAt7SP&amp.

     2016c. *"Semiotic, Adj. And N."* Oxford University Press.

     2016d. *"Society, N."* Oxford University Press. www.oed.com/view/Entry/183776?redirectedFrom=society&amp.

Ogden, Richard. 2003. Voice Quality as a Resource for the Management of Turn-Taking in Finnish Talk-in-Interaction. In *Proceedings of the XVth International Congress of Phonetic Sciences, Barcelona, August 3–9, 2003*. M. J. Solé, D. Recasens, and J. Romero, eds. Pp. 123–126. Barcelona: ICPhS Archive. www.internationalphoneticassociation.org/icphs/icphs2003.

Oller, D Kimbrough. 2014. Phonation Takes Precedence over Articulation in Development as Well as Evolution of Language. *Behavioral and Brain Sciences* 37(06):567–568.

Ortner, Sherry. 1984. Theory in Anthropology since the Sixties. *Comparative Studies in Society and History* 26(1):126–166.

Ottenheimer, Harriet J. 2012. *The Anthropology of Language: An Introduction to Linguistic Anthropology*. Belmont, CA: Cengage Learning.

Pascendi. 2009. John Paul the Great and Hugh Hefner the Magnificent. Mary Victrix. https://maryvictrix.com/2009/05/08/john-paul-the-great-and-hugh-hefner-the-magnificent/.

Paul, Benjamin D. 1950. Symbolic Sibling Rivalry in a Guatemalan Indian Village. *American Anthropologist* 52(2):205–218.

PBSKids.org-PBS-Learning-Media. 2016. When You Feel So Mad That You Want to Roar: Strategy Song and Activity | Daniel Tiger's Neighborhood. PBSLearning Media. PBSKids.org.

Peden, James Hunter. 2012. The Provider's Black Box: Language, Technology, and Participation in General Practice Medical Encounters. MA thesis, Northern Arizona University.

Peirce, Charles S. 1931–1958. *Collected Papers of Charles Sanders Peirce*. Cambridge, MA: Belknap Press of Harvard University Press.

   1960 *The Simplest Mathematics*, Vol. III. Cambridge, MA: Belknap Press of Harvard University Press.

Pennisi, Elizabeth, and Wade Roush. 1997. Developing a New View of Evolution. *Science* 277(5322):34–37.

Percival, W. Keith. 2011. Roman Jakobson and the Birth of Linguistic Structuralism. *Sign Systems Studies* 29(1):236–262.

Perrino, Sabina M. 2002. Intimate Hierarchies and Qur'anic Saliva (Tëfli): Textuality in a Senegalese Ethnomedical Encounter. *Journal of Linguistic Anthropology* 12(2):225–259.

Philips, Susan. 2013. Method in Anthropological Discourse Analysis: The Comparison of Units of Interaction [Forum: Methods and Analysis in Linguistic Anthropology]. *Journal of Linguistic Anthropology* 23(1):82–95.

Phillips, Susan A. 1999. *Wallbangin': Graffiti and Gangs in L.A.* University of Chicago Press.

Phillips-Silver, Jessica, C. Athena Aktipis, and Gregory A. Bryant. 2010. The Ecology of Entrainment: Foundations of Coordinated Rhythmic Movement. *Music Perception* 28(1):3–14.

Pickering, Judith. 2015. Acoustic Resonance at the Dawn of Life: Musical Fundamentals of the Psychoanalytic Relationship. *Journal of Analytical Psychology* 60(5):618–641.

Poedjosoedarmo, Soepomo. 1968. Javanese Speech Levels. *Indonesia* 6(1):54–81.

Pollock, Sheldon. 1996. The Sanskrit Cosmopolis. In *Ideology and Status of Sanskrit: Contributions to the History of the Sankrit Language*. J. E. M. Houben, ed. Pp. 197–245. Leiden: E. J. Brill.

Preethi. 2016. A Preschooler's Social and Emotional Life – Daniel Tiger's Neighborhood. Behaviour, Parenting, Tech Reviews. http://sumo.ly/hM6U/.

Preloran, H. Mabel, Carole H. Browner, and Eli Lieber. 2005. Impact of Interpreters' Approach on Latinas' Use of Amniocentesis. *Health Education & Behavior* 32(5):599–612.

Preucel, Robert W., and Alexander A. Bauer. 2001. Archeological Pragmatics. *Norwegian Archaeological Review* 34(2):85–96.

Price, John A. 1973. The Superorganic Fringe. Protoculture, Indioculture, and Material Culture. *Ethos* 1(2):201–218.

Proust, Joëlle. 2016. The Evolution of Primate Communication and Metacommunication. *Mind & Language* 31(2):177–203.

Pyers, Jennie E., and Ann Senghas. 2009. Language Promotes False-Belief Understanding: Evidence from Learners of a New Sign Language. *Psychological Science* 20:805–812.

Radcliffe-Brown, Alfred Reginald. 1940 On Social Structure. *The Journal of the Royal Anthropological Institute of Great Britain and Ireland* 70(1):1-12.

Rakhlin, N., S. A. Kornilov, J. Reich, M. Babyonyshev, R. A. Koposov, and E. L. Grigorenko. 2011. The Relationship between Syntactic Development and Theory of Mind: Evidence from a Small-Population Study of a Developmental Language Disorder. *Journal of Neurolinguistics* 24(4):476–496.

Ramnarine, Tina Karina. 2003. *Ilmatar's Inspirations: Nationalism, Globalization, and the Changing Soundscapes of Finnish Folk Music*. University of Chicago Press.

Rampton, Ben. 1995. Language Crossing and the Problematisation of Ethnicity and Socialisation. *Pragmatics* 5(4):485–513.

Ranjan, Geetika. 2012. Tribe as a Category: Perspective from Within and Without. *The Oriental Anthropologist* 12(1):153–163.

Rasmussen, Susan J. 1992. Ritual Specialists, Ambiguity and Power in Tuareg Society. *Man* 27(1):105–128.

Reber, Stephan A., Markus Boeckle, Georgine Szipl, Judith Janisch, Thomas Bugnyar, and W. Tecumseh Fitch. 2016. Territorial Raven Pairs are Sensitive to Structural Changes in Simulated Acoustic Displays of Conspecifics. *Animal Behaviour* 116:153–162.

Reddy, Michael J. 1979. The Conduit Metaphor: A Case of Frame Conflict in Our Language About Language. *Metaphor and Thought* 2:164–201.

[1979] 1993. The Conduit Metaphor: A Case of Frame Conflict in Our Language About Language. In *Metaphor and Thought*. A. Ortony, ed. Pp. 164–201. Cambridge University Press.

Reich, Adam. 2012. Disciplined Doctors: The Electronic Medical Record and Physicians' Changing Relationship to Medical Knowledge. *Social Science & Medicine* 74(7):1021–1028.

Reyes, Angela. 2014. Linguistic Anthropology in 2013: Super-New-Big. *American Anthropologist* 116(2):366–378.

Reyna, B. A., L. F. Brown, R. H. Pickler, B. J. Myers, and J. B. Younger. 2012. Mother–Infant Synchrony during Infant Feeding. *Infant Behavior & Development* 35(4):669–677.

Reynolds, Jennifer F., and Marjorie Faulstich Orellana. 2014. Translanguaging within Enactments of Quotidian Interpreter-Mediated Interactions. *Journal of Linguistic Anthropology* 24(3):315–338.

Richardson, Michael K., and Gerhard Keuck. 2002. Haeckel's Abc of Evolution and Development. *Biological Reviews of the Cambridge Philosophical Society* 77(4):495–528.

Richo, David. 2007. *The Sacred Heart of the World: Restoring Mystical Devotion to Our Spiritual Life*: Paulist Press.

Robbins, Joel. 2001. God Is Nothing but Talk: Modernity, Language and Prayer in a Papua New Guinea Society. *American Anthropologist* 103(4):901–912.

2004. *Becoming Sinners: Christianity and Moral Torment in a Papua New Guinea Society,* Vol. IV. Berkeley: University of California Press.

2014. The Anthropology of Christianity: Unity, Diversity, New Directions: An Introduction to Supplement 10. *Current Anthropology* 55(S10):S000–S000.

Rosaldo, Michelle Z. 1973. I Have Nothing to Hide: The Language of Ilongot Oratory. *Language in Society* 2(2):193–223.

1982. The Things We Do with Words: Ilongot Speech Acts and Speech Act Theory in Philosophy. *Language in Society* 11(2):203–237.

Rosaldo, Renato. 1984. Grief and a Headhunter's Rage: On the Cultural Forces of Emotions. In *Text, Play and Story: The Construction and Reconstruction of Self and Society*. S. Plattner and E. M. Bruner, eds. Washington, DC: American Ethnological Society.

Rose, Nikolas. 1999. *Governing the Soul: The Shaping of the Private Self.* London: Free Association Books.

Rosenblatt, Jay S. 1969. The Development of Maternal Responsiveness in the Rat. *American Journal of Orthopsychiatry* 39(1):36.

Ruusuvuori, Johanna. 2005 "Empathy" and "Sympathy" in Action: Attending to Patients' Troubles in Finnish Homeopathic and General Practice Consultations. *Social Psychology Quarterly* 68:204–222.

Sacks, Harvey. 1984. On Doing" Being Ordinary". In *Structures of Social Action: Studies in Conversational Analysis*. J. M. Atkinson and J. Heritage, eds. Pp. 413–429. Cambridge University Press.

Sameer, Sharanbir Kaur. 2012. Strategy and Repositioning the Brand Mcdonald's in India. *International Journal of Scientific and Research Publications* 2(9):1–5.

Santiago-Irizarry, Vilma. 1996. Culture as Cure. *Cultural Anthropology* 11(1):3–24.

2001. *Medicalizing Ethnicity: The Construction of Latino Identity in a Psychiatric Setting.* Ithaca, NY: Cornell University Press.

Sapir, Edward. 1927. The Unconscious Patterning of Behavior in Society. In *The Unconscious: A Symposium*. C. M. Child and E. S. Drummer, eds. Pp. 114–142. New York: Knopf.

1929. The Status of Linguistics as a Science. *Language* 5:207–214.

Sass, Louis A. 1992. *Madness and Modernism: Insanity in the Light of Modern Art, Literature, and Thought*. New York: Basic Books.

Saussure, Ferdinand de. [1916] 1959. *Course in General Linguistics*. New York: Philosophical Library.

Sawyer, Robert Keith. 2001. *Creating Conversations: Improvisation in Everyday Discourse*. Cresskill, NJ: University of Michigan/Hampton Press.

Scalise Sugiyama, Michelle. 1996. On the Origins of Narrative. *Human Nature* 7(4):403–425.

2001. Food, Foragers, and Folklore: The Role of Narrative in Human Subsistence. *Evolution and Human Behavior* 22(4):221–240.

2005. Reverse-Engineering Narrative: Evidence of Special Design. In *The Literary Animal: Evolution and the Nature of Narrative*. J. Gottschall and D. S. Wilson, eds. Pp. 177–196. Evanston, IL: Northwestern University Press.

2011. The Forager Oral Tradition and the Evolution of Prolonged Juvenility. *Frontiers in Psychology* 2:1–19.

Scheff, Thomas. 2000. Shame and the Social Bond: A Sociological Theory. *Sociological Theory* 18(1):84–98.

Schegloff, Emanuel A., Elinor Ochs, and Sandra A. Thompson. 1996. Introduction. In *Interaction and Grammar*. E. Ochs, E. A. Schegloff, and S. A. Thompson, eds. Pp. 1–51. Cambridge University Press.

Schegloff, Emanuel A., and Harvey Sacks. 1973. Opening up Closings. *Semiotica* 7(4):289–327.

Scheper-Hughes, Nancy. 2000. Ire in Ireland. *Ethnography* 1(1):117–140.

Schick, B., P. de Villiers, J. de Villiers, and R. Hoffmeister. 2007. Language and Theory of Mind: A Study of Deaf Children. *Child Development* 78(2):376–396.

Schieffelin, Bambi B. 1979. Getting It Together: An Ethnographic Perspective on the Study of the Acquisition of Communicative Competence. In *Developmental Pragmatics*. E. Ochs and B. Schieffelin, eds. Pp. 73–108. New York: Academic Press.

    1990. *The Give and Take of Everyday Life: Language Socialization of Kaluli Children*. Cambridge University Press.

    2000. Introducing Kaluli Literacy: A Chronology of Influences. In *Regimes of Language*. P. Kroskrity, ed. Pp. 293–327. Santa Fe, NM: School of American Research Press.

Schieffelin, Bambi B., and Elinor Ochs. 1986. Language Socialization. *Annual Review of Anthropology* 15:163–191.

Schieffelin, Edward L. 1976. *The Sorrow of the Lonely and the Burning of the Dancers*. New York: St. Martin's Press.

Schilbach, Leonhard, Marcus Wilms, Simon B. Eickhoff, Sandro Romanzetti, Ralf Tepest, Gary Bente, N. Jon Shah, Gereon R. Fink, and Kai Vogeley. 2010. Minds Made for Sharing: Initiating Joint Attention Recruits Reward-Related Neurocircuitry. *Journal of Cognitive Neuroscience* 22(12):2702–2715.

Schutz, Alfred. 1962–1966. Making Music Together: A Study in Social Relationship. In *Collected Papers*. A. Brodersen, ed. Pp. 159–178. Phaenomenologica, Vol. 2 (Studies in Social Theory). The Hague: M. Nijhoff.

    1967. *The Phenomenology of the Social World*. Evanston, IL: Northwestern University Press.

Schwartz, J. H., R. L. Holloway, I. Tattersall, D. C. Broadfield, and M. S. Yuan. 2004. *The Human Fossil Record, Brain Endocasts: The Paleoneurological Evidence*. Hoboken, NJ: Wiley.

Scribner, Sylvia, and Michael Cole. 1981. Unpackaging Literacy. In *Writing: The Nature, Development, and Teaching of Written Communication*, Vol. I: *Variation in Writing: Functional and Linguistic-Cultural Differences*. M. F. Whiteman, ed. Pp. 71–87. Hillsdale, NJ: Lawrence Erlbaum.

Searle, John. 1969. *Speech Acts*. Cambridge University Press.

Seedhouse, Paul. 2004. Transcription Conventions. *Language Learning* 54(S1):267–270.

Senghas, Richard, and Leila Monaghan. 2002. Signs of Their Times: Deaf Communities and the Culture of Language. *Annual Review of Anthropology* 31(1):69–97.

Seyfarth, Robert M., Dorothy L. Cheney, and Peter Marler. 1980a. Monkey Responses to Three Different Alarm Calls. *Science* 210:801–803.

    1980b. Vervet Monkey Alarm Calls. *Animal Behavior* 28(4):1070–1094.

Sherlock, Steve, and Lawrence Kielich. 1991. Medication and the Patient Role: Implications for the Labeling Theory of Mental Illness. *Michigan Sociological Review* (5):90–102.

Sherzer, Joel. 1987. A Diversity of Voices: Men's and Women's Speech in Ethnographic Perspective. In *Language, Gender, and Sex in Comparative Perspective*. S. U. Philips, S. Steele, and C. Tanz, eds. Pp. 95–120. Cambridge University Press.

Shoaps, Robin Ann. 2002. "Pray Earnestly": The Textual Construction of Personal Involvement in Pentecostal Prayer and Song. *Journal of Linguistic Anthropology* 12(1):34–71.

2009. Ritual and (Im)Moral Voices: Locating the Testament of Judas in Sakapultek Communicative Ecology. *American Ethnologist* 36(3):459–477.

Shohamy, Elana. 2008. At What Cost? Methods of Language Revival and Protection: Examples from Hebrew. In *Sustaining Linguistic Diversity: Endangered and Minority Languages and Language Varieties*. K. A. King, N. Schilling-Estes, L. Fogle, J. J. Lou, and B. Soukup, eds. Pp. 205–218. Washington, DC: Georgetown University Press.

Sidnell, Jack. 1999. Deixis. In *Handbook of Pragmatics*. J. Verschueren, J.-O. Ostman, J. Blommaert, and C. Bulcaen, eds. Pp. 1–28. Amsterdam and Philadelphia: John Benjamins.

Silverstein, Michael. 1976. Shifters, Linguistic Categories, and Cultural Description. In *Meaning in Anthropology*. K. Basso and H. A. Selby, eds. Pp. 11–56. Albuquerque: School of American Research/University of New Mexico Press.

1979. Language Structure and Linguistic Ideology. In *The Elements: A Parasession on Linguistic Units and Levels*. R. Cline, W. Hanks, and C. Hofbauer, eds. Pp. 193–247. Chicago Linguistic Society.

1996. Encountering Language and Languages of Encounter in North American Ethnohistory. *Journal of Linguistic Anthropology* 6(2):126–144.

2000. Whorfianism and the Linguistic Imagination of Nationality. In *Regimes of Language: Ideologies, Polities, and Identities*. P. Kroskrity, ed. Pp. 85–138. Santa Fe, NM: School of American Research.

[1981] 2001. The Limits of Awareness. In *Linguistic Anthropology: A Reader*. A. Duranti, ed. Pp. 382–401. Malden, MA: Blackwell Publishers.

2003a. Death and Life at Gettysburg. In *Talking Politics: The Substance of Style from Abe to "W"*. M. Silverstein, ed. Pp. 33–62. Chicago: Prickly Paradigm Press (distributed by University of Chicago).

2003b. Indexical Order and the Dialectics of Sociolinguistic Life. *Language & Communication* 23(1):193–229.

2004. "Cultural" Concepts and the Language–Culture Nexus. *Current Anthropology* 45(5):621–652.

2015. How Language Communities Intersect: Is "Superdiversity" an Incremental or Transformative Condition? *Language & Communication* 44:7–18.

Slobin, Dan I. 1996. From "Thought and Language" to "Thinking for Speaking". In *Rethinking Linguistic Relativity*. J. Gumperz and S. Levinson, eds. Pp. 70–96. Cambridge University Press.

Slotta, James. 2014. Revelations of the World: Transnationalism and the Politics of Perception in Papua New Guinea. *American Anthropologist* 116(3):626–642.

Slyomovics, Susan. 1985. *The Merchant of Art: An Egyptian Hilali Oral Epic in Performance*. Berkeley and Los Angeles: University of California Press.

1987. The Death-Song of ʿĀmir Khafājī: Puns in an Oral and Printed Episode of "Sīrat Bani Hilāl". *Journal of Arabic Literature* 18(1):62–78.

Smith, Benjamin. 2010. Of Marbles and (Little) Men: Bad Luck and Masculine Identification in Aymara Boyhood. *Journal of Linguistic Anthropology* 20(1):225–239.

Smith, K., and Simon Kirby. 2012. Compositionality and Linguistic Evolution. In *The Oxford Handbook of Compositionality*. M. Werning, W. Hinzen, and E. Machery, eds. pp. 493–509. New York: Oxford University Press.

Smith-Hefner, Nancy. 1988. Women and Politeness: The Javanese Example. *Language in Society* 17:535–554.

Solomon, Olga. 2010. What a Dog Can Do: Children with Autism and Therapy Dogs in Social Interaction. *Ethos* 38(1):143–166.

　 2015. "But-He'll Fall!": Children with Autism, Interspecies Intersubjectivity, and the Problem of "Being Social". *Culture, Medicine, and Psychiatry* 39(2):323–344.

Speas, Margaret. 2009. Someone Else's Language: On the Role of Linguists in Language Revitalization. In *Indigenous Language Revitalization: Encouragements, Guidance and Lessons Learned*. J. Reyhner and L. Lockard, eds. Pp. 23–36. Flagstaff: Northern Arizona University.

Sperber, Dan, and Deirdre Wilson. 1981. Irony and the Use-Mention Distinction. In *Radical Pragmatics*. P. Cole, ed. Pp. 295–318. New York: Academic Press.

Stepanova, Aleksandra S. 2012. *Karjalaisen Itkuvirsikielen Sanakirja (Dictionary of Karelian Lament Language)*. Vantaa: Suomalaisen Krijallisuuden Seura [Finnish Literature Society].

Stepanova, Eila. 2012. Mythic Elements of Karelian Laments: The Case of *Syndyzet* and *Spuassuzet*. In *Confluence, Continuity and Change in the Evolution of Mythology: The Case of the Finno-Karelian Sampo-Cycle*. Frog, A.-L. Siikala, and E. Stepanova, eds. Pp. 257–287. Helsinki: Suomalaisen Kirjallisuuden Seura (Finnish Literature Society).

Stern, Daniel N. 1985. *The Interpersonal World of the Infant: A View from Psychoanalysis and Developmental Psychology*. New York: Basic Books.

Streeck, Jürgen, and J. Scott Jordan. 2009. Communication as a Dynamical Self-Sustaining System: The Importance of Time-Scales and Nested Context. *Communication Theory* 19(4):445–464.

Street, Brian, and Niko Besnier. 2008. Aspects of Literacy. In *Making Sense of Language: Readings in Culture and Communication*. S. D. Blum, ed. Pp. 52–69. Oxford University Press.

Stromberg, Peter G. 1993. *Language and Self-Transformation: A Study of the Christian Conversion Narrative*. Cambridge University Press.

Swinglehurst, Deborah. 2014. Displays of Authority in the Clinical Consultation: A Linguistic Ethnographic Study of the Electronic Patient Record. *Social Science & Medicine* 118:17–26.

Tan, Li Hai, Alice H. D. Chan, Paul Kay, Pek-Lan Khong, Lawrance K. C. Yip, and Luke Kang-Kwong. 2008 Language Affects Patterns of Brain Activation Associated with Perceptual Decision. *PNAS (Proceedings of the National Academy of Sciences)* 105(10):4004–4009.

Tannen, Deborah. 2010. Abduction and Identity in Family Interaction: Ventriloquizing as Indirectness. *Journal of Pragmatics* 42(2):307–316.

Taylor, Charles. 1992. *The Ethics of Authenticity*. Cambridge, MA: Harvard University Press.

Tedlock, Dennis. 1983. *The Spoken Word and the Work of Interpretation*. Philadelphia: University of Pennsylvania Press.

Templeton, Christopher N., Erick Greene, and Kate Davis. 2005. Allometry of Alarm Calls: Black-Capped Chickadees Encode Information About Predator Size. *Science* 308(5730):1934–1937.

Throop, Jason. 2010. *Suffering and Sentiment: Exploring the Vicissitudes of Experience and Pain in Yap*. Berkeley: University of California Press.

Thygesen, Bente. 2008. Resonance: No Music Without Resonance – Without Resonance No Group. *Group Analysis* 41(1):63–83.

Tolbert, Elizabeth. 1988. The Musical Means of Sorrow: The Karelian Lament Tradition. Ph.D. thesis, University of California, Los Angeles.

— 2001a. The Enigma of Music, the Voice of Reason: "Music," "Language," and Becoming Human. *New Literary History* 32:451–465.

— 2001b Music and Meaning: An Evolutionary Story. *Psychology of Music* 29(1):84–94.

Trask, Robert Lawrence. 1995. *Language: The Basics*. London and New York: Routledge.

Trawick, Margaret. 1990. *Notes on Love in a Tamil Family*. Berkeley: University of California Press.

Trevarthen, Colwyn. 1979. Communication and Cooperation in Early Infancy: A Description of Primary Intersubjectivity. In *Before Speech: The Beginning of Interpersonal Communication*. M. Bullowa, ed. Pp. 321–347. Cambridge University Press.

Trosset, Carol S. 1986. The Social Identity of Welsh Learners. *Language in Society* 15(2):165–192.

Tylor, Edward Burnet. 1871. *Primitive Culture: Researches into the Development of Mythology, Philosophy, Religion, Art, and Custom*. London: J. Murray.

University of California Regents. 2015–2016. Languages of California. In *Survey of California and Other Indian Languages*. T.R.O.T.U.O. California, ed. Berkeley: The Regents of the University of California.

Urban, Gregory. 1985. The Semiotics of Two Speech Styles in Shokleng. In *Semiotic Mediation: Sociocultural and Psychological Perspectives*. E. Mertz and R. Parmentier, eds. Pp. 311–329. Orlando: Academic Press.

— 1988. Ritual Wailing in Amerindian Brazil. *American Anthropologist* 90(2):385–400.

— 2001. *Metaculture: How Culture Moves through the World*. Minneapolis: University of Minnesota Press.

— 2002. Metasignaling and Language Origins. *American Anthropologist* 104(1):233–246.

Valdés, Guadalupe, Cristina Chavez, and Claudia Angelelli. [2003] 2014. A Performance Team: Young Interpreters and Their Parents. In *Expanding Definitions of Giftedness: The Case of Young Interpreters from Immigrant Communities*. G. Valdés, ed. Pp. 63–98. New York: Routledge.

van der Schyff, Dylan. 2013. Music, Culture and the Evolution of the Human Mind: Looking beyond Dichotomies. *Hellenic Journal of Music, Education and Culture* 4(1):5–15.

Van Puyvelde, Martine, and Fabia Franco. 2015. The Interaction of Music and Language in the Ontogenesis of Human Communication: A Multimodal Parent-Infant Co-Regulation System. In *Proceedings of the International Conference on the Multimodal Experience of Music, University of Sheffield (ICMEM 2015)*. R. Timmers, N. Dibben, Z. Eitan, R. Granot, T. Metcalfe, A. Schiavio, and V. Williamson, eds. Pp. 1–8. HRI Online Publications, University of Sheffield.

Vaux, Bert, Justin Cooper, and Emily Tucker. 2007. *Linguistic Field Methods*. Eugene, OR: Wipf & Stock.

VegasPBS.org. 2015. Vegas PBS ITV Guide 2015–2016. In *Teachers Guide: Instructional Television in the Classroom*. C.C.S. District, ed. Las Vegas: Clark County School District.

Vertovec, Steven. 2007. Super-Diversity and Its Implications. *Ethnic and Racial Studies* 30(6):1024–1054.

Vinkhuyzen, Erik, Luke Plurkowski, and Gary David. 2012. Implementing EMRS: Learnings from a Video Ethnography. In *Ethnographic Praxis in Industry Conference Proceedings, 2012*. Pp. 235–248. Wiley Online Library.

Volfová, Martina. 2013. "And Now We Are All Newenee": A Journey of Becoming and Keeping the Shoshone Language and Culture Alive. Masters thesis, Northern Arizona University.

Volosinov, Valentin Nikolaevitch. [1929] 1973. *Marxism and the Philosophy of Language*. L. Matejka and I. R. Titunik, trans. Cambridge, MA: Harvard University Press.

Waife, S. O. 1958. Medicalese. *Mississippi Valley Medical Journal (Quincy, Ill)* 80(1):10–11.

Waitzkin, Howard. 1991. *The Politics of Medical Encounters*. New Haven, CT: Yale University Press.

Wallace, Anthony F. C. 1952. Individual Differences and Cultural Uniformities. *American Sociological Review* 17(6):747–750.

        2009. Epilogue: On the Organization of Diversity. *Ethos* 37(2):251–255.

Wallace, Anthony F. C., and Robert S. Grumet, eds. 2004. *Modernity and Mind: Essays on Culture Change*, Vol. II. Lincoln: University of Nebraska.

Wang, Xuan. 2015. Inauthentic Authenticity: Semiotic Design and Globalization in the Margins of China. *Semiotica* 2015(203):227–248.

Waxer, Peter. 1974 Nonverbal Cues for Depression. *Journal of Abnormal Psychology* 83(3):319–322.

Waxler, Nancy. 1974. Culture and Mental Illness: A Social Labeling Perspective. *Journal of Nervous and Mental Disease* 159:379–395.

Webster, Anthony K. 2010. On Intimate Grammars with Examples from Navajo English, Navlish, and Navajo. *Journal of Anthropological Research* 66(2):187–208.

        2012. "Don't Talk About It": Navajo Poets and Their Ordeals of Language. *Journal of Anthropological Research* 68(3):399–414.

Wesch, Michael. 2007. What Is Web 2.0? What Does It Mean for Anthropology? Lessons from an Accidental Viral Video. *Anthropology News* 48(5):30–31.

Whorf, Benjamin Lee. [1939] 1956. *Language, Thought, and Reality: Selected Writings of Benjamin Lee Whorf*. J. B. Carroll, ed. Cambridge, MA: MIT Press.

Wiget, Andrew. 1987. Telling the Tale: A Performance Analysis of a Hopi Coyote Story. In *Recovering the Word: Essays on Native American Literature*. B. Swann and A. Krupat, eds. Pp. 297–336. Berkeley: University of California Press.

Wilce, James M. 1996. Reduplication and Reciprocity in Imagining Community: The Play of Tropes in a Rural Bangladeshi Moot. *Journal of Linguistic Anthropology* 6(2):188–222.

        1998. *Eloquence in Trouble: The Poetics and Politics of Complaint in Rural Bangladesh*. New York: Oxford University Press.

        2001. Divining Troubles, or Divining Troubles? Emergent and Conflictual Dimensions of Bangladeshi Divination. *Anthropological Quarterly* 74(4):190–199.

2006. Divining Troubles: Divination as Interaction in Bangladesh. In *Conference on Language, Interaction, and Culture*. University of California, Los Angeles.

2008. Scientizing Bangladeshi Psychiatry: Parallelism, Enregisterment, and the Cure for a Magic Complex. *Language in Society* 37(1):91–114.

2009a. *Crying Shame: Metaculture, Modernity, and the Exaggerated Death of Lament*. Malden, MA: Blackwell Publishers.

2009b. *Language and Emotion*. Cambridge University Press.

2009c. Medical Discourse. *Annual Review of Anthropology* 38(1):199–215.

2011a. Sacred Psychotherapy in the Age of Authenticity: Healing and Cultural Revivalisms in Contemporary Finland. *Religions* 2(4):566–589.

2011b. "Voice" or "Sound" in Two Contemporary Finnish Healing Modalities. *Medical Anthropology and Bioethics* [Moscow] 1(1). http://jmaib.iea.ras.ru/englishversion/issues/001/publications/wilce.html.

2017. Tradition, Emotion, Healing, and the Sacred: Revivalist Lamenting in Finland in Relation to Three Authenticities. In *Spirit & Mind: Mental Health at the Intersection of Religion & Psychiatry*. H. Basu, R. Littlewood, and A. S. Steinforth, eds. Pp. 227–252. Berlin and London: Lit Verlag.

Wilce, James M., and Janina Fenigsen. 2015. Mourning and Honor: Register in Karelian Lament. In *Registers of Communication*. A. Agha and Frog, eds. Pp. 187–209. *Studia Fennica Linguistica 18*. Helsinki: Suomalaisen Kirjallisuuden Seura (Finnish Literature Society).

2016. Emotion Pedagogies: What Are They, and Why Do They Matter? *Ethos* 44(2):81–95.

Wilce, John Woodworth. 1923. *Football, How to Play It and How to Understand It*. New York: C. Scribner's Sons.

Witmer, Robert. 1973. Recent Change in the Musical Culture of the Blood Indians of Alberta, Canada. *Anuario Interamericano de Investigacion Musical* 9:64–94.

Wittgenstein, Ludwig. 1958. *Philosophical Investigations*. G. E. M. Anscombe and R. Rhees, trans. Oxford: Blackwell.

1969. *On Certainty*. G. E. M. Anscombe, D. Paul, and G. H. Wright, trans. Oxford: Basil Blackwell.

Woolard, Kathryn A. 1998a. Introduction: Language Ideology as a Field of Inquiry. In *Language Ideologies: Practice and Theory*. B. B. Schieffelin, K. A. Woolard, and P. V. Kroskrity, eds. Pp. 3–47. New York: Oxford University Press.

1998b. Simultaneity and Bivalency as Strategies in Bilingualism. *Journal of Linguistic Anthropology* 8(1):3–29.

Wyman, Leisy, T. 2014. Youth Linguistic Survivance in Transforming Setting. In *Indigenous Youth and Multilingualism: Language Identity, Ideology, and Practice in Dynamic Cultural Worlds*. L. T. Wyman, T. L. McCarty, and S. E. Nicholas, eds. Pp. 90–110. New York: Routledge.

Wyman, Leisy T., Teresa L. McCarty, and Sheilah E. Nicholas, eds. 2014. *Indigenous Youth and Multilingualism: Language Identity, Ideology, and Practice in Dynamic Cultural Worlds*. New York: Routledge.

Young, Allan. 1995. *The Harmony of Illusions: Inventing Post-Traumatic Stress Disorder*. Princeton University Press.

Yukon Native Language Centre. 2016. *Native Languages in the Yukon*. Whitehorse, Canada: Yukan Native Language Centre. www.ynlc.ca.

Zuberbühler, Klaus. 2001. Predator-Specific Alarm Calls in Campbell's Monkeys, Cercopithecus Campbelli. *Behavioral Ecology and Sociobiology* 50(5):414–422.

Zuberbühler, Klaus, Ronald Noë, and Robert M. Seyfarth. 1997. Diana Monkey Long-Distance Calls: Messages for Conspecifics and Predators. *Animal Behaviour* 53(3):589–604.

INDEX